ST ANTONY'S/MACMILLAN SERIES

General Editors: Archie Brown (1978–85), Rosemary Thorp (1985–92), and Alex Pravda (1992–), all Fellows of St Antony's College, Oxford

Recent titles include

Mark D. Alleyne
INTERNATIONAL POWER AND INTERNATIONAL COMMUNICATION

Daniel Bell, David Brown, Kanishka Jayasuryia and David Martin Jones
TOWARDS ILLIBERAL DEMOCRACY IN PACIFIC ASIA

Judith M. Brown and Rosemary Foot (*editors*)
MIGRATION: The Asian Experience

Anne Deighton (*editor*)
BUILDING POSTWAR EUROPE: National Decision-makers and European Institutions, 1948–63

Simon Duke
THE NEW EUROPEAN SECURITY DISORDER

Christoph Gassenschmidt
JEWISH LIBERAL POLITICS IN TSARIST RUSSIA, 1900–14: The Modernization of Russian Jewry

Amitzur Ilan
THE ORIGIN OF THE ARAB–ISRAELI ARMS RACE: Arms, Embargo, Military Power and Decision in the 1948 Palestine War

Hiroshi Ishida
SOCIAL MOBILITY IN CONTEMPORARY JAPAN

Austen Ivereigh
CATHOLICISM AND POLITICS IN ARGENTINA, 1910–60

Leroy Jin
MONETARY POLICY AND THE DESIGN OF FINANCIAL INSTITUTIONS IN CHINA, 1978–90

Matthew Jones
BRITAIN, THE UNITED STATES AND THE MEDITERRANEAN WAR, 1942–44

Anthony Kirk-Greene and Daniel Bach (*editors*)
STATE AND SOCIETY IN FRANCOPHONE AFRICA SINCE INDEPENDENCE

Leslie McLoughlin
IBN SAUD: Founder of a Kingdom

Rosalind Marsh
HISTORY AND LITERATURE IN CONTEMPORARY RUSSIA

David Nicholls
THE PLURALIST STATE, 2nd edition: The Political Ideas of J. N. Figgis and his Contemporaries

J. L. Porkett
UNEMPLOYMENT IN CAPITALIST, COMMUNIST AND POST-COMMUNIST ECONOMIES

Charles Powell
JUAN CARLOS OF SPAIN: Self-made Monarch

Neil Renwich
JAPAN'S ALLIANCE POLITICS AND DEFENCE PRODUCTION

H. Gordon Skilling
T. G. MASARYK: Against the Current, 1882–1914

William J. Tompson
KHRUSHCHEV: A Political Life

Christopher Tremewan
THE POLITICAL ECONOMY OF SOCIAL CONTROL IN SINGAPORE

Stephen Welch
THE CONCEPT OF POLITICAL CULTURE

Jennifer M. Welsh
EDMUND BURKE AND INTERNATIONAL RELATIONS: The Commonwealth of Europe and the Crusade against the French Revolution

Managing the British Economy in the 1960s

A Treasury Perspective

Sir Alec Cairncross

in association with
St Antony's College, Oxford

MACMILLAN

© Sir Alec Cairncross 1996

All rights reserved. No reproduction, copy or transmission of this publication may be made without written permission.

No paragraph of this publication may be reproduced, copied or transmitted save with written permission or in accordance with the provisions of the Copyright, Designs and Patents Act 1988, or under the terms of any licence permitting limited copying issued by the Copyright Licensing Agency, 90 Tottenham Court Road, London W1P 9HE.

Any person who does any unauthorised act in relation to this publication may be liable to criminal prosecution and civil claims for damages.

This book is published in the
St Antony's/Macmillan series
General Editor: Alex Pravda

First published 1996 by
MACMILLAN PRESS LTD
Houndmills, Basingstoke, Hampshire RG21 6XS
and London
Companies and representatives
throughout the world

ISBN 0-333-65075-1

A catalogue record for this book is available from the British Library.

10 9 8 7 6 5 4 3 2 1
05 04 03 02 01 00 99 98 97 96

Printed in Great Britain by
The Ipswich Book Co Ltd
Ipswich, Suffolk

*To my ex-colleagues in the
Economic Section of the Treasury*

Contents

List of Tables viii
List of Figures ix
Preface x

Part I
1   Introduction 3

Part II
2   The First Cycle, 1957–61 29
3   The July Measures and After, 1961–2 44
4   The Maudling 'Dash for Growth' 65

Part III
5   A Change of Government, 1964 91
6   A Strategy for the Pound? 112
7   The Exchange Crisis of 1965 120
8   The Exchange Crisis of 1966 141
9   The New Strategy, 1967 159
10 The Countdown to Devaluation 180

Part IV
11 From Devaluation to the Gold Rush 195
12 A Long Hard Slog, 1968 211
13 Success at Last, 1969 232
14 Monetary and Financial Policy in the 1960s 243
15 Economic Management in the 1960s: A Summing-up 262

Appendix: An Economic Anatomy of the 1960s 276
Notes 283
Calendar of Main Events, 1960–9 290
Dramatis Personae, 1960–70 299
Index 305

List of Tables

2.1	Gross Domestic Product: forecasts and actual growth, 1958–61	35
3.1	Estimates of increases in stocks, 1959–61	55
3.2	Gross Domestic Product: forecast and actual growth, 1961–4	59
4.1	Successive forecasts of changes in the constituents of final demand, 1962–4	77
7.1	Central government borrowing and lending, 1963–4 to 1969–70	122
11.1	Preliminary forecasts, December 1967	201
14.1	Public borrowing and monetary growth, 1960–9	252
14.2	Net sales of government stocks, 1960–9	252
14.3	Total international reserves in 1949, 1955 and 1969	255
A.1	Changes in the allocation of resources, 1959–69	278
A.2	Balance of payments estimates then and now, 1960–9	279

List of Figures

1.1	British share of world trade in manufactures, 1959–70	19
1.2	The balance of payments on current account and the gold and dollar drain, 1959–70	20
1.3	Half-yearly changes in GDP and unemployment, 1960–70	23
7.1	Public and private investment, 1959–70 (at 1985 prices)	135
12.1	Dollar rate of exchange, 1968–9	213
13.1	Volume of exports and imports, 1959–70	233
A.1	Annual increases in fixed investment, exports and GDP, 1960–70	280
A.2	Unemployment and hourly wages, 1959–70	282

Preface

This is an account of economic management in Britain in the 1960s from the standpoint of the Treasury, in which I served between 1961 and 1969, first as Economic Adviser to HMG and subsequently as Head of the Government Economic Service. It is simultaneously a history of events – how, when and why they occurred – and of the government's efforts to influence events – how policies took shape and what success they had. It focuses on economic fluctuations and economic change and the efforts of the Treasury to influence or control them.

The book is almost entirely confined to macroeconomic policy, with the emphasis on growth, unemployment, inflation and external balance. Issues of industrial and social policy, relations with the European Community, structural changes such as the rise of the Euro-dollar market and the expansion in international capital flows are largely neglected. So also are changes that seized public attention at the time, such as decimalisation, the Channel Tunnel, raising the school leaving age and student unrest. Much that occupied the Treasury is left out of account: changes in the system of public expenditure control (PESC); new financial objectives for the nationalised industries (e.g. the test rate of discount); efforts to improve the competence in economics and administration of young civil servants (first the Centre for Administrative Studies in 1963 and later the Civil Service College); and the host of other concerns with which an administrative staff of nearly 200 wrestled from day to day.

Since I was a participant in the process by which policy was formed, I have drawn on my personal recollections and such records as I retain, including a diary I kept, like my two predecessors, James Meade and Robert Hall, contrary to official regulations. This gives the book a more personal cast than I would have wished and mixes memoir with historical analysis; but it also allows me to offer the counterpart by an ex-official to the various Ministerial surveys of the period in the memoirs of Harold Macmillan, Harold Wilson, James Callaghan, Roy Jenkins and others and in the diaries of Tony Benn, Dick Crossman and Barbara Castle.

The staff of economists who served under me in the Economic Section included some of the most distinguished applied economists in the country. Although none of them are mentioned by name, the reader will appreciate how enormously I depended on them: they worked as a team of a dozen or so, each with his own area of responsibility, while I spent my time preparing briefs, attending committees, and trying to recruit more economists to government service.

I begin in Part I with an introductory chapter discussing prevailing ideas at the beginning of the decade about the economy and how it should be managed, especially the aspiration to faster economic growth and emulation of continental economic success.

Part II (Chapters 2–4) deals with the last years of Conservative government under Macmillan, starting with the economic cycle of 1957–61 and going on to review the efforts of Selwyn Lloyd and Reginald Maudling to accelerate economic growth.

Part III (Chapters 5–10) covers the period of Labour rule from 1964 to the devaluation of 1967. The Labour Government, believing like its predecessor that it could raise the rate of growth if it kept up the pressure on the economy whatever the deficit in the balance of payment, soon found itself struggling to avoid devaluation and finally succumbed. Part IV (Chapters 11–15) describes how, for a further two years after 1967, in the midst of turmoil in international currency markets, the struggle continued, this time to avoid a second devaluation. There was then a brief interregnum of external surplus before the pound was allowed to float in June 1972.

It is a story with strong overtones of more recent events. As in the early 1990s, one of the central issues of policy was what to do about the exchange rate. Should the pound be devalued? Should it be allowed to float or should a fixed parity be maintained? Could changes in the international monetary system help to stabilise rates of exchange in face of speculative pressure?

In the 1960s, the problem was complicated by sterling's role as a reserve currency and the accumulation of liquid liabilities to other countries (in sterling) dating back to the war. In the 1990s the complications related more to the effort to keep in step with other members of the European Community and the vulnerability of exchange rates to the pressure of international capital flows on an unprecedented scale.

Devaluation was seen very differently in the 1960s from the current view of it as largely ineffectual. It was then represented as capable of exercising an early and powerful effect on the balance of payments and encouraging export-led growth at a faster rate. From this point of view, the long delay in devaluing was widely regarded as a cardinal error in policy. Even a temporary check to the rise in production from year to year in order to preserve the existing parity was attacked as wrong-headed. The point of view common at that time is in striking contrast to the assumption in the 1990s that little is lost by putting an end once and for all to the possibility of devaluation by establishing a common currency within the European Community. It will be remembered that in 1992 the then chancellor in more picturesque language than his predecessors had used in 1949 and 1967, stigmatised devaluation before he was obliged to let the pound float as 'fool's gold'.

I have thought it useful to supplement the narrative by a more systematic treatment in Chapter 14 of monetary and financial policy during a decade lying between the Radcliffe Report of 1959 and the rise of monetarism in Britain from about 1970 onwards. Chapter 15 gives a brief assessment and summing up.

The book is intended to throw light not only on the practice of economic management, the problems it faces, its effectiveness and limitations, but also on its administrative and political aspects. How was the work of economic management divided within the Treasury between administrators and economists, officials and Ministers? How did the Treasury and the Bank of England divide responsibility for monetary and financial policy? What part was played by other departments of government, by the press and by outside commentators such as the National Institute and the London and Cambridge Economic Service? These are questions that are not addressed directly, but the reader will find contributions to an answer scattered through the book.

I am indebted to an old colleague, Sir Fred Atkinson, for much useful advice in preparing this book for publication and to Dr Kenneth Morgan for reading the entire manuscript and making many helpful suggestions. I have also profited from comments by Richard Lamb and Hamish McRae. As on many other occasions, I am indebted to Mrs Anne Robinson (assisted on this occasion by Mrs Martha Kempton) for converting my assorted scribbles into a readable and orderly text.

ALEC CAIRNCROSS

Part I

1 Introduction

In the early post-war years in Britain there was little thought of the growing prosperity that lay ahead. The public was more concerned with the recovery of pre-war living standards, the threat of nuclear war and the danger of a post-war slump. As one crisis followed another, the government for some years held back consumption in the interests of industrial reconstruction and the balance of payments. Unemployment rather than economic growth was the dominant preoccupation.

In the 1950s a different world opened up. An increase in the volume of consumer spending of a mere 7 per cent in the six years 1946–52 gave way to an increase of 30 per cent in the eight years 1952–60. Rationing had completely ceased by 1954. In the course of the decade to 1960 real weekly earnings rose on the average by 33 per cent and gross domestic product by 30 per cent. These were rates well above experience before the war or, indeed, at any earlier time. No wonder Butler was moved as early as 1954 to prophesy a doubling of the standard of living in the next twenty-five years – a prophecy that proved to be just a little too optimistic – while Macmillan at the end of the decade could assure the public that they had 'never had it so good'.

By 1960 there was evidence in plenty of a new prosperity. Car ownership had more than doubled since 1950 and the rise was accelerating. Cheap air travel had become commonplace and was expanding by leaps and bounds. Holidays were more universal, more frequent and more exotic. A revolution in household equipment was in progress, transforming the life of the housewife and releasing women for paid work elsewhere. Apart from what was bought by the consumer, an expanding volume of services was provided by the state in health, education, pensions, etc. Above all, employment prospects had been transformed. Unemployment had not completely disappeared. But in 1960 it was nearly twenty years since it had been as high as 3 per cent.

This did not mean that workers could count on staying indefinitely in the same job. Some industries contracted and employment in them fell: but since other industries were expanding, new employment opportunities were created and employment in total continued to grow. In the four years 1956–60, for example, coalmining, rail transport and shipbuilding shed 220,000 workers but the increase in unemployment in those industries was under 4600. In the same way, the process of technical change and reorganisation within enterprises resulted in redundancies in some directions and shortages of labour in others. Between 1950 and 1960, employment grew by over 1 million while the number unemployed remained virtually unchanged at about 300,000.

Increasing wealth and the greater security of employment changed the temper of society. There was a greater consciousness of rights among those who had been accustomed to accept their lot for good or ill; a recognition that the social and economic set-up was not permanent and unchanging but could be made to yield to the power of the state, to the advantage of those who were able to wield that power; a new questioning of established practice; a more critical and satirical spirit. The young were both more experimental and more insistent that they be allowed to have their way. Wage-earners and their representatives in the trade unions were more militant. The greater the evidence of wealth, the larger the place it took in life and thought, the more it sowed discontent along with its obvious benefits: stirring envy on one side and disenchantment with material wealth on the other. Economic success was sought for but despised; economic failure was humiliating and frustrating.

Britain's experience was shared by other industrial countries. There was a buoyancy in the world economy that appeared to be self-sustaining and allowed markets to expand without much need for economic management by governments. Indeed, for much of the time the concern of governments was to rein back demand when it was in danger of pressing too hard on available capacity and either driving up prices or overflowing on to imports and producing imbalance in the international accounts.

Inflation and the balance of payments had been the outstanding economic problems of the 1950s and they were to prove just as intractable in the 1960s. As had been foreseen in 1945, continuous full employment conveyed to the trade unions the power to press for, and in most circumstances obtain, higher money wages. In all probability, however, there would be no lasting improvement in the average level of real wages since employers working at full capacity were in a position to make a corresponding upward adjustment in prices. If, however, foreign competitors did not share the same experience, British employers would forfeit competitive power, the balance of payments would move into deficit, and a devaluation of the currency might become necessary if balance was to be restored. The value of the currency, in other words, was to some extent in the hands of wage-earners in conditions of full employment; and if the domestic value fell, the external value would have to be adjusted.

We shall come later to the controversies attending the problems of inflation and the balance of payments. The first of these had come to a head in 1957 when Thorneycroft attempted to put a stop to inflation by limiting expenditure, public and private. He appeared at the time to be giving expression to views now identified with monetarism and claiming that if the quantity of money were held constant its value would also remain unchanged. But the language he used was somewhat confused and it was the money value of gross national product (GNP) rather than the quantity of money that he sought to stabilise. The role of money, as opposed to demand or wage-bargaining, in producing inflation became a subject of increasing controversy after the report of the Radcliffe Committee in 1959. The policies appropriate to a balance of payments crisis were also a matter of debate from about that time.

It was, however, the idea of economic growth that dominated discussion on economic policy at the beginning of the 1960s. The public had gradually come to recognise the importance of growth without much appreciation of its causes. Their earlier concern for greater stability and a higher level of employment appeared to have been met and they were now able to observe that stable employment carried a bonus of rising productivity and a continuous improvement in living standards. At first this improvement was thought of as recovery from the burdens of war. But as the years of rationing drew to an end in the early 1950s they became aware of a steady and continuous expansion in purchasing power.

The consciousness of growth and the benefits it brought was coupled, as the 1950s progressed, with a feeling of disquiet at the more rapid progress abroad, especially in continential Europe. It was not enough to be doing better than ever if others did better still. While industrial production in Britain grew at just over 3 per cent per annum in the 1950s, West German production had grown three times as fast; and for the six countries of the European Economic Community (EEC) growth had averaged two and a half times the British rate. That might be thought to reflect different rates of recovery from wartime destruction and dislocation which was much more extensive on the continent and left a large amount of unused capacity on which to draw. In comparison, the United Kingdom had remained fully employed and close to the ceiling of its capacity, which remained largely intact. As the 1950s wore on, however, the disparity in rates of growth showed no sign of narrowing. Between 1955 and 1958, for example, industrial production hardly changed in Britain but increased by 18 per cent in West Germany and at the same rate in the EEC. By 1961, France and Germany had probably overtaken Britain in income per head for the first time since the Industrial Revolution.[1]

Even more disquieting was Britain's failure to take advantage of the booming export markets that were supplied increasingly by continental competitors. It had been reasonable to expect that the trade of countries disrupted by war would recover rapidly at rates comparing favourably with Britain's; after all, in 1950 Britain was still exporting more than France, West Germany and Italy combined and there could be no expectation of sustaining such a lead. But if one passes over the first ten post-war years and looks at the change between 1955 and 1960, when British exports increased by 21 per cent in value, West Germany nearly doubled her exports and by 1959 was already outstripping Britain. Italy and Japan both doubled their exports, too, and France showed a 40 per cent increase. Every year without exception, for the entire decade, Britain's share of world trade in manufactures fell. Over the decade the fall was from 25.5 per cent to 16.1 per cent; and there was no sign that the rate of decline was flattening out.

These trends made Britain look abroad with different eyes. In the early post-war years there had been confidence that Britain had a clearer view than her neighbours of what economic recovery entailed and there was a reluctance to be too closely bound up with them for fear they would prove a drag on the economic strategy required for recovery. Now there was a disposition to look abroad in search of new economic models that had proved their worth elsewhere and might provide a means to faster growth in Britain. The country that monopolised attention as an exemplar was France; and it was widely assumed that France's economic success could be attributed largely to the system of indicative planning that was in use.

It may seem a little odd to have picked on France as a role model when it was not the fastest growing country in Europe. Little attention was paid to Italy and West Germany where growth had been appreciably faster. The explanation appears to be that there was already a disposition to look to economic planning to improve performance in Britain and hence to dwell on such evidence as could be found that planning had been an element in successful performance elsewhere. Commentators, in other words, were predisposed to believe that economic planning was what was needed in Britain, and were correspondingly ready to accept that it accounted for faster growth in France.

Little convincing evidence was produced that this was so. The Commissariat au Plan itself made no such claim, contenting itself with the proposition that planning had been helpful to growth. The rest of the EEC grew just as fast as France, and some countries faster, without indicative planning; but it was France that was singled out for attention and imitation.

It might be thought that since Britain had many years of experience in planning during and after the war, there was little need to look to France to learn about it. But there are many different kinds of planning; and the attraction of the French variety lay precisely in the fact that it worked successfully in conditions of peace and could be shown to bring government and industry together in a common endeavour. *How* it worked in France was not at all well understood in Britain: what mattered was that no one doubted that it worked.

What was surprising was that the appeal of planning extended to the Conservatives as well as to the Labour Party. In 1951 when the Conservatives came to power, anything that smacked of planning was anathema to Ministers. They were in revolt against government interference in industry, anxious to allow business a freer hand and almost as full of trust in market forces as their successors in the 1950s. Rab Butler objected even to the inclusion of forecasts in the annual *Economic Survey*; he hoped to 'free the pound', i.e. allow it to float at rates dictated by the market. Yet by 1961 Selwyn Lloyd had swung back to support planning through a National Economic Development Council with the full approval of the Cabinet.

It would seem from what he told the Cabinet that he was as much concerned to slow down inflation as to speed up growth. He intended to enlist the help of the Council in securing agreement to some restraint on wage demands in order to reduce inflationary pressure; and he hoped to achieve this agreement by allying it with the prospect of faster growth. How faster growth would result from planning except via more stable prices he had not considered: it was enough to announce a target higher than the current rate of growth without any preliminary examination of the potential for the proposed acceleration. In other words, he regarded planning as a *political* activity, not a highly technical examination of options and a co-ordination of the available means to secure the selected ends.

The Economist, which had studied planning procedure in France, was highly critical of the Chancellor's approach. The French might have a Conseil Supérieur, with 57 members drawn from employers, trade unionists, ministers and independent members, but it was fortunately 'completely dormant'. The real planning was undertaken by the technocrats in the Ministry of Finance who drafted the plan and set a target for the growth of Gross Domestic Product (GDP) on the basis of past performance; and on the staff of the Commissariat who co-ordinated the detailed production plans in conjunction with the industries concerned. In the view of *The Economist* there was 'an element of lunacy in the United Kingdom debate where the big question is supposed to be whether the Chancellor can get the TUC on the Council'[2] when he should be sending them to sleep. However, since Norman Macrae, who wrote all *The Economist*'s articles on planning, could see little difficulty in making incomes policy effective, he could hardly be expected to share the Chancellor's anxieties.

The appeal of planning in 1960–1 lay in the prospect of faster growth. It was assumed that by looking further ahead and selecting targets that could be shown to be self-consistent and attainable, planning offered the prospect of steadier and faster growth. It was represented as the antithesis of the sudden changes of policy, labelled 'stop–go', that were liable to interrupt the process of growth and discourage the enterprise on which it depended.

The idea of stop–go was linked in the public mind with a weak balance of payments and inadequate reserves. The immediate cause of the adoption of a restrictive policy was usually a deterioration in the balance of payments, coupled with withdrawals of capital and a loss of reserves. But balance of payments difficulties often originated in a loss of competitive power that could be traced to inflation. When restrictive measures were taken, symptoms of excess demand were rarely absent, the labour market was invariably tight, and the rise in prices and wages was showing signs of accelerating. The repeated efforts in the mid-1950s to check the expansion in production when a boom was developing in 1955 had as much to do with inflation as with the balance of payments, which by 1957 appeared to be in healthy surplus. Thorneycroft's announcement of a package of restrictive measures in September 1957, which brought to a halt a slow rise in production at 1.5 per cent per annum over the two preceding years, can be traced primarily to his determination to get on top of inflation. It was only at a late stage, when withdrawals of capital were eating into the reserves, that it was decided to include in the package a rise in bank rate to 7 per cent. The measures were successful in reducing domestic inflation to the extent that retail prices in 1958–60, for the first and last time since the war, remained steady for eighteen months. As unemployment decreased rapidly in 1959–60, however, wage-pressure built up again and the rise in prices recommenced.

Planning was thought to offer a remedy for inflation as well as a recipe for steady growth. Rising prices were associated with rising wages and the cure for cost inflation was sought in the reform of wage bargaining or in agreements to limit wage increases through some form of incomes policy. If the economy was planned, wages should form part of the plan; and it would be easier to obtain the agreement of wage-earners to moderate settlements in the context of economic growth. When the National Plan was abandoned in 1966, the prospect of a link between wage settlements and the planned rate of growth – never very likely – disappeared simultaneously while the struggle to control inflation continued with undiminished zeal.

Balance of payments difficulties were a more peremptory incitement to stop–go policies than the danger of inflation. It was nearly always possible to put off for a time counter-inflationary measures: there was usually room for argument that the limits of capacity had not yet been reached and that only by persevering with expansion would industrial investment be encouraged and bring with it the increased productivity that was the substance of real growth. Long before capacity operation was reached, expanding demand tended to overflow on to imports, causing a drain on reserves that could only be checked by urgent action. Such action, especially after direct control over imports was abandoned, was liable to bring expansion to a halt and arrest promising developments in industry: new investment, new practices, new products.

Critics of deflation pointed to these long-term losses on top of the loss of current production. Their views were most fully developed in two articles in 1961–2 by R. C. Tress and J. M. Fleming.[3] These articles, which attracted the attention of the Prime Minister, called for some form of incomes policy if cost inflation was to be avoided; and for corrective mechanisms including variations in exchange rates in preference to deliberate interruptions of economic growth if inflation nevertheless occurred.

The Tress–Fleming articles were perhaps the most sophisticated exposition of the case against stop–go. Others, in *The Economist* and the *National Institute Economic Review* expressed themselves equally strongly but from different angles. Norman Macrae in *The Economist*, for example, believed that, with the help of incomes policy, cost-inflation would yield to a resolute government, and so make possible a healthier balance of payments. He also thought that more use should be made of bank rate to check an outflow of capital and that the government was at fault in 1961 in delaying its use.

Were the critics right in calling for 'sustainable growth'? First of all, was it within the power of the government to maintain steady growth at or near the ceiling? Could demand management ever achieve the necessary skill and foresight? Were the fluctuations associated with stop–go in Britain wider than those in other industrial countries? The answer given by those who have looked into the matter is 'no'. The fluctuations elsewhere were just as large but they were around a trend that was rising more steeply than in Britain so that when output was checked it continued to grow in continental countries but stopped growing in Britain.

Again, was the lower rate of growth in Britain the consequence of the instability and uncertainty summed up in the phrase stop–go? Some economists wrote as if there could be only one answer. If the growth of demand kept being checked it would be the new and expanding products that would suffer most and the enterprising that were hit hardest. How could innovation help but be slowed down? To this there are three rejoinders. First of all, if Britain was typical rather than unique in the fluctuations it experienced, as research appeared to indicate, why should the set-back to growth be greater? Secondly, on an occasion such as occurred in 1968–71, when demand grew at a steady pace for three successive years, there was no evidence of a spurt in productivity growth. Uncertainty does not spring exclusively from the rate of expansion of aggregate demand. Thirdly, if stop–go is thought to explain the difference in economic performance between Britain and her neighbours on the continent, how does it come about that growth was no faster in the eighties than in the sixties despite the disappearance of stop–go? And why has the rate of growth in Europe fallen decade by decade to about the same rate as in Britain while in Britain it continues at a long-familiar rate?

Looking back on the constant harping on 'stop–go' as an explanation of Britain's disappointing rate of growth, one is struck by the emphasis on factors on the side of demand to the exclusion of factors on the side of supply. Output growth does, of course, depend intimately on the expansion of market demand. But productivity growth, the main source of long-term improvements in the standard of living, is another matter altogether and responds to commercial innovation of all kinds. Much as an expanding market may smooth the path of the innovator, it still remains necessary for him to be alert to the possibilities of innovation, to work on alternative ways of giving effect to them, to recognise the concomitant changes required in working practice, and to persuade the market of the advantages offered. If one takes the obvious example of motor car manufacture, market fluctuations associated with 'stop–go' may explain some of the difficulties of British producers but they do not explain why Japanese producers have been able to offer a superior product.

Whatever the impact of stop–go on productivity it did imply a loss of production during the stop phase; and it was a loss that could never be made up. If growth was at a steady rate and not too far below capacity, the loss would no longer occur. Demand management had not succeeded in maintaining a steady rate of growth. Could planning in some form achieve such a result?

It soon became clear that different people had different ideas of what planning involved. There were those who thought of planning as a way of framing government policy by giving more weight to long-term considerations and trying to ensure cor-ordination between the different elements in the policy adopted. To those who thought along these lines it was the activity of planning that mattered: planning could be highly flexible, based on a continuous review of economic prospects, and subject to frequent adjustment. Others took it for granted that planning meant the preparation of a plan that would remain unchanged until completion, with fixed objectives and fixed targets. It obviously involved a relationship between government and industry: but how the macroeconomic objectives of the plan were to be translated into the microeconomic targets of individual businesses was obscure. Was the government to lay down targets for particular industries after discussion with representatives of each industry? If so, what was the government to do to help in achieving the targets? And how were the representatives to proceed in harnessing individual businesses to the plan under competitive conditions? In a command economy the plan was a set of instructions, but even that was far from guaranteeing its fulfilment. With indicative planning it was not possible to do more, after consultation with a sample of those affected, than to issue a set of figures that was both self-consistent and judged to be feasible if appropriate policies were adopted. But what notice would the individual business take of the figures?

In wartime, government planning involved a direct relationship with every enterprise supplying government requirements or dependent on the government for its materials or labour supply or authority to proceed. In the absence of such a direct relationship, the government had to rely on influences of a different kind: appeals, promises, tax incentives, subsidies, protection in one form or another. How successful all this would be in procuring fulfilment of a plan was hard to say. In the French case the plan was prepared initially in the Treasury on the basis of the rate of growth already achieved: there was no attempt to use the plan in the 1950s to jack up the rate still higher. So long as the pace was maintained, it could be claimed that the plan was fulfilled even when, industry by industry, there were substantial shortfalls or oversupplies that offset one another. In Britain where it was hoped to raise the rate of growth, such an outcome would have been tantamount to failure.

A popular idea was that if only the government would commit itself to a higher rate of growth and win the support of industry in such a commitment, higher growth would automatically result. Each industry, by expanding production, would afford a larger market to the others and when they in turn responded by expanding, it would find the wider market for its output for which it had hoped.

As the National Institute put it in 1962:

> a necessary, and almost sufficient, condition for rapid growth is for businessmen in general to expect that demand for their products will continue to grow rapidly. Otherwise they are unlikely to increase their investment expenditure, to engage in expansionary (rather than defensive) investment or to exert themselves in finding ways of increasing productivity. For businessmen to hold confident expectations about the long-run demand for their products, they must also be confident that total demand in the economy as a whole will expand unhampered by balance of payments difficulties or excessive price rises.[4]

This emphasis on demand factors to the exclusion of influences on the side of supply, and on investment rather than on technical and organisational change, seemed to go much too far, especially in versions of the doctrine that disregarded the qualifications at the end of the paragraph and were little more than economic Couéism. To the extent that business confidence generated its own justification, the preparation of a plan seemed superfluous except as a kind of totem. The fluctuations that occurred were not just the product of the come and go of business confidence. They resulted from imbalances and uncertainties which had to be corrected if growth was to be faster; and it was from these imbalances and uncertainties, not a series of industrial targets, that planning ought to start.

The most obvious of these uncertainties related to the balance of payments. This was where the British economy was most vulnerable. The most frequent interruptions to the expansion of output had come from difficulties with the balance of payments and there was every indication that these interruptions would continue unless something could be done to improve Britain's competitive position and allow exports to take the lead over imports. This was a view fully endorsed by the officials who prepared The National Plan in 1964–5 some of whom assumed an eventual devaluation not approved by the Ministers in charge of the Plan. Paradoxically, had Ministers been of the same mind, there would probably have been no Plan. By the time the pound was devalued in 1967 the Plan had disappeared and was never revived.

Not that devaluation was the only way of fortifying the balance of payments. There were a number of other possibilities. One was a long-term loan such as had been raised after the war from the United States on generous terms. This would have strengthened the reserves and made it easier to ride out speculative pressure on the balance of payments without higher interest rates or an approach to the International Monetary Fund (IMF) for short-term assistance. The difficulty was to see how a loan of the size required could be raised in the United States when the American balance of payments was itself running into difficulties. A second possibility was to restrict foreign lending and investment. There was already control over long-term capital flows to countries outside the sterling area but this still left a large net outflow throughout the 1950s to countries within the sterling area – an outflow that continued in the 1960s. Short-term capital flows, including leads and lags in commercial credit, were extremely difficult to regulate; one of the few forms of control that worked was the periodic ban on the provision of credit for the finance of trade between third parties. Other possibilities, of which much was heard in the 1960s, included the use of import quotas, import deposits, an import surcharge and export subsidies, open or disguised, although the last two of these were infringements of international agreements.

We shall come later to the issue of devaluation. For the present we need only take note that by 1960 there were already hints and suggestions implying an eventual need for it. The pound, it was thought, was overvalued and holding back economic growth. On these propositions, three comments can be offered.

First of all, whatever view one took of the parity, the reserves were too low, especially for a reserve currency like sterling. At the beginning of 1960 they stood at $2736 million, not much bigger than at the end of the war, far below the total of sterling balances held in London, and less than the equivalent of three months' imports. Efforts to increase the reserves by running a balance of payment surplus were liable to frustration because of the inability of Britain's trading partners to provide gold or dollars in settlement. Over one-third of Britain's trade was with other members of the sterling area and settled in sterling. A surplus with other countries was not easy to obtain or enlarge.

Secondly, whether the pound was overvalued could not be decided independently of the pressure of demand at which it was intended to operate the economy. A deficit that appeared when unemployment reached 1.3 per cent might disappear when unemployment was slightly higher. In the years 1956–9 the surplus on current account had averaged £240 million and the reserves had increased by a total of £220 million while unemployment had averaged 1.7 per cent. These figures hardly suggest consistent overvaluation. If unemployment had remained throughout at 1.7 per cent, there would have been still less evidence of overvaluation and if it had been maintained at 2 per cent the chances are that there would have been even less again. It is by no means certain that output would have risen more slowly with this relatively small reduction in pressure.

Thirdly, it can be argued that the 'slow' growth of productivity in the British economy had little to do with stop–go and the loss of production that accompanied it. In a decade like the 1980s, when there was no suggestion of balance of payments difficulties or of stop–go policies, the growth rate was much what it had been in the 1960s when balance of payments problems were acute. There was no spurt in the growth of productivity in the years following devaluation in 1967. What has dominated talk of Britain's industrial decline in recent years has been, not stop–go, but lack of training, defects of management, inflexibility in various forms and other factors of a more persistent kind.

Growth implies change and change is greeted with more enthusiasm in some countries than others. It was more likely to be welcomed in countries that had been occupied or fought over in wartime, and left at the end of the war with a severely damaged physical, institutional and cultural infrastructure, than in a country like Britain that had been on the winning side, retained a well-established social and economic structure more or less intact, and regarded its existing institutions and habits with satisfaction. Full employment in Britain encouraged conservative and protectionist attitudes that slowed down change, while on the continent unemployment and underemployment called for more drastic action. Managements in Britain had a booming home market from the start and workers could insist on sticking to established practice without fear of unemployment.

Economic growth is not only a function of the acceptability of change. It is also a function of the rate at which markets expand. In 1945, the main continental economies were operating at very low levels in relation to their potential. Once expansion started, it had a long way to go before all the slack in the system was absorbed; and as it expanded it could suck in additional resources of manpower from agriculture and from abroad. This meant that as expansion proceeded, and provided it was not diverted by inflation or balance of payments difficulties, the domestic market would grow too. Productivity would rise as the market expanded as a result of economies of scale, investment in the latest types of equipment, and all the pressures that an expanding market exerts on managerial ingenuity. The growth in productivity in turn enhanced competitive power in foreign markets and a higher level of income and spending in the domestic market, reinforcing the whole process of market growth begun under other influences. In the United Kingdom, on the other hand, (and in the United States), an economy already fully employed as the war ended could enjoy a rapidly expanding market only abroad and only until former exporting countries re-entered world markets. There was less chance of generating the momentum of growth attending the absorption of extensive slack. It is perhaps some such explanation as this that accounts for the wide differences in rates of growth in the 1950s and their progressive narrowing decade by decade since then. As the end-war slack was absorbed, and other forms of slack proved more difficult to draw upon, continental rates fell to the British rate, while that continued unchanged at what was still thought of as the low rate of a country in decline.

One thing that contributed to faster economic growth was the higher level of capital investment. In total, fixed capital investment was 60 per cent higher in the 1960s than in the 1950s and fixed investment in manufacturing industry, which was about a quarter of the total, increased in much the same proportion. The only decade in which total investment was as high as in the 1960s was the 1980s; but investment in manufacturing industry was then slightly lower than in the 1960s.

INFLATION

The main economic problems, apart from how to accelerate growth, were inflation and external imbalance. The two were related since it was rising costs, and particularly rising wage-costs, that pushed up prices, whittled away competitive power and left the balance of payments in chronic deficit. Excess demand played its part by creating an environment of labour scarcity in which workers demanded and employers conceded large increases in pay that were met by putting up prices. The process was one that ate into competitive power, except in so far as other countries were caught in the same vicious circle; and the loss of competitive power in turn propelled the balance of payments into deficit.

In the 1950s, the only remedy the government had been able to find was deflation, putting an end to excess demand by a 'stop': a package of measures that usually included higher interest rates, higher taxes, cuts in public expenditure and hire purchase restrictions. The tax component could only be included at budget time until the introduction of the tax regulator in 1961; the cuts in public expenditure were always very slow to take effect; the variations in interest rates were usually small and without much effect domestically, although they could be quite powerful externally in improving the attractiveness of sterling to foreign holders. Hire-purchase restrictions were the quickest-acting and perhaps the most powerful influence on consumer spending, but affected only a narrow range of economic activity and could have damaging effects on the efficiency of an industry such as motor-car manufacture. In total, however, the government had quite enough power to limit demand when so minded. The difficulty was to foresee when action would be required and how much. There was certainly a risk of not doing enough, as was evident from mid-1964 to mid-1966; but there was also a risk of doing too much, as may well have happened in 1961 and, through overexpansion, in 1963–4.

In the effort to limit inflation there was little thought of reliance on monetary policy, much less *exclusive* reliance on monetary policy, such as became popular doctrine in the 1970s. The prevailing view was that of the Radcliffe Committee, based on the experience of the 1950s: monetary policy by itself had limited usefulness in controlling inflation. There were a few convinced monetarists whose views received increasing prominence in the late 1960s; but their influence on policy was at that time negligible. The IMF expressed concern that the United Kingdom attached so little importance to monetary policy as an instrument of domestic policy and in 1968 sent a mission to discuss the matter with the Treasury. But the IMF itself did not hold strict monetarist views and the Treasury continued to regard monetary policy as of limited value in demand management and not a very effective weapon to use against inflation except in rather extreme circumstances.

Inflation in the 1960s never assumed the proportions it did in the 1970s. There were none of those bouts of rapid price increases such as occurred when world commodity prices soared upwards in 1950–1 and 1973–4. The rise in prices was propelled almost entirely by inflationary wage-bargains in Britain and not by outside influences. It stood to reason that the remedy must be one that affected these bargains either through greater restraint or by reducing demand. If output was not to suffer, greater restraint was the natural recourse. Demand management was not an appropriate instrument since it was designed to act not on prices but on output.

Much thought was given to various forms of incomes policy that would act directly on prices or on the costs to which prices responded. One possibility was a wage freeze. There had been occasions in the early post-war years when a freeze was successful in stabilising prices for a time – notably after the 1949 devaluation. Ministers in the Conservative government hesitated to use a wage freeze but in 1961 Selwyn Lloyd called for a voluntary 'wage pause'. This was succeeded by the appointment of a National Incomes Commission and when this proved to be a flop, Maudling did his best to reach agreement with the TUC on wage restraint in 1963–4 but had no success.

Under the Labour Governments of 1964–70 George Brown gave incomes policy a new start and a more and more elaborate machinery for monitoring wage and price movements was introduced. A National Board for Prices and Incomes was created and the policy, at first voluntary, became statutory. But in spite of the great effort that was made, wages rose at least as fast as before. In the first half of the decade, hourly wage-rates increased by 29 per cent, in the second half by $37\frac{1}{2}$ per cent. The devaluation of 1967 added to pressure on wages and may be thought to upset the comparison. But there were other circumstances that could have worked the other way: for example, the higher level of unemployment in the second period made for more moderate wage-bargains. The wage-freeze in July 1966 did have a marked effect on wage-bargains and helped to limit the rise in hourly wages in the next six months to less than 1 per cent. It was succeeded, however, by an average rise of 6.8 per cent per annum over the next three years – appreciably higher than the average of 5.2 per cent between 1960 and 1965.

Seen in a wider perspective, the acceleration in prices in the late 1960s might seem the prelude to the far more rapid inflation of the 1970s. However, the acceleration was not very marked until the end of 1969. It was not until 1970 that wage inflation, climbed above 10 per cent per annum, and continued at that level. It is difficult to put much of the blame for the faster rise in prices on the devaluation in late 1967 and more plausible to associate it with the militant temper of those years. The forces at work as discussed in Chapter 13.

Was price inflation faster in Britain in the 1960s than abroad? For the period 1956–73 there was not a great deal of difference between Britain and the average for industrial countries. Prices rose by 4.5 per cent a year in Britain and by 4 per cent a year in the Organization for Economic Cooperation and Development (OECD). In the 1960s, the rise in consumer prices in Britain was somewhat lower than this – 3.8 per cent per annum. Whether this was higher or lower than on the continent depends on the countries entering into the comparison. It was slightly lower than in France or Italy but higher than in Germany where inflation averaged 2.7 per cent per annum.

Price inflation speeded up at the end of the decade in most industrial countries, but less so in Britain in spite of devaluation. The figures of hourly earnings also show some acceleration on the European continent but very little in Britain. In the late 1950s, the slower rise of productivity in Britain was largely offset by the slower rise in wages: money wages rose twice as fast in France and thrice as fast in Germany. In the 1960s the divergence was much less: money wages rose about 45 per cent faster in France and 30 per cent faster in Germany.

THE BALANCE OF PAYMENTS

The central problem of the decade for the United Kingdom was the balance of payments. It had been a problem in the 1950s as other countries recovered and gained a larger share of world trade. In the first eight years of the 1950s, exports had increased in volume by a mere 10 per cent and over the decade as a whole the increase was no more than 20 per cent. In every year between 1950 and 1970 Britain's share in world trade in manufacturing fell (Figure 1.1). The current account surplus of a little over £100 million a year on the average in the 1950s had been more than offset by the outflow of long-term capital, making it impossible to add to the reserves, which did not regain the level reached in early 1951 until twenty years later. What saved the day in the 1950s was a favourable shift of 10 per cent in the terms of trade (which represented a windfall of about £300 million a year in foreign exchange) and an unrecorded credit hidden in the 'balancing item' which was reckoned to be worth some £60 million or more annually.

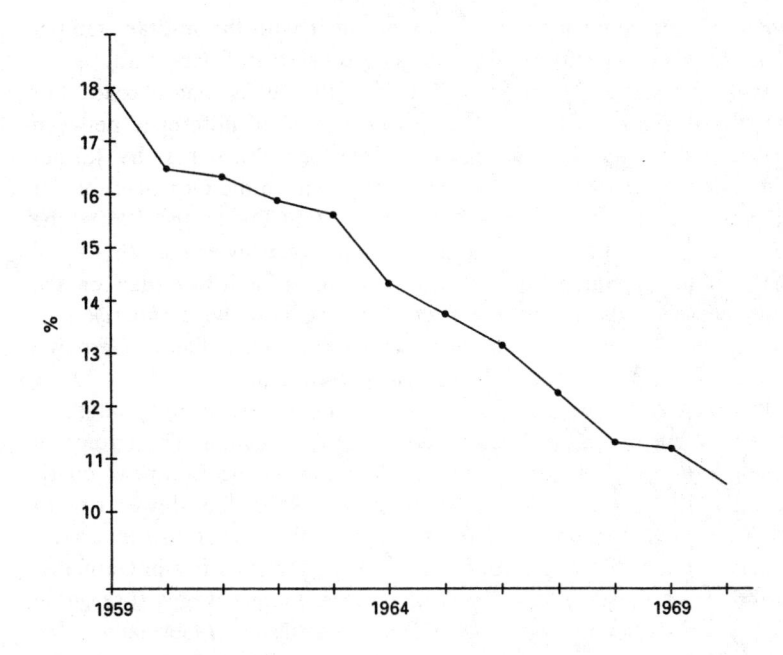

FIGURE 1.1 *British share of world trade in manufactures, 1959–70*

The precariousness of the situation first became apparent in 1960 when the current account was thought to be £344 million in deficit (revised many years later to £237 million). A crisis was avoided in 1960 as a result of a large inflow of funds from abroad, but it proved only to have been postponed to 1961 when the funds began to be withdrawn. The deflationary measures then taken restored a small surplus in the current balance of payments in 1962–3 (see Figure 1.2) but as recovery gathered momentum in 1964, a fresh balance of payments crisis occurred shortly after the election in the autumn. The current account deficit in 1964, now put at £362 million, was aggravated by heavy investment abroad, much of it by the oil companies, amounting to a further £300 million. The reserves fell to their lowest level since 1957 so that the deficit could be covered only by heavy short-term borrowing from abroad.

Over the next three years a great effort was made to maintain the parity. Many different measures were devised to improve the current account and to reduce the outflow of long-term capital. The current account moved into surplus by the end of 1965, remained close to

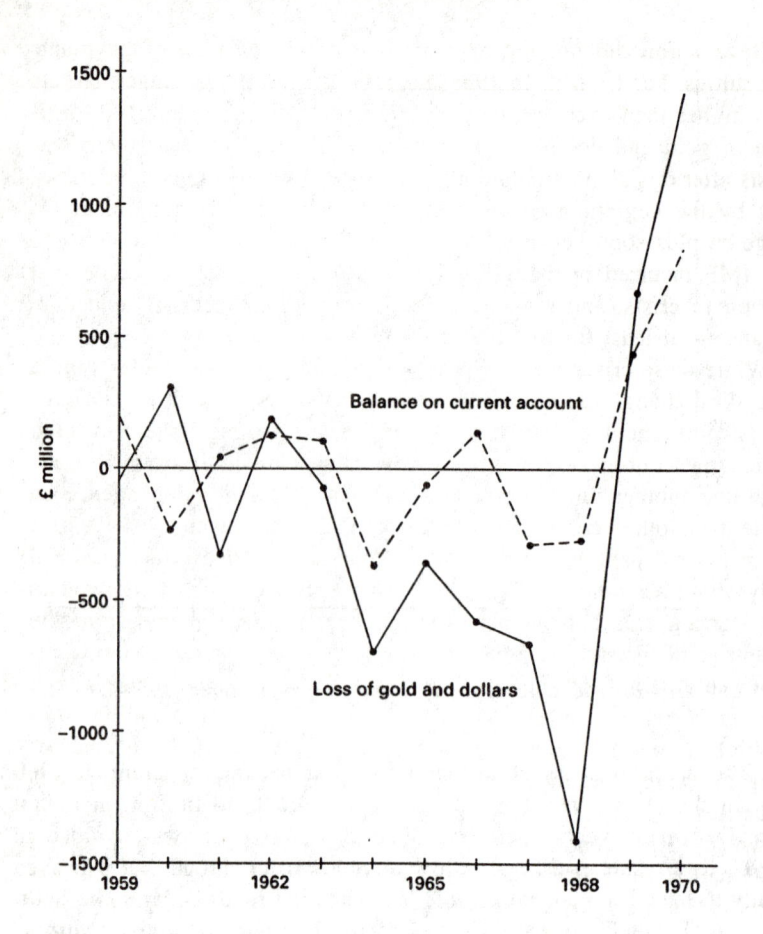

FIGURE 1.2 *The balance of payments on current account and the gold and dollar drain, 1959–70*

balance until the autumn of 1967 and then plunged again into heavy deficit as world trade temporarily lost its momentum. Meanwhile the outflow of long-term capital had subsided a little; but investment within the sterling area remained unrestricted. Monetary movements were on a far larger scale. The withdrawal of funds continued year after year and made it necessary to borrow heavily from the IMF and other monetary authorities. In the four years 1964–7 the drain of foreign exchange added up to £2300 million. When devaluation ultimately occurred in November 1967 the debts contracted had reached nearly $5 billion, all of them short-term.

Devaluation did not put an end to Britain's balance of payments difficulties. Far from it. In 1968 the pressure in the exchange markets was higher than ever and the authorities had to find over £1400 million in gold and dollars to hold the rate. During the year there was crisis after crisis, more palpitating than any in the previous three years. But by the beginning of 1969 the outlook was more hopeful and a large surplus soon began to appear. Three years later all the debts to the IMF incurred in the 1960s had been repaid. Thus a decade that started in crisis, and remained almost throughout in crisis, ended in balance – at least for the time being.

While these crises were in progress, British trade was undergoing a structural change. Before the war it had been largely with other continents: only about a quarter was with Europe. In this Britain differed from other European countries which carried on most of their trade with one another. In the early post-war years, Britain's dependence on trade with other continents was even more pronounced. By 1950 a more normal pattern had re-appeared but trade with Europe was still only about a quarter of the total. Nearly half British exports went to the sterling area and 38 per cent of British imports came from the countries of the sterling area, nearly all of them members of the Commonwealth. By 1960 the rapid expansion in continental markets, and the much greater competition in sterling area markets (including competition from domestic suppliers of those markets), was already beginning to change the direction of British trade. Exports to sterling-area countries had been flat or actually falling for some years and were down to 35 per cent of the total while exports to the six members of EEC had risen from about 11 per cent to about 15 per cent and exports to European Free Trade Association (EFTA) countries were over 10 per cent. These proportions rose rapidly in the early 1960s and had reached 22 per cent and 16 per cent by 1970 while the sterling area's share of exports had fallen to 23 per cent.[5]

The shift to West European markets had still a long way to go, but it was already clear by the 1960s how the wind was blowing. The big expansion in intra-European trade in the mid-fifties had paved the way for the Treaty of Rome in 1957. Similarly, the change in the direction of British trade helped to move the government to seek entry to the European Community in 1961 and was an even more powerful influence on the second occasion in 1967.

Other changes in the structure of trade were becoming visible in the 1960s. After convertibility of currencies was established at the end of 1958, discrimination against imports from America was gradually withdrawn. This contributed to a surge in imports of manufactures, which continued long after the 1960s. From 31 per cent of total imports in 1960, they had risen to 51 per cent ten years later and the proportion was still increasing. It took just over another ten years for Britain to become a net importer of manufactures.

UNEMPLOYMENT

While unemployment in the 1960s may seem in retrospect almost negligible, it was politically of the highest importance. To let unemployment rise by 1 per cent was to risk losing the next election. As an object of policy, unemployment took precedence over almost every other consideration.

At the beginning of the 1960s unemployment was extremely low. A boom had developed in 1959–60 that continued until the middle of 1961. The pound came under threat and the Chancellor took deflationary action in July 1961 which depressed the level of production without causing an actual fall. This re-established confidence in the currency but raised unemployment. The 'stop' was highly unpopular, especially as the check to activity was prolonged into 1963. A rapid recovery then began which continued in spite of an exchange crisis in 1964 and persistent balance of payments difficulties in 1965. Fresh deflationary measures were taken in July 1966 and this once again checked the growth of production and produced a sharp rise in unemployment. Nevertheless, the Central Statistical Office's (CSO) index of GDP continued to rise from half-year to half-year as it had done in 1961–3 (Figure 1.3).

Unemployment was more sensitive than production to these measures. In January 1960 it had fallen to 1.7 per cent and a year later stood at 1.3 per cent. In the ensuing recession, unemployment climbed to 2.4 per cent early in 1963 and then fell steadily to 1.3 per cent at the beginning of 1965. There was then very little change until the measures of July 1966 which caused unemployment to climb steeply from a low point of 1.2 per cent in the first half of the year to 2.3 per cent in the second half of 1967, i.e. from about 300,000 to 570,000. After devaluation in November 1967 the rate changed very little over the next two years. It did not rise above 2.4 per cent until 1970.

Unemployment was thus at a very low level for most of the decade and never very high compared with later years. In 1960–1 the average rate was under $1\frac{1}{2}$ per cent and in the south of the country it was, for

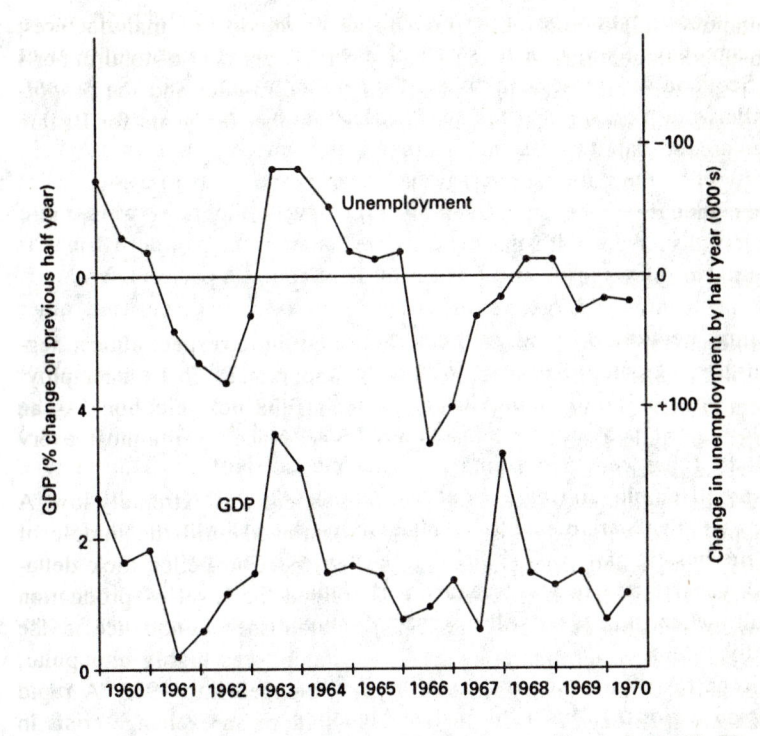

FIGURE 1.3 *Half-yearly changes in GDP and unemployment, 1960–70*

long spells, under 1 per cent. Even in the appalling weather at the beginning of 1963 the peak in unemployment (including 226,000 temporarily stopped) fell well short of a million; and for the wholly unemployed the rate in Britain never reached 2.5 per cent then or later in the decade. There were, however, some indications that a given unemployment percentage represented a somewhat tighter labour market in the 1960s than it did in the 1950s. When unemployment was at its lowest in the first half of 1966 at 1.2 per cent, and it seemed almost impossible that it should fall further, it was appreciably higher than at the low point in the 1950s, when for six months at the end of 1955 it was down to 0.9 per cent. The minimum feasible level of unemployment seemed to be rising slowly from one cycle to the next.[6]

Regional Differences

The level of unemployment differed a good deal from one part of the country to another and the differences tended to persist, each area remaining in much the same relationship to the others. In 1960, when unemployment was near its seasonal low point in June, unemployment in Scotland was more than double the national average of 1.5 per cent, while from Yorkshire to the south coast (but not in the south-west) it was around half the national average. The same was true in 1964. In 1970 when the national average had risen at mid-year to 2.5 per cent (then thought to be an intolerably high level), the rates were more widely dispersed, with the highest rate (apart from Northern Ireland) in the Northern region at 4.6 per cent, Scotland at 4 per cent, Wales at 3.8 per cent, the large South-East region at 1.6 per cent and other regions between 1.8 and 2.5 per cent.

These regional differences were seen as a major problem in employment policy. If full employment meant keeping the national average below 2 per cent, the rate in the south-east and the Midlands would fall to 1 per cent and signal an acute labour shortage. This in turn disposed employers there to accept, and workers to press for, wage increases that were bound to be inflationary since the settlements reached in the busiest parts of the country set the pace for the rest and ended in a general rise in wages and prices. Inflation would then lead to a 'stop' when there were still reserves of unused resources in many parts of the country.

Repeated efforts were made in the 1960s to assist the less fully occupied regions. In his 1963 budget Maudling introduced 'free' depreciation for businesses in the development areas where unemployment was highest (i.e. firms could write off plant and machinery at whatever rate they chose). Later, in 1967, a regional employment premium was introduced, offering a bounty on the employment of workers in 'underemployed' regions. These incentives may have brought more work to the regions concerned but they did not operate to bring unemployment rates closer together. Their principal effect would seem to have been to slow down the outflow of labour to jobs in other regions.

INDUSTRIAL STRUCTURE

The fluctuations over the decade were accompanied by longer-term changes in industrial structure. Some industries contracted and lost labour while others expanded and took on more workers. One of the most significant changes occurred in 1966 when employment in manufacturing reached an all-time peak and started on the decline that has since cut employment in manufacturing in half.

Employment contracted appreciably between 1960 and 1970 in coal-mining, agriculture and horticulture, rail transport (including locomotive building and the supply of railway equipment), shipbuilding and marine engineering, and cotton spinning and weaving. These five groups, employing between them 2.41 million workers in 1960, had shed 400,000 by 1964 and nearly 500,000 in the next four years, employment falling to 1.54 million in 1968. On the other hand, employment in other parts of the economy absorbed over 1 million workers in those eight years. The six groups most prominent in absorbing more labour were: national and local government service, educational services, medical and dental services (which together absorbed 100,000 a year), motor vehicle manufacture and repair, road haulage contracting, and printing and publishing (which absorbed 200,000, nearly all in the first four years to 1964). The biggest single changes were in coal-mining, which contracted in eight years from 700,000 to 430,000, and in educational services which expanded from 900,000 to 1,340,000. While the expanding group took on over 1 million more workers, the contracting group shed nearly 900,000.[7] In addition, changes in employment were in progress *within* the groups and in the much larger area of employment not covered by the eleven industries listed.

The comparative steadiness of total employment during those years thus conceals movement on a very considerable scale within the total from job to job. Adjustments to the industrial structure were assisted by a net increase in the number of workers in employment by over 600,000 (from 24.18 million in 1960 to 24.84 million in 1968). But, as we have just seen, the contribution of the contracting industries in releasing nearly 900,000 workers was even larger.

THE ROLE OF THE STATE

Finally, a brief word on the role of the state. In some ways the 1960s represented the apogee of the state's influence in economic affairs.

It is true that a higher proportion of GDP was taken in rates and taxes and social security contributions in 1988 than in 1968 (36.7 per cent against 34.8 per cent). But what makes the 1960s stand out is the large *increase* that occurred then in the resources surrendered by the citizenry for use by the authorities. In 1958 the proportion of GDP surrendered had fallen below 30 per cent; ten years later it had risen by over 5 per cent to 34.8 per cent. So large an increase had never previously occurred within a decade in peace-time.

Another illustration of the expanding role of the state is the growing proportion of capital investment taking place in the public sector in the 1960s. In the early post-war years public investment had been of the same order of magnitude as private investment – not surprisingly when the state had to undertake a large part of the community's saving through its budget. In the 1950s, public investment fell behind and by 1960 accounted for 40 per cent of gross fixed investment. In 1967 the proportion had risen to over 48 per cent, although it had fallen back to 44 per cent by 1970.[8] The rapid increase in public investment in the mid-1960s was an important source of the government's financial difficulties.

The influence of the state is not to be measured only in statistical terms. What was more striking was the acute sense of dependence on the state to take the initiative and the presumption that if something was amiss it was up to the state to put it right. The presumption was that whatever was thought its duty to do, it could do. There was little sense of the state's impotence, the limits within which it could act effectively, the time required to frame feasible policies, the dangers of undue reliance on officials.

On the other hand, the 1960s were also a time of release from custom and wont, when permissiveness became the watchword and satire the prevailing mode. Prosperity allowed constraints to be relaxed and the assurance of employment made for a spirit of independence and experimentation combined with a certain indiscipline and insubordination. It was a time of student revolt when the young came to power and revelled in it. At the same time as the state was being deified it was also being defied.

Part II

2 The First Cycle, 1957–61

THE ECONOMIC SECTION

Before I begin to trace the development of policy, let me briefly explain what my job was, what staff I inherited and how we all fitted into the Treasury. Although I was given the rather grand title of Economic Adviser to HMG, my job in practice was that of a Treasury official advising the Chancellor (or more frequently the Permanent Secretary) on economic and financial affairs. I had the assistance, as Director of the Economic Section of the Treasury, of a group of economists who had been since 1940 the principal source of economic advice to the government.[1]

They were a distinct group, meeting regularly even when some members worked in another Treasury division (but not when they worked in another department in Whitehall or were posted abroad). Each member had his own area of responsibility, with economic forecasting the main area and the exclusive responsibility of the Section. There was a close association with both Home and Overseas Finance but less involvement with the expenditure divisions dealing with Defence, Agriculture, Transport, Social Services and so on. So far as available personnel allowed – and it did not allow very much – I tried to brigade more economists with the expenditure divisions. This was an arrangement that developed later with an absorption of economists into Treasury divisions so that economists could come to head these divisions – a process which culminated in the appointment in the 1990s of an economist (Sir Terence Burns, Head of the Government Economic Service) as Permanent Secretary of the Treasury.

There were rarely more than fifteen economists in the Treasury, while a few others served in other departments or abroad on secondment. They were thus a relatively small part of the total administrative staff of the Treasury (assistant principals and upwards) which numbered about 200 in the 1960s. Unlike other Treasury officials, few of them were established, most of them being on five-year contracts or on leave from their universities for two years. Given their responsibilities and capabilities they were nearly all poorly graded and poorly paid.

The ground covered by the Section was enormous because the

responsibilities of the Treasury were enormously widespread, including at least five different functions, each of which might be (and in some countries is) entrusted to a separate agency. It acted as a Ministry of Economic Affairs before the creation of the Department of Economic Affairs (DEA) (and some would say after as well); a Ministry of Finance in charge of taxation; a Ministry of the Public Sector controlling public expenditure and public enterprise; it had a responsibility for monetary policy and international financial affairs; and it was the ministry responsible for the civil service until that function was briefly taken over by a separate department in 1969. In addition to all this, the Treasury took a leading past in issues of foreign economic policy. That may seem a rather terrifying catalogue. There was indeed a great deal of detailed information to be absorbed and a host of decisions to be made. But from the point of view of the Chancellor, there were relatively few decisions, compared with, say, the Home Office, that he and only he could take, and they could usually be taken at leisure and after due deliberation, especially once a Chief Secretary had been appointed in 1960 to take over most of the work on public expenditure.

Time set limits to what could be done and time was limited by meetings, minutes and memoranda – both the memos one had to read and the memos one had to write. When photocopying arrived, the number of minutes I received almost doubled and as I had no staff to act as a filter, I could only discover what it was important to read after I had read it. In my $7\frac{1}{2}$ years in the Treasury I must have written or dictated at least 4500 minutes of varying length – at a guess about 2 million words – much of it written or dictated in the evenings or at weekends. On top of that was all that went to recruiting staff to the Government Economic Service: innumerable letters and interviews, together with arguments on pay and gradings with the Establishments division. That took up about a third of my time.

Such pressures gave one a keen sense of priorities: and there could be no doubt where priority No. 1 lay. What Chancellors most wanted from me was an assessment of the economic outlook. They might revile and distrust the forecasts we produced; but they knew that there was no escape from forming a view of the future and that such a view had ultimately to be in quantitative terms.

Forecasting took up much more of our time than anything else. The preparation of three full forecasts each year was a co-operative effort involving the CSO, the Board of Trade and other departments; and key elements might be incorporated without endorsement by the Economic Section, as happened in 1962 when we issued a highly optimistic national income forecast based on an expansion in the volume of exports in that year by 9 per cent.

Incomes policy, although the prime responsibility after 1964 rested on DEA and the management side of the Treasury, raised issues central to economic management and we had constantly to brief the Chancellor. There were issues of monetary policy and debt management which, as a signatory of the Radcliffe Report, I could hardly neglect. These involved me in regular contact with the Bank of England – more regular than my contacts with the Home Finance Division of the Treasury. Equally, there were issues of international finance and liquidity that were constantly under discussion. I was drawn by past experience to matters of industrial policy on which the Treasury was often not well-informed. In energy policy alone, there were all the problems of nuclear power and electricity generation; the future of coal-mining; the development of the gas industry once North Sea supplies became available; investment by the oil companies and at a later stage (but already under discussion by 1967) in North Sea oil. There were also the problems of transport policy by road, rail, air and sea. These in turn led into the problems of the nationalised industries, the pricing policy they pursued, the investment they proposed to undertake. When railway revenue was no more than £1000 per employee and the low prices forced on the nationalised industries were fuelling inflationary pressure by adding to the purchasing power of consumers, these were not matters the Treasury could neglect.

Even more important were questions of industrial efficiency and competitive power: questions that were not confined to private industry. How could productivity be raised and the rate of innovation improved? What were we to do about restrictive practices or about monopolies and mergers? Half our exports came from the metal and engineering industries, but Whitehall's contact with engineering was minimal in comparison with its contact with agriculture, coal-mining and textiles – the declining industries.

From my point of view, finding staff was perhaps the most time-consuming duty of all. There were less than a score of posts for economists within the Treasury but other departments were constantly seeking an economic adviser and those who were recruited to the Treasury had to be of high calibre. Senior members of the Economic Section might be serving in Washington, Paris or elsewhere; in the Foreign Office, the DEA or some other department; or, on release for a year or two, in the National Institute. Of the most senior of my colleagues in 1961–4, for example, Jack Downie and Christopher Dow had to be seconded during that period to OECD, Bryan Hopkin and Christopher Dow were seconded in the 1950s to the National Institute, Wynne Godley was there for two years in the 1960s, Fred Atkinson was lent for a year to the Foreign Office and Bryan Hopkin was seconded for a time to the Ministry of Overseas Development. In 1968 I was under pressure to release another colleague, Andrew Roy, to the Bank of England.

I came to the conclusion that we needed to breed more economists to serve in government. I proposed towards the end of 1965 that we should recruit as cadets up to fifteen graduates who had taken a first at their university and were willing to undergo re-training as economists at government expense. I reckoned that, even if they elected, once trained in economics, to abandon their government job and take employment elsewhere, some contribution would still have been made to relieving the shortage of economists. I am glad, therefore, to be able to point to the example of Andrew Britton, a former cadet economist who began as a graduate in classics and, after a spell at the London School of Economics (LSE) and service in the Treasury, became Director of the National Institute.

THE FIRST CYCLE, 1957–61

When I entered the Treasury in June 1961 I had only a limited knowledge of the policies pursued over the preceding years and how the Treasury viewed the events of those years. Although I had been in fairly close touch with members of the Treasury staff, including Sir Frank Lee, the Permanent Secretary, in 1940–1 when I was in the War Cabinet Offices and again in 1946–9 when I was Economic Adviser to the Board of Trade, many years had passed since then. In the 1950s, I had not been brought much into contact with Treasury officials except when they appeared as witnesses before the Radcliffe Committee in 1957–9 and my interests had been more in developments in industry and trade than in the management of the British economy.

I had no sooner taken up my duties than the first signs of an exchange crisis appeared. To understand the situation it is necessary to go back a little, since 1957 was at the end of one cycle and the beginning of another. The crisis in 1961 was seen by economic commentators and government officials in the light of events in the cycle that was just ending. Since there is no adequate published account of that cycle,[2] I have thought it desirable to preface an account of events in the 1960s with a sketch of developments between 1957 and 1961.

The cycle of 1957–61 opened with the measures taken by Thorneycroft in September 1957. These took shape largely at ministerial level and were designed primarily to bring inflation under control. At a late stage an increase in bank rate to 7 per cent was added so as to cope with an outflow of short-term capital. Thorneycroft is often represented as an early monetarist. It was the flow of money expenditure (i.e. demand) rather than the stock of money that he sought to limit although he used language in a way that confused the two things. He did seek to get agreement to a 5 per cent reduction in bank advances (which would have led to a corresponding fall in the stock of money) but was unable to persuade the clearing banks, found that the Governor of the Bank of England was unwilling to issue a directive, and was advised that he had neither the power to force the Bank to issue a directive nor the power to dismiss the Governor, both of which courses he was contemplating.[3]

Nothing of this emerged in the proceedings before the Bank Rate Tribunal which was set up to enquire into allegations of a leak before the increase in bank rate. Nor was there any disclosure of a disagreement between the Chancellor and the Governor over the size of the increase. The Governor had pressed for a rise to 7 per cent while the Chancellor favoured a rise to 6 per cent, but gave way when it was pointed out to him that if he intended to sack the Governor he would be in difficulties if it transpired that the Governor had favoured tougher action than he did.[4]

All I knew of this episode was that there had been such a serious rift between the Chancellor and his advisers that Sir Robert Hall, Economic Adviser to HMG, had offered his resignation – indeed, according to Lord Franks, had offered it twice. It was not until April 1961, however, that Robert Hall finally retired at the age of 60.

The September measures produced a shallow recession in 1958 when, for the first time since the war, output fell below the level of the previous year. Unemployment, which had been as low as 1 per cent for most of 1955–6 and was still under 300,000 in the autumn of 1957, rose to a peak of 467,000 (or 2.1 per cent) in November 1958.[5] This produced a powerful reaction. Reflationary measures were taken one after another from May 1958 onwards but were slow to show results. At the end of the year, when unemployment was already past its peak, there were doubts whether what had been done would be sufficient to produce a fall in unemployment in 1959 and there was talk of production a year later still running at least 5 per cent below 'normal potential'. In the months before the 1959 Budget, although the outlook was a little less gloomy, proposals for tax concessions multiplied and if they had all been adopted would have involved an overall deficit (above and below the line) of £800 million (nearly 4 per cent of GNP). The prospect of so large a deficit alarmed the Chancellor (Heathcoat Amory), who had throughout urged caution, and rather fewer concessions were made. They amounted, however, to a record in comparison with any earlier Budget (except that of 1946) and were accompanied by a substantial increase in public expenditure.

The explosive effect of the measures taken was not foreseen. After the Budget, a 4 per cent increase in GDP, year on year, was forecast and a 5 per cent increase between the last quarter of 1958 and the last quarter of 1959 (see Table 2.1). No further action seemed to be required except a step-by-step reduction in bank rate from 6 per cent in March to 4 per cent in November. The pace of expansion aroused no expressions of disquiet until near the end of 1959. By that time the recovery had gathered more speed than could be easily checked.

At the end of July, Robert Hall rejected comparisons with the boom of 1955, pointing out that industrial production in May was only 4 per cent above the low point in 1958 and suggesting that 1953, when recovery was only beginning, was a nearer comparison.[6] This was fair comment. It was only in the second half of 1959 that the upswing developed its full momentum. As was pointed out in a *post mortem* by Bryan Hopkin, subsequently circulated to the Cabinet Committee on Economic Policy in January 1963,[7] one reason why the Government's measures had been much too expansionary was the way in which the various measures interacted with one another in a cumulative process to generate more demand than seemed likely if one merely added together the separate effects of each.

One neglected factor contributing to the boom was the complete removal of restrictions on the banking system in the middle of 1958. Bank lending had been held down by a series of government requests that went back to Butler's call for 'a positive and significant reduction' in bank advances in July 1955. These 'requests' had been endorsed by the Bank of England with increasing reluctance and had given rise to the confrontation between the Bank and the Treasury in September 1957 referred to above. In the three years 1955–7 there had been a net fall in total advances while in the next three years, 1958–60, the total nearly doubled. As Sir Robert Hall pointed out, the removal of restrictions in 1958 had been the first step in the expansion that

TABLE 2.1 *Gross Domestic Product: forecast and actual growth 1958–61*

Date of forecast	Period covered	Forecast growth (%)	Actual growth (%) (1)[a]	(2)[b]
12.12.58	1958–1959 1958 IV–1959 IV	1 1½	4 6¾	4 6½
25.2.59	1958–1959 1958 IV–1959 IV	1½ 2	4 6¾	4 6½
28.5.59	1958–1959 1958 IV–1959 IV	3½ 4/5	4 6¾	4 6½
10.12.59	1959 IV–1960 IV	3.5–3.8	3	3½
9.2.60	1959 IV–1960 IV	3–3.5	3	3½
12.5.60	1960 1st half–1961 1st half	2½	3	3½
12.12.60	1960 III–1961 III	about 1	3	1¾
9.3.61	1960 IV–1961 IV	2¾	1¾	2½
14.6.61	1961 1st half–1962 1st half	3½/4	¾	1

[a] Derived from estimates in *Economic Trends*, October 1968, using average of seasonally adjusted figures for expenditure and output measures of GDP
[b] Derived from *Economic Trends Annual Supplement 1990*, Table 1; average estimate of GDP at factor cost (1985 prices)

SOURCE: R. F. Bretherton, *The Control of Demand, 1958 to 1964*, p. 89.

followed and it was a mistake to put all the blame on the Budget of 1959.[8]

The Macmillan government was re-elected on 8 October 1959, and shortly afterwards the Chancellor became concerned about the balance of payments which in the second half of the year got steadily worse. He already suspected that he would have to raise taxes again in April and was concerned that inflation might reappear.[9] He had studied what could be done to promote stability of wages and prices and was quite clear what lines of policy he wished to follow. He called a meeting of employers' organisations towards the end of November at which he came near to enunciating a 'guiding light' of 2½–3 per cent as the limit of the wage increase that the economy could stand if there were to be no inflation. The employers' representatives thought that in the long run wage-bargaining had to be between employers and workers but were prepared to sound the TUC on how to secure wage restraint.[10] In the current wage round they expected the increase to settle at 4½ per cent and extend over a period of eighteen months.

There were no immediate results of this exchange of views. Amory was right, however, to expect a faster rise in wage-rates in 1960. Hourly wage rates were not much over 1 per cent higher at the end of 1959 than a year earlier, but in the course of the next year they rose by over 6 per cent and by July 1961 had risen by 3 per cent more. Hourly earnings rose much faster: in the two years from October 1959 to October 1961 they increased by nearly 16 per cent.

Even in October 1959, the speed with which output was expanding was imperfectly appreciated. Economic indicators of demand took a long time to become available, were subject to correction for months and often years afterwards, and were liable to be inconsistent with one another so that, as Robert Hall put it, 'the hardest thing to forecast is where we are now'. The growth of GDP over the first three quarters of 1959, for example, was put at under 5 per cent per annum by the National Institute of Economic and Social Research in November 1959 while up-to-date estimates in 1990 indicate a rate of over 6 per cent — a much less sustainable rate. Other indicators have changed much more. Fixed investment, then shown as increasing at 7.5 per cent per annum in the first half of the year, is now reckoned to have increased over the year at 12.7 per cent per annum. Estimates of the movement in stocks and work in progress have undergone repeated changes since first publication as is illustrated later in Table 3.1 (see p. 55).

The main reason why the rate of expansion was underestimated was the unexpectedly rapid increase in exports. Instead of falling in volume as had been expected, they rose between the final quarters of 1958 and 1959 by about 8 per cent. Even so, the large favourable balance of payments with which the year opened had disappeared as it ended. The demand for imports was swollen by the soaring of real incomes in the boom of 1959 and to a lesser extent by the easing of import restrictions that accompanied convertibility at the end of 1958.

With the deterioration in the balance of payments the reserves were beginning to drain away. This alarmed the Chancellor who asked the Bank of England in November to give consideration to a rise in bank rate. The possibility of bringing the new Special Deposits scheme into operation was also under discussion.

Early in December the Chancellor tried without success to persuade the Deputy Governor to act at once or, if not, to send for the Governor, who was abroad. Treasury officials, like the Bank, saw no need for a higher bank rate although they recognised that interest rates in Britain were low in comparison with Germany and the United States. Germany had the excuse of an inflationary situation and the United States of a large external deficit, but the United Kingdom, they argued, could hardly say that the internal situation needed restraint and the reserves had yet to come under serious strain. William Armstrong, in charge of debt management, would have liked to give a jerk to the long rate of interest to help overcome his funding difficulties.[11] The Permanent Secretary, Roger Makins, pointed out that prices had been steady for the past eighteen months while the Economic Adviser, Robert Hall, thought a rise in bank rate inconsistent with the government's efforts to stimulate private investment and likely to 'rouse evil passions' if it was defended as called for by higher rates abroad or, as the Chancellor had argued, as a way of keeping down imports by checking expansion. In Robert Hall's view, which proved to be mistaken, the November figures showed that the rate of expansion was slowing down and restraint in such circumstances would reflect on an election victory that 'was largely won on prosperity'.[12]

The Chancellor nevertheless carried his worries to the Prime Minister on 4 December taking the President of the Board of Trade with him. The Prime Minister, who regarded support for the forward market as the appropriate way to cover a balance of payments deficit by bringing in funds from abroad, assured him that there was nothing to worry about. Having just won an election with an enlarged majority on a promise to preserve prosperity, he thought a deflationary budget 'either very foolish or very dishonest'.

Although nothing was settled, debate continued in January 1960 with the Chancellor maintaining that bank rate should go up as soon as possible and the Prime Minister anxious not to check recovery when it was only just beginning.[13] Robert Hall produced two further minutes on 5 and 13 January, emphasising that the outlook for investment had altered with the new Board of Trade survey of investment intentions and that new and large wage claims were creating a more inflationary atmosphere. At a meeting between the Chancellor and the Governor and Deputy Governor on 18 January, it was agreed to raise bank rate to 5 per cent on the 21st, the Chancellor maintaining that the rise was at least a month late, Robert Hall that it was a little too early and the Governor that the timing was just right.[14]

A month later the Bank withdrew support from the gilt-edged market and let prices fall by about a point, partly in order to discourage sales by the Clearing Banks to improve their liquidity and partly as a way of edging up long-term interest rates so as to allow more funding. The banks had been expanding credit at a very fast rate – by 50 per cent in six months – and had been able to do so by disposing of government debt in order to add to their liquid assets.[15] The government was now trying, rather late in the day, to increase the cost of acquiring additional bank reserves and put a brake on credit expansion.

By February 1960 the Treasury was fully alive to the strength of the boom. The forecasts prepared after the election had envisaged a slowing down of the economy in 1960. A growth of 3.5 per cent or a little more in output was expected between the final quarter of 1959 and the final quarter of 1960. This proved to be remarkably accurate but it bore little relation to the state of affairs at the beginning of the year. Output continued to rise fast in the first quarter and fixed investment in manufacturing industry was just beginning to accelerate. It was not until the second quarter that there was any perceptible slowdown and by then the labour market was becoming very tight and exports were being crowded out.

When a fresh forecast was under preparation in January it was recognised that the surge in production had gone further and faster in 1959 than had been appreciated in November. Inflationary pressures were building up, the economy was nearer capacity limits and restraining action was clearly necessary in the Budget. The bulk of the income tax remissions in the 1958 budget would be in operation in the first quarter of the year and with two debt maturities due there would be greater liquidity. If all demand could be met, output would grow at 4 per cent but the construction industries were overloaded and would be unable to keep pace with demand. The likely increase in output would therefore fall short of 4 per cent and was expected to be between 3 and $3\frac{1}{2}$ per cent.

In a note to the Cabinet at the end of January the Chancellor commented that 'the new forecasts indicate a very marked change in the economic outlook' and suggested that, in view of the overloading of the building industry, public investment in the next financial year should be 'cut back ... in any feasible ways'. The Budget, he was now convinced, should be 'definitely deflationary'.

Shortly afterwards, the Budget Committee (of Treasury officials) recommended that tax revenue should be increased by £100 million (about $\frac{1}{2}$ per cent of GNP). It was not easy, however, to find ways of raising this amount without putting up income tax or purchase tax, both of which had been reduced only a year previously. What was proposed eventually was a rise in profits tax from 10 to $12\frac{1}{2}$ per cent (which would bring in no revenue until 1961–2 or later, when it would raise £65 million annually) and an extra £29 million in tobacco duty. Since even the £29 million was largely offset by a number of minor tax concessions, the budget in its impact on 1960–1 was virtually neutral.

This was something of an anti-climax after all the talk of a deflationary budget. Even so, the Budget was received in the House of Commons with some consternation on the government benches and such cheers as there were came largely from the opposition. Outside opinion also was taken by surprise that the Budget offered no further encouragement to industry. The TUC and the FBI had either pressed for further measures to reduce unemployment or for some remission of taxation.

The Prime Minister in particular had been difficult to persuade of the seriousness of the situation. He was greeted on his return from Africa in February with a note warning him of 'an intolerably tight labour position', inflationary symptoms and the danger of another autumn crisis. A note prepared by the Economic Secretary, Sir Edward Boyle, argued that it would be a mistake to risk a balance of payments crisis which would require very drastic measures if it occurred when, if consumption were curbed by monetary and fiscal weapons, the standard of living could continue to rise satisfactorily with a growth in output that might average 3 per cent. The Prime Minister was more impressed by how foolish the Tories would look if they checked economic activity just when it was at last getting up speed.

In the end it came to a matter of presentation. The Prime Minister did not mind some action of the kind proposed, so long as it was not presented as a brake on activity while the Chancellor wanted to give the country something of a shock.[16]

The Chancellor from an early stage had envisaged that after the Budget monetary policy should be tightened in line with fiscal policy and announced his intention to restrict credit in the Budget. The Budget Committee had considered possible measures to limit credit expansion and favoured a call for special deposits although the proposal received no support from the Bank of England, the Governor arguing that special deposits were not suited to the day-to-day control of the economy and should be reserved for emergencies.[17] William Armstrong would have preferred action to raise long-term interest rates such as a new issue of government securities at 6 per cent. The feeling was growing, he maintained, that the long-term rate was too low and a rise was widely expected. The Governor, however, was against the issue of stock below the market price on the grounds that it would discourage other holders of gilt-edged securities if prices were forced down. The most effective step in his view would be to raise income tax and couple it with a 6 (or even a 7) per cent bank rate.[18]

The use of hire-purchase restrictions was also considered, but the Committee was anxious not to discourage Ford and Vauxhall from proceeding with their new plants on Merseyside. The Board of Trade were opposed to the reimposition of hire purchase controls and preferred the use of direct control over the provision of finance by the hire-purchase finance houses. The Governor of the Bank complained of the 'indiscipline' of the less reputable finance houses and would have liked to adopt the Radcliffe proposal for the extension of control to all lending institutions. Even the more limited proposal of the Board of Trade, however, would have required new legislation and a joint Bank/Treasury study, of which the Governor took no notice, threw doubt on the chances of its being effective.[19]

Shortly after the Budget, in accordance with the plans agreed at the talks with the Chancellor, and following a sharp expansion in bank lending in April, the Bank made its first call for special deposits. Hire-purchase restrictions were reimposed, but they were much milder than the restrictions withdrawn in 1958. They may have done little more than impose the commercial terms offered by reputable hire purchase finance companies, but they did produce a small reduction in outstanding debt.

The call for special deposits was not a powerful weapon since the banks could replenish the liquidity removed by selling securities which the Bank felt obliged to buy. It would have been a more effective brake if, as William Armstrong suggested, government securities had been allowed to fall sufficiently to allow increased sales and so contract the monetary base.

The measures announced in April were insufficient to exercise much of a check and in June fresh discussions began about what should be done. The Prime Minister once again saw no need for restraint but agreement was finally reached to make a second call for special deposits and to put bank rate up at the same time to 6 per cent on 23 June.

A month later Heathcoat Amory left office and was succeeded by Selwyn Lloyd on 27 July. In his final speech in the House of Commons it was to rising public expenditure and rising money incomes that Amory directed attention. Public expenditure was growing faster than GDP; and, as the Chancellor pointed out, the trend if allowed to continue left no hope of the lower taxation that his party so much desired. The rise in prices which the Chancellor also feared remained comparatively modest in 1960: consumer prices rose over the year by 1½ per cent. Weekly wage rates, however, increased over the year by 4 per cent, in spite of a 2½ per cent reduction in hours.

Amory had been an able Chancellor, very much alive to the danger of inflation. He had a good working understanding of economic problems and was sensible in his aims. Nevertheless, the measures he took in 1958–9 to counter depression misjudged the amount of slack in the economy and the momentum that they would develop.

His successor, Selwyn Lloyd, had little instinctive 'feel' for the economic forces at work but had clear objectives and showed ingenuity in pursuit of them. At bottom his interests lay in tax reform: in simplification of the tax system and in extending the shift from direct to indirect taxation that was in progress. He also showed boldness and ingenuity in the introduction of his tax 'regulators', in his efforts to develop a viable incomes policy, and in his creation of the National Economic Development Council (NEDC). Like Amory, he attached particular importance to reducing inflation: much more importance than the Prime Minister, who told him in June 1962 that 'too much had been made of the danger of inflation'.[20] Lloyd commented conversely on Macmillan that his big mistake was 'thinking unemployment a worse enemy than uncontrolled inflation.'[21]

The replacement of Amory by Selwyn Lloyd, and his replacement two years later by Maudling, were part of a general changing of the guard. Robert Hall, the Economic Adviser of HMG, retired in April 1961, Cobbold, the Governor of the Bank of England, in July 1961 and Frank Lee, the Permanent Secretary, in July 1962. The changes had little immediate effect on policy but major changes soon began to occur.

At first, production seemed to flatten out in the second half of 1960: the index of industrial production was more or less unchanged throughout the year. Employment, on the other hand, increased steadily over the year by nearly half a million and unemployment fell in each quarter. The conflict of evidence was puzzling and led Ministers to think that 'the fundamental weakness of the economy is not so much excess demand as failure of production to respond'.[22] The Treasury put its money on the production figures and concluded, wrongly, that credit restriction was working and holding down output.

If output, and hence income, was flat why were imports increasing so fast and helping to throw the balance of payments into heavy deficit? The contemporary estimate for 1960 was a deficit of £344 million, of which £265 million (seasonally adjusted) fell in the second half of the year. For the time being the deficit was being offset (and more than offset) by short-term borrowing in the form of an inflow of funds from abroad, attracted by the high bank rate. This inflow was embarrassing to the United States, from which much of the capital came and which was continuing to lose gold at a high rate. There was some pressure, therefore, on the United Kingdom to lower bank rate and reduce the attractiveness of sterling to American lenders. A reduction of ½ per cent was made on 27 October and a second reduction by ½ per cent to 5 per cent on 8 December. At the end of the year the United Kingdom tried to ease the pressure on American gold stocks further by paying over $47 million to the IMF in exchange for sterling.

In the last thirty years the picture of 1960 has greatly altered and the figures of production and employment are now more readily reconciled. Output in the second half of 1960, so far from being flat, is estimated to have increased at about 3 per cent per annum; and for the year 1960 as a whole (last quarter to last quarter) the increase in output is put at 3½ per cent. For unemployment to go on falling in those circumstances is not at all peculiar. The balance of payments deficit has also been revised: instead of £344 million it is now put at £228 million, making the inflow of short-term capital all the greater in relation to the current account deficit.

One result of the belief that production had flattened out in 1960 was that a very slow rate of growth was projected for 1961. In December 1960 the rate was expected to be about 1 per cent, and unemployment was expected to rise by about 80,000 during the year. In the first half of the year, however, before the Chancellor's restrictive measures in July, production was growing at a rate approaching 4 per cent per annum and unemployment was steady at 1.3 per cent.[23] The labour market remained very tight and the balance of payments continued in deficit. Stockbuilding, which had been a major element in sustaining growth in 1960, and had contributed largely to the unexpected surge in imports, fell quarter by quarter in 1961 (although this was not realised at the time – see Table 3.1) while fixed investment took over as the main source of expansion. The balance of payments benefited from the fall in stockbuilding and the reduction in the level of imports, but not quite enough to move into surplus in the first half of the year. On the other hand, the up-valuation of the German mark in March alerted the markets to the possibility of further currency changes and gave rise to a large withdrawal of funds from London – including, no doubt, some of the capital attracted by high interest rates in 1960.

The experience of the first half of 1961 suggests that the maximum annual rate of growth of the British economy at that time, when working at full stretch and with no slack to take in, was probably about $3\frac{1}{2}$ per cent. When higher rates were achieved it was always to the accompaniment of falling rates of unemployment. Whether one could envisage an indefinite prolongation of such a rate of growth is another matter.

First of all, there was what was called a balance of payments constraint – a tendency as output and income expanded for imports to rise faster than exports and jeopardise the expansion in progress. It could not be taken for granted that the constraint would disappear if the currency was devalued: it might reappear after a time and require another devaluation, or alternatively a downward float of the pound. Secondly, a tight labour market affected wage bargains, raising costs and prices and threatening competitiveness. Even where fear of inflation had not entered into the public consciousness, the pressure of demand, if left unchecked, could produce a spiral of rising wages and prices. It was necessary to refrain from operating at too high a pressure; and it was not self-evident how growth would be affected if pressure were less but constant. Thirdly, it was necessary to allow for the accidents of economic life: the sudden uncertainties, the swings in the terms of trade, the shortages of skill and materials, and so on, that forced a retreat from time to time from full capacity operation.

The experience of 1960 carried a warning that was neglected in 1964. When the pressure in the labour market built up, output might at first remain flat while imports flowed in to meet the expansion in demand. The figures might then be misinterpreted as showing that the economy was stuck; and action to curtail demand might be deferred while the growing external deficit was met by foreign borrowing. As in 1961 the cycle might then end with a fresh stop that earlier action would have helped to avoid.

3 The July Measures and After, 1961-2

The Chancellor of the Excheque when I took up my duties in the Treasury on 5 June 1961 was Selwyn Lloyd. He was a lawyer by training, with no knowledge of economic theory and little experience of economic policy; shy and rather diffident in discussing matters where he felt himself at a disadvantage in expertise, and at the same time distrustful of would-be experts. He had no ready flow of language, stuttering more than any Minister I have known, and was given to taking up the time of his officials in long meetings to draft speeches and memoranda. On the other hand, he did not lack boldness or originality and had firm ideas of his own. He had held senior office as Minister of Defence, and subsequently as Foreign Minister, and in June 1961 had been Chancellor for nearly a year.

THE 1961 BUDGET

Two months before I arrived Selwyn Lloyd had introduced his first budget. It had several novel features showing originality of mind, notably two tax 'regulators' allowing the use of tax changes between budgets in order to stabilize demand. One empowered the government to raise or lower indirect taxation across the board by up to 10 per cent at any time. The second, which was abandoned at birth, gave the Chancellor power to impose a payroll tax of up to four shillings per week on all employees through increased national insurance contributions. In a full year the first regulator could vary taxation in either direction by up to £200 million while the second, used to its full extent, would also have brought in £200 million. Other changes in the Budget included an increase in profits tax by $2\frac{1}{2}$ per cent for the second year running and increases in car licence duties and petrol duty. The main concessions were to surtax payers: from 1962-3 the starting level would be raised from £2,000 to £4,000 and the earned income allowance would be increased, making the actual starting level £5,000.

The July Measures and After, 1961–2

The estimated effect in a full year was more or less neutral – a net increase in revenue of £55 million.

In the first half of 1961 there was thus little attempt to rein back demand. On the contrary, Bank rate was left at 5 per cent, and in January hire purchase restrictions were eased. No further action was taken until late July. Meanwhile, from March onwards funds continued to drain away into foreign currencies. In the first six months of 1961 it was necessary to borrow $900 million under the Basle Arrangements (see Chapter 14), and draw a further £164 million from the reserves. By the time the Chancellor announced his 'July measures', the total withdrawn was in the neighbourhood of £600 million. This represented a rate of loss that could not be allowed to continue for long when the reserves at the end of June stood at under £1,000 million. The balance of payments on current account presented a further difficulty. The large deficit of 1960 had certainly dwindled but the deficit was still running in the first half of 1961 at £160 million a year in contemporary estimates (even if it has since been transformed into a tiny surplus. A particular source of anxiety was a dramatic fall in net invisible income which had been estimated to average £250 million a year in 1957–9, but was put at no more than £77 million in 1961 and looked like disappearing altogether. (By 1969, however, net invisible income was yielding an estimated £680 million.)

Treasury officials, reporting on balance of payments trends, voiced the pessimism natural in these circumstances. 'There was no prospect under present policies', they declared, 'of reversion to a surplus of the order of £200 million or more such as was achieved in 1958 and earlier years.'[1] What then was to be done? Perhaps a reduction in the pressure of home demand in relation to capacity would effect an improvement in the balance of payments. There had been 'no period since the war when the economy was slack and world demand strong, so the effects of moderate deflation were as yet untested'. An opportunity might arise in 1961.[2]

The winter of 1960–1 also saw the emergence of public interest in planning. In part this reflected concern over Britain's lower rate of growth: the FBI Conferences at Brighton in November 1960, the Conference on French planning at the National Institute in June 1961, and reports such as one by PEP on 'Growth in the British Economy', urged the need to plan for a higher rate of growth with targets laid down in advance and an end to 'stop–go' policies. In July the Cabinet was told of 'a surge of public interest' in growth: 'the pre-war process of mass unemployment has gone and the problems of this country today are primarily those of expansion and of price stability!'[3]

PLANNING PUBLIC EXPENDITURE

A second source of interest in planning was the need to take a longer view of public expenditure and plan its growth over the next five years on a comprehensive footing. The case for such an approach was developed in the report of a committee under Lord Plowden (but written largely by a Treasury official, R. W. B. Clarke) which was published in late July 1961.[4] The Cabinet had already been invited by the Chancellor to endorse the preparation of a five year plan for public expenditure at the end of March and an outline of the plan was presented by the Chancellor three months later.[5]

In the 1950s public expenditure had been sufficiently controlled to allow taxation to be cut by an average of £100 million a year and one factor behind the preparation of the plan had been the hope of further tax cuts within the life of the current Parliament. The governing condition of the plan was that the ratio of public expenditure to GNP should remain fixed at 42.5 per cent (on the definitions then in use). Labour productivity was assumed to rise at $2\frac{1}{2}$ per cent per annum and employment at $\frac{1}{2}$ per cent per annum, with a 5 per cent increase in wages and salaries (and presumably a 2 per cent rate of inflation). It was assumed that public expenditure would increase between a 1961–2 and 1965–6 by £1,100 million at constant 1961 prices although this did not comply with the fixed ratio to GNP of 42.5 per cent which indicated a limit of £1,000 million. This was not the only respect in which the plan erred on the side of optimism. It assumed that exports would grow twice as fast as in the recent past, labour productivity also somewhat faster, and that the public would be content to consume a smaller proportion of the addition to their income. The natural conclusion was that public expenditure would outpace GNP and offer little opportunity for tax cuts. It was a conclusion borne out by events. The proportion to GDP (not appreciably different from GNP) rose from 33.8 per cent in 1961 to 34.5 per cent in 1964 and to 35.3 per cent in 1965–6 under the Labour Government. Two years later it reached a peak of 40.2 per cent (on the definitions in use in the 1990s.

Most of this background was unknown to me when I arrived in the Treasury. But there was every indication that an exchange crisis was rapidly approaching. I had hardly set foot in the Treasury when the

Chancellor sent for me to discuss the outlook. He was in an expansionist mood with his eye fixed on the domestic situation, puzzled and disappointed by the failure of production to increase more rapidly, but with no particular anxiety about sterling. He enumerated the sources from which he could meet the mounting pressures on the pound – £2,000 million in reserves, IMF drawing rights, the portfolio on US securities, loans under the Basle Arrangement – and they certainly added up to a formidable total. I was inclined to agree that he had good grounds for confidence. But, as has so often happened, the pressures that the market could exert, especially if it saw any chance of a change in the parity, were only too easily underestimated.

It was not, however, the drain of foreign exchange that moved me to recommend immediate action. It was evidence that demand in 1962 would be on a larger scale than had been assumed hitherto and was already at the danger limit. Unemployment throughout the southern half of England was down to 1 per cent or less in July and lower, at under 300,000, than in any month for four years. Demand, it is true, had been more hesitant in the second quarter and exports had ceased to increase. But the latest forecasts, covering the first half of 1962, pointed to a continuing expansion of demand not evident in forecasts extending only to the end of 1961.

After discussion with my colleagues in the Economic Section and examination of the latest economic forecasts I submitted a paper to the Budget Committee which was taken next day on 6 June. I pointed out that after three successive years of deficit in the balance of payments there was an urgent need to make room for a big expansion in commodity exports. But the pressure on manpower was already very high; and if exports were to rise at 5 per cent per annum so as to restore external balance instead of at the forecast rate of 1 per cent, the increase in pressure would bring it to 'a point not far short of the highest levels reached since the war' with effects on wages and prices that could not be disregarded. The reduction in domestic purchasing power necessary to free resources for exports and prevent a further increase in the pressure of demand would be about £600 million a year. As a first step I proposed a cut of £300 million (a little over 1 per cent of GNP) which would still allow output to keep pace with the growth of industrial potential.

Rather to my surprise, this proposal was accepted without challenge. I was not then conscious that budgetary action on the scale proposed was roughly double any measures of deflation proposed by my predecessor in similar circumstances or I might have been more hesitant.

The Committee accepted my estimate of £300 million and recommended the use of both regulators as soon as the Finance Bill became law, together with measures of a longer-term character. The first regulator would add 10 per cent to all commodity taxes and would bring in an additional £200 million or so while the second regulator, with a surcharge of 2 per cent on employers' national insurance contributions, would add about another £100 million. It was not until late July that the first regulator could be used; the second would have had to wait until early November.

Almost simultaneously with the Budget Committee's recommendation, the Bank of England warned the Chancellor to expect a rapid rundown in the reserves unless measures were taken to reassure the markets. Discussion took place with the Chancellor on 6 and 15 June at which the Governor and junior Treasury ministers were present and on the 16th the Chancellor put the Budget Committee's proposals to Cabinet.

At that stage he was not in favour of monetary measures, dismissing a rise in bank rate as damaging to confidence abroad and a call for special deposits as likely to prompt bank sales of government securities. Foreign central banks had been helpful in advancing a substantial amount of foreign exchange against sterling swaps under the Basle Agreement and they would continue to help if the government was seen to be taking adequate steps to bring the situation under control.

The Chancellor attached particular importance to a reduction in government expenditure overseas. He hoped to find ways of reducing defence expenditure abroad from £235 million to £200 million although it would mean drastic cuts in the Far East and in South-east Asia. Military expenditure in Germany involving transfers across the exchanges would be limited to £25 million per annum. He also proposed to limit foreign travel allowances to bring down the total permitted expenditure to £50. An emergency scheme designed to restrict imports had been prepared, but it would have inflationary consequences and was likely to provoke retaliation. Another possibility was the use of the tax system to encourage the remission of profits from abroad.

For the domestic economy he wanted to reduce the overload on the building industry but rejected the reintroduction of building licensing as likely to be made ineffective by forestalling during the lengthy period required in order to set up the machinery. Instead, he hoped to slow down the building of houses and offices by administrative means. He was also examining what he described as 'unconventional policies': unilateral tariff reductions, new encouragements for savers, the establishment of a national economic planning council (the first hint of NEDC). Wage demands would have to be restrained in order to reduce inflationary pressure: 'a standstill for a period in wage and profit levels [*the famous 'pause'*] should not be ruled out'.

Many of these were the Chancellor's own ideas: his advisers confined themselves largely to proposing the use of the regulators and cuts in public expenditure. R. W. B. ('Otto') Clarke, for example, argued for a six months 'pause' in the authorisation by the government of starts in building and civil engineering projects on government and local authority account. He suggested also that subsidies to agriculture and industry should be cut and major changes made in spending on defence and education.

When the Cabinet next discussed the economic situation on 30 June, the Chancellor told them that it was 'more serious than at any time during the past ten years'. Some of the Chancellor's suggestions were rejected and few new ones put forward. Since it would take two months to recreate the machinery required for import quotas the emergency scheme was abandoned. The Minister of Agriculture (Soames) would not accept the proposal for a standstill in agricultural support. The Minister of Defence (Watkinson) saw no possibility of a quick, substantial saving in overseas defence expenditure and nothing came of the proposal to make a reduction of £35 million. It was agreed, however, that the government should appeal for wage restraint and take firm action in the public sector. Direct investment in the non-sterling area (but not in the sterling area) was to be limited by exchange control. Several ministers (no doubt including Maudling) spoke in favour of floating the pound, presenting this as necessary in the longer term but without pressing for its immediate adoption.

There were two further Cabinet meetings on the Chancellor's measures before he announced them on 25 July. At the first, on 20 July, the Chancellor expressed his intention of limiting the increase in supply expenditure in 1962–3 to $2\frac{1}{2}$ per cent in real terms. But without agreement to specific cuts he was in no position to hold to such a limitation, nor did he succeed in doing so. He also spoke in favour of legislation against restrictive practices such as retail price maintenance and on the need to tax short-term capital gains, both of them proposals to which the Conservative government gave effect. The frustration that he must have felt in introducing one more 'stop' after looking forward to faster economic growth was summed up in his remark that 'the fundamental weakness of the economy was not so much excess demand as the failure of production to expand'.

At the second meeting of Cabinet on 24 July, the day before his statement, he told his colleagues that his advisers were doubtful whether the measures he proposed would be sufficient to restore confidence in the pound. This reflected prolonged discussions over the previous fortnight with the Governor of the Bank, Sir Thomas Padmore and myself. Unfortunately for the Chancellor all three of us were either new boys or deputising for someone more experienced. Lord Cromer had succeeded Cameron Cobbold as Governor on 1 July, I had taken up my duties just over three weeks earlier and Tom Padmore was taking the place of his Permanent Secretary, Frank Lee, who was ill and out of action throughout June and July. I have little doubt that a combination of Cobbold, Robert Hall and Frank Lee would have offered better advice and been more persuasive than we were. But I doubt whether the measures taken would have been very different.

On 12 July Padmore and I were summoned to what proved to be a long session with the Chancellor that began with a question about the likely effect on our national income forecasts of a wage pause. After we had expressed doubts whether it would make much difference to the level of consumption he turned to regulator No. 2 on which doubts had been expressed in Cabinet on the grounds that it would raise industrial costs. The Chancellor was now adamant in his opposition to it, calling it 'a dead rat', and was strongly supported by Tony Barber, the Economic Secretary.[6] At one point the Chancellor said he would rather think of an autumn budget. When I suggested that if all that was involved was an increase in income tax, he hardly needed a budget, he was momentarily attracted by the idea and wanted to go and discuss it with the Prime Minister who, however, happened not to be free.

Just before the weekend, Padmore attempted to resurrect regulator No. 2, stressing the awkwardness of any change in direct taxation in mid-year. The material question, as Edward Boyle pointed out, was whether the Chancellor was doing enough already and there was a good case for thinking that he was. In any event he had already left for Hawarden.

On the 13th he had given the Governor a summary of what he proposed to say. He made no mention of regulator No. 2 or of monetary measures and appeared to intend a deliberately unalarmist presentation. The Governor was obviously a little taken aback by this low key approach as indeed we all were. But he in turn was hesitant over using any monetary weapons and would have preferred hire-purchase controls (which the Cabinet later ruled out). Leslie O'Brien, the Deputy

Governor, argued for a 1 per cent call for special deposits, for which the Bank had not previously expressed much enthusiasm, but neither he nor the Governor proposed a rise in bank rate and the Chancellor wanted to keep it up his sleeve. I insisted that this was the one thing that could not be done and was backed up by Padmore who thought that a package that left out bank rate would look odd. In the end an increase in bank rate from 5 to 7 per cent formed an important part of the July measures.

The measures, when announced, included the rise in bank rate, a further call for special deposits of 1 per cent, a 10 per cent surcharge on existing customs and excise duties and purchase tax, and a promise to reduce public expenditure (including expenditure overseas) by £300 million in 1962–3. There was to be tighter control of private investment outside the sterling area and encouragement of United Kingdom firms operating abroad to remit a higher proportion of their earnings. The Chancellor also announced two measures of a different kind. There was to be a six months' 'pay pause' in the public sector (with an injunction to the private sector to join in) and a new planning council, the National Economic Development Council.

The July measures were followed shortly afterwards by two other important events. First the Chancellor sought and obtained, on the the strength of the measures, a credit of $2 billion from the IMF which put an end to pressure on the pound. Then on 10 August the United Kingdom applied for membership of the European Economic Community, leading to negotiations that lasted until de Gaulle's veto on 14 January 1963.

I deal first with the reception of the July measures and then with their impact on the economy.

THE RECEPTION OF THE JULY MEASURES

The press showed little sympathy with the deflationary measures and was more or less unanimous in claiming that demand was already falling off and in denying that it had been excessive. *The Economist* thought that there was evidence that 'demand was moderating' and declared that the measures, taken together, 'probably add up to the biggest immediate cut in demand that has been deliberately imposed by a British government on any single afternoon in British history'. In industries where prices were being raised by pressure of demand, some restraint might be necessary but in others more demand would reduce 'the high costs of working below capacity'. There was also agreement on the need for restraint in wage settlements without much appreciation of the difficulties.

The FBI was confident of an expansion in exports and saw no need to check domestic demand. They put their faith in a 'shock' resistance to wage increases and a drive for cost reduction. The TUC had urged further expansion on the Chancellor in mid-June, coupled if necessary with selective controls such as building licensing. They now denounced both the pay pause and the deflationary measures and called for their withdrawal. They attacked the very idea that rising wages were to blame for a loss of competitiveness or that costs and prices would be under less pressure as activity fell off. If their figures were to be believed, real wages were actually falling. They also maintained that the effect of underemployment would be to diminish competitive power by raising overhead costs per unit of output. One result of this opposition to the July measures was to delay acceptance of the government's invitation to join the proposed planning organisation. Even the Prime Minister and some of his colleagues were inclined to look to further credit restriction, with the possible addition of import controls, as an appropriate and adequate response to the balance of payments difficulties.

Part of the trouble was the reluctance of commentators to contemplate *any* check to demand even when the current level could only be met with the help of an excess of imports. No doubt only a fraction of any reduction in demand would serve to improve the balance of payments, the more so if there was spare capacity. But was it right to add to demand when the economy was virtually fully employed and domestic output had to be supplemented increasingly from imports bought on credit? Again, was there not a danger of exaggerating the loss in domestic production resulting from the check to demand? The higher the pressure of demand, the less that loss would be since the greater would be the recourse to imports that were not particularly competitive and the more potential exports would be diverted to the domestic market. The adjustments required between domestic and international markets were small in relation to total imports and exports and not easily observed. If exports and imports both formed up to 30 per cent of GNP, the loss of domestic production resulting from a cut in demand was likely to be limited under conditions approaching full employment.

There was also a readiness on the part of the government's critics to turn to devaluation of the currency as a way of avoiding checks to demand. But of course devaluation has its price, too, and part of that price is precisely a loss of production if inflation is not to follow. It is one thing to contemplate devaluation every eighteen years but quite another, especially for a reserve currency, to devalue whenever the balance of payments runs into a substantial deficit.

Yet the critics had a point. Demand was not as buoyant as the government supposed. Exports in particular did not show the sustained rise in 1962 that was expected in July 1961.

Very little attempt was made to offer to the public a reasoned justification for the measures. In the middle of July the Chancellor assured us that there would be time enough to find the words so long as we decided on the appropriate measures. But in fact when he came to announce the measures he confined himself to a short exposition lasting about twenty minutes and made no attempt, then or later, to get across to the public an explanation of the situation that had prompted the measures and how he expected them to take effect.

All this reflected the view that the only real decisions concerned the cuts and that their presentation to MPs and the public was a quite subordinate matter. It may be that we exhausted the Chancellor with our protracted discussions of regulator No. 2 or that we left him inadequate time to prepare his statement. I once thought so but no longer do. Even the short presentation got things out of perspective. It put the pressure of home demand in the foreground when it was the drain from the reserves that needed to be emphasized. Unfortunately the Overseas Finance Division and the Bank would not hear of the disclosure of the true position in advance of the receipt of IMF help.

One of the curious features of the situation was that the Chancellor kept warning the public of the lightning that was about to strike but was powerless to act before the passing of the Finance Bill on 25 July. This built up expectations of drastic government action to which the actual measures seemed an anti-climax. The long wait did nothing to improve the government's standing, but it may have served to inure the public to the action the government took.

THE IMPACT OF THE MEASURES

Looking back at the July measures, we were puzzled how they had worked. The official figures for 1961 showed a different picture two years later and have changed again many times since. Our interpretation at the time was that the check to production after July came from the impact of higher indirect taxes on consumer spending. Later figures, however, indicate a small *rise* in consumer spending (in real terms) between the first and second halves of the year. Revised figures for GDP also show no fall in the second half of the year and instead a slow but steady growth from one half year to the next all through 1961 and 1962. What has changed most is the picture for stockbuilding, which originally remained very low and rather flat throughout 1961 but now appears to have fallen progressively over the year (after seasonal adjustment) by as much as £1 billion per quarter (at 1985 prices) between the first and last quarters (see table 3.1). If we can accept this very different version and set aside the indications that some fall in stockbuilding was in progress before July, there can be no doubt that the main impact of the July measures was on stockbuilding, partly perhaps because of the increase in bank rate but probably more because of the jolt to confidence. The official figures merely served to mislead us.

The July measures checked the growth of production but, after a slight dip in the autumn, a slow expansion began, accompanied by a gradual rise in unemployment that continued through 1962 until it reached a peak of 3.6 per cent (or 2.7 per cent excluding temporarily stopped) in the middle of the fearful weather at the beginning of 1963 ('the worst winter of the century'). The Board of Trade assured us that exports would increase by 9 per cent in volume in 1962 and this estimate was built into the official November 1961 forecast in spite of our scepticism. On the other hand, a substantial fall in manufacturing investment was likely, to judge from the replies received from industrialists to the latest questionnaire. I saw no great likelihood of a deep recession and indeed expected a rather slow recovery in the first half of 1962, gathering speed in the second half largely under the influence of a rapid growth in exports.

Things happened in 1962 the other way round. In the first six months exports of goods increased by 5 per cent but in the last six months they flattened out and seemed to fall away slightly (although the fall virtually disappears once an allowance is made for seasonal factors and exceptional items). The change in trend followed a sharp decline on Wall Street in May and was a response to a marked check to the expansion of markets abroad, particularly in the European Community. Other factors making for a slowing down in production were a slight falling-off in fixed investment and a move by the nationalised industries to raise their prices in order to finance a higher proportion of

The July Measures and After, 1961–2

TABLE 3.1 *Estimates of increases in stocks, 1959–60 (seasonally adjusted)*

		May 1962 (£m at 1958 prices)	October 1968 (£m at 1958 prices)	1990 (£m at 1985 prices)
1959	Q1	5	31	158
	Q2	28	42	81
	Q3	43	48	398
	Q4	100	58	542
1960	Q1	94	128	870
	Q2	172	167	653
	Q3	145	157	968
	Q4	173	143	1189
1961	Q1	85	149	921
	Q2	83	101	743
	Q3	12	43	187
	Q4	78	32	−79

SOURCE: *Economic Trends Annual Supplement* 1990; *Monthly Digest of Statistics* 1962 and 1968.

their investment programme out of profits. This involved a withdrawal from the public of an additional £100 million, much as higher indirect taxes would have done, and had the same effect on demand as bringing the tax regulator into play in an upward direction to half its full extent.

Thus although the level of output in the first half of the year was closely in accordance with our expectations, the apparent failure of production to rise during the second half took us by surprise. Even in the first half there had been much public agitation for more rapid expansion – so much so that when Selwyn Lloyd was sacked in July, I assumed at first that it must be because he was thought to have deflated too long. A day or two before, I had reassured Anthony Barber, the Economic Secretary, on our immediate economic prospects and he had laid on the reassurance much too thickly in a subsequent briefing of the press, so that it was for his future rather than Selwyn's I feared. (I was entirely mistaken: Barber moved on to become Financial Secretary on 16 July.)

Our February forecast had been for a 5 per cent rise in GDP over the year, but only if exports increased by 9 per cent which I did not expect. In the 1962 Budget discussions the working assumption was a 4 per cent expansion – far above the rate of 1½ per cent actually realised.

Even then, alarms of various kinds were expressed. The Board of Trade feared that exports would be held down by the expansion of home demand; the Bank of England were troubled by the high borrowing requirement; and there were rumours that if the United Kingdom gained admission to the Common Market devaluation of the pound would follow at once.

At one stage it even seemed possible that an increase in taxation might be recommended in order to permit a relaxation of the credit squeeze and so encourage more industrial investment. My own recommendation, which was accepted, was for a neutral budget.

The net reduction in taxation was negligible and such relaxation as was made was entirely on the side of monetary policy. Bank rate had been lowered at intervals from 7 per cent to 5 per cent and was cut by a further $\frac{1}{2}$ per cent in late April. A month later the Bank reduced its July 1961 call for special deposits from 3 per cent to 2 per cent and after a few days a relaxation was made in hire purchase restrictions.

In those days the Chancellor used to be sent short notes by the Prime Minister, pointing him in this direction or that. The prevailing tone of the notes was expansionist and they were sometimes remarkably naive. In October 1961, for example, he wrote to the Chancellor: 'I suppose you read the *Daily Worker*. It is much the best paper for us to study.'[7] Frequent themes were the need for more international liquidity and a higher price of gold.

He was clearly unhappy with the April Budget and sent one of his notes immediately after it.[8] There was no need, he told the Chancellor, to waste three months on the Finance Bill – Stafford Cripps had got away with absenting himself and there were others who could see the Bill through Parliament. He should review right away the possibilities for the next Budget, which should be expansionary and include substantial cuts in taxation. These should be selected to benefit those who were 'most squeezed', such as pensioners and married couples with children, rather than give preference to a cut in the standard rate of income tax. 'Do not', he concluded, 'leave it too late.'[9]

He also urged the Chancellor to get the long-term rate of interest down, whatever happened to Bank rate. But 'the most urgent problem', he told him, 'is incomes policy'.[10] The Prime Minister's ideas on incomes policy, although no doubt they developed, had been fairly elementary at the time of the 'pause' in 1961. He suggested beginning by assessing how much was available for wage increases and then proceeding to a share-out, as if the government could fix wages and suppress wage bargaining.[11]

On 28 May 1962 the Dow Jones Industrial Index dropped by 35 points – the steepest fall since October 1929 – and gave rise to fears of a world deflation. The *Financial Times* index fell steeply next day but had almost completely recovered a day later. Similarly on Wall Street there was a sharp rise by 20 points on 28 June, and little sign of the threatened collapse. *The Economist*, however, thought the slide on Wall Street 'no momentary aberration' and continued on 29 June to draw parallels with 1929.

The Prime Minister was in no doubt that world-wide deflation was at hand. 'All this', he told Selwyn Lloyd on 23 June, 'which I foresaw coming a year ago, seemed then to your advisers the ravings of a kind of political King Lear. But now the storm is clearly approaching.'[12] The Chancellor should consult his officials and propose 'radical changes' in international payments arrangements (i.e. more international liquidity). If the Americans would not revalue gold in terms of the dollar, others would have to take the lead. 'If the pound, mark and franc force them to, they will have to follow.' A World Economic Conference might not be the best way of proceeding since panic might be caused by the 'mere meeting' of such a conference. Perhaps it would be better to use the machinery of OECD, with Heads of Government taking part behind the scenes.[13]

A week before he was ousted from the Cabinet, Selwyn Lloyd sent Macmillan a lengthy Treasury memorandum expressing very different views, with which the Chancellor said he agreed. There was no need for undue alarm over the situation in the United States. The downturn was 'more in the nature of a general sagging of production rather than a complete collapse' and in Europe expansion was continuing. There were 'no indications of a general inadequacy of international liquidity'. Moreover it was 'not in the interests of the United Kingdom to initiate movements in respect of the gold price'.[14]

Two days earlier Macmillan had had a very different note from Maudling asserting that 'there seems an ever-growing case for really imaginative measures to increase the volume of world liquidity'.[15] It is difficult to believe that these exchanges had no influence on the change of Chancellor on 13 July.

By the summer months, with unemployment beginning to rise faster and approaching 2 per cent, there was increasing public impatience at the lack of more decisive reflationary measures and accusations that the Treasury was out of touch with business views and the evidence of a continuing fall in manufacturing investment. Starting in June there had been signs of a slowdown in activity. Although we were not yet aware of it, exports had ceased to grow. In July the Board of Trade's survey of investment intentions pointed to a need to revise downwards estimates of future industrial and commercial investment.

In spite of pressure to reflate from Cabinet colleagues and industry, the Chancellor made it clear to me that it suited him to delay action for the time being. At the end of June I was still inclined to dwell on the few hopeful signs: a rise in new car registrations, an increase in bank advances, the prospect of additional spending in response to the relaxation of hire-purchase restrictions. I mistakenly advised the Chancellor and the Budget Committee that the growth expected in 1962 had been delayed but was now getting under way.

The forecast prepared early in July took a different view (see Table 3.2). Although it presented an optimistic picture of growth in 1963, it showed little increase in GDP in the second half of 1962. Instead of public investment more than offsetting the expected fall in private investment, a fall in the total was forecast over the rest of the year. This forecast may not have been absorbed by the Chancellor before his replacement by Reginald Maudling on 13 July: what other advice he received concurred in recommending no reflation.

THE EMERGENCE OF INCOMES POLICY

The July measures were announced in a month when many other things were happening. On the first day of the month a new Governor, Lord Cromer, took office at the Bank of England; on the last day the Council on Prices Productivity and Incomes (COPPI) – an earlier effort to educate the public in the sources of inflation – issued its fourth report and expired. In between came preparations for an application for membership of the European Economic Community, made on 1 August.

The measures themselves were accompanied by hints of two important new government initiatives: one in the direction of an incomes policy and a second in the direction of joint planning of the economy. The move towards an incomes policy did not go beyond a wage 'pause' involving a freeze in the public sector and an encouragement of the private sector to follow suit. The move towards planning took shape in mid-August with a letter from the Chancellor to the TUC and four employers' organisations inviting them to join a national economic planning council.

Both of these moves were pursued at a rather leisurely pace over

TABLE 3.2 *Gross Domestic Product: forecast and actual growth 1961–4*

Date of forecast	Period covered	Forecast growth (%)	Actual growth (%) (1)[a, c]	(2)[b, c]
15.11.61	1961 IV–1963 I	3[d]	$2\frac{1}{2}$[d]	$3\frac{1}{4}$[d]
20.2.62	1962 I–1963 I	nearly 5	nearly 4[d]	$4\frac{3}{4}$[d]
6.7.62	1962 I–1963 I 1963 I–1963 III	$4\frac{1}{4}$ $3\frac{1}{4}$	nearly 4[d] $5\frac{1}{4}$[d]	$4\frac{3}{4}$[d] $3\frac{1}{4}$[d]
30.11.62	1962 III–1963 III	nearly 3	4	4
19.2.63	1963 I–1964 I	$3\frac{1}{4}$	$6\frac{1}{4}$[d]	$5\frac{1}{4}$[d]
10.7.63	1963 II–1964 IV	6[d]	$5\frac{1}{4}$*	$4\frac{1}{2}$[d]
13.11.63	1963 II–1964 IV	$5\frac{3}{4}$[d]	$5\frac{1}{4}$[d]	$4\frac{1}{2}$[d]
11.2.64	1963 III–1965 I	nearly 6[d]	5[d]	$4\frac{1}{2}$[d]
1.7.64	1963 1st half–1964 1st half 1964 1st half–1965 1st half 1965 II–1965 IV	6 4 $3\frac{1}{4}$[d]	$7\frac{1}{4}$ 3 $3\frac{3}{4}$[d]	$7\frac{1}{2}$ 3 $3\frac{1}{4}$[d]

[a] Derived from estimates in *Economic Trends*, October 1968 using average of seasonally adjusted figures for expenditure and output measures of GDP.
[b] Derived from *Economic Trends Annual Supplement 1990*, Table 1; average estimate of GDP at factor cost (1985 prices).
[c] Where the period covered refers to the first quarter of 1963, the figures in these columns substitute the second quarter in arriving at an annual rate.
[d] Annual rate.

Source of column 1: Bretherton, op. cit., p. 89.

the winter. The TUC was attracted by the invitation to join a planning council but deterred from accepting by the pay pause. There were a number of meetings between the Chancellor and TUC representatives at the Treasury at which little progress was made. Both sides were suspicious of one another and spoke a different language. There was also the difficulty that what seemed to meet with the agreement of union representatives one day was liable to be rejected the next.

I was doubtful whether Selwyn Lloyd was the man to win acceptance of an incomes policy. As I noted in my diary he was inclined to take a false-bellicose stand on wages. He thought that demand hardly mattered and that costs did. He therefore almost welcomed the prospect of strikes in the autumn so that there could be a show-down and treated the wage-pause as a means of waving employers on to tough resistance. Naturally the unions responded by treating the measures as a declaration of war and were not in the least reassured by the Chancellor's claim to be defending the workers' interests. Thus the Chancellor put himself in a weak position to secure an agreed wage-policy and had no guarantee that he could enforce a pause, with or without the cooperation of employers.

Early in August I had gone to see George Woodcock, the TUC General Secretary, whom I knew as a fellow member of the Radcliffe Committee. He had shown a keen interest in the planning proposals but was indignant that there had been no consultation with the unions before the announcement of the 'pause'. In these matters he felt that he and his colleagues were the experts and their advice had not been sought. George himself thought that there were distinct limits to what incomes policy could do in conditions of acute labour shortage and that wage restraint could be maintained only for a limited period.

It was soon evident that this was so even in the public sector. At the end of November the Electricity Council, anxious to avoid an interruption in the supply of electric power, agreed to wage increases that were clearly in breach of the policy. Earlier, the Minister of Labour had been obliged to endorse recommendations by two Wage Councils for increases in pay. There was a further breach in December over the M rate, payable to workers in a wide variety of jobs in government factories and workshops. In the private sector there was no halt to the rise in wages. There was, however, a perceptible slowing-down in the rise, whether because of the wage 'pause' or, more probably, because of the easing in the labour market. Between July 1961 and March 1962, when the 'pause' came to an end, the rise in average weekly wage-rates was 2.1 per cent while in the corresponding period in 1960–1 it was 3.3 per cent. In the same period in 1962–3, when the 'pause' was a thing of the past, the rise in wage-rates was still lower at 1.9 per cent; from which it would appear that unemployment was a more powerful influence than the 'pause'.[16]

The pay pause was only the first move towards an incomes policy. During the winter of 1961–2, the Treasury led by Frank Lee, tried to work out a set of principles or guidelines that ought to govern the movement of wages. The conclusions of the group appeared as a White

Paper in February in *Incomes Policy: the Next Step*. For the first time this gave government approval to the idea of a 'guiding light', i.e. an indication to the public of the increase in wages that would be consistent with stable prices. This was put at 2–2 $\frac{1}{2}$ per cent, the current estimate of the trend growth in productivity.

This was, of course, an average; and the White Paper discussed also the grounds on which a wage increase higher than the average could be justified. It did not give its blessing to cases of rapidly increasing productivity unless they could be shown to involve extra effort or hardship on the part of the workers. Nor did it regard low rates of wages as in themselves sufficient justification if there was an over-supply of workers at those rates. Later White Papers took a somewhat different view but the 1962 White Paper was more rigorously in accord with economic principles.

The fundamental problem, however, was not one of economic principle but of implementation. There was a tendency to think that the pressure of public opinion, if guided by clear statements of principle, would suffice. Others thought that arbitrators should be instructed to give effect to the guidelines. But the parties to a labour dispute had to find a settlement acceptable to both sides and might, like George Woodcock, regard the intrusion of an uninvited third party, as an 'impertinence'. Press comment often took for granted that if the government was sufficiently determined it could make incomes policy work. But it was even more difficult to regulate wages than to control prices. A wage freeze, like a price freeze, could be imposed and might, for a limited time, be effective. But a freeze was not a policy: it was an expedient that, by treating all alike, had a certain appeal. It was not a device providing for appropriate changes in wage relationships when these could not for long be avoided.

If incomes policy was to become a reality, machinery must be set up to give effect to it. The need for such machinery was particularly evident in May when two wage settlements – those with the nurses and the dockers – received enormous press publicity as in breach of government policy: in the case of the nurses, with public sympathy for what was seen as unjustifiably low pay; and in the case of the dockers, because their threat of a strike was seen as a major challenge to government policy and the final capitulation was dramatized accordingly. What part Ministers played in the dockers' settlement is not altogether clear. The Treasury had no hand in the affair and the employers had already made concessions well before the settlement that were not far short of what was eventually accepted. The public drew the conclusion that incomes policy was ineffective. As Sir William Hailey, editor of *The Times*, commented, they would have felt more favourable to the pay pause had they seen some prospect of useful results. But the idea that prices might stop rising still seemed implausible to them.

When the Chancellor failed to put forward new long-term proposals, the Prime Minister took the matter up and called a meeting at Chequers on Sunday, 20 May. This was the starting-point in the discussions leading up to the appointment of a National Incomes Commission in July to pronounce on wage settlements referred to it. It also led, as the Prime Minister felt himself shouldering more of the burden of preparing a long-term policy while the Chancellor bore correspondingly less, to the eventual replacement of the Chancellor by Reginald Maudling on Friday, 13 July.

It was only after Selwyn Lloyd's departure that the new Commission was announced. It did not hear its first case until 1963, heard only four cases in all, was boycotted by the unions and was wound up when the Labour government took office in October 1964, the first of several institutions to administer incomes policy that failed to survive a change of government. It cannot be said that its contribution to a long-term incomes policy had much significance.

PLANNING

Early in July 1961 the Chancellor told his colleagues that he proposed to plan for a higher rate of growth, with targets laid down in advance. There had been 'a surge of public interest' in planning since the FBI Conference at Brighton in November 1960 and the conference six months later on French planning at the National Institute.[17] The government itself had accepted in March 1961 the need for longer-term planning in public expenditure, anticipating a main recommendation of the Plowden Committee Report in July on the Control of Public Expenditure.[18]

This enthusiasm for planning implied a volte-face in Conservative thinking and took for granted that plans brought stability and did not undergo changes as substantial as those made in shorter-term arrangements. It was not many years since 'planning' in the vocabulary of a Conservative chancellor had been a dirty word – as in due course it became once again. It was also not many years before a highly elaborate National Plan had to be abandoned because of difficulties with the balance of payments. It did not bode well for the success of planning that the Chancellor coupled the idea with the suggestion that 'we should also consider whether our present powers to control the economy are sufficient'.

It was soon clear that the decision to embark on planning did not rest on a clear understanding of what it implied, how it worked elsewhere and whether it would remove the main obstacles to faster growth. While the government's enthusiasm for planning was widely shared, some had reservations about the kind of planning proposed. *The Economist* attacked the view that the staff of the proposed Planning Council should be 'quite distinct and independent from the Treasury' urging instead a division between a Minister for the Economy (or Chancellor) and a Minister for the Budget (or Finance). Planning was an activity for economic technocrats, not for organised interest groups.[19] The technocrats should prepare and make available to everybody a 'series of top class market research and investment research surveys on a national scale'.[20] The staff would also set targets for the increase in national output and the rise in wages.[21]

The creation of what became the National Economic Development Council ('Neddy') was a prolonged affair. The TUC had given their provisional agreement to join on 20 November but withheld final agreement for two more months out of disagreement over the pay pause. When the Council met at last on 7 March 1962 it included six employers from private industry, six trade unionists, two representatives of the nationalised industries, two independent members (Lord Franks and Professor Henry Phelps Brown) and three Ministers (the Chancellor, the President of the Board of Trade and the Minister of Labour), making twenty in all when the Director-General (Sir Robert Shone) is included.

A month later Selwyn Lloyd introduced his second budget. He was anxious to specify a target rate of growth so that Neddy could get to work on the details of a plan on that basis and he had in mind a rate of 5 per cent, well above any sustained rate previously achieved. I had difficulty in persuading him to be content with 4 per cent which was also higher, but perhaps not impossibly higher, than current performance.[22] If the rate was set too high, it was a recipe, not for faster growth, but for inflation. If it was set too low, it meant planning for less than was within the capabilities of producers. In France, indicative planning was designed to maintain the existing rate of growth, while in Britain the whole purpose of planning was to improve what was seen as a disappointing level of performance. But the mere preparation of a consistent set of figures called a plan did not of itself raise output unless in the process obstacles to higher productivity were removed or forces making for higher productivity were released. This was well understood in 'Neddy' and useful studies of what was needed at the micro level were published. But it was less apparent that the studies were successful in changing industrial practice.

There were three major difficulties about a plan directed to producing faster growth. One was the absence of an effective link between discussions round the table in Neddy on what made for higher productivity and action on the factory floor and round the boardroom table to change current attitudes and practice. Secondly, there was the party division that led each party when it came to power to repudiate the measures and institutions inaugurated by its opponents. Agreement between employers and employed (for example, to an incomes policy) was difficult in the absence of agreement between Labour and Conservatives. As Maudling found, concessions made readily to a Labour Chancellor might be denied to a Conservative. Thirdly and most important of all, the United Kingdom was not a closed system and was exposed to influences from the international economy over which it had little or no control. The balance of payments was the Achilles heel of the British economy and could upset domestic plans geared to fixed objectives. Things might have been different with less debt and higher reserves (including reserves of competitive power). But in fact the economy was highly vulnerable to upsets and made itself still more so by the very anxiety to grow faster to which planning was a response.

In due course Neddy got to work on the implications of a 4 per cent rate of growth. But it had not had time to get far when Selwyn Lloyd left office. When planning began, it was on the basis of a 22 per cent increase in GDP between 1961 and 1966: and this, since the growth rate was currently falling well short of 4 per cent, appeared to imply acceleration by 1966 to a rate *above* 4 per cent. In addition, as I discovered rather late in the day, the Treasury had committed itself to a $4\frac{1}{4}$ per cent per annum increase in public expenditure and was in fact sanctioning an increase in public investment at a much faster rate. The private sector was in no position to commit itself to 4 per cent growth but the public sector could and did.[23] In 1964 fixed investment in the public sector increased (in *real* terms) by no less than 17 per cent over 1963. How this came about under a Public Expenditure Survey Committee (PESC) régime of long-term planning I have no idea; but nothing I could say or do in 1964 reduced the programme one whit.

4 The Maudling 'Dash for Growth'

The new Chancellor was a good deal younger than his predecessor. He had a relaxed, almost off-hand manner, as if he never took anything very seriously, but was invariably well-informed and always considered deeply how he should run his risks. He was at home in economic problems and took an intellectual interest in them, relying much less than Selwyn Lloyd on his advisers. After the first six months I noted in my diary:

> The Chancellor keeps his own counsel.... There is undoubtedly some coolness between him and the Department. They don't like his preference for gimmicks, for putting his own individual mark on things. He has also been fairly free in rejecting advice... or in indicating distrust.... I have had no real opportunity ever to discuss with him alone the state of the economy in the way I sometimes did with Selwyn.

It is a nice question how far there was a fundamental difference between Maudling's policies and Selwyn Lloyd's. Both hoped to effect a transformation in Britain's economic performance by mobilising all possible reserves of foreign exchange in support of sustained expansion. Neither had any real insight into the mainsprings of economic growth, especially if that is taken to mean growth in productivity; they simply assumed that if expansion was sufficiently prolonged, industrial productivity would move upwards to a new, steeper curve. Selwyn Lloyd drew back when the reserves dwindled fast. Maudling was luckier in escaping the final crunch. But he also contemplated, with the encouragement of the Prime Minister, a way out that Selwyn Lloyd had either overlooked or, more probably, rejected – floating the currency.

The press, which was impatient to see expansion, took for granted that he was of the same mind. 'Mr Maudling's difficulty from the outset,' according to *The Economist*, 'is that his job has been to reverse the policies of his predecessor, while all the time pretending that he was not doing so.'[1] He was certainly in no hurry to reflate. For the first two months he spent much of his time reviewing the situation, consulting officials and industrialists, and considering possible lines of action. It was not until his Mansion House speech on 2 October after his return from the annual meeting of the Bank and Fund in Washington, that he announced his first cautious measures of reflation.

While still in Washington he had used the opportunity, amid great publicity, to propose the establishment of a Mutual Currency Account as a means of improving international liquidity. The scheme, which was the brain-child of Lucius Thompson-McCausland of the Bank of England, provided that countries in temporary surplus, acquiring the currency of the debtors, would be allowed to establish claims on an account held by the IMF which they could then draw upon when their situations were reversed. It was presumably an attempt to generalise the system of currency swaps that had been created on the initiative of the United States, under which bilateral arrangements were made for the central banks of two countries to hold an agreed amount of each other's currency as an addition to their reserves. The United Kingdom, for example, had entered into a pilot arrangement of this kind with the United States for a $50 million swap in 1961 and the US Secretary of the Treasury had discussed an extension of the arrangement in May 1962.

The scheme for a Mutual Currency Account was given no support by the United States, which made clear its opposition to it. R. V. Roosa, the Treasury Under-Secretary in charge of currency swaps (and indeed the originator of the swaps scheme) saw no need for concern over international liquidity during the next five years and preferred to make progress by developing swap arrangements. I return to the question of international liquidity in Chapter 14 on 'Monetary and Fiscal Policy in the 1960s'.

In the summer and autumn of 1962, the economic outlook darkened. By the end of July the signs of a slowdown were already increasingly apparent. Manufacturing investment was well below the level in 1961 and was likely to go on falling. Stockbuilding (as we later discovered) was negative and showed no sign of picking up. Exports were feeling the effects of the American recession. Unemployment continued to rise.

An important element in the slowdown was the completion of a large investment programme in the iron and steel industry. Between 1959 and 1961 capital expenditure had doubled, from just under £100 million to nearly £200 million. In the next two years it fell away, first to £170 million in 1962 and then to £77 million in 1963 and lower figures in later years. The turning point must have been near the middle of 1962: when total manufacturing investment had already fallen by over 10 per cent below its peak in the second half of 1961. Important as was the falling off in steel investment, it neither initiated the general decline in investment nor accounted for more than a fraction of it.

The slowdown was world-wide. From the second quarter of 1962 the increase over the next three quarters in world industrial production was trifling and the growth in trade between industrial countries was equally small. World trade in manufactures in those three quarters stood still and Britain's share in the total ceased to fall for the time being. In the two winter quarters a rise in consumer spending and government expenditure on goods and services was insufficient to offset the fall in fixed investment and stockbuilding. GDP fell in those quarters – something that did not happen again until 1967 – and the rise in unemployment continued through the freezing weather, the first (seasonally adjusted) drop coming in April 1963.

On the basis of the first signs of these trends, I pressed in July for immediate action but without success.

In the recess, action was difficult and none was taken. The Chancellor did, however, decide towards the end of August to prepare a package of measures for announcement in October. These included a release of post-war credits, an extra £60 million in public investment, various monetary measures including a 1 per cent reduction in bank rate (which the Bank of England successfully resisted) and a release of special deposits.

In August and September I hesitated to urge any drastic expansionary measures since industrial production was still increasing and unemployment appeared to be flattening out. In October, however, the crude unemployment figures (excluding school-leavers) increased by nearly 50,000, a jump that removed any hesitations over recommending immediate action. I at once advised the Chancellor to make use of the regulator to the full extent. The Budget Committee, however, offered no support, arguing that the rise in unemployment represented 'a continuing shake-out of labour, which is good in the long run'. I was, in fact, overimpressed by the rise in unemployment since two-thirds of the increase was seasonal; in retrospect, however, it would have been quite reasonable to bring the regulator into play, although not to the full extent. Instead, the Budget Committee recommended a reduction in the rate of purchase tax on a single item – motor cars – from 45 per cent to 25 per cent. This had the merit of bringing the tax into line with tax on many other consumer durables and it assisted an industry that was working well below capacity. But new car registrations were higher than a year previously and the car industry was in an area where acute shortages of labour tended to recur. I thought that a stimulus should not be so narrowly concentrated.

Other reflationary measures followed. When the reduction in purchase tax on cars was announced on 5 November, the Chancellor promised to include in the 1963 Budget substantial increases in investment allowances on machinery and industrial buildings and in depreciation rates on new purchases of heavy plant, the improved rates to come into effect immediately on all future expenditure. Action of this kind had long been favoured by the Economic Section but was anathema to the Inland Revenue which had persuaded itself that to use the tax system for economic purposes was wrong in principle. The return of the remaining special deposits to the clearing banks was announced in two stages, on 27 September and on 29 November; and in December local authorities in three selected areas in the North were allowed to embark on public works to provide winter employment, while consumption was given a further stimulus through a reduction to 25 per cent of purchase tax on radio and television sets and other items.

These measures were introduced one by one without any attempt to assess their total effect. The time for such an assessment was in the February forecast in advance of the 1963 Budget. In the meantime there was little reason to regard their impact as excessive. The repayment of post-war credits and tax concessions represented a release of about £130 million a year in purchasing power, to which had to be added the public investment, to the value of £80 million, authorised in October and December, the cost of the additional investment allowances (which would not affect the Budget until 1964 or later), and the effect of the easing of credit through the release of special deposits and the withdrawal of restrictions on lending by the banks.

The December forecast was not able to take account of all the Chancellor's measures since it was submitted at the beginning of the month. It showed GDP growing by about 3 per cent between the third quarter of 1962 and the third quarter of 1963, little rise in exports and a slight recovery in total fixed investment. The balance of payments would be a little higher than in 1962 when there had been a small surplus on current account.

This faced us with a familiar dilemma. There was a margin of unused resources which appeared to be fairly substantial and was not only increasing but seemed likely to increase still further in 1963. On the other hand, the balance of payments was far from secure and faster expansion meant taking the risk of throwing it into deficit. There was the further uncertainty as to how the bid to join the Common Market would end.

Having weighed up these different considerations, I concluded that there was scope for further expansion and once again suggested a much more powerful stimulus than had been customary in similar circumstances – 1959 apart. I even suggested the use of the regulator before Christmas and the release in all of £300 million in purchasing power. This I took to be what was required to raise the rate of expansion from 3 per cent to 5 per cent. The Budget Committee again rejected my suggestion, recommended against the use of the regulator, and were unwilling to name any specific figure for a release of purchasing power.

I was unaware at that time that £300 million (which had caused not a murmur in June 1961) was roughly twice the dose that Robert Hall had been accustomed to recommend in a recession. I was also not yet conscious that Christmas is no time to play around with indirect taxation. On the other hand, looking back, I see that the expansionary action for which I pressed in July was taken some months later; and the release of £300 million that I proposed in December was duly made (although differently composed) in the April Budget.

Nevertheless, in retrospect, I take no pride in my record as an adviser in 1962. First of all I was rash to allow Selwyn Lloyd to indicate in the 1962 Budget that personal consumption was likely to rise by 4 per cent over the year and that the pressure of demand would grow when it was already obvious that it was falling. It was not that personal consumption was expected to be particularly buoyant or the principal agency in causing production to increase. It was simply that, by convention, the government did not publicly predict the change in production in the year ahead but was less reticent about consumption. In suggesting 4 per cent, we thought that we were being cautious, since we had deliberately reduced the export forecast and advised the Chancellor that the official forecast of a 5 per cent rise in GDP was too optimistic. To the public as the year went by, 4 per cent was in cloud cuckoo land. Revised figures show a rise in consumption over the year of about $2\frac{1}{3}$ per cent and in GDP at a rate of at best, nearly 2 per cent.

There were other forecasting errors, nearly all in the same direction. It was soon evident that fixed investment, instead of increasing by up to 2 per cent, would be level or falling. Prices in the nationalised industries were unexpectedly high.

It was not these errors that troubled me. It was rather that I continued to offer reassurance too long, that I acquiesced too readily in

Selwyn Lloyd's inclination to wait, and that in the summer and autumn I dithered, first calling for a boost in July when it was too late and then waiting until the end of the year before making fresh proposals.

When we contemplated recovery in 1963 we had to reckon with the pressure of the NEDC for plans to be based on a 4 per cent growth rate. Ever since Selwyn Lloyd had announced a 4 per cent target in the spring of 1962, it had persisted under Maudling and ultimately became the corner-stone of the National Plan when Labour came to power. It was all too easy to move from regarding 4 per cent growth as something that might yet be achieved if all the right things were done, to taking it as a basis for forward planning and going on to insist that the elements of policy should all be consistent with a 4 per cent rate.

The matter was complicated by the contention that growth was accelerating towards 4 per cent and that if expansion were smoother, the incentive to invest would be stronger, and higher investment would yield faster growth. It was an argument that I often encountered, especially from those who thought stop–go peculiar to Britain and saw no great difficulty in following a smoother path of expansion. If one drew attention to repeated balance of payments difficulties, the answer given was that chronic difficulties could be met by devaluation and lesser difficulties by capital controls and in other ways. The chances that excess demand might renew the difficulties after devaluation and undermine competitiveness by opening the door to inflationary wage claims tended to be set on one side.

Were we in fact within sight of 4 per cent growth? I was sceptical. The CSO had shown that in the 1950s the annual improvement in labour productivity had averaged 2 per cent while employment had risen at a little under 1 per cent so that the growth in GDP was a little below 3 per cent. On the other hand, over the five years 1955–60 the improvement in labour productivity had been somewhat higher at 2.5 per cent per annum and there was some evidence of a still higher rate in the 1960s. These were years when there was much talk of large economies in manpower through automation and a popular belief that technical progress was more than usually labour-saving. It was at least conceivable that labour productivity might be improving at 3 per cent per annum in a year or two – a low rate by continental standards. But the most I was disposed to concede was that the underlying rate of growth in GDP appeared to be at $3-3\frac{1}{2}$ per cent and any faster rate would be possible only by drawing idle resources into employment – a finite process.

Britain was not alone in setting growth targets. The OECD, rallying its members to the expansionist banner, had called for a 50 per cent increase in production between 1961 and 1970. This was an aggregate target which each country could interpret as it chose; but in 1963 members were invited to set individual targets for the next twelve months. These had no necessary connection with the aggregate target and seemed little more than an exercise in public relations.

Another difficulty was to judge the margin of spare capacity in an upswing. In two large regions – London and the South East/East Anglia and Yorkshire and Humberside/East Midlands – unemployment in July 1961 had been down to 0.7 per cent, while in a third – the West Midlands – it had been as low as 0.6 per cent in 1960. In other regions such as Northern Ireland, Scotland and the North, the boom-time rates were much higher, the lowest rates touched in 1960–1 being 5.8, 2.8 and 1.9 respectively. On the other hand, in bad times, as in April 1963, the rates in these regions stood at 8.3, 5.2 and 5.1 per cent compared with a national average of 2.7 per cent. These differences gave an expansionist – indeed inflationary – bias to policy since to bring rates in Scotland, for example, down to 3 per cent the national average had to be held at about 1.5 per cent.

The winter of 1962–3 was so severe and so protracted that it was difficult to judge the underlying trends. The crude unemployment figure, including temporarily stopped, reached a peak of 933 000 in February, but the seasonally adjusted rate in Great Britain for the wholly unemployed was estimated to be no higher than 2.4 per cent. The national income forecast, when produced in February concluded that production in the second half of 1963 would be $3\frac{1}{4}$ per cent higher than a year previously with some slight slowing down towards the end of the year. Consumer spending was expected to rise fast early in the year and then fall away in the absence of a fresh stimulus. Fixed investment, on the other hand, would accelerate over the year. Public service investment, indeed, would be higher than in 1962 by 12–14 per cent and manufacturing investment, which had fallen heavily in 1962, would begin to recover. Exports, however, would grow by only 3 per cent. On these assumptions, unemployment would continue to grow slowly for a time in 1963 and then flatten out. The amount of spare capacity was not expected to contract.

In mid-February 1963 I submitted my pre-budget assessment of the situation. If we could assume an underlying rate of growth of $3-3\frac{1}{2}$ per cent and spare capacity that might provide a further $3-3\frac{1}{2}$ per cent, there might be a margin to spare over the year ahead of about 7 per cent. Since it was necessary to allow for a period in which expansion subsided again to a normal level, however, it would be unwise to take up all the slack in 1963. A target of 4 per cent was quite enough for the current year; but if we looked ahead to the first quarter of 1965, a 10 per cent expansion was possible by that time. These were reasonable targets. In fact the increase in GDP from the last quarter of 1962 to the first quarter of 1965 was over 11 per cent. What was much more in question was what would happen to the balance of payments and whether, as the pressure mounted, the old problem of rising wages and prices could be avoided.

Pressure was already making itself felt on the foreign exchanges. After the French veto at the end of January on the British application to join the European Community and a fall in the bill rate in January and February to the lowest level since 1959, the dollar rate fell below par in March for the first time for eighteen months. Between January and May covered interest rate differentials were against the United Kingdom and an outflow of funds began that reached £170 million by the end of April. To meet this, recourse was again made to the Basle Arrangements and $250 million borrowed from foreign central banks. Nevertheless. Bank Rate was left at 4 per cent throughout the year, the Bank seeking to drive market rates closer to Bank Rate by threatening to charge more than Bank Rate on occasion for future loans to the discount market. Efforts were also made to keep long rates from falling below $5\frac{1}{2}$ per cent by large-scale funding but without preventing a fall from about 6.25 per cent in the second quarter of 1962 to 5.2 per cent in the third quarter of 1963 with some reversal of the fall at the beginning of 1963.

The outflow of funds ceased and the fresh borrowings made under the Basle Arrangements were repaid in the second quarter but the background to the Budget was far from reassuring: particularly so had we reflected that in one year we were moving from a Budget in 1962 that aimed at a rare overall surplus to a Budget in 1963 that provided for a deficit above the line – something no post-war Conservative government had done.

Even before Maudling's first budget in April 1963, the Prime Minister had outlined to him the strategy to be followed. In a lengthy memorandum he argued that:

> an expansionary budget, together with accompanying measures in various fields, would, before it had started to achieve its target, be snookered by a balance of payments crisis, a run on the pound, and

all that. The orthodox measure of dealing with this could defeat the purpose of the Budget.[2]

Instead one should either strengthen the reserves by borrowing, using the dollar portfolio as collateral, and drawing as large a credit as possible from the IMF, or alternatively let the exchange rate float. The first possibility would be coupled with a declaration that the Government:

> were now going to expand the economy with a view to the ultimate strengthening of sterling; that they thought this would be possible within, say, three years and that in the meantime they were prepared to spend every penny of the reserves to defend the pound.[3]

The alternative would be to let the pound drop when the Budget was announced, declaring that:

> we saw no way of getting through our exchange difficulties; on a fixed exchange rate we might be forced to adopt monetary measures which would inhibit economic expansion at home: we did not intend to do this; and therefore the only alternative was to float.[4]

The Prime Minister accepted that there might be difficulties. But a fall in the exchange rate offered 'the only effective and immediate form of import control', and he did not expect the fall to be a large one, once exports had had time to respond. It would be possible to plead the breakdown of the Brussels negotiations as the occasion, if not the cause, of 'this radical change in British policy'.[5]

It was not a convincing prescription. But it sums up the policy that Maudling adopted. He did indeed try to reinforce the reserves, for example by arranging a standby of $1 billion with the IMF. He was also (privately) ready to float the pound. Above all, he shared the confident belief that an expansionist policy, if persisted in, would make for faster growth.

When it came to deciding how expansionary the Budget should be, the Prime Minister hesitated between the National Institute's proposal to cut taxation by £400 million and a more modest proposal for a cut of £200 million attributed to the Treasury.[6] In discussion with the Chancellor on 21 February, he urged the higher figure as more likely to make it possible to 'break through the vicious circle of stop and go'. Maudling was more cautious and thought £250–300 million nearer the mark. Both were well aware of the risk to the balance of payments. Maudling told the Prime Minister that he had asked the Treasury to consider a variety of measures including straight devaluation, a floating rate, multiple rates and an import surcharge (I have no recollection of any mention of the first three of these: the choice was between import quotas and a surcharge). Macmillan backtracked on floating, commenting that 'it might be thought a gimmick' and would encourage a mood of indiscipline.[7]

In a discussion at Chequers a few days later, it was agreed that tax cuts should not exceed £250 million. This would cover the abandonment of Schedule A (which the Orpington by-election had shown to be electorally popular), the measures Maudling had already promised, and a cut of 50 per cent in fuel oil duty (subsequently omitted because of the repercussions on the coal industry).

Earlier, I had recommended to the Budget Committee cuts of £250 million in revenue, coupled with a statement that more would be done later if necessary. There was some uneasiness about this in the Budget Committee since the balance of payments at that (pre-budget) stage was expected to the £150 million in deficit. Moreover there had been a big increase in the Supply Estimates for 1963/4 – the biggest since 1951/2 – and this, together with the proposed cuts in revenue, would mean budgeting for a deficit of £100 million above the line. There had also been increases in National Insurance benefits and contributions, the effect of which would be to transfer about an extra £180 million from contributors to beneficiaries with a net increase in consumer spending. In spite of the doubts, the Budget Committee recommended tax reductions of £200–300 million.

When the recommendation was put to the Chancellor, he decided to take what he recognised as a calculated gamble. There would be a substantial growth in exports over the next two years and only a moderate rise in imports, attributable in part to the stocking up of materials to meet the expected growth in production. In these circumstances, and allowing for an abnormal amount of investment abroad, he argued that the expected deficit in the balance of payments could be represented as temporary and met, if necessary, by drawings from the IMF. He did, however, ask the Treasury to study emergency measures in case things turned out less happily and indicated a leaning towards import surcharges rather than import quotas as the appropriate response. He made clear to me subsequently that if the worst came to the worst he would be prepared to let the pound float.

His Budget speech expressed no such doubts. 'I absolutely reject the proposition', he declared, 'that a vigorous economy and a strong pound are incompatible.' He hoped for 'some continued improvement' in the current balance of payments in 1963 but admitted that the outflow of long-term capital was likely to increase. In the early stages of expansion, imports might rise faster than exports while stocks were being built up. But to finance such a build-up it was 'perfectly reasonable and sensible' to make use of reserves and the borrowing facilities provided by the IMF. He had already drawn $250 billion from other central banks in February and March (repaid in the second quarter) and stood ready to use the $1 billion of dollar securities held by the government and its drawing rights of nearly $2¼ billion.

The budget measures went a little beyond the Budget Committee's recommendations. The tax concessions added up to a sacrifice of revenue in 1963–4 estimated at £269 million and produced a borrowing requirement of £687 million compared with one of £66 million the year before. In a full year the loss of revenue would be much higher, mainly because of the eventual cost of the higher investment allowances promised in November and of what was described as 'free' depreciation in the development districts. 'Free' depreciation, which allowed firms in those districts freedom to decide the timing of depreciation for tax purposes, was designed to attract more investment to areas of high unemployment but seemed an expensive way of accomplishing this and was superseded in January 1966 by investment grants.

The Inland Revenue's estimate of the eventual cost of the investment and depreciation allowances was £240 million and the effect in a full year of all the concessions was put at £638 million. Thus instead of providing a powerful initial stimulus that would fade a little after the first year, which was what was required, the budgetary stimulus was due to acquire added force in 1964.

Apart from the additions to the programme of public investment that kept being made in spite of the Treasury's efforts to check them, no further expansionary measures were taken. Bank rate had finally been cut after over 8 months from 4½ per cent to 4 per cent on 3 January 1963 and remained there for over a year. Other measures were taken to reinforce the reserves: the $50 million swap with the Federal Reserve was increased to $500 million in May; and in addition to a drawing of £100 million in March, a stand-by of $1 billion was arranged with the IMF in August.

The budget also contained a modification of the 'guiding light'. Maudling had attached importance from the start to securing the agreement of the trade unions to an incomes policy. 'Without expansion' he maintained, 'you can't have an incomes policy; without an incomes policy you can't have expansion.' As a first step he included in the budget a change in the 'guiding light', raising it at the urging of the National Institute and other commentators from 2–2$\frac{1}{2}$ per cent to 3$\frac{1}{2}$ per cent in the hope that this would seem more realistic and acceptable to the unions and no doubt also because it seemed more consistent with a 4 per cent growth target. But as recovery gathered speed, 3$\frac{1}{2}$ per cent proved no more effective than 2$\frac{1}{2}$ per cent. If expansion reflected higher productivity it might help to make an incomes policy acceptable; but if it led to an increasing shortage of labour it had quite the opposite effect.

Our picture of economic prospects changed rapidly after the budget and went on changing in successive forecasts. In June, before the budget had had much time to influence employment there was a record fall of 73,000 in unemployment. This did not prevent the TUC from arguing for more rapid expansion in 1963, but it reminded other observers of the headlong expansion in 1959. Where our February forecast had been of an increase of a little over 3 per cent in GDP in 1963, by July we were expecting a 3$\frac{1}{2}$ per cent increase in the next six months alone, followed by a 5 per cent annual increase in 1964. Even so, we continued to assume a favourable balance of payments in 1964 with a surplus on current account of £60 million – an extraordinary misjudgment.

Meanwhile in May monetary problems had become pressing. The government was taking the opportunity of a strong demand for gilts to undertake extensive funding rather than let long-term rates of interest fall heavily. This left the clearing banks short of the Treasury Bills they needed in order to maintain a liquidity ratio of 30 per cent and also risked letting short-term rates fall too low to offer support to the exchange rate. The Bank of England in May wanted an immediate reduction in the minimum liquidity ratio to 25 per cent but this seemed to go too far when a large budget deficit was in prospect. A reduction to 28 per cent was agreed and other ways were suggested of adding temporarily to liquidity such as repurchase agreements (which had been in regular use before 1914) and the deposit of larger cash balances with the clearing banks by the nationalised industries.

When the conference season opened in the autumn the TUC passed two contradictory resolutions on incomes policy. They supported the report of the General Council, which argued that under the new planning arrangements money incomes should not rise faster than output, but coupled this with a resolution denouncing wage restraint. A month later, on 4 October, the Labour Party conference was also in agree-

TABLE 4.1 Successive forecasts of changes in the constituents of final demand, 1962–4 (£ million, quarterly rates)

	February 1963	April 1963 (post-budget)	July 1963	November 1963	February 1964	Actual increase (at 1958 prices)[a]
Change forecast between Q2–4 (average) 1962 and Q1 1964 in:						
Exports	28	24	51	75	86	94
Civil public investment	68	77	94	90	99 }	169
Other investment	−32	−16	−13	−8	8	
Total domestic investment	36	61	81	82	107	263
Stockbuilding	11	8	3	2	25	79
Public consumption	57	66	59	64	50	29
Personal consumption	148	229	244	264	311	323
Final expenditure	252	364	387	412	493	694
GDP (% per annum)	2.4	3.3	3.9	4.6	5.0	5.2

[a] *Economic Trends*, October 1968, expenditure measure.

SOURCE: National Income Forecasts.

ment on a 'planned growth of incomes'. More significantly, it accepted a proposal to create a Ministry of Economic Planning. What the new Ministry was to do had not been worked out but it was likely to take over most of the staff of the National Economic Development Office (NEDO) and was clearly intended to limit the role of the Treasury.

Shortly afterwards, the Prime Minister was removed to hospital and on 10 October announced unexpectedly his intention of resigning from office just as the Conservative Party Conference in Blackpool was about to open. The Chancellor, who had thought his chances of succeeding might be 50 : 50, was unsuccessful in the subsequent contest. The choice fell instead on the Foreign Secretary, Lord Home, who formed a new government on 19 October and was subsequently elected to the House of Commons as Sir Alec Douglas-Home.

As production accelerated, people began to ask whether anything fundamental had changed over the past four years and whether in a year or so it would be possible to avoid another balance of payments crisis. The Chancellor, in his Mansion House speech, had dwelt on incomes policy and international liquidity; and in addressing NEDC he had concentrated on the need to keep down costs and remain competitive. But might not the greater danger be a recurrence of excessive pressure of demand that found an outlet in higher imports and an adverse balance of payments? Investment was rising strongly and might be accompanied by a fresh bout of stockbuilding that could quickly absorb the slack in the system. It would be a mistake to assume too readily that universal acceptance of the need for an incomes policy would prevent money incomes from rising and the competitive position from becoming endangered. There could be no certainty how far expansion could proceed without running into bottlenecks or how effective incomes policy would be in conditions of labour shortage.

It would, of course, take many months for the pressure to build up. But if it was intended, as the White Paper on Public Investment (Cmnd 2177) indicated, to increase public investment in 1963–4 by some 20 per cent over 1962–3, action would have to be taken well in advance of the expected peak to make sure that no overheating resulted. The Chancellor made speeches warning of the danger of overinvestment but he ran the risk that the public would assume that the danger was immediate, not many months away, and was advised by the press to act as he thought necessary, not make speeches about matters under the government's own control.

On 25 October I prepared a note for the new Prime Minister on the economic situation. Production had been expanding since the spring, latterly, I suggested, at too hot a pace to be sustained and it would probably grow in 1964 at an annual rate of at least 5 per cent. Three powerful influences had united to propel the economy forward. One was exports which had grown quarter by quarter and were 8 per cent higher than a year previously. A second was the tax cuts of November 1962 and the Budget in April which were reflected in a boom in car registrations, up by nearly a third since the summer of 1962; and in a sharp increase in retail sales beginning in July and continuing throughout the autumn. A third influence was the large increase in public investment set on foot over the past eighteen months.

The improvement in production was widely spread and was even more apparent in the recovery of business confidence. Order books were lengthening, most conspicuously in the engineering industries, where export orders in July and August were 18 per cent and home orders 24 per cent above the level in those two months a year earlier.

The balance of payments appeared to be in a relatively healthy state and confidence in the pound had remained steady since the Budget, but there were big uncertainties. A little later it became apparent that a current account surplus of £70 million in the first quarter had been falling quarter by quarter and was no longer sufficient in the second half of 1963 to balance the usual net outflow of long-term capital.

I cited four problems that would assume increasing importance in 1964. The first was the gradual disappearance of spare capacity implicit in the divergence between the growth of demand at between 5 and 6 per cent per annum and the slower growth at about $3\frac{1}{2}$ per cent per annum of the capacity to produce. The pace was likely to be set by fixed investment, but stockbuilding would not be far behind and the momentum of expansion would carry into 1965. The margin of spare capacity would probably not disappear before the second half of 1964; but given the slowness with which some elements in demand responded, action could not wait even if results were not needed until the early months of 1965. This was particularly true of public investment which was planned and committed for several years ahead and could not easily be altered at short notice.

The timing and scale of restraining action by the government over the next year would depend on its success in dealing with the other three problems. Of these the first was the more rapid decline of unemployment in London and the Midlands than in the rest of the country. Unemployment in the London region was already down to 1.2 per cent and still falling so that labour shortages would become more acute. The concessions offered in the 1963 Budget in favour of capital investment in the development areas would take a long time to exert their influence and would not have much effect on the regional balance within the next year or two.

There were also signs that wages would rise more rapidly in 1964. Superficially the Government's incomes policy appeared to be remarkably successful. But current wage settlements showed an average increase of $5\frac{1}{2}$ per cent and the tightening of the labour market and the rise in profits were bound to lead to some bidding up of the price of scarce labour and increased pressure from the trade unions.

This would lead, thirdly, to a weakening in our competitive position and make for a more anxious outlook in the balance of payments. We did not expect at that stage any serious deterioration in the current balance or any large deficit on current and capital account; but there were 'big uncertainties and this outlook could easily change'.

By mid November I took a more decided view. I thought it almost inconceivable that expansion at the forecast rate of $5\frac{1}{2}$ per cent could continue throughout 1964 to be matched by the resources available. The momentum was increasing and the balance of payments would weaken with some loss of confidence and outflow of funds. There should be some check to activity before the end of 1963, with firmer control over public investment and some limitation of non-industrial building. The 1964 budget should follow this up with higher indirect taxation and some addition to profits tax. What was most needed was an early reconsideration of investment plans which would otherwise overload the construction industry in 1964 and spill over into 1965. The Budget Committee was in sympathy with this diagnosis but saw no point in recommending the measures proposed until Ministers also accepted it.

The Chancellor appeared to accept the diagnosis but held out no prospect of higher taxes. As he saw it, with some wry amusement, the course of events was likely to be a splendid burst of expansion in the spring, followed by an election in June, and then efforts on the part of Callaghan and Co. to cope with the resulting exchange crisis. He did, however, put a warning paper to the Economic Policy Committee and followed it up at the end of the year with a paper to the Cabinet that began 'We are again facing the problem of how to control a boom.' He went on, however, to claim more power to do so than in the past and refrained from suggesting any of the unpopular measures, such as cuts in public investment, that his advisers had proposed.

Thus as 1963 ended, output was growing at an unsustainable rate; and in spite of the study that had gone to the experience of 1959, a very similar situation had been allowed to arise. No action had been taken to check the momentum and as a general election approached, it would be increasingly difficult for Ministers pledged to policies of steady growth to take the restrictive measures required.

In December came a nasty shock. A study of five sets of possible seasonal adjustments to the unemployment figures revealed that while four of them showed a progressively larger decline in unemployment month by month since June, the Ministry of Labour's seasonal adjustment showed, if not the precise opposite, at least a flattening out in the monthly rate of decline. The implication was that the margin of spare manpower was smaller and disappearing faster than we had imagined.

There were other grounds for uneasiness. I was moved to protest in December at 'the increasingly unqualified acceptance of the NEDC target of a 4 per cent rate of growth between 1961 and 1966' when all the evidence suggested little change from a perceptibly slower rate. I was also concerned over forecasting arrangements that made the reports of the various committees involved bear too much the character of treaties between contending powers. They yielded forecasts, particularly of exports and imports, that were often neither reliable nor plausible (for example, the November forecast indicated no deterioration in the current account between the first half and the second half of 1964). Those working on national income and long-range forecasts were 'largely detached' from the work on world economic problems and the balance of payments, and those who prepared export forecasts were separated from those who reported on world economic problems. Christopher Dow urged the creation of a forecasting unit in the Treasury responsible for all economic forecasts and drawing on information supplied by the Board of Trade, Ministry of Labour and other departments. This went beyond what I hoped to do; but closer co-ordination was certainly necessary not only between the forecasters but in the economic information reaching Whitehall departments through different channels from abroad.

As 1964 opened, the natural first move would have been to put up bank rate and this was urged both in the press (by *The Economist*) and in the Treasury. I had supported the idea of a 1 per cent rise in bank rate when it was first proposed in mid-December, but two complications had to be considered. The first was that the banks had returned to a proposal made earlier that they should be allowed to raise their overdraft rates as well as some deposit rates. The Governor, in putting the banks' case pointed out that their costs had been rising for a long time and they would sooner or later have to offset higher costs by higher rates. The banks might run a cartel but the rates they charged were competitive, to judge from the rates established by competition in the United States. While an announcement of higher bank interest rates would not look well against the background of prices and incomes policy, it was not clear that they could be stopped or would ask for the government's agreement. But if they put up their rates would it still be possible to raise bank rate?

The second complication was proposal from Bill Martin of the Federal Reserve Board for a co-ordinated rise of $\frac{1}{2}$ per cent in the US and UK. This followed earlier discussion with Roosa who told us he was holding down US bill rates with the UK situation in mind. The Governor intended to pursue this idea and I discussed it with him at some length on 17 December. It emerged that he favoured a straight 1 per cent increase, as I did, but recognised that the Chancellor was unlikely to go for a 1 per cent rise if the US limited itself to $\frac{1}{2}$ per cent. On the other hand, a rise of $\frac{1}{2}$ per cent might simply unsettle the market. Towards the end of January, after a long talk with Maurice Allen of the Bank, I argued strongly against a move of $\frac{1}{2}$ per cent, whether in conjunction with the US or without, although most of my colleagues favoured a movement of $\frac{1}{2}$ per cent. I pressed instead for a 1 per cent increase, convinced that such an increase would cause the banks to scrap their proposal to raise overdraft rates. I put it to the Chancellor that interest rates would have to go up by the budget and that he had to choose between an extra 1 per cent and something like £50 million more in taxation.

In mid-February the matter was discussed between the Prime Minister and the President (in spite of general agreement that it should *not* be discussed). The President was anxious for agreement on a rise of $\frac{1}{2}$ per cent and explained that a larger rise would be very awkward for the US. The Prime Minister remained non-committal and the Chancellor at once cabled to say he had more or less decided on a 1 per cent rise. Then he had cold feet as he reflected on the need for American help later in the year and the other sources of friction with the United States (for example, over the sale of Leyland 'buses' to Cuba). What, he asked, would a 1 per cent increase do that could not be effected in other ways? So after nearly three months of discussion that seemed to have yielded a firm conclusion, we were back again in doubt. At last on 27 February, fourteen months after the drop in the rate to 4 per cent, it was raised to 5 per cent just as the morning press had concluded that no change was in the wind. The exactly similar rise from

4 to 5 per cent after 14 months in January 1960 was a depressing parallel.

The slack in the economy was meanwhile rapidly disappearing. By mid-February the press had begun to talk openly of the need for restraint. In 1963 production had risen by over 5 per cent (although we did not yet have the figures) with an abnormally sharp increase in the final quarter of the year. A fall of 17,000 in unemployment was announced in January and one of 22,000 in February (after seasonal adjustment), bringing the total under 400,000 and leaving the rate of unemployment in the South East only a little over 1 per cent. The Chancellor recognised that there must be a transition from 6 per cent to 4 per cent expansion but when and how this was to be done was still obscure. If the transition was accomplished, we had no confidence that growth at 4 per cent, which remained the target, was sustainable.

To complicate matters, 1964 was an election year. The Chancellor would have preferred an early election but other Ministers were in favour of waiting as long as possible so as to regain electoral support as the economy entered on a boom. I recall Nigel Lawson advising Ministers that 1964 would be 'annus mirabilis', with a rapid increase in production all through the year – indeed our own forecast was that manufacturing output would grow by 8 per cent between the autumn of 1963 and the autumn of 1964. What made the prospect less appealing politically was that the balance of payments had ceased to be in surplus, and the forecast indicated a growing deficit. I warned that there were likely to be substantial losses of reserves, beginning about the middle of the year even if there were no confidence crisis.

In the pre-budget forecast, the outlook for the domestic economy was dominated by the prospects for investment. Public investment in particular was expected to go on climbing rapidly at an average annual rate of 16 per cent in the seven quarters from the middle of 1963 to the beginning of 1965 and total fixed investment at about 10 per cent, with some slowing down towards the end. Demand would grow even faster and outrun the capacity of the construction industries to keep pace, causing some demand to be pushed back into 1965. House-building was already at a high rate and manufacturing investment was expected to accelerate. A second expansionary thrust was likely from stockbuilding, which had been at a low rate in 1963, but would now account for about an eighth of the rise in domestic activity. While some elements would slow down a little, others would gather speed and the forecasters were confident that, in the absence of policy changes, there was not likely to be any appreciable deceleration in the growth of demand.

The counterpart of this picture of rising pressure was a sharp fall in the current balance of payments from a surplus of £120 million in 1963 to a forecast deficit of £60 million in 1964 and a larger deficit at an annual rate of £150 million in the first half of 1965. Exports had been rising at about 4 per cent per annum and this rate was expected to continue. But a 4 per cent rise in exports would fall short of the rate implied in a 4 per cent growth of GDP and far short of a predicted increase in imports by 10 per cent. The actual growth in imports in 1964 was even faster and no doubt corresponded to the high rate of stockbuilding during the year. Exports, although growing in volume by 4 per cent in 1964 as forecast, reached a peak in the first quarter and expanded no further thereafter.

To the deficit on current account had to be added net overseas investment by the oil companies of £150 million and a further £200 million to cover the balance on portfolio account and the net outflow on official account. Some of this and some of the current account deficit could be regarded as temporary but probably not more than half. But a deficit of over £400 million on current and long-term capital account in 1964 was likely to be still larger in 1965 and continue in 1966. Even in years of high unemployment and fairly rapidly expanding world trade such as 1962 and 1963, there had been no more than a bare balance on current and long-term capital account. There seemed to be 'an underlying weakness in the economy which makes it extremely difficult to combine a reasonably full use of productive potential and a viable balance of payments'.

There could be little doubt that taxes should be increased in the budget. Apart from anything else, the steady upward drift in public expenditure made increase sooner or later inevitable. It was estimated that, with existing policies and commitments, an extra £100 million a year would be needed over the years 1964 to 1967 simply to keep the budget in balance. I saw little chance, however, that the Chancellor would consider any larger increase in 1964 than £100 million, especially as it was not many months since he was being urged to *reduce* taxation. Accordingly, £100 million was what I recommended to the Budget Committee at the end of January. If nothing were done in the budget either the use of the regulator during the summer or an autumn bud-get would become inevitable. At that stage the general view was that the most Ministers could be expected to accept was an increase of £50 million.

In February, however, the seriousness of the situation began to be appreciated by the press. Where a few months previously there had been talk of using the regulator to encourage expansion, now some commentators were advocating higher taxation to check it. The National Institute foresaw a deficit of £375 million in the balance of payments in the eighteen months to the middle of 1965 – without being aware that the current account was no longer in surplus but in heavy deficit and without knowing of the extra £150 million the oil companies were planning to invest in 1964. They proposed an additional £200 million in taxation in the budget as a first instalment with more to come at a later stage. About the same time the January trade returns showed a large increase of nearly 20 per cent in imports and alerted the public to the widening gap between exports and imports. Before the end of February the press had taken fright and was clamouring for action.

The Budget Committee was still doubtful whether it was 'politically feasible' to increase taxation by a minimum of £100 million especially if an early election made it necessary to keep the Finance Bill short and uncontroversial. But they accepted the need for such an increase and recommended it to the Chancellor who accepted the Committee's judgment of the economic requirement and assured them that a necessary increase in taxation should not be prevented by a decision in favour of an early election.

On 8 March he was able to indicate October as the likely date for an election and agreed to increase indirect taxation by about £100 million, holding the regulator in reserve and making it more flexible. He was not prepared, however, to make any increase in income tax, which no Tory government had raised in all the years they had been in power since 1951. Accordingly the Finance Bill on 14 April increased the tax on drink and tobacco and modified the regulator powers to permit the exclusion from its use of any of the major blocks – tobacco, alcohol, oil, and purchase tax.

In justifying the increase, the Chancellor attributed it to the need for a smooth transition from too high a rate of growth to the rate of 4 per cent accepted by the government as a long-term target (but one that officials regarded as unrealistically high under conditions in which there was no remaining slack in the system). The Chancellor was also able to claim that without increased taxation he would be budgeting for a deficit for the second year in succession. In fact, however, things had turned out differently in 1963–4 from budget expectations. There had been a surplus of £73 million above the line instead of the deficit expected; and the borrowing requirement had fallen short of the estimate by £200 million.

At the end of May the Chancellor suggested 'another tweak at the reins'. What he had in mind was a rise in the 'liquidity ratio' of the banks, not, he insisted, a call for special deposits. When I suggested delay until we had another month's figures he pointed out that after July it would be impossible to take action with a general election in the offing. After further discussion the Chancellor agreed early in June that he would aim for a call for special deposits on 26 June. This seemed an appropriate date since it was expected to follow the publication of banking figures showing a big increase in advances as well as other economic indicators that might cause some alarm. The Bank of England agreed without enthusiasm, the Governor representing the effect as marginal although he estimated the check to advances at £30 million a month (which would have meant a sudden halt to a 9 per cent per annum increase).

At a later meeting it was decided to defer action. Opinion during the month had been so robust and the Chancellor had been so successful in convincing the Press that everything was under control, that a call for special deposits would have come as a shock. The Chancellor now proposed to prepare the ground in a speech in Cardiff for a move later in July, probably the 23rd. The speech did nothing to debamboozle the journalists; and a first quarter current deficit of £300 million at an annual rate passed without mention, much less comment, in *The Economist* and little indication of concern elsewhere in the Press. Still more remarkable, the exchange reserves had grown in the first six months of 1964 in spite of a deficit on current and long-term capital account of £400 million (or £800 million a year).

The explanation did not lie entirely in market confidence. In June there had been a large increase in forward sales of sterling so that part of the deficit was masked by these transactions. We had also begun to make use of swap facilities but only to meet an unexpected bill and for no more than $15 million.

Discussion continued on special deposits and possible alternatives such as a rise in bank rate or the use of the regulator. It now emerged that the banks were fully lent with a 55 per cent advances ratio in the case of the Midland and a 29.5 per cent liquid assets ratio for the clearing banks as a group. To call for special deposits, as the Governor pointed out, would merely oblige the banks to sell gilt-edged securities on the same scale to the government and put a complete stop to credit expansion. There was some support for a 1 per cent rise in bank rate, but in the end it was decided to keep bank rate in reserve until the external situation required its immediate use. At a final meeting on 21 July the Chancellor, doubtful whether there was much expansion to check, opted to do nothing. And so, between the budget and the election, as a balance of payments crisis drew steadily nearer, the government was transfixed and made no move of any kind – not even a rise in bank rate.

The prime difficulty was that the figures seemed to imply that the economy was stuck. Ever since January, the index of industrial production had remained unchanged and it was not until October that any change occurred. To take restrictive action in those circumstances meant a major change in policy and a public rejection of the 4 per cent target.

But was the index of production to be trusted? The index of industrial production, shown as unchanged through the first nine months when published in 1964, climbed by nearly 3 per cent in six months when re-estimated in 1966 and was flat when again recalculated a year or two later. There was some supporting evidence of a lull. Unemployment, for example, fell much more slowly in mid-1964, and in August it was only 7000 lower than in March. The employment figures, on the other hand, increased in the first two quarters of 1964 by nearly 200,000 or at much the same rate as in the previous two quarters in 1963. The output measure of GDP, which is perhaps the best check, rose quarter by quarter but at a decreasing rate. The economy was certainly not stuck: nor did it seem so at the time. That there was some slowing down was never a matter of dispute from May onwards. But that output had ceased to grow was most implausible. In fact, 1964 was a repetition of 1960 when there were similar complaints while all the time, as later figures showed, output went on growing. In the second half of 1964, as in the second half of 1960, GDP was up by 4.4 per cent on a year earlier.

By the time the election was held, the size of the expected deficit had become headline news. There was an exchange of letters in *The Times* between Nicholas Kaldor and the Chancellor, an article by Dr Balogh appeared in the *New Statesman*, and the National Institute published yet another forecast – all pointing ineluctably to an overall deficit in the balance of payments of the order of £800 million. It was of no use to explain that half of the deficit was on capital account and that much of the rest was associated with stockbuilding and likely to be temporary. A crisis atmosphere was created just as the election was about to take place.

Part III

5 A Change of Government, 1964

The General Election in October 1964 brought Labour to power by the narrowest of majorities after thirteen years of Conservative Government. The result was uncertain until the last. First one and then the other party took the lead as the results were announced. In the end, Labour had a majority of five and another election seemed almost inescapable within the next year or two.

The election had been accompanied by much publicity for the precarious state of the balance of payments. This was taken fairly calmly by the markets, no doubt in the expectation of early action by the incoming government, but also because its attention was diverted by world events, including the deposition of Khrushchev and the explosion of an atomic bomb by the Chinese. It helped also that much of the external deficit was with the sterling area (notably Australia and the Middle East) and exerted no immediate pressure on the exchange rate.

Maudling had contemplated a rise in bank rate before the election but was persuaded to wait until there was real pressure on the pound. On the morning after the election, the Prime Minister again proposed an increase. But again the suggestion was rejected as likely to smack of panic. In any event it could not have been done without the agreement of Harold Wilson who was travelling from Liverpool and inaccessible until his arrival in London at 12.45 p.m.

The usual set of briefs had been prepared in the Treasury reviewing the various courses open to the government. Maudling had fully expected a large deficit to emerge by the autumn and had set on foot contingency planning to deal with it. One possibility was to resort to import restriction through the use of quotas: this had been done on earlier occasions and was accepted by the General Agreement on Tariffs and Trade (GATT) as a legitimate way of dealing with a balance of payments deficit. It was, however, an arbitrary way of reducing the volume of imports and would be harmful to the suppliers and importers affected. Maudling was more attracted to the alternative of a surcharge on imports such as the Canadians had used in 1962, although this did not have the blessing of GATT.

On our calculations, either scheme for import restriction was capable of improving the balance of payments by about £250–300 million. On the other hand, both would be inflationary unless purchasing power were withdrawn simultaneously with the limitation of imports. The surcharge might by itself do as much as about two-thirds of the work of deflation required while the quota scheme would do nothing at all. This strengthened our inclinations to regard the surcharge as the better bet. As I put it to Sir William Armstrong, 'in circumstances in which some form of deflation may be inescapable and any form of stop–go appears to be anathema, we should not dismiss the fiscal aspects of the matter as of subordinate importance'.

Having reviewed the Canadian experience, the Treasury recommended the imposition of a surcharge to deal with the external deficit. The Treasury also urged the rejection of more radical measures such as devaluation or allowing the pound to float. It refrained from including in its recommendations anything that could be interpreted as a 'stop'. But there could be little doubt that it would not be possible to eliminate the deficit without deflationary action of some kind. All that the surcharge could do was to buy time and permit a more gradual limitation of demand. For that purpose a loan would have been just as effective but no attempt was made to raise one: not even by getting the nationalised industries to borrow abroad under government guarantees as I suggested.

In recommending against devaluation, we had little doubt that our recommendation would be accepted. William Armstrong and I had both been intimately involved in the devaluation of 1949 and remembered how little support Harold Wilson had provided. We expected him to show equal reluctance in 1964 to saddling his party with the reputation of always choosing the devaluation option. Any government deciding to devalue had in any event to act wholeheartedly if the measure was to succeed and take resolute accompanying measures to restrict demand which there seemed no chance whatever of a Labour government's adopting. Devaluation might yet be necessary; but it was preferable to wait until the government had learnt its lesson. Meanwhile if it was determined to maintain the parity it might just possibly succeed provided it could find a way of holding down costs and improving the competitive position of British industry as costs elsewhere continued to rise.

The Treasury was also against allowing the pound to float since this would forfeit any assistance that the IMF might offer. They feared that a floating pound would release inflationary forces that would cause a progressive rise in prices and wages cancelling out much, or all, of any improvement in Britain's competitive position. At least a devaluation set limits to the impact on prices; and it would be easier to hold wages after a finite fall in the pound than when there was no assurance of an end to the decline. Professor Kaldor was later to argue in favour of a progressive fall in the pound, with exports expanding after each drop to a level sufficient to raise Britain's share of world trade in manufactures by about three percentage points. Given the fast rate at which world trade was expanding, this would have implied a large progressive rise in the proportion of British manufacturing output exported and a rapidly growing favourable balance of payments far beyond what was required. It would also, like devaluation, have added to inflationary risks. Kaldor's was no doubt an extreme view of the transformation that floating the pound could bring about. But many economists in those days were in favour of floating and, like Kaldor, had a lively sense of its advantages unaccompanied by any sense of its dangers. Economists in the 1960s had a faith in the healing powers of devaluation and floating that has since become less common.

Whatever advice they were offered, the incoming government had no hesitation in deciding to maintain the parity. A small group of Ministers met within a couple of days of the election and decided firmly against devaluation or floating and in favour of the surcharge. A week or so later, with calculated swiftness, a statement of policy was issued from the Prime Minister's office. This gave full publicity – more perhaps than was prudent – to the balance of payments deficit, estimated at £800 million, which the government had inherited. On the other hand, it maintained that the pressure on resources was not excessive. There would be no 'stop' and other means would be sought to deal with the deficit. A promise was made to review government expenditure and a start would be made by scrapping the Concorde, a supersonic airliner under development in conjunction with the French. The French, however, had not been consulted, were not prepared to abandon the aircraft and were in a position to demand very substantial compensation if Britain pulled out. A few months later, after reconsideration, it was announced that the Concorde would go ahead.

A similar situation arose over the surcharge. Simultaneously with the issue of the Prime Minister's statement, it was announced that a 15 per cent surcharge would be imposed on all imports of manufactures and a system of export rebates would be introduced. There had been no consultation with other countries before the announcement of the surcharge and it soon came under strong attack, particularly in

EFTA, but also in GATT and OECD. The justification offered by Ministers was not well received. At the EFTA meeting soon after the announcement of the surcharge, Ministers insisted that the economy was not overheated when the contrary seemed obvious to other governments; and they seemed to make light of the breach of international obligations – a breach formally confirmed by GATT in December. Complaints in OECD were met by a promise from William Armstrong that the government would take 'brutal' measures though this hardly squared with the Prime Minister's statement. Both the Dutch and the Swiss emphasized, as others did later, that a 15 per cent surcharge would be widely interpreted as the forerunner of a devaluation. Although the government was remarkably indifferent to foreign criticism, it was plain that it would be wise to make some reduction in the surcharge by the Budget and on 27 February 1965 it was announced that in two months time it would be reduced to 10 per cent.

If the government rejected devaluation and would not deflate, was there any other course open to it? The surcharge would not last for ever, there was a limit to what could be borrowed, and meanwhile the reserves were draining away. Something had to be done to improve the balance of payments, with or without deflation, either by acting on it directly or by restoring Britain's ability to compete in international markets. We shall discuss the measures taken with those aims in Chapter 6. The immediate need was, at the every least, to prevent the further expansion in demand after which some Ministers still hankered – an expansion that would suck in more imports and eat into competitive power by making for still higher wage settlements.

The Economic Section's view was that since devaluation could only succeed if measures were taken to restrict home demand, the right course was to begin by introducing these restrictive measures as soon as possible and see whether they restored balance without resort to devaluation. The balance of payments was fairly sensitive to the pressure of demand; and a moderate reduction in pressure, coupled with other measures, might be enough to remove the need to devalue.

The danger was that we should embark yet again on a kind of Maudling experiment. All British governments seemed to believe that if they ran the economy at full pressure and met any resulting external deficit out of reserves or by borrowing, there would sooner or later be a breakthrough to a higher rate of growth that would make exports more competitive and restore external balance. Instead, the breakthrough had been to faster inflation and bigger balance of payments deficits. There was hardly a single major industrial country that had failed so conspicuously as Britain to increase its exports over the previous twelve months. In the engineering and building industries what had resulted was an overload that did not make for efficiency; and indeed in the electrical engineering industry, which accounted for much of the expansion in investment, the prospect was one of an accumulation of incompletely developed large generating sets.

THE NEW CHANCELLOR

It appeared to be the intention of the Treasury to ship me off to Washington as soon as possible to take over from Eric Roll as Treasury Representative, now that Eric had returned as Permanent Secretary of DEA. I was disinclined to go if it meant leaving the Economic Section in charge of a political appointee and assumed, wrongly, that the new arrangement had the blessing of the Chancellor, James Callagnan. When we met by chance in the corridor soon after the election, I made my disgruntlement plain and walked away. I was then overwhelmed by the evident anxiety of the Chancellor to retain my services. The post of Economic Adviser to HMG which I had held for three and a half years, had been abolished by the incoming government; but it was agreed that I should continue as Director of the Economic Section and became head of the newly created Government Economic Service.

This first contact with the new Chancellor was the beginning of a long and, on the whole, happy association. I could not but admire his constant good humour and approachability and his efforts to preserve friendly relations with almost everyone who came in contact with him. Not without reason was his soubriquet 'Sunny Jim'. I had first met him at a Nuffield Conference in the late forties and had been impressed by a certain directness and honesty in his interventions. I thought then that he would go far in politics, but did not foresee that I should one day be one of his advisers. His political gifts were demonstrated by his successive appointments to the Treasury, the Home Office, the Foreign Office and the Premiership. To his regret, he had never attended a university and he was certainly no tax lawyer or economist like his immediate predecessors. But if he was not as deep a thinker as some of his colleagues, he had an appetite for political problems and absorbed them with an open mind and an abundance of common sense. The one major exception was devaluation, which he saw as largely a moral issue and was brought to accept with great difficulty.

He took pains to discuss matters with a wide range of Treasury staff. He gave the impression of enjoying meetings even on such abstract subjects an international liquidity. When he lunched in the City he might entertain his hosts by bursting into song. His main difficulty was that in Cabinet he often failed to carry his point, speaking well initially but allowing a more vehement speaker like George Brown to persist successfully. While I did not regard him as the ablest of my four Chancellors, I did find him the most agreeable to serve.

THE SYSTEM OF GOVERNMENT

1 The Department of Economic Affairs

Life under the Labour Government was in many ways different from life under its predecessor. Hitherto, the Chancellor of the Exchequer had enjoyed sole responsibility for economic policy, subject to the agreement of the Prime Minister and the approval of the Cabinet. Macmillan had been in the habit of sending periodic notes in extravagant terms to Selwyn Lloyd but he was unlikely to intervene over specific measures: nor did he consistently act the back-seat driver with Maudling. These days were over. The Labour Party viewed the Treasury with suspicion as the author of stop–go policies and an important source of Britain's slower growth in comparison with her continental neighbours. It had been known for at least a year that, if successful at the polls, a Labour Government would bring into existence a new department under George Brown to engage in economic planning and try to accelerate economic growth. What was to be planned, and how, was left vague and little was known about how the new department would be staffed. It seemed inevitable, however, that it would overlap in its responsibilities with the Treasury.

The prospect of sharing its responsibility for economic policy with another department was viewed with some apprehension in the Treasury which recalled an earlier split under the post-war Labour Government that had proved anything but satisfactory. From 1945 to 1947 Herbert Morrison as Lord President attempted to co-ordinate economic policy while Dalton as Chancellor of the Exchequer handled the urgent issues of domestic and international finance. Sir Stafford Cripps who had reunited the different elements in economic policy commented afterwards that no attempt should ever be made to repeat such a division.

The Treasury had given consideration in advance of the election to arrangements for a new department in the event of the Labour victory and had made tentative plans for the filling of top posts in it. Eric Roll was to come back from Washington to be Permanent Secretary, Donald MacDougall was to join the Department as Economic Director, a few officials including Douglas Allen and Fred Atkinson were to be transferred from the Treasury and a large section of the staff of NEDO was to move to DEA.

Responsibility for economic policy was split in a rather ill-defined way between the Treasury and the Department of Economic Affairs, with the Prime Minister acting as umpire. On the key issue of devaluation, there was no discussion in Cabinet, no request by Ministers for a statement of the Treasury's views, no way of engaging the Prime Minister, who had a power of veto, in argument with officials, or even with other Ministers except the First Secretary and the Chancellor. For the Chancellor, devaluation meant resignation and he was not, until the end, open to argument. The First Secretary began by suppressing discussion and when he changed his mind had no way of changing the Prime Minister's.

The organisation of economic advice from officials was also unsatisfactory. With the arrival of four senior economists in Whitehall, all expecting to participate in the framing of economic policy, there were simply too many for the efficient dispatch of business. They added to the load on other economists and officials – especially the Permanent Secretary of the Treasury, William Armstrong – by multiplying meetings, multiplying paper and making the co-ordination of official advice far more time-consuming and imperfect. The administrative machine became more cumbersome. In addition, the departmental officials who normally advised on policy tended to be left out of Ministerial meeting. This was most obviously so in the meetings at No. 10 in the winter of 1964 when economic advisers were automatically included and departmental officials – apart from permanent secretaries – never appeared. On top of all this there was the problem of coping with Dr Balogh, widely regarded as the Prime Minister's spy, who felt free to attack and revile each department in turn and became the *bête noire* of nearly all the Cabinet ministers, not just of their officials. The operations of the Labour Government, particularly in 1964–6, seemed remarkably amateurish and ramshackle.

No clear line of division was drawn between the duties of the DEA and the Treasury. Much earlier I had expressed scepticism about the proposed division of responsibilities which I thought 'retrograde and unsustainable'. Economic co-ordination, I argued, which had hitherto been the Treasury's function, was an indivisible process; and 'co-ordination' was simply another word for 'planning'. It was inconceivable that the short-term management of demand (and the devising of measures for that purpose) could remain the responsibility of one minister while some other minister was in charge of overall economic policy. 'A division of duties', I pointed out, 'that left the Chancellor in charge of the Budget, bank rate, the rate of exchange, the use of the Regulator, and all the other instruments of economic control from day to day, must put him in a position of such overwhelming strength in relation to his colleagues that it is inconceivable that any other Minister could imagine himself to be in charge of economic policy.... Whoever controls [those instruments] becomes Minister for Economic Affairs whatever title he is given. The only satisfactory delimitation that I can imagine is between decisions calculated to regulate the economy within its existing structure and decisions calculated to change that structure.'

While the key instruments of policy that I listed remained attached to the Treasury, the DEA took a close interest in all of them and George Brown, the First Secretary who headed the department, expected to be consulted on their use. A concordat between the two departments was prepared after some weeks and tried to distinguish their separate roles. There was a presumption that long-term issues should be the province of DEA and short-term issues the province of the Treasury. But this was not a sustainable division in matters of policy, as I argued later in an address to the World Bank in 1966 (*The Long Term and the Short in Economic Planning*). All major issues of policy have long-term and short-term aspects which need to be considered together, not by separate agencies. In any event, DEA was automatically involved in short-term problems through its responsibility for incomes' policy which William Armstrong had seen to it was assigned to them in order to give them more immediate duties than drawing up a National Plan.

After a year's experience of the new régime I concluded that:

> we still do all the short-term economic forecasting in the Treasury; we are obliged to take part in, and frequently to take charge of, much of the work of long-range projection; and on top of this we have still to give what time we can to considering long-term issues of financial, commercial and fiscal policy alongside the other Treasury Divisions. The D.E.A.'s attention in the meantime seems to me to wander irresistibly towards the short end of the spectrum and to desert a wide range of major problems of longer-term strategy that

would repay study. If, for example, one looks through the Plan to see how it is proposed to manage the private sector with a view to raising productivity and exports and getting the kind of expansion (or contraction) that the Plan foreshadows, there is an almost complete blank.... I would not be far wrong if I summed up by saying that in the Treasury the economists are inclined to be frustrated because they cannot give sufficient time to long-range problems while the economists in the D.E.A. seem to be frustrated if they cannot gravitate to short-term issues.

2 The Triumvirate

One purpose served by the new Department was to provide a Cabinet post in keeping with the ambitions of the First Secretary of State, George Brown, and ranking ahead of that occupied by the Chancellor, James Callaghan. It also suited the Prime Minister if these two were at odds and he was in the position of umpire. The 'creative tension' between the two departments of which the Prime Minister talked might enhance his authority but it did not make for a clear economic strategy.

It was a triumvirate of these three Ministers and not the Cabinet that settled major issues of economic policy in the first two years of the Labour government. Even at the discussions at No. 10 described below, Ministers from other departments such as the Foreign Office, the Board of Trade or the Department of Employment were rarely present, although they might attend the larger meetings from time to time at Chequers. It was only after the deflationary measures of July 1966 that the Prime Minister was obliged to bring in other Ministers and channel discussion through a new Ministerial Committee on economic strategy.

All three Ministers were agreed that an alternative to devaluation and deflation must be found but failed to take the measure of the scale of action necessary in order to restore external balance. The Prime Minister offered a long list of trivial proposals (what the Treasury described as 'the 57 varieties'), of which an automated shipyard and a Post Office unit trust were typical examples. In his speeches he represented a succession of minor cuts as highly deflationary while all the time unemployment continued to fall.

George Brown took an equally extravagant view of the effect on employment of any effort to restrain demand, equating the least reduction in government expenditure with two million unemployed. He threw himself into the preparation of an incomes policy in the confident belief that the TUC could hold down wages when unemployment had fallen to 1.2 per cent and there were nine vacancies for every unemployed skilled engineer in the Midlands. He was as determined on expansion as on avoiding devaluation but was bound sooner or later to convince himself that the parity was a prime obstacle to the growth for which his department was planning.

The third of the trio, James Callaghan, was the most level-headed and reasonable and accepted from the start that some check to demand was necessary sooner or later. But even he was reluctant to take decisive action and in any event had little chance of converting the other two. He, even more than they, was dead set against devaluation, which he thought of as bilking Britain's creditors. He had no intention of staying on as Chancellor if devaluation took place and as his advisers came to realise this, it was borne in on them that to recommend devaluation to him was tantamount to calling for his resignation.

All three were not only united in rejecting devaluation. They wanted no mention of it and consequently no discussion of it. Apart from what was submitted when they took office, and papers submitted and destroyed unread on 25 November, as described below,[1] no position paper on devaluation was ever submitted to Ministers. Nothing at all got as far as the Cabinet from start to finish. It might be expected that Ministers would ask for Treasury views on how devaluation was to be avoided. But that, too, did not occur. The Chancellor was certainly told of changes in policy that officials thought were required. But until the end of 1966 when he indicated how far he was prepared to go, there was no comprehensive strategy aimed specifically at avoiding devaluation; even then the strategy was not submitted to full Cabinet although it did go to a Cabinet committee on 'Strategic Economic Policy'.

3 Consultations at No. 10 and Chequers

The way in which policy was considered also changed. A series of meetings took place over the winter of 1964–5 between Ministers and officials, some at No. 10 in the late evening and some at Chequers at the weekend. As a rule there were no papers, no definite agenda, no minutes. There were usually five or six Ministers – more when the meetings were at Chequers – and about the same number of officials. The Ministers always included the triumvirate while others, such as the Foreign Secretary or the President of the Board of Trade, made occasional appearances. Dick Crossman, to the best of my recollection was never included at No. 10. The officials were either Permanent

Secretaries (William Armstrong, Eric Roll, Richard Powell) or Economic Advisers (the four new arrivals mentioned below and myself). Established civil servants within whose area of responsibility the evening's discussion at No. 10 fell were unlikely to be included. Sir Denis Rickett, the Head of the Overseas Finance Division of the Treasury was never invited. Nor do I recall Sir Richard Clarke, even on occasions when public expenditure was the subject of discussion The Bank of England were rigorously excluded so that rude comments about the Governor could be freely made.

The discussion was highly informal, at times random, the Prime Minister steering as far as anyone did. There was no attempt to reach agreement and one subject would follow another when it seemed time to move on. At some point there was usually a round-the-room poll of opinion.

It did not seem to me an efficient or successful way to consider issues of high policy. For one thing George Brown was liable to be drunk and rather quarrelsome at that time in the evening. He would pose questions such as: 'Does anyone in this room think business is expanding?' when it was only too obvious that it was, or declare that 'everybody who comes to see me says he is cutting out new factory building', when manufacturing investment was expanding at 10 per cent per annum (and did not reach its peak until 1967). Tommy Balogh was even more effective in blocking coherent discussion, denouncing everything and everybody at great length in extravagant terms.

The discussion at these meetings was usually on some favourite wheeze of the Prime Minister's. At the early meetings there was a great deal about exchange control and the handling of the forward market, with an emphasis that became customary with Ministers on the inadequacy of the statistics. The Prime Minister still hankered after an enquiry such as he had conducted in 1947 into speculation in foreign exchange. Another theme was the need for intervention to make industry more efficient and absorb the fruits of modern science and technology. Investment allowances or grants to help the export industries, encourage automation, and assist the expansion of new science-based industries had been suggested by the Prime Minister before the election and half a dozen different plans to meet these and other purposes were under preparation. In the spring of 1965, the progress of these plans was reviewed at the No. 10 meetings and one result was the eventual replacement of investment allowances by investment grants.

4 Economic Advice to the Labour Government

Little thought had been given to the future of the economists remaining in the Treasury. The new government brought in as economic advisers several eminent economists of their own political persuasion: Dr Balogh, nominally to advise the Cabinet; Professor Kaldor nominally to advise on tax matters; Robert Neild as Economic Adviser to the Treasury; and Sir Donald MacDougall as Economic Director in DEA. All of them expected to be consulted on the major issues of economic policy and the first two in particular expected to be given access to all official papers (including in Dr Balogh's case papers of the outgoing government). All of them (except for Dr Balogh in the first month or so) favoured immediate devaluation or allowing the currency to float. My colleagues – administrators as well as economists – found it rather piquant and somewhat embarrassing that the advisers to whom the government now turned, and with whom they had to associate without reserve, held views on the most important single economic issue confronting it that were diametrically opposed to the government's declared policy.

It looked for a time as if Robert Neild, a former member of the Economic Section, would be put in charge of it on my departure to America: and since I knew that this would not be acceptable to the key members of the Section, I decided that I ought to stay, in my capacity as Director. Some months previously I had pointed out to Sir Laurence Helsby, Joint Permanent Secretary of the Treasury on the Management side, the need to give thought to the place of the Economic Section if a new Department of Economic Affairs was created but had received no reply Such a department, I suggested, might 'expect to have first pick of the limited supply of trained economists in Government service'. 'Is it conceivable,' I asked, 'that it would be prepared to acquiesce in the recruitment and management of Government economists by the Head of the Economic Section of the Treasury?' I recall no answer to this question before the election. It was only after I had made it plain that I was not prepared to go to Washington that it was decisively answered (without consultation with DEA) by my appointment at the end of October as Head of the Government Economic Service, charged with exactly the duties my minute described.

Not that I was left free to carry out these duties. Ministers appointed private armies of economists without reference to me and frequently without notifying me. Salaries were fixed without regard to the position of long-serving members of the Economic Section. Dr Balogh took it on himself to recruit independently, denounce appointments already made, and generally do his best to take over the job and make a nuisance of himself.

ECONOMIC POLICY

The main elements of economic policy in the early days of the Labour government were threefold: the preparation of a National Plan; the formulation of an agreed policy for money incomes; and the management of demand. Of these, the first two were primarily for the Department of Economic Affairs and the third was the business of the Treasury. We can leave aside for the time being the work in progress on the National Plan; something, however, must be said about incomes policy in which the Treasury had previously been deeply involved and in which it continued to take an interest; demand management calls for more detailed analysis.

1 Incomes Policy

The Labour Party had pinned much of its hopes on a successful incomes policy as a means of combating inflation, preserving the competitive power of British industry, and improving the balance of payments. In the early post-war years the unions had rallied to the support of the Labour government and had helped to keep wages and prices down after the devaluation of 1949. In those days, however, all that was attempted was a wage freeze for a limited time. In the 1960s what was aimed at was a more sophisticated approach to wage settlements that would link them more closely with the growth of productivity. The efforts of the Conservative government had yielded little result. George Brown hoped to do better.

He began by approaching the TUC and on 16 December, after lengthy discussions, he was able to announce a 'joint Statement of Intent' on prices and incomes policy. New machinery, agreed by the TUC and by both organisations of employers (FBI and BEC), was due to come into operation in February. It would rely very heavily on the full cooperation of employers and employed on claims as well as settlements (which could be referred to a National Board for Prices and Incomes) and envisaged no other sanctions than 'persuasion and the pressure of public opinion'. This seemed highly optimistic, given the rise in average weekly earnings of 8.3 per cent between October 1963 and October 1964. If the conditions of labour shortage giving rise to such increases continued – as they did – it was natural to wonder how the new machinery could come into effective operation without either lending itself to the whitewashing of larger increases than the economy could stand or clashing with the underlying pressures that sustained the upward trend

A little later the First Secretary accepted that it might yet be necessary to go beyond persuasion and the 'pressure of public opinion' but continued to imply that it was only through such pressure that costs and prices could be influenced. He gave no indication that there was another form of pressure affecting costs and prices – the pressure of demand – and that this pressure was likely to swamp any other in 1965–6, with unemployment falling below 1.5 per cent and in large parts of the country below 1 per cent. Reliance on incomes policy might go too far and come to be regarded as the only effective way of slowing down the wage/price spiral when in fact its contribution might become negligible.

2 The Management of Demand

Within its first month in office the government introduced a budget that seemed likely to be neutral in its impact on demand. The surcharge was expected to withdraw purchasing power at an annual rate of £200 million and an increase in petrol duty would withdraw about another £100 million. On the other hand, an export rebate was introduced, costing £75 million a year, while the surcharge increased substantially the demand on domestic resources.

The budget also announced a number of measures to come into effect in the spring: sixpence would be added to the standard rate of income tax and at the same time pensions and national insurance benefits would be increased at a cost estimated as £300 million. National assistance benefits would also be increased and prescription charges would be abolished. On the other hand, national insurance contributions would be raised. The net effect of all these changes was expected to be to leave the pressure of demand unchanged. Two new taxes were also announced for inclusion in the April budget: a capital gains tax and a corporation tax.

The November Budget alarmed the city. It promised fundamental changes in the tax system whose effects the government did not appear to have fully appreciated and it did nothing to limit the obvious pressures on the economy. Soon after, on 11 November, a run on the pound began. If the government intended to do no more than was proposed in the Budget there was every likelihood of real trouble. Five days later the Prime Minister, at the Mansion House Dinner, asserted the Government's firm determination to protect the pound against speculations in a rhetorical but unconvincing speech, unaccompanied by resolute action. Bank Rate remained at 5 per cent. The loss of foreign exchange mounted instead of diminishing.

The Governor proposed a rise of 1 per cent on the 13th but this was at first resisted by the Treasury as reflecting on the Budget and contrary to assurances given to the United States. The Chancellor, however, decided the following week on a 1 per cent increase on the 19th and was overruled by the Prime Minister and the First Secretary (George Brown). On the same day EFTA was promised that the surcharge would be reduced in a matter of months. Next day (Friday 20 November) there was a loss from the reserves of over £60 million which made the Chancellor propose a rise to 7 per cent on the following Monday. While this created difficulties for the Americans, the rise was agreed: a one point rise made little sense if it was likely to be followed soon after by a further rise.

The exchange losses continued to grow. On the 25th they reached over £90 million. A meeting was called at No. 10 for which papers were prepared in haste. The government's new advisers advocated devaluation and hesitated between floating and moving to a new fixed rate. The Economic Section outlined the deflationary measures they thought necessary. Neither paper was discussed. Instead, the Prime Minister opened the meeting by announcing that the Bank of England had raised $3 billion from other central banks with no strings attached. George Brown told us we must not even think of devaluation which must henceforth be 'unmentionable'. The two papers by advisers were collected and sent for destruction.

After November the pressure eased a little but by the end of the quarter it had been necessary to feed £582 million into the exchange market. Even in the third quarter, when things were remarkably calm, the exchange losses had amounted to £126 million (an annual rate of £500 million). In both quarters, however, the reserves increased thanks to the drawing of $1 billion from the IMF arranged for by Maudling. This was used to repay swaps with other central banks while an additional $600 million was drawn from the $3 billion credit. In addition, the Bank of England was already beginning to offer support, to an undisclosed extent, through the forward market.

It has been argued that any errors in the conduct of policy over those early months of the Labour government counted for little in the light of the prolonged speculative pressure over the next three years.[2] It is true that the really serious error was to refrain then from more decisive deflationary action. But the initial impression left by the actions taken – the harping on the size of the deficit, the delay in raising bank rate, the bald announcement of new taxes at unspecified rates, the hesitations over the surcharge – was of an indecisive government unfamiliar with its responsibilities and one in which it was difficult to have confidence. That impression lingered and underlay the continuing drain on the reserves in 1965–6.

Meanwhile the forecasters were trying to size up the economic outlook for 1965. They had first to decide what was happening currently to output and why. It was important to recognise that output had not been stagnant, as Maudling, with some reason, believed. The difficulties in expanding production lay, almost certainly, on the side of supply, not demand. The metal and engineering industries in particular, accounting for about half the index, were affected by a large increase in work in progress as orders took longer to complete. Exports were affected in the same way: order books grew but deliveries lagged badly behind. Once it became clear that production was overloaded but still expanding the case for an early check to demand became more telling.

At the beginning of December I argued that we were 'already committed to a degree of deflation in step with the rate of withdrawal of the surcharge'. We were deflating (for example, through a 7 per cent bank rate) but we were simultaneously insisting that we had no wish to deflate. This injected the maximum amount of uncertainty about our long-run intentions. If we wanted to get back into balance we needed to make available on external account something like £600 million in domestic resources. A large part of that would come almost automatically in 1965 from reduced stockbuilding. But this would still leave excess pressure that could only be got rid of by cuts in consumption or investment.

Cuts could be made to two kinds of investment so as to benefit manufacture for export or permit a reduction in imports. One was electricity investment, where the programme had risen by about 50 per cent in two years and was geared to a 4 per cent rate of growth that had not been achieved. The other was housing where again investment had risen by 50 per cent above its previous peak. Each of these programmes was more than half the size of the entire programme of investment in manufacturing.

Proposals to cut investment had no effect. Although we ended up, as I feared, with a vast excess of capacity for electricity generation, Otto Clarke stuck by the programme throughout and no cuts were made. In housing, Dick Crossman was aiming to go up to 500,000 houses a year and was quite prepared to conceal from the Treasury the scale on which new building was being authorised. In any event, housing was felt to be too politically sensitive to be the subject of a cut. So those two massive programmes continued to overload the building industry.

Later in December, the forecasters reported on the outlook for 1965 and 1966. Although they were in the dark as to how the surcharge was operating, and the rate of decline in stockbuilding – principally of imports – was highly uncertain, they forecast quite correctly a large improvement in the current balance of payments in the first quarter of 1965. They also predicted, less successfully, a slight surplus – again on current account – over the year. (The official estimates show a deficit of £43 million in 1965 after a deficit of £362 million in 1964.) This was on the assumption that the surcharge would be retained at $12\frac{1}{2}$ rather than the 10 per cent ultimately fixed for the period from the Budget until at least the end of the year. The improvement expected in the current account would not, however, wipe out the balance of payments deficit completely since there would still be a substantial debit balance on long-term capital account.

Production was expected to rise by about 3 per cent or a trifle more, with little or no change in unemployment and the main expansionary force would continue to be fixed investment, although some falling off was likely in private investment during the year. In most respects this was a pretty accurate forecast, in striking contrast to the wild predictions that were being made by Ministers at evening gatherings in No. 10. The forecasters admitted that they had little first-hand evidence of how any loss of confidence and change in the business climate had affected investment intentions. But they proved, if anything, too conservative in their predictions for manufacturing investment and exports.

In mid-December reserve losses remained heavy – £200 million had gone by the 17th – and $400 million dollars of the banking credits had already been used. The credits were for three months only and there was no guarantee that they would be renewed. It might be difficult to point to any real improvement in the trade balance until the January figures became available in mid-February, shortly before repayment was due. There was strong feeling in EFTA against the use of the surcharge and there were threats of retaliation which might bring in the European Community as well. We kept being advised by foreign economists to devalue.

There was some tendency to regard the pressure on the pound as the work of speculators but I was assured that most of the business, in November at least, had been on behalf of industrial clients, such as the tobacco companies, with large forward commitments. Since little was published on the extent to which the borrowings had been drawn upon, I was interested in the views expressed at dinner in January by a group of well-known financial journalists and bankers. None of them expected devaluation; they forecast a reduction by $2\frac{1}{2}$ per cent in the surcharge in April; and they put the drawings on the $3 billion credits no higher than $250 million or, at most, $500 million.

Shortly afterwards I talked to another group of business economists, academic economists and officials at the Centre for Administrative Studies and found a remarkable degree of agreement on economic prospects for the next twelve months. The National Institute expected the existing high pressure of demand to increase over the first half of the year, with some very slight easing only in the final quarter. The business economists, after starting from some rather pessimistic conclusions about the likely behaviour of output, had come to accept forecasts not unlike our own. The members of the Business Economists Group, drawn from twelve quite important firms, expected that the Budget would be either neutral or more probably deflationary, bank rate might be reduced in March and the surcharge might be cut in half in June. Wynne Godley (then at the National Institute) was concerned at the effect on wage-costs of shorter hours and high pressure of demand but thought that a fall in import prices would keep the rise in consumer prices lower than in 1964. Wadsworth of the Midland Bank told us that the banks were having difficulty in providing finance for industrial expansion and that they were now restricting advances in good earnest.

On the basis of the December forecast I warned the Chancellor that we were liable to have to take further action to restrict demand in the April budget. This would be all the more true if he hoped to lower bank rate from 7 per cent. If we looked ahead to 1966 we were likely to have a continuing basic deficit in the balance of payments, even with a surcharge of 10 per cent, which we could not hope to go on financing indefinitely out of short-term credits. Sooner or later, too, we would have to abandon the surcharge unless we were prepared to risk retaliation on the one hand and disbelief in our ability to maintain the parity on the other. Without the surcharge there was little chance of getting back into balance unless some reduction took place in the pressure of demand.

Fortunately the credits were renewed on 10 February and on 12 May it was possible to draw a further $1.4 billion from the IMF. The

$1 million standby that had been negotiated much earlier by Maudling had all been drawn by the end of 1964 and it was then clear that further support would be required if the drain from the reserves continued. The IMF loan of $1.4 billion did not last long.

While European central bankers had played a full part in supporting sterling, there had been a particular dependence on the United States. But the dollar, too, was in difficulties. The United States continued to be in substantial deficit and the deficit was swollen by the flow of American investment to other countries. The dollars that this left in the reserves of foreign central banks helped to keep the world in a liquid state that contributed to the prosperity of those years. But there were those who thought the liquidity excessive and responsible for world inflation. France in particular resented, or affected to resent, the acquisition of European businesses by Americans out of the dollars that, in their view, European banks were required to hold. Early in February the French decided to ask for gold in exchange for their dollar holdings, beginning with a first encashment of $350 million. Not long after, on 4 February, General de Gaulle called for a return to the gold standard and an end to reserve currencies. To the General, reserve currencies were a way of printing money to pay foreigners and he had just as strong views about sterling as he had about dollars, except that French holdings of sterling were very much less.

The weakness of the dollar, to which the French attitude contributed, made it necessary for Britain to tread carefully in turning to America for help and to avoid action (for example, on interest rates) that might be embarrassing to American economic policy. The United States, however, was almost as anxious as the British Cabinet to avoid a devaluation of sterling since it might oblige the dollar to follow suit. For the next three years Britain enjoyed consistent American support.

As the April Budget approached, all the indications pointed to a large increase in the deficit. In February the Vote on the Account was up on the previous year by 9 per cent. On 22 February it was announced that for the next five financial years public expenditure would be limited to an annual increase in real terms of $4\frac{1}{4}$ per cent. This differed little from the earlier limit announced in December 1963 of 4.1 per cent. These were rates of growth intended to keep public expenditure roughly in line with the growth in GDP. But since public expenditure in fact grew faster, and GDP slower, than these rates of increase, public expenditure absorbed an increasing proportion of GDP. The limits proved to be illusory and were exceeded in all except the first and last of the five years.

The year 1964–5 was one in which GDP did outstrip public expenditure by a narrow margin. The illusion in that year was that when the economy was seriously out of balance it was enough to allow public expenditure to grow at about the same rate as GDP. Had expenditure been more restricted, there would have been less need for higher taxation.

At the beginning of February Emil Van Lennep, who was Chairman of Working Party No. 3 of the OECD, visited London with Christopher Dow and told us that continental countries doubted whether British policies justified the renewal of the $3 billion credits. They advised us that nothing less than an extra £200 million in taxation in the Budget would reassure them. The Chancellor was not thinking in these terms and it was not easy to see how we could convince him. Part of the trouble was that we had no strategy for the balance of payments into which the Budget would fit. At the meeting of Working Party No. 3 later in the month we were given little advice: the members seemed curiously apathetic, as if they felt that it was now up to us to find a way out of our difficulties and that there was nothing more they could do for us. The same tone governed the letter sent to the government from the Working Party.

The Governor, who had given the Chancellor a figure of £300 million as his assessment of the extra taxation required, felt that it was more important to get public expenditure down. He had had a difficult time in Basle in securing agreement to the renewal of the $3 billion central bank credits and was pessimistic about the likelihood of a tax increase in excess of £100 million. This would not be enough to prevent increased pressure on the pound. The exchange losses were continuing and some holders of sterling in Scandinavia and the Middle East were getting nervous. On the other hand, it would not be possible to draw on the IMF until April.

As we prepared for a meeting on 27 February at Chequers where the general outlook was to be discussed, the DEA was still strongly against deflation (without avowing the implied preference for devaluation). Others went further. Roy Harrod, for example, wrote to me twice, arguing for an extra £1000 million of demand and the withdrawal of the extra 6*d* on income tax. At Chequers the Prime Minister took the line (which was also George Brown's) that while an extra £600 million in tax made sense as a deflationary solution there was no point in doing half as much. The favoured way out of balance of payments difficulties, though it failed to convince the Chancellor, was by cutting capital exports. As for Working Party No. 3, it was regarded as just a bunch of officials with no political clout.

Although the emphasis at Chequers was on limiting capital outflows, nothing was done to extend exchange control to sterling area investment. The main economy sought by the Prime Minister was £50 million to be taken out of the switch market. But, as emerged later, £50 million was already being milked from the market and the chances of getting more were poor. There was no prospect of increasing purchases of the switch dollars to equal net private investment overseas (including reinvestment of profits), as the Prime Minister seemed to hope. The Budget did, however, include a provision, suggested by Tony Rawlinson, requiring all sellers of foreign securities to surrender 25 per cent of the takings at the official rate instead of the higher rate in the market for switch dollars.

At the beginning of March, William Armstrong warned the Chancellor that the planned increases in taxation were insufficient. Soon after, Ministers agreed on an extra 6d on tobacco but wanted to take 1d off the petrol tax. There seemed little hope of reaching £200 million. Only the Chief Secretary, Jack Diamond, was prepared to insist on an extra £200 million, and not just in a full year, but in 1965–6. We spent some part of the month getting ready for a possible devaluation after the Budget if there were a large run on the pound.

By the time we got to the Budget on 6 April, however, agreement had been reached that taxes would go up by £164 million in 1965–6 and £217 million in 1966–7. £123 million was to be raised in higher taxes on tobacco and drink and an extra £49 million in motor vehicle duties. The TSR 2 aircraft was to be cancelled – the one measure included to give effect to the promised 'stern review' of defence expenditure. The total effect was assessed by the Chancellor as a reduction in domestic demand by £250 million.

Thus at the end of its first six months, the government had at last taken modest action to check the growth of demand and begun to frame an incomes policy. The balance of payments had improved as stockbuilding of imports fell off. The immediate danger to the pound appeared to have passed. But the government was still far from taking the measure of what was required. The pressure on the economy continued to grow, the government remained committed to further expansion, and continental opinion, to which the government paid little attention, was increasingly critical. A fresh crisis was only a few months away.

6 A Strategy for the Pound?

If there was to be no devaluation and little or no deflation, how was the deficit in the balance of payments to be got rid of? How were the external debts that were mounting up ever to be repaid? It was not possible to count on the continuation of the surcharge for more than a year or two and there was a limit to what should or could be borrowed abroad. A long-term foreign loan received scant consideration. Instead a whole series of measures was taken to improve the balance of payments directly or to make British industry more competitive and narrow the gap between imports and exports. These measures were spread over several years, many of them during the exchange crises in July 1965 and July 1966, without any effort to frame a comprehensive programme and assess its adequacy.

The direct measures are set out in some detail by Brian Tew in Chapter 7 of *British Economic Policy, 1960–74* (ed. F. Blackaby, 1978) and need only be summarised. Among the more important were efforts to improve the capital balance and to reduce military expenditure overseas.

THE CAPITAL BALANCE

One deterrent to overseas investment was associated with the introduction of corporation tax in the 1965 budget. The Chancellor maintained that foreign investment yielded less to the national economy than domestic investment since tax paid remained in the country of origin and did not accrue to the British government. He made a number of changes reducing the tax relief or tax credit on earnings and dividends from abroad and expected a substantial gain in tax and reduction in foreign investment from the changes. Exchange controls over capital outflows were also tightened after April 1965. From July 1965 to January 1968 no official exchange was made available for any foreign projects, but it remained possible to use 'investment currency' (with permission) or borrow abroad. A third change affected portfolio investment in foreign securities, which United Kingdom residents could acquire or dispose of for 'investment currency' at a variable premium over the official exchange rate. As from the 1965 budget, 25 per cent of the proceeds of sales of foreign securities and other assets (including switches into another foreign security) had to be surrendered at the official rate. Finally, from May 1966 efforts were made to reduce net investment in the overseas sterling area, which had hitherto been free of control, apart from tight restrictions on capital issues in the London market. Under a 'voluntary programme', British companies were asked to postpone or finance abroad plans for direct investment in Australia, New Zealand, South Africa and Eire; and institutional investors were asked to refrain from making any significant increase in their investments in those countries.

These measures seem to have had little effect on outward investment. There was no marked divergence between the course of sterling and non-sterling investment. There was also little sign that investment by the oil companies, which formed a high proportion of direct investment, was much affected by changes in the regulations. The main effect seems to have been to encourage borrowing abroad, both for the finance of direct investment and for the purchase of foreign securities. As Tew points out, 'the grand total of British private investment outside the sterling area was financed in the second half of the 1960s without leading to any drain on official reserves'.[1] He adds that in the years 1965–70 the only important category of overseas investment discouraged was overseas investment by private individuals who sold off a substantial part of their holdings.

The use of foreign finance meant a large saving in foreign exchange. In 1968, for example, £133 million was borrowed abroad or in Eurocurrency to finance direct investment outside the sterling area and £85 million to finance portfolio investment. In addition, the 'bleeding' of the investment currency market brought in £104 million, making £322 million in all. A further contribution came from foreign currency borrowing by nationalised industries and local authorities with forward exchange cover by the Treasury, introduced in January 1968. But although the government was prepared to borrow by proxy, it at no time contemplated long-term borrowing on its own.

What proved to be the most expensive measure of support to the capital balance was the intervention of the Bank of England in the forward market. High short-term rates of interest could only attract funds if there was confidence that the funds could be freely withdrawn without depreciation or, if such confidence did not exist, by maintaining the forward value of sterling at a level guaranteeing a satisfactory return when the funds were sold forward. Unfortunately, if sterling was devalued – as in the event it was – forward contracts were bound to involve the Bank in a loss proportionate to the depreciation; and the forward contracts could be entered into not only by those who sought cover for the transfer of funds but also by speculators betting outright on a devaluation of the pound.

THE CURRENT ACCOUNT

Efforts to reduce military expenditure overseas were one of a number of measures intended to improve the current account. In his 1965 Budget the Chancellor pointed out that this expenditure had increased year by year since 1959 from about £179 million to over £300 million. In the *National Plan* later in the year it was proposed to save £50–100 million by restricting the Defence Budget at constant prices to the level of the 1964-5 estimates and to make an absolute reduction in expenditure incurred overseas. A series of major decisions had been taken by February 1968 reducing the burden of defence and effecting economies of foreign exchange. These included offset agreements with Germany and the United States to promote British exports in settlement of defence costs in marks and dollars. Outgoings in overseas military expenditure, which had grown from £213 million to £306 million between 1960 and 1964, rose only by a further £8 million over the next six years, involving a fall in real terms.

A second economy in foreign exchange was on the programme of aid to developing countries. A ceiling of £205 million was imposed in 1965-6, raised the following year to £225 million, and cut again in 1967-8 to £205 million where it remained for the next three years.

Other savings in foreign exchange included a bisque in December 1964 and again in December 1965, each of which deferred payment of £32 million due under the Loan Agreement with the United States in 1946. There was also a saving on tourist account from the limitation of the allowance for foreign travel outside the sterling area to £50 a year for three years, beginning in November 1966. This seems to have cut expenditure overseas by about £40 million a year; but if the money was spent instead at home, some part of this would still have gone on imports from abroad.

Efforts were also made by the Labour government to promote exports and save imports. The export rebate, introduced in October 1964, was intended to recompense exporters for indirect taxes (for example, the hydrocarbon duties) on goods 'incorporated' in exports. It was maintained that this was not an export subsidy and hence not in contravention of GATT, but other countries took a different view and it was repealed in March 1968, some months after devaluation. The amount refunded was a little over £80 million a year and represented about 2 per cent of the total value of exports.

Other assistance to exports was given in the form of improved export credit facilities and various schemes, aimed at smaller firms, that supported collective market research and encouraged selling missions abroad. On the import side, NEDC and the National Plan both sought to reduce the growth of manufactured imports: but in none of the industries specifically mentioned – machine tools, chemicals and mechanical engineering – was there much effect on the upward trend. The one decisive intervention to reduce imports was in the aluminium industry where three new smelters were built *after* devaluation with the inducement of cut-price electricity – a project code-named 'Uncle' which seemed to me to make little sense.

To all these measures have to be added:

(a) industrial policy so far as it improved the competitive efficiency of British industry;

(b) incomes policy so far as it succeeded in slowing down the rise in wage-costs;

(c) the surcharge over the period 1964–6;

(d) import deposits from their introduction in November 1968.

Of these four, incomes policy is discussed elsewhere and import deposits did not affect the struggle to maintain the parity in 1964–7. I see little reason to suppose that competitive efficiency was much improved. That leaves the surcharge.

Were we right in expecting that the surcharge would reduce imports by about £300 million a year? The behaviour of imports in the 1960s kept taking us by surprise so that it was difficult to have much confidence in any equation from which one could arrive at an estimate. There is the further difficulty that part of the effect took the form of a run-down in stocks, inflating the immediate effect to an unknown extent. Tew, basing himself on National Institute calculations but making no explicit allowance for a rundown in stocks, suggests a total effect of £250 million spread over two years. This may be a slight underestimate but it is likely that our initial figure, which was equivalent to about £440 million over the two years, was a good deal too high.

It was conceivable that the combined effect of all these measures would be to reduce the pressure on the balance of payments sufficiently to safeguard the parity. For 1965 as a whole, the deficit on current account was a mere £43 million and for the entire period from the end of 1964 until a couple of months before the devaluation of November 1967 the current account was roughly in balance. But we never, except briefly in the winter of 1965–6 and in the early months of 1967, regained the confidence of the market. With the exception of these periods, foreign exchange totalling £1500 million had to be fed almost continuously into the spot market over a three-year period and another £1000 million in forward contracts was outstanding by the beginning of November 1967.

No subject occupied us more than devaluation in the first three years of Labour government when I was the only senior economist among the government's advisers not pressing for it immediately. In November 1964 I had urged the necessity of deflation whether followed by devaluation or not. But as time went by and the pressure on the economy increased instead of diminishing, I was increasingly doubtful whether devaluation could be avoided. As Keynes put it in August 1931: 'When doubts as to the prospects of a currency ... have come into existence, the game is up.'[3]

In the middle of 1965 I wrote a number of personal notes to clear my own mind, sending some of them to William Armstrong or the Chancellor. I started from the proposition that:

> it doesn't do any good just to delay devaluation if you are going to jib later at paying the price. We don't know what the price will be but we do know that it is inconsistent with the ideas underlying "The Plan". I happen to think ... that we ought to welcome a means of reducing the overload on the economy as a first step towards faster growth. But I recognize that the government cannot suddenly be converted to ideas they associate with Selwyn Lloyd....
>
> On top of this, I agree that the present parity is not the one that we should choose if we were free to start again.... We can't be sure that a retreat to lower levels of employment and production would do enough or do it fast enough.... So although it seems absurd to devalue with unemployment under 1.5 per cent ... the

alternative that can be offered involves an act of faith both in the way the economy would respond and in the capacity of Ministers to persevere with highly uncongenial measures over what might prove to be rather a long time. If we were as firmly persuaded as Ministers that the right way to run the economy was to keep unemployment at 1.5 per cent (with fluctuations above *and below*) would we have any case for arguing against devaluation (except the international repercussions)? And if we thought that unemployment [in the absence of devaluation] might have to increase to 2.5 per cent *and stay there*, would we not hesitate to [opt for a deflationary solution?].

In a later note I pointed out that devaluation

is widely regarded here and abroad, as inevitable or even desirable whether it comes now or later; and this is coming to be a settled expectation or mood not easily shaken by new declarations or measures of policy.... Even if the immediate danger is avoided, therefore, there is a continuing prospect of pressure with no end in sight.... What we have to weigh up are not only the chances of surviving a run on the pound but the chances of regaining balance at the existing parity without having to pay a still higher price than devaluation would involve.

The strange fact is that this has not been done. Ministers have neither asked nor wanted to be told. There has been no confrontation at the official level of the opposing views. No recovery programme has been drawn up on realistic assumptions about the balance of payments to show what degree of deflation might be required over the next two or three years in order to hold the present parity and honour our international obligations. Instead, a series of measures has been adopted in response to immediate threats, with a cumulative deflationary effect that has been greatly exaggerated.

I went on:

On present expectations the growth in production over the next 18 months will be at about 2 per cent per annum ... [and] is likely to involve an increase in unemployment to about 1.8 per cent.... A rise in unemployment to 1.8 per cent is hardly a retreat from full employment.... Many economists would regard some easing of the pressure in the labour market as highly desirable for its own sake.

But suppose we went further. If Ministers had to choose between devaluation at 1.8 per cent unemployment and no devaluation at 2.3 per cent unemployment (the figure put to them last October) or even 2.5 per cent unemployment, what would they prefer?

On the rule of thumb we used, a 1 per cent increase in unemployment would be likely to reduce output initially by 5 per cent and imports would be reduced in about the same proportion. If unemployment were allowed to rise to 2.3 per cent in 1966, we would expect a 4 per cent fall in imports and an improvement in the balance of payments by over £225 million. If the surcharge were retained the deficit forecast for 1966 would disappear.

While my view of the mainsprings of economic growth disposed me to look favourably on a less acute shortage of labour such as a rise to 2.3 per cent unemployment would eventually imply, I was in no doubt that proposals that would halt the growth of output for over a year stood little chance of acceptance except in crisis conditions. But sooner or later, if devaluation was to be avoided, some such proposals seemed unavoidable. If rejected or deferred, the chances were that the reserves would dwindle month by month, with a run on the pound all too likely in the autumn.

Some months later I drafted yet another note. This began from the need for more slack if costs and prices were to rise less rapidly, if the parity was to be held and if it was hoped that devaluation, if it came, would redirect resources into exports or import substitutes. The amount of slack expected, however, measured in terms of unemployment, was no more than 1.8 per cent at the end of 1966. How did that square with the need to repay all debts by 1970?

I suggested that if all debts had to be repaid by 1970, unemployment would have to rise to 3 per cent and stay there. If half the debts could be postponed, it would be enough to raise unemployment to $2\frac{1}{2}$ per cent. If all debts could be postponed, unemployment could be limited to 2 per cent. These conclusions assumed that nothing was done to reinforce deflation by more direct action on the balance of payments.

In my judgment, deflation to raise unemployment to 3 per cent was unthinkable. It would be wise to devalue if all debts had to be repaid by 1970. On the other hand, if we could fund all our debts there was a strong case for sticking to the existing parity provided it was clearly understood that unemployment would not be driven below 2 per cent. On what should be done if only half our debts had to be repaid I remained undecided.

The reader may be interested in how these various eventualities worked out. So far as unemployment is concerned, it did in fact rise to just over 1.8 per cent at the end of 1966 and was at 2.3 per cent when devaluation took place in 1967. It did not rise above 2.5 per cent until the 1970s. More debt continued to be contracted throughout 1966–8 and although a start was made on repayment in 1969, it was mid-1972 before it was all discharged.

Looking back, some of my arithmetic carries little conviction. What seemed to be required in order to restore the government's credibility was a symbolic gesture indicating a clear change of policy. But then, didn't just such a change occur in July 1966? Unfortunately it was followed by a slowing down in world trade combined with a major dispute in the shipping industry that was very quickly reflected in the balance of payments. Had the government acted in 1964 things might have been different, but two years later it had drifted into a position where only consistent good luck could save the parity.

7 The Exchange Crisis of 1965

THE BUDGET

The April budget created no great stir – at least not in Britain. The controversial new taxes on capital gains and corporate profits had already been discounted after their announcement in November. The increase in tax revenue proved just large enough to keep the market quiet. It was obvious, however, that trouble lay ahead. The pressure on the economy continued to mount and unemployment to fall. Wage-rates were rising at 8 per cent per annum and eating into competitive power. The balance of payments might have improved but there was still a small deficit on current account and a large outflow of capital that together made it necessary to offer support at the rate of £650 million a year out of borrowed funds.

Foreigners were also troubled about the budget with its borrowing requirement of £848 million – more than twice as large as in 1964–5 – and were baffled by the claim that it would yield 'some easing of home demand as the year progresses'.[1] I had evidence of the reactions of continental bankers when I visited Rome for a meeting of the Anglo-Italian Economic Committee – one of a number of time-consuming bilateral committees set up after de Gaulle's veto of our bid to join the European Community. I dined with Dr Carli, Governor of the Banca D'Italia and some of his colleagues after giving a short talk on the Budget to the staff of the Bank. Carli was just back from a meeting of central bank governors in Basle and described their reactions to the Budget.

Many of the Governors had argued that the large budget deficit could not fail to have inflationary consequences. They found it hard to see how an economy as strained as Britain's could find room for so much additional investment, for the accompanying increase in consumer spending, and for the improvement in the balance of payments that we claimed would occur. From their own experience they knew how a large increase in government borrowing was liable to add to the liquid assets in the hands of the banks and provide a base for the erection of a superstructure of additional credit. Carli himself was emphatic that if we wanted European backing for a drawing on the IMF we should need to provide a more convincing explanation of our view of the Budget.

Brian Rose of the IMF told me on my return to London that nobody in Washington could understand our budget or the way we ran our economy. When his Mission reported, his colleagues would find the report largely unintelligible. They took the simple-minded view that countries with big budget deficits ended up with balance of payments deficits and that the cure for the second was usually a cut in the first.

If one pointed out that Exchequer Accounts were a very unsatisfactory basis for assessing a country's economic prospects and that what was required was a national income forecast such as we prepared, one was open to the retort that the forecast was secret and that in any event it had not saved us from a crisis in 1964. The alternative was to analyse the Budget figures and show that the large borrowing requirement was consistent with a big increase in saving on the part of the central government. In 1965–6 the government was expected to add £1000 million to its net assets compared with £693 million in 1964–5 and an estimate in the Budget of April 1964 implying a figure of no more than £336 million.

The fact was that the government included in its Budget borrowing and lending operations that had little to do with its demands on the country's resources and were essentially banking transactions. Lending 'below the line' which was expected to reach £1268 million in 1965/6 – represented borrowing not only for the government's own purposes but in order to advance funds to the nationalised industries and local authorities which would otherwise have been raised on the capital market. In his Budget speech the Chancellor made clear that £1043 million out of £1268 million was intended for such purposes and that he was budgeting for an excess of revenue over expenditure of £380 million, leaving a borrowing requirement of £848 million. A year later the recorded surplus turned out to be £688 million and the central government's borrowing came to no more than £499 million, allowing £551 million to be lent to local authorities and £597 million to the nationalised industries (see Table 7.1).[2] There was nothing unsound about the Budget provided the activities of the local authorities and nationalised industries did not overstretch the available resources.

If the borrowing requirement was thought to imply the creation of too much money, the answer was that the banks were just emerging from a shortage of liquid assets and had been *reducing* their advances

TABLE 7.1 *Central government borrowing and lending, 1963–4 to 1969–70 (£ million)*

	Net lending by central government[a]	=	Central government financial surplus	+	Other capital receipts	+	Central government borrowing requirement
1963–4	562		49		138		375
1964–5	524		117		94		313
1965–6	1261		706		56		499
1966–7	1591		813		51		727
1967–8	1804		352		117		1335
1968–9	210		34		449		−273
1969–70	1595		2383		328		−1116

[a] Nearly all to local authorities and nationalised industries

SOURCE: *Bank of England Statistical Abstract 1970.*

in the early months of 1965. Thanks to the large external deficit, Treasury bills had been run down in 1964–5 by £500 million. In 1965–6, although the external deficit was much lower and the finance borrowed from abroad correspondingly less, the entire requirements of the central government for loan finance seemed unlikely to call for any addition to market instruments of debt, whether long-term or short.

Indeed, since 1959 the market Treasury bills had shown a steady contraction in every year except 1963 and British government securities had shown an extremely small net sale.[3] The banking system was only able to go on expanding the stock of money by working on a reduced liquidity ratio, making increased use of commercial bills, and disposing of a substantial part of its holding of British Government securities. There was nothing in the budget figures to imply a massive creation of credit or even a marked easing of the monetary situation in 1965–6.

From the perspective of the central government the situation in retrospect was as shown in Table 7.1. The government was lending large sums to the local authorities and nationalised industries in support of rapidly expanding programmes of public investment. Some of the money to finance this came from a surplus on the government's operations – the excess of current revenue over current expenditure, less the government's own outlay on investment, and after a few other adjustments for capital grants and receipts from capital taxation. Some came from miscellaneous capital receipts as shown in column 3. The shortfall, if any, had then to be met by government borrowing. The money mobilised from these sources might reach a formidable and growing total, rising to over £1800 million 1967–8. But the money went on the capital expenditure of local authorities and public corporations totalling £3200 million in 1967.

In the light of some of these points, a paper was prepared for submission to Working Party No. 3 of the OECD and copied to Carli for circulation to the Monetary Committee of the EEC. This was supplemented later by a report prepared by the IMF embodying information supplied to them by the Treasury on the expected economic impact of the Budget.

One element in the Budget that caused more difficulty than had been foreseen was local authority borrowing from the Public Works Loan Board. Since they raised money more cheaply from this source, it paid the local authorities to make the maximum use of it. In the first three months of the financial year a net total of £200 million had been raised while the Budget estimate for the year was £360 million and the total at the end of the year reached £550 million. The loans had been offered on pegged terms since November 1964 as a transitional device and no limit had yet been set to the transition. It was not until the end of May 1967 that the rates charged for loans within the local authorities' borrowing quotas at the PWLB were brought into line with market rates, causing a sharp drop in lending.

MONETARY POLICY

However the figures were presented, the financial position had its difficulties. The Prime Minister was anxious to see bank rate reduced and the Chancellor was conscious that it would soon have stood at 7 per cent for longer than under any other administration. The Treasury and the Bank had both recommended that the Budget should include a call for special deposits but the Chancellor had decided against it. He had contemplated reacting to a possible influx of funds after the Budget by combining a call for special deposits with a cut in bank rate but dropped the idea and resisted it successfully when the Prime Minister put it forward. Then at the end of April a rise in bank advances made him change his mind: a call for special deposits on 29 April was followed by the imposition on 6 May of a 5 per cent limit on the growth of advances in 1965–6.

The call for special deposits affected only the clearing banks. But advances to United Kingdom residents by the accepting houses and overseas banks had grown by 40 per cent in 1964 and the addition amounted to £235 million compared with £575 million for the clearing banks, so that it was far from negligible. The clearing banks were also reacting to the recent shortage of Treasury bills by increasing their holdings of commercial bills and appeared to be promoting a switch from advances to bill finance on the part of their clients. Bank advances, however, on a seasonally adjusted basis, were virtually unchanged over the first half of 1965.

The Prime Minister continued to press for a reduction in bank rate. As William Armstrong put it, 'he had talked himself into a view of the future in which a fall in Bank Rate would complete the restoration of the Government's image'. He found a supporter in the Governor of the Bank and the proposal became linked with one for hire purchase restrictions. Lower interest rates, however, involved serious risks for a country in deficit since they had to be high enough to make capital flow internationally in the right direction. A setback in the exchange markets in May seemed to rule out the idea and the Chancellor abandoned it. The Prime Minister, however, did not.

Officials had hesitated over a reduction in bank rate even if coupled with hire purchase restrictions. But in May, William Armstrong had argued that bank rate should come down unless there was a very strong case the other way and we had come close to suggesting an immediate cut. When over £50 million was switched out of sterling during the month, the risks seemed too high. Robert Neild felt this even more strongly than I did and we both advised against a move.

When we all met at the House of Commons on 2 June (Prime Minister, Chancellor, Governor and officials) the Chancellor cited our earlier attitude in justification for accepting the Governor's advice. When Denis Rickett asked how a fall in bank rate could strengthen confidence if a rise was intended to do the same, the Governor took the view that it would show that the authorities had the situation under control. On the hire-purchase side of the proposal, he advised that what would most impress foreigners would be an increase in minimum down-payments although the Board of Trade regarded the alternative of a contraction in the maximum period of installment repayments as likely to exercise a more powerful effect on demand.

That seemed to settle the matter. Not a bit of it. George Brown had taken no part in the discussion and, when told, would not agree to any hire-purchase restrictions. A furious argument began and continued until after 2.30 a.m. In the morning the Governor had breakfast with the Prime Minister and they agreed to couple the cut in bank rate with restrictions limited to higher down-payments as the Governor had suggested. This was put to Cabinet and after further debate, ending only at 11.20 a.m. on 3 June – too late to have the Order printed for distribution – agreement was finally reached.

UNEMPLOYMENT

Unemployment had continued to fall through the winter of 1964–5 and at the time of the April Budget was running at 1.3 per cent after seasonal adjustment. In the southern part of the country (including the Midlands and even Yorkshire but not the south west) this meant that the rate was down to 1 per cent or less. It was hard to see how efficient firms could recruit the manpower they needed for expansion or what incentive they had in a booming domestic market to give priority to building up export sales.

After April the unemployment figures seemed to rise until August when they resumed their fall. We were uncertain how to interpret these movements, lacking confidence in the seasonal adjustments and seeking to reconcile the continuing fall in unemployment with the slower growth of output. Had a change in school-leaving arrangements produced a large influx of school-leavers into the labour market in the early spring? Had the labour force ceased to grow in the fourth quarter? Had there been a lag in adjusting employment to the slower growth in output? Before restrictive measures were taken in July we expected unemployment, seasonally adjusted, to increase by about 40,000 over the second half of 1965 and, after the measures, by a further 40,000 in the first half of 1966. This would have involved a rise from about 320,000 in July to 360,000 in January and 400,000 in July 1966. In fact, if one can trust the seasonal adjustments, unemployment *fell* by 35,000 from July to January, and in July 1966 was nearly 20,000 lower than a year earlier. Long before the end of 1965, however, we had concluded that unemployment was changing very little and was likely to remain flat for some time.

Falling unemployment may have been welcome to Ministers with an election in prospect; but how was it to be reconciled with the Chancellor's aim (in his Budget speech) to restore balance on current and long-term capital account in the course of 1966? Unless the pressure on the economy was reduced, there was not the slightest chance of such an improvement, even if the surcharge were retained at 10 per cent until the end of 1966. In any event, the measures taken by the government in the Budget and earlier were presumably intended to provide a check to demand even if there was little or no evidence in the unemployment figures that the check had been effective. The Prime Minister kept listing the various cuts that had been made as if they involved the most drastic economies. In May 1965, however, the National Institute had listed the government's measures and assessed their impact on demand on *a priori* assumptions. On their showing, all that the government had done up to May had had no net effect on demand but would raise the cost of living by 2 per cent.

THE PLAN

When the IMF produced its staff report on the United Kingdom at the beginning of May, George Brown expressed concern that we seemed to be committed to restricting growth in demand to $2\frac{1}{2}$ per cent per annum from the second half of 1964 to the second half of 1966. It was necessary for the Chancellor to point out that there was no absolute limit but that any more rapid expansion would have to be consistent with getting back into balance in the course of 1966. What was said to the IMF and to Working Party No. 3 echoed the Budget speech except for the more precise undertaking to aim at balance in the second half of 1966. However unattractive expansion at $2\frac{1}{2}$ per cent might be, the Plan under preparation was not likely to be credible and consistent with external balance within a measurable period of time if it provided for a faster rate; and it was difficult to see how such a target could be pursued for long without disclosure to the public. Indeed, within a few days the National Institute issued a forecast showing an annual rate of growth of about $2\frac{1}{2}$ per cent between the first quarter of 1965 and the second quarter of 1966. Even this was somewhat higher than the target put before the IMF.

The Treasury viewed the Plan with some apprehension. The drafts submitted to us did not make very clear what was at issue in preparing a plan for 1970 in the very uncertain conditions facing us over the yeas ahead. In our view it was important to stress that there could be no guarantee that it would be possible to allow output to rise more or less steadily towards the assumed 1970 level. Our hands might be tied by balance of payments difficulties, particularly over the next year or two, that obliged us to pursue more restrictive demand policies than were consistent with steady growth. We also had reservations about DEA's views on the acceleration in productivity growth which they claimed to detect, although in January 1965 we did not dispute that '25 per cent is a reasonable figure to take for planning market-oriented capacity, either in private industry or in the public sector, for 1970'.

By March, when a draft White Paper on the plan was circulated, I expressed to William Armstrong the hope 'that we have not closed our minds to seeing the whole idea of issuing this White Paper abandoned' [AKC 1659].

> The present draft [I argued] does very little to convey the immensity of the task before us. Nobody reading it would have much of a clue as to the short-term dangers ... and they might very easily be tempted to take for granted the increase of 25 per cent in GDP.... The only phrase in which there is any reference to difficulties in the initial years seems to be in para 28, and it is about as pussy-foot as anything could be. The publication of this series of figures [showing the allocation of resources in 1970] not only does nothing to prepare people for trouble ahead, but is bound to tie our hands when we come to try to work out future prospects in more detail.

The draft still contained no reference to the threat that an adverse balance of payments hung over the current rate of growth. Instead the discussion was all in terms of the contribution to improving the balance of payments that might come from more rapid growth.

After March we heard little about the plan: attention was concentrated on the Budget, the new taxes and incomes policy. In mid-July a draft was circulated in a form very different from what we had seen but as William Armstrong commented on Chapter 1, it gave 'a rather sketchy account of the next 12–18 months'. By the time it reached Ministers we were on the verge of the exchange crisis that culminated in the statement of 27 July. On 21 July Ministers had a kind of 'second reading debate' on the plan at No. 10. The Chancellor wanted to know 'the latest date when we can turn this juggernaut back' and suggested giving priority over growth to the restoration of external balance. George Brown was prepared to give the balance of payments equality of treatment with growth but both he and the Prime Minister agreed that to aim merely at restoring the balance of payments was a recipe for stumbling from one crisis to another.

The Prime Minister was particularly unrealistic. He appeared to want control over private investment as a means of clearing the way for public investment, not in order to limit it to $4\frac{1}{4}$ per cent per annum or to ensure fulfilment by the private sector of the plan. He thought it 'inconceivable' that the plan should not be published. It was not until 16 September that it appeared but by that time the government had made the first move towards a policy of deflation and the plan, although not dead, had lost credibility.

THE JULY CRISIS

The Budget had done little to restore confidence: at best it prevented things from getting worse. In the second quarter the loss of reserves was just as high as in the first and the forecast for the last two quarters, *excluding* short-term capital movements, showed the drain continuing at a slightly faster rate, £720 million per annum, and stretching out into 1966. Foreign opinion was increasingly pessimistic and saw the economy as teetering on the edge of devaluation.

The trade balance, which had improved sharply from a deficit of £42 million per month in the last quarter of 1964 to only £13 million per month in the first quarter of 1965, worsened again to £30 million in April and £49 million in May, which was as bad as in the second half of 1964. A run on sterling began on the publication of the May figures and was not halted by an improvement in the deficit to £33 million in June.[4]

The Chancellor was increasingly conscious of his difficulties. As he prepared for a visit to Washington at the end of June he called us in and asked us for ideas to put to the Americans for ways of helping us. We could think of nothing but more credit. Nicky Kaldor would have liked us to engage in a joint float with the Americans but there were too many snags in any proposal of that kind.

I was able to sound foreign opinion at a meeting of Working Party No. 3 in Paris on 5 and 6 July. The Swiss and German representatives at the meeting emphasised that lack of confidence in the pound seemed to be greatest in the City of London. The discussion made clear that if confidence was to be restored, additional measures would have to be taken soon.

In replying to the discussion, I enquired whether the feeling that further measures were required arose from a changed assessment of the adequacy of our measures and the way in which they appeared to be working out or from a change in the state of confidence that had a different origin. Van Lennep, the Chairman of the Working Party, said that the adequacy of our programme had been questioned at its May meeting and the line then taken was that the margin of safety might prove to be too small since no one could guarantee that our forecasts would be completely fulfilled. It was natural that there should be increased concern when we had raised our forecast of the deficit in the balance of payments from $400 million in the seven months from May to $550 million in the second half of the year. In addition, there had been disappointment over the trend in exports as well as the developments in the labour market reflected in the rapid increase in wages and the very low level of unemployment. The high capital outflow in the first quarter emphasised the danger that there, too, our forecast might be too optimistic.

Other delegates amplified these points. The IMF representative mentioned as reasons for disquiet the deterioration in the outlook for the sterling area, the high level of long-term capital outflow, and the recent tendency to switch out of sterling which might be intensified at current interest rate relationships. The Swiss delegate underlined the contradictions in British policy: more purchasing power was being put at the disposal of public authorities when purchasing power needed to be restricted; costs were going up when we needed more exports; hire purchase restrictions were being imposed at the same time as bank rate was being brought down; and so on. The German representative thought that our measures had been too cautious and did not operate quickly enough. Any measures of restraint should be extended from consumption to investment, both private and public. We should be thinking of heavier pressure on the rather alarming wage situation and a crash programme for incomes policy.

The undertone of the discussion was that we were having too much regard to preserving our chances of long-term improvement and insufficiently alive to the short-term dangers which might oblige us to do more than enough if we wanted to restore the conviction that what we were doing was genuinely enough. It was not the last time that such a message was conveyed to a Labour government.

On my return to London I naturally provided for the Chancellor an account of the views expressed. A meeting with the Prime Minister was held in his room at the House of Commons on 9 July but without agreement on the need for any new measures – at least not if they were deflationary. The Prime Minister, as usual, identified deflation with two million unemployed. In his view, the economy had always been hit when it was on the way down, and it was going down now, so there could be no case for further deflation. In any event, each Minister ruled out the action open to him and united only in arguing for import deposits.

Two days earlier the Prime Minister had dictated a long memorandum with twenty-eight points for examination (including foreign language training courses). One proposal calling for serious consideration was a moratorium on building, subsequently limited to civil engineering. There was clearly to be no restriction on housing: on the contrary the Prime Minister wanted 500,000 houses at subsidised interest rates.

For one more week the Prime Minister refused to admit that there was a problem and gave assurances to the press in non-attributable interviews that there would be no restrictive measures. The Chancellor created a stir by speaking off the cuff in the House of Commons about the 'temptation' to deflate and the need to resist it until there had been time for past measures to take effect. The Governor became increasingly agitated in his letters on the situation and a letter of advice promised earlier by the IMF arrived. Meanwhile we continued to prepare a package of measures that we felt fell short of the full seriousness of the situation. The danger was that Ministers, with the support of some of the bankers, would content themselves with some gimmick such as import deposits. At the end of the week I noted that the Anglo-German Economic Committee which I attended half-expected devaluation while the Board of Trade Regional Controllers half-expected deflation and the Prime Minister ruled out both.

Losses of foreign exchange continued and reached £48 million on Thursday 22 July. At that point my four fellow advisers again pressed for immediate devaluation (but without a word to me) and were unhesitatingly turned down by the Prime Minister. I was persuaded to submit a personal note to the Chancellor and minuted William Armstrong as well, but have no recollection of the argument I developed.

Ministers continued to meet to discuss Plans D, E and F for investment grants and the National Plan but had each strong objections to any of the more obvious components of a package of measures. There seemed no way of getting over to the Cabinet how serious the situation was and what action was required. Then on Sunday 25 July George Brown returned from a weekend in the company of Roy Jenkins and Tony Crosland, converted to devaluation. For the first time there was a serious discussion between Ministers on the merits of a drop in the exchange rate. After a long wrangle between the Prime Minister, the

First Secretary and the Chancellor that ended at 1 a.m. on 27 July, a package of measures was agreed and announced by the Prime Minister later in the day. The rate of exchange remained unaltered.

THE MEASURES

The measures included a contraction in the period for hire purchase repayments, tighter exchange controls, cuts in public investment estimated at £200 million in a full year and a system of building licences for private projects over £100,000 excluding housing and industrial building. Since the building industry was very much over-loaded it was difficult to judge what effect the measures would have on current activity.[5] A moratorium on starts by local authorities excluded houses, schools and hospitals and might do little more than allow such work to go ahead more quickly. Private investment was higher in each quarter of 1965 than in the corresponding quarter of 1964 but did flatten out in 1966; much the same was true of private house-building. Public investment grew rapidly year by year from 1962 to 1967 with no more than a slight easing in the rate of growth in 1965. There is little evidence of a decisive break in the upward trend in the autumn or winter of 1965.[6]

Whatever their impact on the domestic economy, the measures failed to stop the run on the pound which was on a scale in August comparable with that in November 1964. By the end of the month, however, the danger had passed and the Prime Minister, the Chancellor and the Governor had all gone on holiday as originally planned.

THE AFTERMATH OF THE 1965 CRISIS

The immediate effect of the measures of 27 July on the market in foreign exchange was to add to the pressure, not reduce it. The delay in announcing the measures was taken as a sign of unpreparedness or irresolution: first the Prime Minister had issued assurances that there would be no 'mini-budget', then he had made it plain that there would, but for a week he had been unable to say what he proposed to do. When the reserves were announced on 2 August the markets remained uneasy. People thought that things must be really bad if it was not possible to wait until the end of the month before making the July statement, or at least quote the exchange losses at once. The run on sterling grew instead of falling away and it was some time before the market regained its calm. When figures for the third quarter were eventually released later in the year, they showed a drain from the reserves during the quarter of £195 million, not much greater than in each of the first two quarters. The figures, however, showed only the spot position, while the Bank of England was operating also in the forward market to an unknown extent.

How the measures would affect economic activity over the next twelve months had to be hastily assessed. It was thought that domestic demand would be reduced by about £200 million, made up in roughly equal parts by lower spending on hire purchase, cuts in new construction work by central and local government, and a reduction in capital investment in the private sector. The visible balance of payments might improve by about £70 million a year as the pressure of demand was reduced and the balance in invisibles by about £45 million through the further tightening of exchange control.

An improvement in the current account by £100 million or so would be helpful. But was it enough? In early July, before the measures, we had prepared a forecast on the assumption that the surcharge would be entirely removed by the April Budget in 1966. The forecast indicated a deficit on current account of £140 million in 1965, deteriorating to one of £210 million in 1966. To these figures had to be added the net capital outflow; and for long-term capital alone we expected a net outflow of £200 million in 1965 and £140 million in 1966. An improvement of £100 million a year on these figures would still leave us with an external deficit totalling over £500 million in two years. That was bad enough. But had these figures proved to be correct, they concealed an inconsistency. It would not have been possible to run deficits of £250 million a year until 1967 and yet maintain confidence in the pound at home and abroad. There would have been an outflow of short-term funds, of which the forecast took no account, on a scale which we might have been unable to finance.

Apart from any withdrawals of funds, covering of obligations in the forward market, and outright speculation against the pound, other uncertainties might begin to tell. We were counting on some helpful disinvestment in external assets as a result of the tax changes in the Budget; but what if there were no confidence in sterling? Long-term capital flows might turn much less favourable. We had to reckon also on possible drawings by sterling area countries on their reserves, an increase in outstanding export credit of perhaps £100 million, and a balancing item that might well be negative.

Balance of payments forecasts are never altogether reliable and in the circumstances of 1965 were peculiarly difficult. The record shows an outcome very different from our forecast: a deficit on current account of only £43 million in 1965 succeeded by a surplus of £113 million in 1966. We were far too pessimistic about exports, which we expected to show little or no increase in volume from the middle of 1965 to the end of 1966 because of rising costs and a growth in world markets at perhaps only half the previous rate. Such a forecast might have been interpreted as an incitement to devalue but had no such origin. In fact exports grew in volume by 12 per cent by the end of 1966 and had been the fastest growing element in demand. We also miscalculated fixed investment, underrating like others the persistence of the investment boom.

Commentators in the press speculated on the chances that the balance of payments would improve sufficiently to meet the Chancellor's target of a surplus by the second half of 1966 and enable Britain's accumulated debts to be repaid. The National Institute thought in August that balance might possibly be reached but only at the cost of virtually stopping the rise in output. At that stage they thought that there was 'a choice between quasi-stagnation ($2-2\frac{1}{2}$ per cent growth of output, combined with rising unemployment) or an inability to pay by 1970 the debts incurred in the last year'.[7] The definition of 'quasi-stagnation' might be rather bizarre – it was close to the average rate of growth in the 1950s and above the late nineteenth century average – but it was expressive of the expansionist ambitions prevalent at the time.

The *London and Cambridge Economic Bulletin* contented itself with a forecast on unchanged policies and concluded that a deficit on current and long-term capital account at an annual rate of about £150 million was not unlikely by the end of 1966.[8] If the surcharge was to be abolished by that time it was highly unlikely that it would be possible to maintain a significantly favourable current balance. In an earlier issue, Peter Oppenheimer had reviewed the policy alternatives in such a situation and had pointed to devaluation as an effective instrument. 'The onus of proof', he argued, 'is on those who maintain that measures other than devaluation can do the job within a reasonable period or, indeed, at all.'[9] The arguments for and against devaluation were becoming increasingly ventilated in the press but usually, as in the example just quoted, without any indication that when devaluation is prescribed it is unlikely to be effective unless accompanied by other, less acceptable, measures.

The July measures appeared to be impressive and were clearly intended to impress the markets. Their impact on the balance of payments might be appreciable but what of domestic demand? Were the measures, as the Prime Minister was given to predicting, the prelude to a large rise in unemployment? It was widely assumed that, taken in conjunction with the Budget and other measures, they would put an end to the boom that began in 1963. Comparisons were drawn with the previous cycle from 1958–62, and 1965 was depicted as a 'stop' year like 1961.[10] Investment, which had been rising strongly in 1964 and 1965, was expected to flatten out in 1966.[11] Unemployment, it was thought, would increase slowly over the next eighteen months while output would grow at a snail's pace.[12]

THE INVESTMENT BOOM

All these forecasts proved to be wrong. Fixed investment did *not* slow down, as we forecast, from an annual rate of 8 per cent to one of $3\frac{1}{2}$ per cent over the next twelve months and to $1\frac{1}{2}$ per cent between the first and second halves of 1966, but accelerated slowly from half year to half year, speeding up to a fast rate of growth in the first half of 1967 (Figure 7.1). The forecasters – including the Treasury forecasters – underrated the extraordinary buoyancy of investment in the mid-1960s. Whatever one may think of the economic policies pursued, they sustained a major boom in investment and allowed manufacturing investment to reach an all-time peak in 1970.

Similarly with the forecast of rising unemployment. There was no consistent rise until the second half of 1966 after a second and more decisive deflationary package: from August 1965 unemployment fell steadily and in the first half of 1966 it remained month by month below the level in the corresponding month in 1965. As for output, it increased quarter by quarter in 1965 and 1966 at a rate close to $2\frac{1}{2}$ per cent. This was perceptibly below the rate of expansion in the winter of 1964–5 when the growth rate was about $3\frac{1}{2}$ per cent per annum. But it was no more than the 'marked slowing down in the growth of home demand' that we were already predicting *before* the July measures were even contemplated.

Whatever the check to output there was no easing in the labour mar-

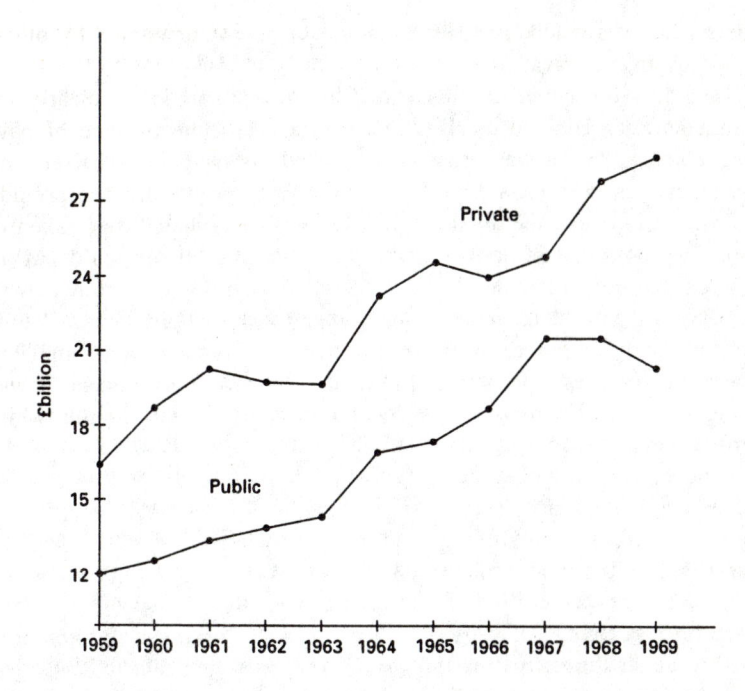

FIGURE 7.1 *Public and private investment, 1959–70 (at 1985 prices)*

ket. Instead of increasing, as generally expected, unemployment fell slightly over the year following the July measures and in June 1966 was still at 1.2 per cent. The movement in unemployment was out of line with the movement of output, partly because of a reduction in standard work-ing hours. This reduction, or part of it, appears to have reflected a genuine desire for a shorter working week rather than served as a means of obtaining more pay at overtime rates.[13] It therefore curtailed the increase in production from a given labour force as productivity improved.

The investment boom was concentrated in the public sector where the increase between 1963 and 1967 was a little over 50 per cent, whereas in the private sector it was just under 25 per cent. Of the increase in the public sector it was government investment, not investment by the nationalised industries, that rose most and fastest. Indeed, by 1968 government investment was on a scale only exceeded since in 1973 (and possibly in 1970): twice as large as in the 1980s. Much the same was true of investment by the nationalised industries. The all-time peak was reached in 1967 and was only ever approached again in 1975–6. In the private sector, on the other hand, investment rose comparatively little between 1964 and 1967 (and fell slightly in 1966) but went on after 1967 to much higher levels. In manufacturing industry, on which attention was often concentrated, there was not only no investment boom in the mid-1960s but the level of investment remained consistently below the level reached in 1964 (or, for that matter, 1960–4). The boom was in housing, power stations and infrastructure, not in manufacturing.

One of the problems in handling an investment boom was the difficulty of translating programmes into probable performance. When programmes were not fulfilled, the explanation was often labour shortage and this was acute in most parts of the country in the mid-sixties. If cuts were made – as they were in July 1965 and again in July 1966 – they might do no more than substitute a realistic for an unrealistic forecast. Indeed, if deflationary measures released labour elsewhere, investment might speed up and exceed expectations. In 1965–6 we were constantly at a loss to know how much less slippage would occur in programmes that were never fulfilled if something happened to make the labour market less tight.

Moreover the indicators that were used were hard to interpret: they might consist of no more than a balance of ups over downs in investment intentions in an industrial survey. In the autumn of 1966, for example, the Confederation of British Industry's (CBI) inquiry was showing a dramatic change in the excess in the number of firms authorising less capital expenditure in 1967 over those authorising more: an increase to 39 per cent. This was interpreted in the press as indicating a corresponding drop in industrial investment by 39 per cent whereas our own analysis of the figures yielded a drop of 15 per cent and the Board of Trade Survey of investment intentions pointed to a fall of under 7 per cent. In fact, the fall in investment in manufacturing industry in 1967 was no more than $3\frac{1}{2}$ per cent and investment in the whole of the private sector (excluding housing) actually *rose* by $1\frac{1}{2}$ per cent.

The economy was working so close to full employment that output was limited as much by supply difficulties as by any inadequacy of demand. This was particularly true of construction: after the big increase starting in the middle of 1963 there was only a moderate rise of 6 per cent from the end of 1964 to the end of 1966 and it was not until 1967, when the labour market eased at last, that rapid expansion was resumed. Exports, on the other hand, provided much of what expansion there was in 1965–6 but fell off steeply in 1967. Imports, which showed little increase in 1965 and 1966 while the surcharge remained in place, surged in 1967 and 1968 after its removal

One outcome of these movements in exports and imports was that the trade balance and the balance on current account were unusually favourable in 1965–6. In the second half of 1965 the current account (as now estimated) was slightly in surplus where a year before it had been in deficit at an annual rate of £450 million. In the first half of 1966 the current account was back in deficit but over the year as a whole there was a surplus of over £100 million. The Chancellor's target of balance on current and long-term capital account before the end of 1966 was met in a formal sense but only because of a quite exceptional drop in imports in the last quarter of 1966, presumably in order to take advantage of the removal of the surcharge at the end of the year.

The low level of imports in 1965 was largely attributable to the surcharge, coupled with a drop in the level of stockbuilding, a US dock strike which reduced shipments across the Atlantic, and the good harvest of 1964 which kept down food imports. In 1966 imports rose a good deal faster than in 1965, except in the final quarter, but even so, showed none of the buoyancy that was to follow. As a result, the anxieties of 1965 and 1966, while real enough, owed nothing to the underlying strength of the demand for imports of which we were too little conscious and which became so apparent and alarming in 1968.

THE COURSE OF EVENTS AFTER JULY

Three events dominated the months of August and September. One was the publication of *The National Plan* on 16 September. From our point of view that was of little interest: the Plan was already obsolete and more of an embarrassment than a guide to action. A second development was the organisation of a 'Great Bear Squeeze' in sterling after the meeting of the Group of Ten early in August. Allied with this was a move to make incomes policy more effective.

The run on sterling after the measures made it clear that sterling was in need of fresh international support and talks took place between British and American officials and simultaneously between the Bank of England and the Federal Reserve Board. A paper was drawn up by Charles Coombs of the Fed. setting out the proposed strategy, approved as a basis of action by the President, and taken in hand by Henry Fowler, Secretary of the Treasury. The Americans would have liked Britain to follow the model of their own policies in 1950–1: a freeze of prices and incomes; further deflation, preferably making use of the regulator; and various dramatic measures such as the recall of Parliament. Not much of this survived, but Ministers concentrated on proposals for an early warning system for prices and wages and for putting the National Board for Prices and Incomes on a statutory footing. In the middle of August, with most officials still on holiday, there were almost nightly talks by telephone hook-up between the Prime Minister (in the Scilly Islands), George Brown and James Callaghan; and between them and the Americans, notably Henry Fowler, Secretary of the Treasury.

The support operation took place at two levels. Fowler toured the European capitals to drum up support. He was preceded by a Bank of England official, Rupert Raw, who had made tentative arrangements, unknown to Fowler before the tour began. The Chancellor sent a message to the Finance Ministers of the Group of Ten but made no mention in it of the support operation. When a public announcement was made – by the Bank of England – on 10 September it embraced eight European countries, Canada and the United States. France, however, after some delay, refused to participate: de Gaulle was not prepared to take part in what he saw as an American scheme. The Chancellor, learning of the French decision and of the insistence of some other countries on the use of swaps as the mechanism of support, was still uncertain to the last whether to call the operation off.

Within a day or two the Bank was taking in foreign exchange from the market and went on doing so. Throughout the winter months the inflow of foreign exchange continued and on the stock exchange stocks and bonds both rose in price in September and October. The dollar exchange rate, which had been held a little above 2.79 in July and August, rose to over 2.80 at the end of September for the first time since May 1964 and remained above par until March 1966. The Chancellor was even tempted to think of another cut in bank rate and other Ministers contemplated various reflationary proposals; but no action was taken.

INCOMES POLICY

Progress with incomes policy remained unconvincing. There were, first of all, administrative difficulties. There was a gulf between Ministers and officials and another gulf between different sets of officials. George Brown did not use the official machinery and his officials had limited influence on him. He could be effective in personal dealings with trade unionists but his persuasive powers did not prevent them changing their tune when out of his presence. Within the Treasury there was little contact between the management side under Helsby and the policy side under Armstrong and the Chancellor did not take to Helsby as he took to Armstrong. There were limitations, too, to the number of cases that the National Board for Prices and Incomes (NBPI) could handle effectively; and the kind of recommendations they made followed a pattern that seemed unlikely to exercise much influence on the rate of wage inflation. By October 1965 hourly earnings (excluding overtime) were rising at 9.5 per cent per annum and even hourly wage rates were rising at 7.3 per cent per annum. Not since the Korean war boom in the winter of 1951–2 had wages risen as fast.

It was not easy to see how, under those conditions, the policy could be made effective. There was none of that lasting horror of inflation that kept German workers from pressing their claims too far when unemployment was negligible. So long as labour was as scarce as it was throughout the southern half of the country, the most one could hope for was to set up procedures to delay and hamper the satisfaction of wage claims and inject, whenever possible, conditions likely to enhance productivity. A wage freeze, in which all alike were held back from exerting their bargaining power, might provide an emergency stop that worked more or less for a few months; but it was never completely effective, or effective for long, and might leave no trace after a year or two as workers sought to recover what they thought they had forfeited.

In 1965 there was no freeze. The policy continued to rest on persuasion and consent. But it was not in the government's power to command consent. What the government was able to legislate for was that advance warning should be given of wage claims and price increases. Moreover the government felt obliged to offer a quid pro quo for greater wage stability by promising greater price stability: not by relying on competition but by exerting pressure on price-fixers. This had two consequences. So long as wages continued to rise, employers relied on their freedom to raise prices in compensation; if that freedom ceased, what incomes policy implied was a government-sponsored increase in real wages. More obviously, the government would be expected to limit price increases in the public sector and was likely to do so more effectively than it could limit wage increases. The nationalised industries, when obliged to keep their prices down, inevitably failed to meet their financial targets and, what was worse, were putting an extra £100 million in purchasing power in the hands of the public when there was already too much. Price control, far from assisting in the control of inflation, was apt to give it a boost.

By the end of 1965 practically all public sector wages and prices came within the purview of the National Board and it was being taken for granted that the Board's recommendations would be respected. But over the winter of 1965–6 wages rose faster than ever. The Board may have had some influence on the growth of productivity: but there is no evidence that it had a perceptible effect on the rise in wages.

8 The Exchange Crisis of 1966

Over the winter of 1965–6 there was a marked improvement in the balance of payments. In the final quarter of 1965 the current account was in surplus and the outflow of long-term capital was relatively small. As a result, the dollar spot rate rose above par in September and remained there until February. The three month forward premium on dollars fell from 2.5 per cent in August to 0.8 per cent in January 1966 and 0.5 per cent in May. The forward commitments of the Bank of England started to fall in September, continued to fall until in January 1966 they were less than in January 1965 and fell heavily in February. In the first quarter of 1966 it was possible to repay £200 million and, by transferring £316 million from the dollar portfolio, to increase the reserves by a net £200 million.

The outlook, however, was not reassuring. Unemployment continued to fall and the labour market became increasingly tight. Early in November 1965, after the preparation of a fresh economic forecast, the Chancellor briefly contemplated new measures. He was well aware that the Prime Minister would resist further deflation and thought first of using hire-purchase restrictions. At that stage he wanted to be ahead of events and take immediate action, accepting that everything pointed to renewed pressure on resources. A week later he was more cautious, recognising that George Brown, too, would be strongly opposed and thinking perhaps of a spring election. When I pointed to the serious risks he was running both at home and externally and urged prompt action to get the pressure down he merely asked whether I would be coming to him again in a few months' time asking for another £150 million off demand in the Budget and I had to admit that he read my mind correctly. He hoped for a substantial cut in defence expenditure and proposed to find relief for the balance of payments in another bisque under the American loan agreement.

At the beginning of December officials agreed that it would be necessary to wait until January and that even then higher taxes might undermine efforts to limit public expenditure. The choice seemed to lie between the regulator and hire-purchase restrictions with the Chancellor very doubtful about the latter. I argued that public expenditure cuts would be slow to take effect, and that, since programmes were not being met, they might do no more than tally with existing forecast assumptions. We should go for a 5 per cent rise in indirect taxation with 10 per cent on purchase tax. The Chancellor was advised to wait for a month without concealing his wish to act. He had already issued a warning which the press had taken up. When he approached the Prime Minister, there was, rather surprisingly, no challenge to our forecasts and diagnosis, perhaps because the National Institute had just issued almost identical forecasts. The Prime Minister agreed that public expenditure should be cut severely but thought that it would be wrong to put up taxation in the Budget. By mid-December the Chancellor was talking of cuts of £150–200 million in public expenditure and £50 million through hire purchase restrictions. He was toying also with introducing a value-added tax in 1967 or earlier although nothing came of this.

The proposed cuts seemed inadequate in relation to the danger of an early exchange crisis. They would not prevent an alarming increase in the estimates and they were unlikely to have large immediate effects – or change much even by the second half of 1966 – especially if half the reduction in public expenditure was to be in defence. There was a growing feeling that devaluation in the course of 1966 was almost inescapable and that if that was so it would be best to act while markets were relatively calm.

Whatever was done about the exchange rate, every deflationary weapon that could be employed was required. But how could agreement be reached on the necessary measures if the government was adamant against devaluation, against letting prices rise with costs in the public sector, against increasing taxation, and powerless to adjust its expenditure within six months?

A major problem was the attempt to hold down prices in the nationalised industries. Coal was being sold well below costs, enabling steel prices also to be held down but laying a mine that would sooner or later be sprung when prices had to be allowed to follow costs. In January DEA insisted that if only prices could be kept down for a few months more, wage incomes would respond and inflation be brought under control. The gamble had not paid off in 1965 because of the reduction in hours of work, but this was now almost over and the rise in wages could be expected to moderate. Nothing of this kind happened in 1966.

In the winter of 1965–6 we had many other things to worry about than macro-economic policy. One of these was Rhodesia. As the Chancellor told us, 'when I talk to the Prime Minister about the Governor now, he thinks I mean the Governor of Rhodesia'. Treasury and Board of Trade officials felt the additional burden. Then there were all the discussions on alternative plans to encourage investment with grants instead of tax allowances; the problems raised by the introduction of corporation tax whose effect on investment abroad seemed to be the reverse of what was originally promised; the continuing negotiations on international liquidity that led eventually to the creation of a new reserve asset in the form of the SDR.

PUBLICATIONS

In mid-December the Chancellor returned to a proposal he had made earlier in the year for the issue of an official publication giving a reasoned account of Treasury views. He had wanted us to take over *Economic Trends* from the CSO and nothing had been done. Why did DEA issue broadsheets extolling its activities in fulsome terms, while the Treasury kept quiet? If anyone spoke for the government on economic policy it should be the Treasury. DEA had stolen a march on us and would be in a still stronger position the longer we waited. William Armstrong asked why it should matter to us as servants of the government if DEA published and the Treasury did not. To this the Chancellor replied with a warning that he would not be there indefinitely to help us and rubbed in what we would have to endure by reading us some random samples of what DEA were putting out and telling us: 'I bet you won't have anything like this in *your* articles'.

I was not at all sure that we should enjoy much freedom to issue an objective view of events in difficult times but I pursued the idea – dating from February 1963 – of reprinting our monthly economic assessment as an article in *Economic Trends*. Although this did not meet the Chancellor's proposal, he agreed without enthusiasm. As I feared, we soon ran into difficulties in getting the text approved, had to postpone its introduction till a later issue in June 1966 and again were obliged, at the very last minute, to arrange for a postponement. It took many months before our anodyne assessment was included regularly in *Economic Trends*. Even then, enquiries were made by DEA as to why the report should be the handiwork of the Treasury and we became aware that anything including the word 'economic' in its title was liable to excite proprietorial claims from George Brown.

The Chancellor had also been annoyed by comments in the Bank of England's *Quarterly Bulletin*. The government ought not, he argued, to speak with two voices. How did the Bank come to have such freedom to express its views without clearance with the Treasury? I explained that it all went back to the Radcliffe Committee of 1957–9 which had pressed for an authoritative exposition of financial developments and regarded the Bank as the natural agency to take on the job. Were we then content to leave everything to the Bank, the Chancellor demanded, and go without any publication of our own?

FORECASTING

In mid-December Norman Macrae published an attack on the Chancellor in *The Economist* under the heading 'Crystal Ball.' It was part of his argument that the government was falling badly behind practice elsewhere in not issuing official forecasts of GDP. Other journalists were also pressing strongly for the publication of government forecasts. They exaggerated the openness of European governments and paid no regard to the unique position of the Chancellor in his power to act at once on a forecast in a way none of the Europeans could, so that a government forecast on which no action was taken was virtually a plan. In some countries 'official' forecasts were made by agencies which, unlike the Treasury, had no responsibility for policy; in others they were rather rough and ready affairs, based on annual data, and related only loosely to policy decisions. At that time only one comprehensive set of forecasts (in the *National Institute Economic Review*) was published in Britain and they originated in an effort by Robert Hall, my predecessor, to ensure that the Treasury should not be the sole source of economic forecasts. We had done our best to assist the National Institute by seconding staff and looked forward to seeing more forecasts by other bodies as a check on our own efforts.

The publication of official forecasts could be both embarrassing and misleading: embarrassing if they showed a deteriorating balance of payments or increasing unemployment; and misleading because it was not the figures that were the effective forecast but the policy advice that was offered on the basis of the forecast. Both in short-term forecasting and in long-term planning, each figure had its own uncertainties and qualifications and what mattered was not the collection of figures but the series of decisions of policy to which they pointed. It would be much easier to publish forecasts *after* the Budget when all the key decisions had been taken and the forecasts would neither disclose policy decisions that were not already public knowledge nor fail to take decisions of a kind that the figures suggested to be necessary.

My view was that forecasts were in danger of being taken too literally. Their primary purpose, when prepared by the Treasury, was to assist the Chancellor in deciding how to run his risks. To issue a set of figures representing the best single judgment available might seem highly advantageous. But it could do more harm than good if it failed to bring home the uncertainties surrounding the forecast. This being so, there was everything to be said for encouraging research and discussion *outside* government into longer-term trends and helping industry to prepare a do-it-yourself kit rather than tie everything to one set of officially endorsed statistics. This was, of course, subject to the government's own policies being as consistent and publicly known as possible.

The Chancellor took a keen interest in the debate on forecasting, arranged for Norman Macrae to discuss his article with him and spent nearly an hour talking things over before bringing me in. 'Sit over there, Alec' he said as I came in, 'we have the enemy on this side.' He suggested that we should arrange a conference at Nuffield College on what forecasts should and should not be published and offered to promote it so long as he was not required to come. This suggestion was acted upon and a conference was held in May.

The journalists who attended the conference regarded it as an opportunity to bring pressure on the Chancellor and in this, with the support of William Armstrong, they were successful: publication of government forecasts began in the next budget.

HIRE-PURCHASE RESTRICTIONS

At the beginning of January I was asked to prepare a paper analysing the economic situation and prospects with the other economic advisers (Balogh, Kaldor, Neild and MacDougall – in practice Jukes as MacDougall had pleurisy). Although a diagnosis was asked for, they were all determined to put forward recommendations for policy. There was no likelihood of agreement on recommendations when Jukes opposed deflation of any kind and wanted its disastrous consequences (non-fulfilment of the Plan) to be spelled out. Balogh and Kaldor, as usual, could find no common ground. Kaldor, without expecting confidence in sterling to be disturbed, agreed that there was a risk of a forced devaluation before the Budget and on those grounds favoured early action. Balogh was unable to follow his usual tactics of voicing anathema against his various hates and endorsing the views of somebody else. Everybody except Jukes accepted the need for action in January, even Balogh favouring hire-purchase restrictions but making such action dependent on the date of the election. Kaldor and I submitted a note of our own to supplement the main report.

When the paper went to Ministers there was no agreement. As I was in the United States, Robert Neild was asked to organise a paper with the other three advisers on the 'relevance' of hire-purchase restrictions to current circumstances and was taken off his aeroplane to Geneva to undertake the work. The Chancellor was empowered to go ahead after the Hull by-election in February with restrictions estimated to reduce demand by £135 million. It was also agreed to consider guidelines for exports of capital to the sterling area and to tighten monetary policy as the Bank of England was only too ready to do.

There was, however, some doubt whether, with the continued strength of sterling, Ministers would hold to their decision. George Brown was trying to hedge his agreement, Douglas Jay wanted to cut the proposed restrictions in half and Balogh wanted to withhold action till the February trade figures were available. A victory for Labour at Hull strengthened these reservations. The Chancellor supported the restrictions only to escape raising taxes in the Budget, using arguments which William Armstrong told him resembled those used in the same room in 1955. The oddest proposal from the Chancellor was for a cut in bank rate to 5 per cent – this in the middle of an international boom.

After further delay until the threat of a railway strike had been settled, agreement was reached and the hire-purchase measures were announced on 8 February. These were expected to cut demand by £160 million a year. The Governor at about the same time announced a prolongation of the credit squeeze limiting advances (including commercial bills) to 105 per cent of the March 1965 level. The deferments of capital expenditure made in July were also prolonged. All this was calmly received by the markets.

More or less simultaneously, a firm decision was taken on a March election and a May budget, with a public statement by the Chancellor explaining the situation and keeping the Budget open. There were some indications that the Chancellor might be changing his view on devaluation, and that he might unite with George Brown after the Budget to press it on the Prime Minister, but there was no real foundation for this. The Chancellor's statement, after much re-drafting, was issued on 1 March and was well received, although more attention was given to the official acceptance of a decimal currency than to what was said on the economic situation.

After a sharp drop in sterling on 9 March, the Governor expressed concern which was shared by other members of the Court and proposed a rise in bank rate, then at 6 per cent. He feared a heavy loss if this were not done and maintained that the market had come to expect it (although the press said the reverse). The Chancellor was at first disposed to agree but changed his mind when he saw Edward Heath on television claiming that a Labour victory would damage sterling. The following day the Bank took in £2 million from the market, mainly from French buying.

It had been agreed at the end of February to prepare a paper for 31 March on medium term strategy and Robert Neild prepared a draft. This set a target of £500 million for a balance of payments surplus and offered a threefold choice of policy of which the third was headed 'letting the pound float or changing the parity' – a course strongly favoured by the other four advisers. To my mind the document, which sprouted appendices by Kaldor and Balogh, dealt too exclusively with the balance of payments, had nothing to say about a Plan that was simply not feasible, and was unlikely to persuade Ministers of the need to devalue.

It had indeed become clear, especially after the Ministry of Labour revised drastically its estimate of employment at June 1965 to show a large increase, that productivity was increasing at a rate well below the 3.2 per cent per annum assumed in the Plan, that there had been *no* acceleration in the growth of productivity, and that, as the National Institute agreed, it was not possible to put it higher than 3 per cent per annum. Indeed if productivity was measured as output per head, the reduction in hours in 1965 had lowered it to 2.7 per cent during that year. A post mortem on the growth targets set for 1961–6 by NEDC provided a chastening reminder of the gap between target and achievement: instead of an increase in GDP by 22 per cent, the increase was likely to work out at about 16 per cent. It was the slower growth in productivity in 1965 that accounted in our judgment for the continuing fall in unemployment – by 50,000 over the winter months – when the rise in output was below the current estimate of economic potential.

Many papers for Ministers on economic strategy were prepared while the election was in progress: one by Permanent Secretaries, a revision of the paper by Economic Advisers, a paper by Eric Roll and William

Armstrong, notes of dissent by Balogh and others. There was endless debate and re-drafting, including re-drafting of other people's papers. As constantly happened in those years, the regular civil servants below the level of Permanent Secretary were left in the dark and not consulted. When the Prime Minister became aware of what the economic advisers were up to, he exploded, saying flatly that he was not prepared to receive advice based on a change in the parity. But drafting and re-drafting continued until well into April.

There was also much desultory discussion on the European Community. Those who wanted immediate devaluation (and were not prepared to wait and see what a dose of deflation would do) saw advantage in joining the EEC as a cover for devaluation. Balogh, who in one mood was of this school of thought, was simultaneously against even thinking of joining the Community until we were in a strong competitive position, presumably after devaluation and only after some years. Kaldor saw as the main danger the eagerness of British financiers to pour in British capital to finance mergers, reorganisations, etc. when the balance of payments would be unable to stand it. The Governor, too, had begun to look forward to membership but thought that it would only be possible with larger reserves. The Prime Minister, we were told, was counting on the Americans to bale us out if that proved necessary.

THE SELECTIVE EMPLOYMENT TAX

Discussion with the Chancellor on the budget began on 6 April. He raised the possibility of a surcharge on the national insurance contribution designed to cut labour-hoarding by serving as a payroll tax. Kaldor then produced the idea of a surcharge that would be rebated on manufacturing and confined effectively to services. This appealed to the Chancellor who was determined to avoid a rise in purchase tax. He approached the Prime Minister next day before going off on holiday, leaving Customs with no guidance on the options on purchase tax that he wanted to keep open. The Prime Minister was sympathetic to the idea and was dumbfounded at the alternative of trying to raise £200 million in purchase tax. As the Chief Secretary pointed out, one had to consider how such an increase would look to the Labour Party fresh from its victory at the polls.

However united advisers might be on the need for disinflation, it was obviously going to be difficult to reach agreement on an appropriate package. Both the National Institute and the London and Cambridge Economic Service saw no need for deflationary measures; George Brown was strongly against them; the Chancellor had no positive proposals of his own.

What then was to be done? It seemed inconceivable that, in the short time before the Budget on 3 May, a scheme as complex as Kaldor's could be worked out in final form. But when I returned from leave after Easter I found that the great payroll levy had been virtually accepted by 18 April. The Chancellor had tried in vain to get the Inland Revenue to introduce a tax on services and had fallen back on a surcharge collected through the National Insurance Scheme by the Ministry of Labour.

It had become very different from a simple tax on services. Well over £1000 million would flow into the Exchequer and large sums would flow out again in rebates. These vast surges of money to and fro, as William Armstrong explained to me, were all for the sake of £100 million of disinflation. Moreover it could not come into operation until the autumn so that it would have no effect over the summer when it might be most needed. Even in later months its impact was highly unpredictable. An increase in income tax would have been far more effective. Nevertheless when asked by the Chancellor for an objective opinion, with other duties allowing no time for consultation, I offered a qualified approval. The Chancellor was still troubled, particularly about the 'summer gap', and raised the possibility of increasing petrol tax without in the end doing so.

On 19 April the Prime Minister, Chancellor and First Secretary met to decide on what came to be called the Selective Employment Tax. Their decisions drove Nicky Kaldor, the father of the scheme, to despair. Manufacturing employment was to get no subsidy: it would receive back no more than it paid. All transport and all public services and nationalised industries would be exempt. Ministers had also observed that there would be a lag in repayments so that net revenue would be swollen in 1966–7 and there would be a corresponding credit squeeze to add to the deflationary effects.

THE 1966 BUDGET

When it came to the Budget, SET was fixed at 25*s*. a week for adult men, half that rate for adult women and boys and 8*s*. for girls, yielding an estimated net revenue of £315 million in 1966–7. Manufacturing industry was to receive, after all, a refund of 130 per cent with no refund on constructions and services but a full refund in the public sector and in transport.

The proposal to control capital investment in the sterling area was modified and became a voluntary scheme but with procedures that were not altogether in keeping with voluntary limitation. The Australians had urged the Chancellor – with widespread agreement in Whitehall – not to risk breaking up the sterling area for as little as £40 million a year (the estimated gain to the balance of payments).

It had also been proposed to double the 25 per cent surrender rates on realisations of investment currency. The Bank of England, on the other hand, wanted to exempt switches, for example by investment trusts. Both proposals were rejected. A 50 per cent surrender would make switches too expensive but a nil surrender would be a disincentive to net realisations. On monetary policy I argued that increasing pressure in the gilt-edged market should be allowed to push up interest rates and that we should not be deceived by the strength of the market when the Bank had taken in £350 million of stock in the first quarter. Shortly before the Budget, Leslie O'Brien, the Deputy Governor was appointed to succeed Cromer as Governor of the Bank although he had been told on appointment as Deputy Governor that eventual appointment as Governor was excluded.

A decision had also to be taken on the import surcharge. On 26 November it would have been in force for two years and there was agreement that it could not be retained any longer. There was talk of quotas succeeding the surcharge but this never seemed a starter. The removal of the surcharge on 30 November was announced in the Budget.

THE ONSET OF THE CRISIS

In May a strike of the National Union of Seamen began and continued until the end of June. Sterling weakened and by the middle of June, especially after the devaluation of the rupee, heavy losses of foreign exchange had begun. In the week ending 11 June, losses spot and forward amounted to £130 million. The media began to agitate for a wage freeze but we felt that such a move should be coupled with other measures if it was to succeed. Ministers were remarkably quiescent and business seemed to go on as usual in spite of indications of a growing crisis.

The Chancellor was out of favour with the public because of SET; the First Secretary was baffled by the Plan which was fastened round his neck like a millstone and he was no longer campaigning publicly for incomes policy; the Prime Minister hardly ever made a speech in public. Rhodesia, Vietnam, the seamen's strike, the balance of payments deficit – all seemed to go on indefinitely with no clear solution to any of them in prospect.

The Cabinet was becoming increasingly restive on economic affairs. The practice of confining discussion of major economic issues to the Prime Minister, Chancellor and First Secretary was resented by other Ministers. Some of them felt that they had no opportunity of discussing the economic situation as a whole and that they could not take a view on specific issues, such as matters of incomes policy or devaluation, without an opportunity to debate general policy. Such an opportunity was promised for 12 July.

When I attended a meeting of the Economic Policy Committee of the OECD on 5 July the tone of the discussion of the United Kingdom was elegiac. There was no likelihood now that sterling would recover. The bankers were no longer interested. We had wasted a year. The one thing we didn't have was time and yet it was the one thing we proposed to use most freely. Our forecasts had been mistaken and could not be trusted. What was required was action and action that left no room for doubt.

On my return, I did a hasty minute on the atmosphere in Paris and the dangers the government was running. On the same day Leslie O'Brien called on the Prime Minister before leaving for a meeting of central bank governors in Basle and delivered a warning of the threat to the parity in the heavy losses of foreign exchange that were occurring. As in 1965 the government was caught unprepared. No statement even about the intended credit squeeze had been prepared by 12 July and no increase in bank rate had been made – moves that might have avoided much of the subsequent collapse. Officials were absorbed in SET and international liquidity while No. 10 was putting it about that there would be no mini-budget – exactly as in 1965 – ignoring the implication that the government might therefore be thinking of moving the other way, i.e. towards devaluation.

The first measures to be taken were an increase from 6 to 7 per cent in bank rate and a doubling of special deposits on 14 July. Further measures were not announced until 20 July and, as I had predicted, were almost a caricature of Selwyn Lloyd's July measures in 1961 in that they followed up the rise in bank rate with the full use of the regulator, called for a voluntary freeze in wages and prices, tightened hire-purchase restrictions still further, and made extensive cuts in public expenditure. The investment programmes of the nationalised industries and local authorities for 1967–8 were to be cut by £130 million and building controls on private and office building were to be tightened. £100 million was to be lopped off government overseas expenditure and the travel allowance was to be reduced (from November and in countries outside the sterling area) to £50 a year. These measures were based on a recommendation by William Armstrong that the aim should be an improvement in the balance of payments by £250 million, of which £150 million should come from direct savings and £100 million from domestic deflation through a reduction in demand by £400 million. This was consistent with earlier calculations of what would raise unemployment to 1.8 per cent by July 1967 – an increase that we felt to be justifiable with or without devaluation. The announced total savings were £150 million in overseas spending and £500 million in home demand on an annual basis.

How and why had the government agreed on such measures when even on 12 July the Prime Minister was asking for figures showing the cumulative deflation since 1964 as if nothing more could be required? The answer is twofold. First came events that increased market uneasiness about the rate. On 2 July it was announced that the reserves had fallen by £49 million in June in spite of drawings on foreign credits. Next day Frank Cousins's resignation as Minister of Technology threatened active opposition from the trade unions to the new measures of incomes policy contained in the Bill published on 4 July. The June trade returns were bad and Euro-dollar interest rates were rising. On top of all this it was known in some quarters that George Brown had changed his mind (as had always seemed likely) and now felt that devaluation was preferable to deflation: perhaps it might yet save the Plan. The second and more powerful factor was the scale of exchange losses. These had more effect on Ministers than any warnings from their advisers. For nearly two years the government had resisted a choice between deflation and devaluation but it was now clear that the choice could no longer be avoided.

The week before the measures were announced was full of twists and turns. On 12 July Ministers settled nothing but their common opposition to cuts in public expenditure and it was agreed at official level not to make preparations for fresh hire purchase restrictions on the 14th. At that stage, however, the Prime Minister wanted a package before leaving for Washington and seemed to be contemplating action on the 14th which would have included hire-purchase restrictions, some use of the regulator and a ban on all office building. There was no real possibility of such swift action. On the 13th the 'Big Three' agreed to wait until 2 August. They also agreed to aim at a cut of £100 million in overseas government expenditure. The Chancellor was due to make a statement on the credit ceiling and SET on the 14th and he now proposed to include a warning that further deflationary measures were in preparation while George Brown urged a wage freeze for the next twelve months. All three were united in support of a deflationary package on the scale we proposed (i.e. over £400 million).

The Chancellor, instead of making a statement on the 14th, used a Parliamentary Question to announce an apparent further restriction of credit leaving it to the Prime Minister to make the statement promising further measures at a later date. Once again this advertised the government's unpreparedness. Measures that were at first to be announced in the statement on the 14th were first left to be more fully considered, then put off until 27 July and finally announced on the 20th after the Prime Minister's return from Moscow and just before the Chancellor's departure for Bonn.

Earlier in the month the Chancellor had come to despair of support from his colleagues for the cuts in public expenditure that he felt to be necessary and was beginning to have doubts about the parity. Nevertheless he reacted strongly on the 10th to the argument put to him by William Armstrong that the only way to hold the rate was by massive deflation. The Prime Minister remained firm on the parity and took steps to appeal to the Chancellor's loyalty and so prevent a combined assault by the Chancellor and First Secretary. He drafted a speech to the Australia Club reaffirming his belief in the rate in terms that would commit the government. (Iran had already been assured by Kaldor that there would be no devaluation.)

In the course of the Big Three's discussions George Brown resigned and then withdrew his resignation. Callaghan contemplated resignation but was argued out of it by Harold Wilson. Had he resigned some, at least, of his advisers would have joined him.

As in 1965, the market was far from reassured by the course of events. On the day of the statement the losses reached £100 million, mainly on spot. In the last week of July the losses, spot and forward (mainly forward for lack of spot), approached £350 million. These figures were far in excess of what the press implied. On Friday the 29th, for example, the pressure was reported to be small but the losses were in excess of £80 million. Market forwards had risen to near their previous peak and were still rising. The published loss of reserves on 2 August (£50 million) had little relation to the true position and the Bank had great difficulty in procuring enough spot finance to keep the apparent loss so low. It had both to borrow overnight from the Federal Reserve Board and receive credit from the Bank for International Settlements (BIS), taking care to keep both kinds of transaction strictly secret. The losses, spot and forward, continued into August at up to £90 million a day. It was not until the middle of the month that the market regained its calm. In the third quarter the exchange losses were almost as high as in the last quarter of 1964 and far above any quarter in 1965. Nearly £450 million was borrowed from other monetary authorities, by far the highest total for such borrowing up to that time.

The events of July were a sad reflection on a government that believed in planning. Ministers had been forced in the end to take the action they were unwilling to contemplate in 1964 and had no guarantee such as they might have had then that it would prove sufficient. Their policies had permitted a serious loss of competitive power and at the same time they had piled up debts in defence of a parity that was rapidly losing credibility. Was it possible that these debts could be repaid unless the economy somehow regained its competitive power?

THE AFTERMATH OF THE 1966 CRISIS

The first effect of the July measures was in the political sphere. It broke up the triumvirate, George Brown moving to the Foreign Office on 9 August and being succeeded as First Secretary by Michael Stewart, a more quiescent and also more rational personality. At the same time, the Prime Minister appointed a new committee with himself in the chair to discuss strategic economic policy (SEP) instead of confining it as before almost exclusively to himself, the First Secretary and the Chancellor. How loudly the committee would bark was another matter: the members included neither any of the critics of the Prime Minister's way of deciding policy nor any representatives of the spending departments. No record was to be kept of the committee's proceedings except a single copy kept under lock and key. Only the conclusions would be circulated. The committee was to meet monthly and be serviced by a group of officials who would parcel out the work but engage (so we were told) in no substantive discussion.

Ministers, as always, wanted better statistics, to be circulated along with a monthly report at each meeting, talked of a chart-room, and commissioned both a new short-term and a long five-year look at the prospects for the economy in time for the October meeting. There might also be a look at public expenditure and at the future of relations with Europe and the United States. Import controls, import deposits and reflation were other subjects they itched to discuss. But of the Plan and economic growth not a word was said.

I had supposed that the Ministerial committee would automatically be supplied with the official forecasts once prepared in November and was taken aback when instructed that they should be withheld. The Chancellor was against circulation to other Ministers for fear they would misuse or leak them. Reggie Maudling had had a similar reluctance to trust his colleagues or perhaps a similar desire to keep his cards close to his chest. Neither of them appreciated that since other departments took a hand in the preparation of the forecasts they already had a copy of them. When I asked Peter Baldwin, the Chancellor's private secretary, what SEP was for if it was unable to discuss the forecasts, Peter said that the trouble was that the Chancellor didn't think that it *had* any point.

When we came to assess the likely effects of the July measures, we expected a substantial slowing down, with an expansion in output of only 1.5 per cent over the next eighteen months. This proved to be wide of the mark. In the first half of 1967 output had already risen by 2.5 per cent above the first half of 1966 and if it fell a little in the second half of the year this, too, was unforeseen. Consumers' expenditure did dip by about 2 per cent initially but it recovered by the second half of 1967 to over 3 per cent above its level before the measures. As for fixed investment in the private sector, so far from falling, it was about 4 per cent higher in the first half of 1967 than a year previously while public investment increased not by 12 per cent but by about 16 per cent. The year after what seemed quite savage deflation was a period of at least as rapid economic expansion as in 1965 or 1966.

Although this seems to have been true of output, it was not true of unemployment. From 1.2 per cent in June the number wholly unemployed mounted to 2.7 per cent in January 1967. Part of this was seasonal, a large part represented temporary stoppages, many of them associated with strikes. For the wholly unemployed, excluding school leavers and Northern Ireland, the seasonally-adjusted total rose from 1.2 per cent in June to 2 per cent in February 1967, reached 2.3 per cent in July and remained there until the end of the year. Broadly speaking, the measures eventually added about 1 per cent to the level of unemployment. This may seem almost negligible in the 1990s: in the 1960s it meant doubling the number on the register. In manufacturing it meant that employment had passed its all-time peak.

PUBLIC EXPENDITURE

As 1966 drew on, the rise in public expenditure received increasing attention. The rise was not new: public expenditure had been rising for many years, latterly by about 50 per cent at current prices every five years. In 1965 as part of the National Plan it had been agreed to limit the increase to the planned rate of growth of GDP, namely $4\frac{1}{4}$ per cent per annum. But that rate had been exceeded, while the growth of GDP was falling far short of $4\frac{1}{4}$ per cent. It looked as if 1967–8 would see a sudden acceleration in public expenditure in spite of the cuts in July. There was talk early in October of large increases in spending programmes since July and of fresh cuts that might have to be made of up to £500 million on top of the £500 million in July. There was not much evidence of the first and little chance of the second.

We were chided by the Chancellor and the Chief Secretary on our failure to keep public expenditure from growing. What had happened to the $4\frac{1}{4}$ per cent limit and why had we failed to carry out instructions and show how growth in expenditure might be limited to $3\frac{1}{4}$ per cent? The Chancellor admitted that in July he had not realised just how big the increase in public expenditure would turn out to be; he recognised that if he sought further cuts he and the Chief Secretary would be alone in fighting for them against the rapacity of the big spending departments in the public sector and petted clients such as housing. But to bring the increase within the agreed limit of $4\frac{1}{4}$ per cent should not be regarded as a cut.

He already supported a neutral budget in 1967 and was dead against any increase in taxation. He was also against any increase in expenditure and seemed to hanker after constant money outlay – an attitude not encountered in the Treasury since Thorneycroft. But expenditure was far from constant and there was no second round of expenditure cuts. We were to be faced in April with a central government borrowing requirement of £1115 million and an increase in expenditure on supply services over the outturn in 1966–7 of 17.2 per cent (at current prices). Both figures were underestimates: the borrowing requirement turned out to be £1335 million (nearly twice the level in 1966–7) and the increase in expenditure 22.5 per cent.

Large increases in public expenditure were quite consistent with rising unemployment: indeed, they helped to explain why a fall in private sector activity was so readily contained, the rise in unemployment almost ceasing soon after the turn of the year. As more slack became available in the private sector, it gravitated to the public sector and helped to meet its outstanding labour requirements, so that public investment, after being held down in 1966 by labour shortages, began to rise faster with the help of redundant labour at a rate it was difficult to predict. The fact that public expenditure had a lower import element than expenditure in the private sector helped to restrain imports and delay pressure on the exchanges.

A second consequence of increased government spending came to our attention in November. We had begun to prepare forecasts at current prices alongside the forecasts in real terms. Current price forecasts were of special interest for the picture they gave of the probable movement in profits and liquidity. The November forecast implied a dramatic change under both headings. It showed an increase in company profits by over £400 million between the financial years 1966–7 and 1967–8 and an even larger improvement of £700 million in their liquidity. I had some doubts about this forecast, which was not easily squared with the normal forecast at fixed prices; I suspected that it underestimated the likely addition to stocks. I accepted, however, that the large public sector borrowing requirement in 1967 pointed to a highly liquid private sector. Professor Kaldor not only drew the same conclusion but made it the cornerstone of his budget recommendations. He was as afraid of excess liquidity brought about by government borrowing as any later monetarist and was correspondingly insistent that a large increase in taxation was needed to soak up liquidity.

The November 1966 forecast, the first considered forecast since the measures, took a rather gloomy view of immediate prospects. The initial falling-off in activity had been unexpectedly rapid and industrial production was likely to be flat or falling for some time. A shake-out of labour had taken place sooner and on a somewhat bigger scale than expected. In the near future imports would begin to reflect the removal of the surcharge. The amount of slack in the economy would continue to increase in 1967, but only gradually, and unemployment could be expected to reach about $2\frac{1}{2}$ per cent by the end of the year. Demand and output would show continuing slow growth over the year under the influence of the big investment programmes in the public sector (with a considerable shortfall in 1966 to make good) and the favourable prospects for exports offered by the expansion in world trade and the greater steadiness of production costs.

The outlook for the balance of payments was highly uncertain. Any surplus in 1967 seemed likely to be slender and make at best no more than a small contribution to the repayment of debt. There would be no surplus until well into the year and we should need a substantial surplus in 1968 if we were to begin repaying our debts.

In the background was the question: how is the balance of payments to be further improved? If raising unemployment to $2\frac{1}{2}$ per cent is not enough to secure the necessary swing in the balance of payments, how much further, if at all, would the government be prepared to go? Depressing the level of domestic activity in the interests of external balance could not only raise unemployment beyond tolerable limits but ran the risk of so damaging business confidence that it would prove difficult to restore it. The upward trend in investment and exports minimised these risks for the present; but would Ministers be willing to contemplate further measures in 1967 or had they shot their bolt?

9 The New Strategy, 1967

1967 opened in an atmosphere of low key euphoria. The news was either good or not so bad as it had been. Exports had continued to rise strongly in the second half of 1966 while imports, held down by the expectation of an early end to the Temporary Import Surcharge, fell off a little. The balance of payments had improved quarter by quarter throughout the year. In the exceptional circumstances of the final quarter of 1966 the surplus on current account was an all-time record and even the balance of trade, when seasonally adjusted, showed a surplus for virtually the only time in the whole of the 1960s. Confidence appeared to be reviving and the authorities no longer found it necessary to support the pound.

The domestic situation was not so happy. Unemployment had risen from about 300,000 in July 1966 to nearly 500,000 six months later. So rapid a rise was alarming to Ministers expecting to see the rise continue even if not at so fast a rate. By the end of the year, however, the rise was clearly slackening and in the two weeks before Christmas the (uncorrected) figures showed a slight fall. We were doubtful about the seasonal adjustments and these doubts persisted throughout 1967. It is clear in retrospect that the trend in unemployment remained gently upwards to a peak in September 1967 without raising the unemployment percentage above 2.4 per cent – much as had been forecast at the beginning of the year. What we had then predicted was an increase to a little under 2.5 per cent by the end of the year and a continuing rise for a time in 1968 in spite of a growth in output likely to be at about 3 per cent per annum.

In the week before Christmas the Chancellor developed a new economic strategy with a six-point programme and talked it over with the Prime Minister who said snap to it all. Although some parts of the programme related to the medium term, Callaghan did not mind being accused of doing Michael Stewart's work for him. The elements in the programme were spelled out to us as follows:

(i) around 2 per cent unemployment (perhaps $1\frac{3}{4}$–2 per cent);

(ii) a balance of payments surplus of £100–150 million;

(iii) a rephasing of external debt after repayment in the autumn of maturing debt;

(iv) no reflation in 1967 (or perhaps before September – or even July);

(v) £200 million off defence expenditure

(vi) not more than £300 million to be added to taxation by 1970 (or perhaps £100 million off civil expenditure).

Item (iv) had the explicit agreement of the Prime Minister. The word went round that even hire purchase must not be relaxed until July or later. A test of this very point arose in the first week of January when the President of the Board of Trade circulated to the Steering Group of Ministers a proposal for 'a limited general reflation of demand'. In fact the proposal, apart from a call for lower long-term interest rates, was far from general. It was confined to an easing of hire-purchase restrictions on motor cars, the car industry having been hit disproportionately hard by the July measures. Down-payments on cars were to be reduced from 40 per cent to $33\frac{1}{3}$ per cent and would put cars on the same footing as household appliances. The boost to car sales was estimated at 5 per cent and the expected increase in hire-purchase debt over the next twelve months at £40 million. The Chancellor, however, in conformity with his new strategy, was opposed to any immediate relaxations, and no action was taken.

If the Chancellor's strategy were to be more than an arbitrary collection of targets it would have to be demonstrably self-consistent and calculated to produce the desired results. It rested on some rather speculative estimates which we had prepared hurriedly and were anxious to consider at more length before they were submitted to a ministerial committee. Earlier estimates had been a good deal more optimistic.

A 'medium-term assessment committee' had concluded in 1966 that the public expenditure programmes as they stood implied a large continuing shift from private spending and investment to public spending and investment, requiring as its counterpart higher tax rates and less consumer spending. The required addition to the tax revenue of the central government in 1970 was put at £750 million along with an extra £300 million or so in local rates. In 1967 the estimate of £750 million was reduced to £500 million; and no doubt the Chancellor regarded a cut in defence expenditure of £200 million as consistent with a reduction in the additional revenue required from new taxes to £300 million.

Later work by the Committee in March allowed for an additional £600 million in the surpluses of public corporations and local authority rates by 1970. The additional tax revenue required was now put at £500 million on one hypothesis and nil on another, the figure of £500 million corresponding to a higher public expenditure programme and a larger balance of payments surplus than the alternative hypothesis. On either hypothesis, consumers would receive a smaller share of GNP: an increase of £500 million in taxation would reduce their share from 64.3 per cent in 1965 to 60.8 per cent in 1970.

These calculations, which were obviously highly speculative, were appealed to in the spring when Professor Kaldor argued that taxation would have to be increased by about £1000 million over the next three to five years. They also coloured the approach to the 1967 Budget since if Kaldor was right there was a strong case for making a beginning at once. As we were to find in 1968, much larger budgetary changes were required than we had foreseen.

Other elements in the strategy involved further uncertainties. No one could be confident how world markets would expand or how the balance of payments would react to changes in the economic climate abroad. The rephasing of external debt was also dependent on external conditions. It was not under British control and could not be taken for granted.

I had suggested some time previously to William Armstrong that if the parity was to be held it would be likely to require a 1 per cent addition to unemployment and a 1 per cent addition to interest rates. The Chancellor had accepted intellectually the need for a somewhat higher unemployment rate. But higher interest rates were not part of his strategy. On the contrary, he embarked on a campaign to lower interest rates internationally. Long-term rates in Britain were regarded as very high. They were a little under 7 per cent, with the value of money falling in the months before the freeze at 2–3 per cent per annum.

The nub of the matter was how the balance of payments and the level of production would respond to a slight increase in the level of unemployment. Six months previously we had told Ministers to expect a balance of payments surplus of £300 million (not the Chancellor's £150 million) if unemployment were allowed to rise to 2 per cent. We had also told them that a level of unemployment of $2\frac{1}{2}$ per cent would allow gross domestic product to increase by 13–15 per cent between 1964 and 1970. Now we were substituting a figure of only $14\frac{1}{2}$ per cent at the perceptibly lower level of 2 per cent unemployment while Sir Donald MacDougall in DEA was circulating a much higher estimate of 15–17 per cent (one that in 1970 proved to be closer to the mark). It will be remembered that the National Plan had held out the prospect of a 25 per cent increase in GDP between 1964 and 1970, so that what Ministers were now being asked to accept was a drastic lowering of their hopes.

Although the Chancellor had spoken of 2 per cent unemployment as part of his 'strategy', what he had told William Armstrong was that he now accepted the advice given to him when he entered the Treasury that $1\frac{3}{4}$ per cent (*not* 2 per cent) was the right operating ratio for unemployment. He had also taken the line in discussion with William that he did not propose to run the economy at $2\frac{1}{2}$ per cent unemployment for the sake of joining EEC.

It made a great deal of difference whether these unemployment rates were intended to be operating averages or minima. If the Chancellor was thinking of an average of $1\frac{3}{4}$ per cent, this represented little or no change on past performance: the average for the previous six years for wholly unemployed was 1.7 per cent. If he was thinking of a minimum of $1\frac{3}{4}$ per cent with fluctuations around a higher average, the change would be much more perceptible. But even with a minimum of $1\frac{3}{4}$ per cent for the whole country, unemployment in a boom would fall in some regions to 1 per cent or less and it would be in those regions that the going rate of wages was settled.

There were further uncertainties about items (v) and (vi). The increase in taxation likely to be necessary in 1970 was obviously subject to a wide margin of error, especially as it was highly sensitive to changes in prices; the figure of £300 million was virtually a guess. The Chancellor's strategy, however, revolved round the budgetary actions he was willing to take and the paper he submitted to the Steering Group in January ('Public Expenditure to 1970') was one on public expenditure.

Uncertainty about balance of payments prospects was increased in February by a paper from the CSO analysing the trend over the past ten years. The CSO analysis pointed to an upward trend in the external deficit while our projection to 1970 showed a steady improvement. Where in the middle of 1964 we had put the underlying deficit at £200 million and were now inclined to think that £400 million would have been nearer the mark, we had come to project a surplus of over £200 million by 1970. What confidence could be put in such a projection?

In the case of the trade balance, the CSO painted a picture of an adjusted deficit of about £100 million in 1957–8 rising to about £250 million over the middle 1960s. It could, however, be argued that long-term trends in imports and exports were a mirage. Imports, for example, had undergone two big upswings in the last ten years that were associated with reflation but were very much aggravated, first by liberalisation in 1959–60 and then by rising import prices in 1964. Such jumps were not necessarily recurrent. We had thought in 1961 that we should have to accustom ourselves to living with no net invisible earnings and had found that we were much mistaken. On the other hand, the CSO were assuming a continuing improvement in the terms of trade of just under $1\frac{1}{2}$ per cent per annum or the equivalent of £60 million a year.

Our main reason for thinking the CSO projection too pessimistic was that we were assuming a régime under which unemployment did not fall below 2 per cent and this could not fail to change any previous trend in the balance of payments. But we were conscious of the large uncertainties affecting both the current and the capital account. We could not treat our forecasts as more than a broad indication of the way things might go if we succeeded in doing what we had never yet done since the war: keep on a steady path of expansion without allowing unemployment to drop below 2 per cent.

MASSAGING INTEREST RATES

The Chancellor also included as part of his strategy an effort to lower what was considered a very high long-term rate of interest. He had proposed international action to reduce interest rates to Joe Fowler, the American Secretary of the Treasury, and then called a meeting of Finance Ministers for Saturday 21 January. It seemed to us a case of financial transvestitism, with the Finance Ministers dressing up for a discussion of monetary policy, while the Central Bankers groomed themselves for a meeting in Basle of fiscal policy. The original intention had been to assemble Finance Ministers on 7 January, which would have been more likely to prevent leaks, but the French Finance Minister, Débré, was unable to attend on that date and the Chancellor was unwilling to proceed without him. The revised timing meant that the Conference would be followed immediately by meetings of Working Party No. 3, the Group of 10 and a Joint Meeting with the IMF – a calendar of events that was bound to make journalists suspicious of what was in the wind.

We had little confidence that Finance Ministers would be able to reach conclusions that they could sell to their Central Banks after a discussion in which none of them appreciated just how the others' monetary systems worked. The Governor was rather contemptuous of the whole affair, especially as nobody wanted to have the central bankers present. At a briefing meeting, Jeremy Morse argued that the proceedings were bound to be rather indefinite and inconclusive. Since rates were already falling, it was likely to be 'a Canute quadrille chasing the receding tide'.

As 1966 ended, the Governor had proposed a cut in bank rate of $\frac{1}{2}$ per cent on technical grounds, but in his letter to the Chancellor he made it clear that he expected the December trade figures to be so bad, following the removal of the import surcharge in November, that it would be impossible to make a cut after their publication. (In this he proved to be entirely right.) My own view was that it was a mistake to make a cut in advance of the proposed conference on interest rates and excite foreign opinion by taking the lead; and that a cut of $\frac{1}{2}$ per cent would be liable to lead to a further cut of $\frac{1}{2}$ per cent, perhaps in advance of the conference, so that any cut might as well be one of 1 per cent. The Governor was assuming that the Public Works Loan Board rate would go up simultaneously but the Chancellor would obviously be opposed to such a move and was likely to represent the cut in bank rate to the Prime Minister as one commanding the Governor's support without this or any other condition.

By the end of the first week of January 1967, the proposal seemed to have died, but a week later, after a cut in German rates, it revived. When officials met on 17 January it was agreed to recommend a move within the next week or two. To refrain from doing so was thought to involve a marked shift in policy, not easily squared with the aim of the conference. The Chancellor was at first undecided but contemplated a drop of 1 per cent within the next month or two. It did not look as if conditions would become much more propitious. In the United States, William McChesney Martin did not mean to accommodate the President by cutting rates and resented the arm-twisting tactics of getting Walter Heller's Bank in Michigan to lower its rate. The Governor of the Bundesbank was also resisting an immediate further move. At the Bank of England, the Governor still felt that there was a chance to get rates down and that if it was not taken this would disappoint the market and produce an outflow of funds. The figures, however, indicated just the reverse. A large inflow of funds occurred – the Bank took in nearly £200 million from the market in January – and this was clearly due to London rates staying up.

I had myself come round to the view that a small cut *before* the conference could be used to make it plain that no immediate action was to be expected after it, whereas if we delayed we might be pushed into doing more. A reduction from 7 to 6½ per cent was made on 26 January, just after the conference, and no further cut took place until the middle of March.

When we met the Chancellor on 19 January to brief him for the conference he talked of a reduction in bank rate of 2 per cent, to be made in stages over the cycle in the way bank rate had been cut in previous cycles. William Armstrong put it to him that even abstracting from international pressures we couldn't go down to 5 per cent if public expenditure continued to rise. This made us dependent on a larger sale of gilts unless we were prepared to see a still greater increase in liquidity; and we could not sell more gilts if we were simultaneously aiming to raise their price and force down interest rates. This was a line that I had developed earlier with William but it did not impress the Chancellor who could not see why the creation of more money, or greater liquidity, should matter. So I fell back on the argument that we could not abstract from external pressures that might require high interest rates since these pressures, including our own foreign indebtedness, had already forced on us a conscious slowing down of the economy. (None the less we did get down briefly to 5½ per cent at the beginning of May.)

The Chancellor asked us what he could talk about to other Finance Ministers on Saturday night after dinner when everybody had unbuttoned and was gossiping in the Long Gallery at Chequers. Débré had said that he would not come if he was going to be asked to talk about Europe; Fowler didn't want any discussion of the price of gold; and the Italians (who had been invited late in the day to their considerable annoyance) were not likely to be very interested even in interest rates, having changed their bank rate only once since 1950.

The Chancellor's efforts to arrive at a viable strategy were linked with a least three other subjects under discussion simultaneously. It was his intention, first of all, to invite the co-operation of the unions on the basis of his strategy and work out an agreed incomes policy to succeed the freeze. Discussion was also in progress on the likely cost (in terms of resources and weakening of the balance of payments) of a successful application to join the EEC. Could the Chancellor's strategy meet what might be a substantial additional burden without the devaluation he was so anxious to avoid? Was there a case for an alternative economic association with North America in a North Atlantic Free

Trade Area? A third group of questions related to public expenditure, which was growing rapidly under the initial impulse of the National Plan and then because of the expanding responsibilities of government and the investment appetite of the nationalised industries. Was all public expenditure equally costly in resource terms or were some forms of expenditure more costly than others? This and other issues that could be regarded as methodological were pursued by a group originally set up to discuss export credit and given a wider remit at the suggestion of Sir Richard Powell, Permanent Secretary to the Board of Trade.

We shall leave aside the third set of questions and concentrate on the first two, before turning back to the problems of demand management in the months before devaluation in November.

INCOMES POLICY

The wage freeze introduced in July 1966 virtually arrested the rise in hourly wage-rates over the next six months and even in June 1967 the increase since the freeze began was no more than 2 per cent. Retail prices in August 1967, also under control, had risen over the past year by less than $1\frac{1}{2}$ per cent. These results had been obtained by rigorous restraint with increases in pay only in exceptional circumstances and prices increases only if they were due to a marked rise in the cost of imported materials, or higher taxes, or seasonal factors, or similar reasons.

Part IV of the Prices and Incomes Act 1966, which had provided statutory backing for the standstill in wages and prices in the second half of 1966 and the period of severe restraint that followed, was due to lapse in August 1967. It would be necessary to decide what policy should take its place. Although the primary responsibility rested with DEA, the Treasury had a major stake in the fight against inflation and the Chancellor hoped that his strategy could be the basis of agreement for the coming year.

A report on a possible policy to come into effect in July 1967 was submitted by Lord Kahn and Kenneth Berrill. This took for granted the collaboration of the TUC and CBI as well as government participation in the negotiating process *before* wage settlements. They attached great importance to the right of the government to be directly involved in plant bargaining in addition to nationwide bargaining and envisaged an increase for this purpose in the staff of the Ministry of Labour. Surveillance would be on the basis of criteria still to be worked out and would not prevent subsequent reference of an inflationary settlement to the NBPI, which should be able to apply sanctions for the enforcement of its rulings. The government was also to retain its delaying powers so as to allow cases to be put to the Board. Price control of a loose kind should continue in order to prevent the emergence of excessive profit margins and the wage drift that might accompany it.

A new long-term policy was badly needed as soon as possible to deal with the accumulation of anomalies and new claims at the end of June. The report wanted pressure to be brought for two year agreements from July onwards with a 4 per cent increase as the norm for 1966–8 (i.e. 2 per cent per annum). This would then gradually increase to 4 per cent per annum. As a long-term target – and the report started from a consideration of objectives for the early 1970s – it contemplated a rise in average earnings of $5\frac{1}{2}$ per cent, an annual increase in prices of about 2 per cent and an announced norm for wage increases of 4 per cent (with a smaller increase where earnings were supplemented to a substantial extent by drift).

These proposals 'for a truly tripartite system' were built on sand. There was not much chance that the TUC would accept an indefinite intrusion by the government into wage-bargaining, backed by statutory powers and with fixed norms, when it had long been their view that any wage policy agreed between the government and the unions would decay rapidly after six months or at the outside after a year. Yet the government, having enjoyed an almost unprecedented backing from public opinion over the freeze, could hardly abandon the struggle to contain wage increases when failure to do so would eat into competitive power and ultimately destroy the parity. The prolongation of statutory powers might antagonise the unions and the trade associations. But without them how was it possible to hope for a decisive break with the past in inflationary settlements? Would it not be possible, as DEA suggested, to extend the period of severe restraint in one form or another for a further year on the basis of broad principles accepted by the TUC and the CBI?

The government would retain *some* statutory powers in July enabling it to delay settlements and give time for public opinion to be mobilised. But settlements once arrived at were unlikely to be altered merely in response to a recommendation by the NBPI unless it possessed compulsory powers. Indeed, short of introducing a system of general compulsory arbitration, with legal penalties for failure to implement arbitral awards, there seemed little alternative in the long run to creating institutions capable of giving public opinion a lead and providing a rallying point for opposition to inflationary settlements. If so, it was unlikely that agreements reached at plant level would be much influenced; and the idea of government representation in plant bargaining seemed completely unrealistic.

A final problem was how to move from what was virtually a zero norm to some new norm. Should it, as in the past, correspond to the rate of growth of productivity and hence to stability of the price level? – in which case, at 3 per cent or a little less, it was likely to be dismissed as derisory. Or should a low norm be announced for the two-year period 1966–8, embracing the standstill and the period of severe restraint?

The Kahn–Berrill proposals had little influence on the policy eventually adopted. There was to be no norm and a return to voluntary arrangements. These were to be more flexible and correspondingly less effective in limiting the rise of wages and prices. In a White Paper, *Prices and Incomes Policy after 30th June 1967* (Cmnd 3235) guidelines were provided and the NBPI was given fresh marching orders. In fixing prices, every effort should be made to absorb or reduce costs and wherever possible prices should be reduced. Increases in pay would have to be justified against strict criteria such as an improvement in productivity or an improvement in the relative position of low paid workers (both rather doubtful tests since productivity increases may have little to do with the exertions of workers and wage differentials have a way of re-asserting themselves). There should be a minimum interval of twelve months between successive wage increases.

All these conditions, however, were part of what was now again a voluntary policy. The only powers taken by the government under the 1966 Act were to require compulsory notification of price and pay increases and to impose a standstill for three months (with a possible extension to six months) on such of those increases as were referred to the NBPI unless the Board was able to report earlier. Both the CBI and the TUC undertook to co-operate in the development of the policy over the next twelve months.

THE EUROPEAN ECONOMIC COMMUNITY

Discussion had been proceeding for some time of a fresh bid to join the European Economic Community. The Prime Minister and Foreign Secretary had made approaches to governments on the continent to take the temperature and seemed set on making a renewed attempt. It was unlikely to be successful. When the Prime Minister saw General de Gaulle towards the end of 1966 the General was not encouraging. 'Il parait difficile si non impossible', he remarked in a phrase not recorded in the official record.

Shortly afterwards William Armstrong told me of a conversation with Schweitzer, the Managing Director of the IMF, who had recently met Débré, the French Prime Minister, for the first time and come away very depressed. Débré seemed convinced that there was a US imperialist plot which only the French had spotted and that it was France's duty to protect others from falling victims to it. Britain as a close associate of the US was presumably regarded as party to the plot and seen as a kind of Trojan horse. Schweitzer was satisfied after his conversation that Britain would not be allowed to join the Community.

The French were bound to raise other difficulties. As part of their campaign for European independence of America, they denounced reserve currencies and regarded America's ability to foist dollars on other countries as the source of European inflation (long before prices threatened to rise faster in America than in Europe). They attached similar importance to sterling balances and made light of the difficulty of running them down. Pompidou, according to William Armstrong, had discussed little else. Couve de Murville saw sterling as a currency fundamentally different from other currencies. Britain would remain conscious of her obligations to sterling creditors if allowed to join the EEC: these obligations would influence her policies and might have to be shared by her partners in the Community. But if the question was one of debt obligations there was nothing peculiar about Britain except that the obligations were short term. If because sterling was an international currency other countries had extended credit to Britain, Britain might yet have to extend credit to her European neighbours if Basle Arrangements went into reverse.

Few suggestions were ever made by our continental neighbours as to what should be done about sterling. The only one I can recall was by de la Martinière, the French commercial attaché, who suggested that British payments into the Common Agricultural Fund should go to the repayment of sterling liabilities – not a proposal likely to commend itself to General de Gaulle although it might help to reconcile us to higher food prices. William Armstrong thought that we might pursue the idea of a common European currency; but it was difficult to work up much enthusiasm for this, given French views on international finance.

The United States had from the beginning been an enthusiastic supporter of British membership of the Community. At a Ditchley Conference in January the American participants (including Robert Kennedy) were uniformly in favour of British entry although their enthusiasm diminished as the day wore on. They were full of goodwill but lacking in sustained argument, while the British were full of reservations, only the participants from business coming out hot and strong. Earlier, John Stevens had told me that the attitude of the American administration was changing. The Treasury and the Federal Reserve Board had obvious reservations and the departure of George Ball left the State Department more open to persuasion.

An alternative much in vogue and canvassed at Ditchley was an association, not with Europe but with North America in a North American Free Trade Area (NAFTA). This had the support of Professor Harry Johnson and others but was never taken very seriously by the government. Tommy Balogh, exceptionally, showed some interest because he thought it necessary to keep options open in Washington and distrusted the Ambassador as 'too European' to see the difficulties of joining the EEC. But as I told John Stevens, our Minister in Washington, to whom Tommy expounded his views, he merely thought it useful to keep the idea alive and was not an active supporter of NAFTA. Lots of people in DEA and the Treasury, I explained, were being kept busy doing exercises for Tommy without much conviction.

I was warned at Ditchley by Senator Tydings that while it might be possible to sell a political association to Congress it would not be possible to sell an economic one. Our Ambassador reported from Washington that several high-placed Americans had gone out of their way to warn him that the NAFTA proposal would not lead anywhere. No Minister ever expressed support. The British view at Ditchley was that if the United Kingdom joined such an association it would be dominated and ultimately absorbed by the United States.

Not that British membership of EEC was seen as free from major problems. There was some disquiet at the prospect of becoming dependent on joint European defence. There was no knowing in advance on what terms we would be admitted or what kind of Community would emerge later. It was also true, as I noted, that 'we don't know what we're in for if we're out; and we don't know what we should be out for if we were in'.

From the European point of view there were problems too. The entry of the undisciplined British would disturb the tight-knit Community of Six and change the whole character of the EEC. Other countries would follow and the voting pattern would be altered. The fundamental issue was about the kind of Community to be estblished: all the rest was subsidiary and the various arguments a pretext. There was much talk of the political content of the Community; but its political content for many people did not go much beyond a half-concealed anti-Americanism.

For the Treasury the immediate question was: what costs and benefits would membership entail. The benefits were largely intangible and incapable of quantitative assessment but the costs could be approximated and quantified. Given the weak position of the balance of payments it was particularly important to form a view of the additional external burdens that might have to be shouldered. Whatever the long-term political benefits or even the more advantageous division of labour that might eventually result, there was clearly an immediate danger of being forced to devalue.

It was not a question openly discussed at that stage. John Stevens told me of a lunch party at the British Embassy to discuss British entry into the EEC to which the Ambassador invited Eugene and Walt Rostow, Francis Bator and other high officials. When John mentioned that there might be some 'financial difficulties', everybody looked at him enquiringly and he went on: 'for example, what about devaluation?'. This produced a stunned silence. Bator expressed surprise that John should even mention devaluation and asked him to come to the White House for further discussion. But, as John replied, no realistic assessment could leave out the possibility even although the official line remained unchanged. Not that the possibility had failed to occur to Bator, who was in fact occupying himself in secret with a scheme for a US demonetisation of gold whenever the pound was devalued. This too, since the President was unaware of it, did not supersede the official line. But on both sides of the Atlantic a possible suspension of US gold dealings was already under discussion by the beginning of February 1967. Simultaneously the European Commission was moving towards monetary union and, according to Robert Marjolin, it believed that in another eighteen months devaluation would be virtually impossible for any member of the Community.

At the beginning of April the Cabinet asked for a study of the effects of entry to the Community and a report on the impact on the balance of payments that was to be expected. I circulated a draft memorandum which underwent many revisions before a very different version was issued as a White Paper.

THE 1967 BUDGET

At the beginning of the year it was difficult to know how things stood. The import surcharge had only just been removed in November and it would take some time for the full effects to show themselves. In February, when I had to prepare my usual Budget submission, the latest export figures were far above the level we could hope to see sustained. For the previous three months the increase averaged 10 per cent above the level a year previously. Unemployment was flat; and the Chancellor, when he came to talk to the assembled Economic Section on 9 February, asked us to plan for a *fall* in unemployment. At Christmas I had even thought that if we could count on holding unemployment at a steady 2 per cent we should probably be able to pay our way internationally up to and after 1970 unless there were a sudden change in markets abroad. The Section view was that we needed a bigger margin of unused capacity to stop us constantly hitting the ceiling but that if Ministers insisted on letting up it was better to go a little way at an early stage rather than overdo it under pressure later.

The main problem in the Budget was not unemployment but public expenditure. This had already risen by one-sixth in real terms between 1963–4 and 1966–7 and in the single year 1967–8 it increased by a further 12.8 per cent. In four years the proportion of GDP taken by public expenditure expanded by 6 per cent. The increase in public investment was even more startling. It, too, had risen strongly in the first three years of Labour government but the increase in 1967 was beyond all bounds. The increase in government (including local government) investment was 14.9 per cent in the calendar year while investment by public corporations rose by 13.7 per cent. The result was a large increase of £900 million in the borrowing requirement of the public sector.

One effect of this spending spree was a corresponding surplus in the private sector. Industrial and commercial companies were liquid to a degree that created alarm even before the year began. A financial deficit of £219 million in the first nine months of 1966 in this sector gave way to a surplus of £135 million in the first nine months of 1967. Trading profits during the year benefited from the beginning of repayments of Selective Employment Tax and from the disbursement in the middle quarters of the year of nearly £100 million in investment grants. Companies also borrowed more from the banks. But in spite of the additional liquidity the economy remained comparatively depressed.

The full extent of the impending increase in public expenditure was not apparent until the Vote on the Account on 16 February which created some alarm in the City by heralding an increase of £660 million in government expenditure in 1967–8. The Budget did not, however, appear to show greater increases in public spending and investment than in the previous year. Indeed, in the *Financial Statement* the increase expected in public investment in 1967–8 above the outturn in 1966–7 was put at $8\frac{1}{2}$ per cent (in real terms) whereas the increase in the previous year had proved to be a little over 10 per cent. But in 1967–8 it turned out to be not $8\frac{1}{2}$ per cent but 12.8 per cent. So while I spent January and February arguing that no acceleration in public investment was in the wind, a very perceptible acceleration did occur and the implied slowing down conveyed by the *Financial Statement* was entirely without substance. I was also mistaken in assuming some fall in private investment, which continued to expand gently in spite of the check to economic activity.

Our February forecast in advance of the Budget showed an expansion in output and consumer spending at $2\frac{1}{2}$ per cent per annum between the second halves of 1966 and 1967, with a continuation at the same rate in the first half of 1968. The 'basic' balance of payments (on current and long-term capital account) was expected to be no more than £75 million in 1967 (the same level as in 1966) compared with a forecast of £175 million by the National Institute. The increase in hourly earnings was likely to be about 5 per cent. Unemployment would rise gently throughout the year.

In the Budget Committee and afterwards the running was made by Nicky Kaldor. In January he had argued that Ministers ought to be warned that they might have to raise taxes in the Budget. He expected a renewal of pressure as stockbuilding accelerated and public expenditure rose steeply. In February he was obsessed with the prospective torrent of liquidity flowing from the Budget deficit and wanted a 5 per cent increase in corporation tax to soak up cash, *not* to cut demand. If demand did fall, exports would benefit since in Nicky's view (and Tommy's too) it was domestic demand that was the main constraint on their growth. He kept citing papers none of us had seen and raising issues intended for discussion at another meeting. He was also in process of developing what became the 'New Cambridge' view that the balance of payments deficit was the mirror image of the Budget deficit, so that if we reduced the Budget deficit we could count on a parallel improvement in the balance of payments. The sustainable Budget deficit, he argued, was £700 million, so we must cut the prospective deficit of £1400 million in half. This we could do by raising taxes in

1967 by at least £300 million and repeating the increase in 1968. The increased taxation could be provided by raising corporation tax by 5 per cent in the Budget and SET in October.

All this was produced with passionate conviction and with virtually no reference to his former recipe of devaluation. It was hard to judge whether he now thought that manipulation of the Budget would do all that devaluation was to have done in his previous scheme of things or whether he was still relying on devaluation to bring back into employment the resources released by higher taxation. There seemed to be four different strands in his argument:

(a) the increase in liquidity was itself dangerous and should be reduced;
(b) there was a double risk to the pound because we might not achieve a surplus in the balance of payments and because foreign confidence might evaporate;
(c) the budget deficit could lead to an inflation of prices and profits followed by an inflation of costs;
(d) we ought to make sure that there was enough slack to exploit an increase in export opportunities occurring spontaneously after devaluation.

At a later discussion it became clear that Nicky rejected our forecast of a rise in unemployment. He had bet Wynne Godley £1 for every 10,000 by which unemployment diverged in January 1968 from the total in January 1967. Our forecast rested on unsafe foundations, he said. The only falling elements were business investment – a small element in the total – and stocks which could turn round fast if public expenditure did what he expected it to do. As for exports, he maintained that it was inconceivable that we had been non-competitive all through the past sixteen years. It was the lax approach to fiscal policy that had undermined our competitive position.

Who would have thought two years ago, I asked myself, that I should have to argue against Nicky over a proposed £300 million addition to the tax burden; or over the view that a reduction in home demand would help to put the balance of payments straight? Nicky, for his part, had discovered to his surprise that the Treasury was a hotbed of Keynesians. I told him that he seemed to have reached the point I was at in 1961 when I entered the Treasury and that if he stayed longer he would become a pillar of orthodoxy and 'a good Treasury man'. I shared his emphasis on the importance of economies of scale (but not just in manufacturing), his attitude to deflation, his scepticism of fixed estimates of productive potential. What I did not share was his conviction that changes in taxation would work wonders or even improve the sense of equity. I doubted whether the changes that had been made in the tax system with his support had contributed much to an improvement in economic performance.

Nicky's ideas were challenged by Wynne Godley who reduced Nicky to silence more effectively than I ever saw it done by pointing out that we were not in 1963 as Nicky seemed to suppose but in 1962. Wynne in 1967 had not yet joined the New Cambridge school and challenged the idea of a sustainable deficit. Surely if the building of council houses took the place of private house-building, the 'normal' size of the Budget deficit would change; other switches between one sector and the other would equally impinge on the arithmetic of the Budget without affecting the balance of payments.

My own line was clear. I had no expectation, after hearing the Chancellor broadcast, that he could be persuaded to raise taxation. Any fiscal tightening would have to take the form of a cut in expenditure. Justification for a cut could be found, as Denis Rickett maintained, in that we were at the limit of risk, without reference to liquidity. I had, however, argued for a neutral budget and in this had the support of William Armstrong and Robert Neild. There would, of course, be excess liquidity if we chose to increase public spending in the face of a slump in private investment. But the way to deal with the excess was by keeping money tight, ensuring that interest rates were on the high side of expectations and using Tax Reserve Certificates to mop up some of the liquidity (I wanted three-year certificates at a good rate just as William Armstrong was being pressed to seek a reduction in the rate). If Ministers were induced to raise taxes in the Budget, they might switch too violently towards reflation later in the year.

I was at pains to emphasise that we could not guarantee that there would be no sterling crisis in 1967. On the other hand, there was also quite a risk of appreciably higher unemployment than we were predicting; and we should do nothing to create still more unemployment if we saw the prospect before us of eventual external balance.

A week or two later I told William Armstrong that although I had not changed my view that the Budget should be neutral, I saw force in the arguments for higher taxes, especially if we meant to be taken seriously in Europe. Moreover, I should not want to be told in July that hire-purchase restrictions could not be relaxed because taxes had not been increased in April. Perhaps we could hedge by keeping in mind a possible increase in SET in the autumn. William pointed out that such a move would have to wait until the Finance Bill was passed into law and that it would greatly complicate the new regional proposal if adopted. I let the matter drop and by the middle of March was firmly against a tax increase even if it was intended as a prelude to relaxation of hire purchase restrictions.

THE REGIONAL PROBLEM

The new regional proposal was for a subsidy to the Development Areas in order to reduce unemployment there and bring it nearer to the level in the rest of the country. The proposal did not, however, rest on any clear analysis of the likely effects of the subsidy and tended to equate an increase in employment in the Development Areas with a reduction by at least half as much in unemployment. This seemed to me much too optimistic. The differences in unemployment rates had remained remarkably resistant to all the changes since the war, including the efforts to force industry into underemployed regions and Maudling's introduction of 'free depreciation' in the 1963 Budget.

The regional problem was fundamentally one of differences in the pressure of demand, expressing itself in higher unemployment, lower earnings and, above all, outflows of migrants from the areas of less pressure. It was highly desirable to secure a more even pressure of demand throughout the country so that expansion was not brought to a halt by overheating in some regions while unemployment remained excessive in others. But it was not easy to see how such a result could be secured without heavy expenditure much of which would go to checking the transfer of labour to more favourable locations.

What was now proposed was that the rate of Selective Employment Tax should be lowered in the Development Areas so as to attract additional employment. SET had not proved to be a popular tax and the complications of operating different rates in different areas were bound to be formidable. Nicky Kaldor, the father of SET, was in favour of the proposal and was supported by Robert Neild. I opposed it on the grounds that extra jobs would cut out-migration rather than unemployment and cited other difficulties. The administrators were mixed but unenthusiastic in their reactions. The scheme would have required support from both sides of industry (which seemed unlikely to be forthcoming) and would have required a guaranteed life of several years if it was to affect investment, as was clearly necessary for it to work. There was also a feeling that if you change the calculus of business action too often, you end by getting very little out of a further change.

The Chancellor was well disposed to the scheme but less so when he was told that it would leave out one of the three big Welsh steelworks and include the other two. He made no commitment to include it in the Budget and spoke of consulting outside opinion, which by itself might make it difficult to proceed. Although the other Treasury ministers were in favour – the Chief Secretary very much so – the scheme did not appear in the Budget. A White Paper was issued early in June and the Regional Employment Premium became operative at the beginning of September. It was confined to the Development Areas and was to continue for at least seven years in the form of an additional refund of SET: there would be an extra 30s. a week for men, 15s. for women and boys and 9s. 6d. for girls.

When we saw Treasury ministers to discuss the Budget proposals, the discussion got off to rather a bad start because of too much emphasis on disagreements in diagnosis between Nicky and us. The Chief Secretary and Financial Secretary were obviously foxed by the figures. Diamond (Chief Secretary) argued straight from the Exchequer deficit and the figures of capital investment without regard to the elements we had emphasised. He backed the idea of a rise in corporation tax by $2\frac{1}{2}$ per cent, reinforced by an increase in SET *and* a cut in expenditure. McDermot (Financial Secretary) saw the difficulty of increasing SET when the new regional scheme was in prospect but was impressed by the case for higher taxes. The Chancellor stuck to his objective for unemployment but agreed rather inconsistently that we should consider what form higher taxes might take.

It would have been hard for the Chancellor to bring in a tough budget against the background of consistent good news. Even the trade returns were remarkably good. In the first quarter, the Bank of England took in no less than £500 million from the exchange market. The renewal of the Basle Arrangements, the re-establishment of the US swap facility, the fourth quarter balance of payments surplus had all been announced in the first half of March. On the other hand, the seasonally adjusted figures continued to show a clear upward trend in unemployment of which the public was largely unaware.

REFLATION

At the beginning of April the external position looked deceptively favourable. In each of the first three months the Bank took in over

£100 million from the market and even market forwards had begun to fall at about £100 million a month. But there were still £700–800 million in forwards outstanding and the debts to the IMF and other monetary authorities stood at about £1345 million. Imports had shot up after the removal of the surcharge and it was only unusually favourable export figures that had brought the current account into surplus. There was no reason to think that the United Kingdom had suddenly become more competitive. I warned the Chancellor at the beginning of May that he had had all the good news.

The Bank had pressed at the beginning of March for a cut of $\frac{1}{2}$ per cent in bank rate and although there were objections to acting so close to the Budget and giving the wrong colour to it, the Bank was allowed to go ahead. It was at least a more sensible form of reflation than tax reductions and would be consistent with the easing in American monetary policy. The rate was cut to 6 per cent on 16 March and in April the lending ceilings on the clearing banks were removed. A further cut of $\frac{1}{2}$ per cent in bank rate followed on 4 May. American rates had fallen over the winter even more than the British and so were further below London rates than in the previous autumn. By July 1967, however, US rates had risen steeply and from July onwards the margin in favour of London was rarely much above 1 per cent.

In May the economic situation began to change dramatically. Both the gilt-edged market and the exchange market weakened. The car industry was almost demoralised and pressing for a cut in purchase tax to 15 per cent. The press was discussing devaluation openly and some papers were pressing strongly for it.

The Chancellor was jumpy: at least one journalist had called for his resignation. By July he was in a state of acute depression, conscious that his strategy had crumbled. He had concluded, however, that if it was finally clear that the rate must be changed, it should be delayed until the spring 'when unemployment will be 700,000'. He would be more disposed to favour a change if he could detect any willingness to take the necessary accompanying measures. Yet at the same time he was meditating reflationary measures: a relaxation of hire-purchase restrictions on cars (which had already been considered and rejected in May); a limited use of the regulator; perhaps post-war credits. The possibility that unemployment might reach 700,000 he regarded with horror and had quite forgotten that even in February we were forecasting a level of 680,000 – a level that was well above what we now thought likely. On the other hand, imports were unexpectedly high and pointed to a deficit, not the surplus we hoped for.

Ministers continued to brood on reflation and asked us at the beginning of August for a *factual* paper for a meeting of the Strategic Economic Policy (SEP) Committee to discuss what should be done. The Prime Minister was persuaded by William Armstrong to refrain from proposing a reduction in purchase tax on cars and showed little interest in the reduction on textiles that the President of the Board of Trade was proposing. He was more attracted to a relaxation of hire-purchase terms for both cars and household durable goods. There seemed little doubt that Ministers would do *something* – probably all that the Prime Minister suggested. Meanwhile the Chancellor was reviving the idea of import deposits and was thought to have the support of the Governor.

When I talked to the Governor early in August, he was as strongly opposed as the Treasury to *any* immediate reflation. The Bank was also concerned at the prospect of a large budget deficit. The pound would be in danger until after the IMF conference in Rio de Janeiro and through October. By November the first hints of the size of the 1968 Budget deficit would add to the despondency of the market.

Just before I went on leave in mid-August, the President of the Board of Trade and the Prime Minister both put in papers proposing more reflation. The President, citing the July trade figures in justification, wanted to cut purchase tax on textiles and haberdashery over the seven months from 1 September to 1 April from 11 to 5 per cent (releasing an additional £100 million a year in consumer spending). The Prime Minister rubbished our forecasts as poor and gloomy, predicted an early moderation in imports as 'the fall in commodity prices' reduced their value, and claimed rhetorically that the trade balance had improved between June and July at the rate of £600 million a year. A word with Jack Stafford at the Board of Trade showed that, out of an erratic drop in imports in July of £23 million, over £10 million related to diamonds and could be disregarded. As was soon to be apparent, our balance of payments forecasts were not nearly gloomy enough, import prices *rose* in the third quarter and the trend in imports, whether by value or volume, was about to show a disconcerting tilt upwards.

Ministers were not deterred. On 29 August, against Treasury advice, they relaxed the hire-purchase restrictions more or less across the board. As a result, half of the increase in consumer spending between the first half of 1967 and the second half was on cars, motorcycles and durable household goods. In a quarter when foreign exchange losses were at a rate not far short of the highest in the previous three years, the government was nonchalantly waving on the speculators.

10 The Countdown to Devaluation

From the beginning of May, pressure began to build up again on the exchanges and continued almost without intermission until the eventual devaluation in November.

The starting-point was a change of sentiment after the announcement by the Prime Minister on 2 May that the United Kingdom would apply formally to join the Common Market. Such an application had been in the air since November 1966, when the intention to engage in renewed discussions with the EEC was made public. Although no official estimates of the balance of payments cost of joining the Community had been issued, it was known that it was likely to be substantial, and there was also a natural suspicion that, in view of this, Britain's entry might be made the occasion for a devaluation of the pound. Ironically enough, devaluation preceded by a week or so, not Britain's entry to the Common Market, but General de Gaulle's second veto.

Other factors were tending simultaneously to add to the pressure. Devaluation was increasingly the subject of public discussion, frequently in terms implying that only someone very stupid could fail to see its advantages. Out of forty-five backbench speakers in the Budget debate, ten had either advocated or contemplated devaluation, The successive reductions in bank rate, of which the last came on 4 May, had removed any interest advantage from holding sterling. In the course of the month the gilt-edged market had begun to weaken and the Bank of England had become a net buyer, so adding to market liquidity. Then at the beginning of June came the six-day Arab–Israeli War, the oil embargo and (on 7 June) the closure of the Suez Canal. These events could not fail to have a serious effect both on the balance of payments and on confidence in sterling.

In spite of these developments, the government took no steps to counteract the pressure on sterling and instead embarked on a series of reflationary measures over the summer months, starting with relaxations of the hire-purchase restrictions on cars on 7 June (i.e. on the day when the Suez Canal was closed) and concluding with more extensive hire-purchase relaxations at the end of August. These measures and the simultaneous expansion in public spending had their effect on domestic demand. Retail sales in the second half of the year were 3 per cent by volume above sales in the first half, and real consumer spending over the same period rose by 2.6 per cent (seasonally adjusted in both cases). Unemployment (seasonally adjusted) stopped rising after August and vacancies, which had proved a more reliable guide to the pressure of demand, were on the increase from September onwards.

As the crisis approached, the government was committed to a policy of reflation and was more than making good the drag exercised by falling exports. The drain on reserves, beginning in May, continued throughout the summer months: over £500 million went in the third quarter – almost as much as at the end of 1964.

By mid-September it was clear to me that the government no longer had any option. It would soon be forced either to devalue or to introduce quota restrictions on imports; there could be no doubt which was preferable. My reasoning was simple. It was not possible to do *nothing* for long in face of an estimated deficit in 1967 of £300 million and every expectation of a deficit even in 1968. How would it be possible to justify inaction retrospectively? What action made any sense except devaluation? Quantitative restrictions offered no prospect of restoring equilibrium free of restrictions at the current rate of exchange. We had lost share not only in foreign markets – that was nothing new – but in our home market as well. There was no prospect of levering up exports or displacing imports on a sufficient scale without devaluation. With heavy debts and inadequate reserves that might soon vanish, action was urgent and inaction indefensible.

When I put this to William Armstrong he told me that the Governor had expressed a similar view within the past few weeks. He thought that we might be obliged to devalue before Christmas and that we should be in a position of readiness. The Prime Minister, on the other hand, was quite inflexible about the rate. He was confident that in 1968 Lyndon Johnson would aim to generate a boom in what was an election year and would help sterling over any difficulties even if there were no boom. Speaking to city editors he had given convincing arguments against quantitative restrictions and there seemed no likelihood that he would opt for measures of that kind. As appeared later, the alternative to which he was drawn was a floating rate. At the Labour Party Conference he was able to point to the new downward trend in unemployment and announce an apocalyptic campaign to re-structure each major British industry in turn.

The Chancellor was more realistic about the chances but thought the case not proven and he too intended to wait until the spring. He was still determined to resign if obliged to devalue. However, from mid-September he would be on his travels for several weeks and would not be in the Treasury again until a meeting on SET on 9 October; by which time the September trade figures would be available. I had contemplated putting my views at once to the Chancellor but had now to wait for a month or so. When I talked to my colleagues in the Economic Section they were inclined to counsel delay until a stronger case could be submitted. But discussion went on in the Treasury on the arrangements to be made when the time came.

At Bank Holiday weekend, some important changes were made in Cabinet arrangements. Harold Wilson took personal charge of DEA, with Peter Shore acting as Secretary for Economic Affairs. Fred Lee remained nominally in charge of incomes policy although nobody quite knew where he now came in (according to the wits, DEA was now under a Lee-Shore). With no First Secretary, the Prime Minister and Chancellor shared responsibility for economic policy and had arranged to meet one another every Monday evening. They would act as joint chairmen of NEDC while Peter Shore acted as Deputy Chairman. SEP was to become a regular Cabinet Committee which could be attended by all Ministers involved in the matters under discussion and papers were to be circulated in the normal way. The Chancellor had been offered full responsibility for incomes policy but had declined. He would, however, be chairman of the Prices and Incomes Sub-Committee of SEP. These were changes giving the Treasury a freer hand and, for that matter, making possible a more coherent economic policy.

Changes were also made by the Treasury in the composition of the FU ('forever unmentionable'?) committee laying plans for devaluation. This was a committee going back to 1964 which had continued to meet in spite of a Ministerial ban on all thought of devaluation. It had set about preparing a 'war book' making tentative arrangements as to who should be informed and when, at what point the IMF should be approached and what should be requested, what rate, if any, should be fixed, what measures should accompany devaluation, and so on. Four Bank representatives, including the Governor and Deputy Governor, attended on 21 September. Douglas Allen came from DEA and Michael Posner, the Chancellor's new adviser in place of Robert Neild, was shown the papers and given membership but was unable to attend on this occasion.

ACCOMPANYING MEASURES

What excited most argument was the scale of the accompanying measures required, which we put at £600 million. Douglas Allen thought that our proposals aimed to do too much at once. Kit MacMahon, on the other hand, thought that we could take no chances: the measures must be such as to make the success of the move beyond doubt. William Armstrong reminded us that in the crisis of July 1966 we had suggested a package of deflationary measures adding up to only £400–500 million when the economy was at full stretch. We were now proposing a similar package when there was obvious slack. If Ministers were aware of that, might they not be rather sceptical, especially if it made no difference whether devaluation was to 2.50 or 2.40? As we soon discovered, the Chancellor was indeed concerned at the size of the package we proposed, which grew larger when re-calculated and which he feared might never be given the backing of his Party.

Pressure had increased in early September after the hire-purchase relaxations and an unpopular increase in the price of electricity. The reserves drained away and it looked as if little would soon be left. The Governor shared our concern and intended to seek more support at the monthly meeting of the BIS. He was warned by the Chancellor that he was unlikely to have much success and that the limits of BIS credit arrangements would also soon be reached. The atmosphere in Basle, however, was surprisingly friendly and offers of help came spontaneously from the BIS and the Swiss; indeed, it looked as if yet another international support operation might be mounted. Somehow it fizzled out. Fortunately the pressure in the exchange market died away even although the August trade figures were disappointing.

Unemployment had ceased to rise in September and was likely to fall quite heavily in October. Meanwhile a series of dock strikes had begun, closing Liverpool and Manchester on 18 September and hitting Hull and London as well. The London dockers returned to work a week later but came out again on 4 October, staying out until 27 November after the others had resumed work. These strikes helped to inflate the deficit in the trade balance, which deteriorated from an average per month of £81 million (after adjustment) in the third quarter to a deficit of £159 million in September, £331 million in October and £469 million in November.

Apart from borrowing £37$\frac{1}{2}$ million from three leading Swiss banks on 10 October and negotiating a $250 million credit through the BIS in November to refinance IMF debts, the only action taken by the government was to raise bank rate – a late and inadequate response. The market was first forced into the Bank and then the rate was raised to 6 per cent on 19 October. On 9 November the rate went up by another $\frac{1}{2}$ per cent. By that time it was no more than a pill to cure an earthquake.

LAST TALKS

When the September trade figures were published, my colleagues in the Economic Section agreed that the game was up. But what could we do? If we went to the Chancellor to tell him that there was no option but to devalue we should be inviting him to resign. It was not the Chancellor, however, who had the last word. We had a Prime Minister who had no need to argue things out with anyone – a very dangerous situation on an issue with a large technical component. We did not know how he formed his views on economic policy except that on this matter he did not see eye to eye with any of his advisers at the official level and did not necessarily agree even with his Chancellor, the one Minister with whom he did discuss such matters.

When I put the predicament to William Armstrong, he thought that it rested with the Governor whose tactics were to exhaust all possible lines of assistance before throwing in his hand. He himself had found the Chancellor unwilling to listen although he had put to him the charge of irresponsibility of which I thought him guilty.

Towards the end of October, when there was barely enough in the till for October settlements I drafted a paper on the forecasts setting out the alternatives. At that point a cable from Henry Fowler, the US Secretary of the Treasury, suggested a fresh effort to raise funds from European central banks and in other ways, and expressed the view that our difficulties were temporary and a reflection of the depressed state of world trade. The American government was increasingly anxious that we should not devalue, fearing that if we did so it would expose the dollar to similar pressure. Since Ministers were likely to interpret Fowler's message as something of a blank cheque, I withheld my paper but was encouraged by William Armstrong to put forward to the Chancellor my own professional opinion when I thought it appropriate to do so.

Accordingly I wrote a short memo on 30 October and at William's suggestion sent it under cover of a personal note to the Chancellor on

2 November. There had already been a meeting on 25 October between the Prime Minister, the Chancellor, the Governor and Sir William Armstrong, with Sir Burke Trend, the Cabinet Secretary, in attendance, to discuss the situation. They had covered much of the ground, even to some consideration of accompanying measures. The Chancellor had shown increasing disquiet at the trend of the discussion and had come down strongly in favour of deferring a final decision and waiting until the spring when the trends might again be favourable. The Prime Minister had accepted the Chancellor's line so that, as I had feared, Ministers were proposing to do nothing. But it was impossible to leave things there since we simply did not have the reserves to last out and would have to engage in further borrowing.

When I saw him alone on 3 November I reminded the Chancellor of what we had already borrowed – over £1500 million – the enormous total for market forwards – over £1100 million – and the danger that our lines of credit would run out before the end of the month. As time went on and the bad news accumulated, it would be difficult to explain how we expected to emerge in balance. When he asked if I thought it irresponsible of him not to devalue, I had to say that I did. He for his part thought that it would be wrong to devalue when the future was so obscure and everything at its worst.

On the day of our conversation, the exchange losses (mainly forward contracts) reached over £100 million and in the following week the drain continued. Over a fortnight was to elapse before devaluation and in that time forward contracts appear to have doubled and were well in excess of borrowings. The losses in November, spot and forward, up to devaluation totalled £1000 million, nearly all in forward contracts since there was very little 'spot' in hand. They may have seemed a convenient way of holding back pressure on the exchanges compared with financing a constant drain of gold and dollars, but after devaluation the losses on forward contracts totalled £356 million.

The exchange losses reflected a market expectation that devaluation was imminent. This was based mainly on the sudden deterioration in the balance of payments following a large accumulation of external debt. Rumours after a report from the European Commission in Brussels and a mischievous speech by Couve de Murville intensified the drain.[1]

The Chancellor appears to have been more influenced by our talk than I had gathered.[2] Next day he called on the Prime Minister and expressed his doubts about the parity. For the first time the Prime Minister shared his doubts and was prepared to agree to devaluation if the situation worsened and there was no acceptable alternative. His preference at that stage, however, was that the pound should be allowed to float, and it was only in the course of the next week that he accepted with regret that this would not be possible.[3] He was opposed to what he called 'a major lurch into deflation', and later refused to agree to an increase in the standard rate of income tax.

The Prime Minister also expressed concern that too many other countries might follow the United Kingdom in devaluing their currencies. The main doubts related to Australia (since her example was thought likely to be followed by Malaysia, Singapore, Hong Kong and Japan) and to the EEC (the attitude of the French to a change in the parity of the franc being as obscure as their attitude to a change in the parity of sterling was crystal clear). The Chancellor was assured by Van Lennep, Chairman of the (official) Monetary Committee of the Six, whom he had asked to see him on 8 November, that he would do all in his power to ensure that the members of the Community would not devalue.

On the morning of the 8th there was a meeting of the inner circle of Ministers dealing with economic policy (SEP), at which the issue of devaluation was fully discussed, and the intention of introducing import quotas, which the meeting had been called to discuss, was set aside.[4] That evening the Chancellor, who had been given depressing advice about the chances of holding the rate, called again on the Prime Minister, and by the time he left they seem to have been in agreement that devaluation was 'virtually certain'.[5] It was not until the morning of the 13th, however, that they finally decided, subject to the views of the Cabinet, to go ahead with devaluation plans.

The Chancellor had undoubtedly changed round on 8 November but there was room for doubt whether the Prime Minister had. As late as 12 November he claims to have seen an international package emerging which he, the Chancellor and the Foreign Secretary 'were prepared to go along with', provided the conditions attached were acceptable and it was sufficiently 'solid and lasting' to see sterling through to the New Year.[6]

PARALLEL NEGOTIATIONS

Running parallel with the efforts to come to a decision on devaluation were negotiations based on an entirely different strategy: the organisation of fresh international support for sterling. The negotiations took place in Washington, Basle and various continental countries and were mainly conducted by the Governor or by Sir Denis Rickett. The US Treasury was wholehearted in its attempts to put together a massive package to avert devaluation and President Johnson, when the Treasury began to think the hunt was up, exhorted them to 'go at them' at OECD and drum up support. He would 'put the stack of US resources' right behind us.

The sequence of events was that the Governor first tried to get agreement in Europe to the holding of guaranteed sterling but failed. He then approached the IMF for a standby of $3 billion in agreement with the US Treasury. Schweitzer, although at first encouraging, soon realized that it would tie up too much of the Fund's resources and make it necessary to draw heavily on the General Arrangements to Borrow (GAB). He concluded that it would be better if the UK devalued. Had he agreed to the standby, he would have attached a long string of conditions set out in 'a nice letter'. These the Chancellor was not prepared to accept. Fowler, who conducted the negotiations on the American side, then came forward with a proposal for a $3 billion package which would have included a drawing by the UK of $1.4 billion from the IMF (the remainder of its quota), a further $1 billion from the US, Germany and Italy combined, and $600 million from sources unspecified. When he could find no takers for the European contribution, the idea of a smaller package of $2 billion was canvassed in Basle at the BIS. It suited the United Kingdom to continue negotiations, if only as a smoke-screen, after the Prime Minister and Chancellor had come to regard devaluation as 'virtually certain'. But it proved highly embarrassing when rumours of what was afoot began to appear in the press on 15 November. When asked in the House of Commons next day to make a statement 'on the $1000 million loan being negotiated with foreign banks' the Chancellor neither arranged for the question to be withdrawn nor provided an adequate answer and was taken to imply that the rumours were unfounded. This was assumed to point to the alternative of devaluation and precipitated an unprecedented run on sterling.

The discussions in Basle earlier in the month revealed the attitude of continental countries towards devaluation of the pound. The Dutch and Belgians thought that we should devalue. Italy, Switzerland and, after much havering, Germany, thought not. The French Governor (Brunet) would give no opinion, not even his own, but said that if we devalued by no more than 10 per cent, the French would not move. Other members of the Community, especially Germany, were determined to prevent a French move whatever the size of the devaluation.

It was one of the ironies of the final week, beginning on the 13th, that we were instructed to exclude from the discussions Balogh and Kaldor, who were left in ignorance of the decisions taken.

THE SIZE OF THE PACKAGE

The main issues to be decided – and there was not much time – were the size and composition of the package, guarantees and fixed versus floating. What excited most argument was the size of the package of accompanying measures. Wynne Godley had worked out what curtailment of demand was required in order to release enough resources to improve the balance of payments by £500 million. Devaluation would move the terms of trade against the United Kingdom to an extent which he judged would make it necessary to release an extra £175 million in resources; and a further £75 million would be required to meet the need for more fixed investment as the pattern of demand changed with devaluation. That suggested a total of £750 million as a resource requirement. There would also be a need to prevent the emergence of excess demand in 1969 as the economy developed more momentum and this would require a further reduction in demand of at least £100 million. On the other hand, higher import prices could cut demand more or less automatically by £350 million. These figures were all at factor cost (i.e. net of taxes and subsidies) and would be rather higher, by about £100 million, if measured at market prices. This made the final requirement a reduction in demand of £600 million. Ministers should be warned that if they made no reductions and left output to respond freely, it would take an extra £1200 million in output to yield the planned improvement of £500 million in the balance of payments; and, given the small margin of resources available to be absorbed into employment, it was most unlikely that anything but inflation would result. While it would take time to absorb additional resources into the balance of payments it would also take time for cuts in government expenditure to take effect and free the resources required.

When William Armstrong and I saw the Chancellor on 14 November I argued for a package of £600 million, of which £200 million would be needed to deal with overheating in 1968. There could be no assurance, however, of Parliamentary support for measures of the kind required. Ministers had not seen our forecasts or taken in the full weakness of our position. They were insisting that any measures should be discussed in full Cabinet at leisure when devaluation was only a few days away. They wanted no repetition of the July 1966 measures, pushed through at top speed without debate. The Chancellor spoke of the possibility of fifty Labour MPs voting against the government. We had made it clear to him, however, that without adequate measures devaluation would be futile.

When it came to specific measures he was strongly against an increase in income tax on grounds of incentive. The Prime Minister on similar grounds wanted a *cut* of 6d. (2½p) and the Chancellor suggested a cut half as big until we made it clear that we thought he was joking. He made no great difficulty over hire-purchase restrictions or credit restrictions or an 8 per cent bank rate. But most of his tax proposals were ill-considered or trivial – doubling the duty on fuel oil to protect coal-mining; trebling betting duties; raising corporation tax or imposing a tax on dividends. He preferred to assume cuts of £200 million in public expenditure although such cuts had a way of vanishing as one approached them. I stressed the importance of a large initial package rather than a series of measures spread over time but he regarded this as a political judgment which he 'preferred to take himself'. Was a package of £450 million not enough?

The straightforward answer is that it was not. It came to be accepted that the resources that would have to be fed into the balance of payments amounted not to £600 million but to £1000 million and that the immediate need was to reduce demand by a minimum of £500 million. The measures proposed fell well short of this. They consisted too much of expenditure cuts that were quite a long way off and of which experience made us wary. They did not promise the immediate check to demand that was required.

When Ministers met that evening, it was doubtful whether we could count on any measures. Denis Healey rounded on the Chancellor, asking why anyone should trust him or believe his forecasts after all he had dragged the party through. Both Crosland and George Brown were sceptical of the size of the Chancellor's package of £500 million but were assured by their private economic advisers that it was more likely to be insufficient. The Prime Minister next morning attacked the hire-purchase proposals: if he wanted more exports from the motor industry we should talk to it, not impose restrictions.

On the evening of the 15th the Chancellor supplied his colleagues with our two-page summary of the case for a £500 million package but withheld our paper on accompanying measures. Although he had not decided beforehand what precise measures he would ask for, he was given agreement to most of what he proposed and his package was approved by Cabinet on the 16th although the spending departments (except Defence) had no knowledge of what to expect.

This was not, however, the end of the matter. There was a widespread feeling that the package was inadequate. It was not so much the total of £500 million but the items making up the total. They included the £200 million cut in public spending; the withdrawal of £100 million in SET premia outside the Development Areas; another £100 million from the saving of export rebates from 31 March 1968; an increase in corporation tax by $2\frac{1}{2}$ per cent in the Budget; tighter hire-purchase restrictions on motor cars; and a credit squeeze plus higher interest rates. A proposal for a higher fuel-oil tax had been first watered down, then abandoned. The package might strike the uninitiated as amounting to a severe check to the economy; but the impact would be delayed and diluted, and in particular would do little to check consumer spending, which we aimed to curtail in the interest of releasing resources for the improvement of the balance of payments.

The Governor had the courage to express his disappointment when he saw the Chancellor on the evening of the 16th. The Chancellor reacted indignantly and flatly refused to go back to Cabinet, as would indeed have been virtually impossible. We could, he suggested, make further reductions in the next Budget. This was not much comfort to the Governor. He wrote to the Chancellor next day re-asserting the inadequacy of the measures and asking for assurances about the next Budget and 6d. on income tax at once.

It was at the meeting with the Governor that it was settled, after long discussion, that the IMF and the US President would both be informed at 1 p.m. on the 17th. Earlier the Chancellor had had a cable from Fowler virtually insisting that he should go for a standby to save the pound. To this he decided to send no reply.

Next day, 17 November, was an agonising one. First of all, as kept happening throughout the crisis, personal engagements intruded at awkward moments. The Chancellor left for South Wales and the Prime Minister for Liverpool to meet speaking engagements. In their absence the exchanges were rocked by rumour after the Chancellor's answer in the House of Commons the previous day. Exchanges losses were said to be very heavy – so heavy that we suggested immediate action, such as instructing the Americans to stop supporting the pound. The Governor, however, had already rejected the idea as likely to make a return to a fixed rate impossible. Later it turned out that our losses in the United

States on the 17th were only $50 million, perhaps because rumours of a loan revived.

Devaluation of the pound took place next day from $2.80 to $2.40. The Governor set about organising a standby of $3 billion with contributions along the lines of Fowler's pre-devaluation package, beginning with the IMF. A Mission arrived in the Treasury that afternoon, highly critical of the scale of our measures, possibly after a tip-off from the Bank. They wanted us to accept targets for 1968, one of which took the form of sales of government bonds to the non-bank public. In illustration of the difficulty of forecasting such sales, the Bank pointed out that sales of government securities to the market had reached £75 million over the past week and that even the day before (Friday) they were probably net sellers. (A further £250 million was sold in the first half hour on Monday 20 November.) Nevertheless, we were still asked for a ceiling on government borrowing from the banks. The Letter of Intent to the IMF on 23 November (dictated by William Armstrong) promised a limit of £1000 million to the borrowing requirement, and required us to finance it as far as possible from sales to the non-bank public. A target was also set of an improvement of at least £500 million a year in the balance of payments; this was coupled with a target surplus in the second half of 1968 at an annual rate of at least £200 million.

There were also to be fresh consultations with the IMF after the completion of each forecast. William Armstrong was well aware that acceptance of this condition would hasten agreement. He knew also that the IMF attached special importance to the borrowing requirement.

The Chancellor's transfer to the Home Office and Roy Jenkins's transfer to the Treasury occurred while I was defending British policy at OECD. Crosland arrived in Paris to take part in a meeting of Ministers and was clearly under some emotional strain over the change of Chancellor. My interpretation of what he told me was that he had hoped – or even expected – to succeed Callaghan (who had recommended him to the Prime Minister) and was more than disappointed by Jenkins's appointment.

Part IV

11 From Devaluation to the Gold Rush

THE AFTERMATH OF DEVALUATION

1968 was even more palpitating than 1967 had been. If we had thought that devaluation would prove an instant solution to all our problems we should soon have been disillusioned. One crisis succeeded another, forcing us to contemplate extreme measures, and making us despair of eventual success. The exchange losses showed no sign of falling off; instead of repaying our debts we were obliged to borrow still more; the danger of a second devaluation, or even of being obliged to block sterling held abroad and at the same time letting the pound float, hung over us throughout the year. The crisis might initially seem unconnected with the pound: it could start with a rise in dealings in gold on the London market or with the rumour that the franc was about to be devalued or the mark upvalued. Any aggravation of currency uncertainty tended to rebound on sterling in its weakened condition causing large-scale withdrawals to a safer haven and bringing the exchange reserves near to exhaustion.

In retrospect, the gradual emergence of a large and growing surplus in the balance of payments in 1969 gives a different perspective to events. One can ignore the crises and concentrate instead on the gradual improvement from quarter to quarter in the current account throughout 1968–9, comparing this with estimates of the contribution to an improvement that it would be reasonable to attribute to devaluation. These estimates are substantial: at least £500 million and probably not far from £1000 million. To anyone embroiled in the affair, however, the underlying effect of devaluation is not a single quantity but a development over time that may be overborne one way or the other by the expectations aroused. Exports and imports take time to respond to the stimulus of changed price relationships, the relationships do not remain constant but change over time, the flow of capital and credit reacts incessantly to changing expectations of what is yet to come and the capital account may take precedence over the current account. In singling out from the course of events estimates of what is due to devaluation we are, so to speak, forecasting in reverse; and these 'forecasts', although not as subject to error as true forecasts, since the relevant events are all already in the past, are still no more than rough approximations.[1]

We had an abundance of forecasts before and after devaluation but we had only limited confidence in them. Things changed fast in 1967 and the economy in the second half of the year moved far away from the path along which it seemed to be travelling in the first. This was particularly true of the balance of payments. In February we had expected a small favourable basic balance (i.e. including long term capital movements) of £75 million. By July, with the closing of the Suez canal and early signs of a steeply rising trend in imports, we thought it possible that the balance of payments would show no improvement over 1966 (when the current estimate for the basic balance was a deficit of £175 million). At the end of October, before devaluation, we had reduced our forecast by at least as much as in July and now expected a deficit of around £300 million in 1967 and £200 million in 1968 even if exports in 1968 increased by 5 per cent in volume.

The October forecast should have warned us of increasing pressure on the economy. We were already predicting an increase of $4\frac{1}{2}$ per cent in GDP between the second half of 1967 and the second half of 1968, mainly under the impetus of a continuing surge of fixed investment. We were also predicting a consumer boom. On the other hand, we should have been badly misled if we had counted on holding the increase in the value of imports in 1968 to 3 per cent. If, as we supposed, world trade was about to expand by 10–11 per cent over the year this forecast was much too optimistic: it shows how little we suspected what lay ahead.

It was obviously of the first importance how much of the setback in the last few months of 1967 represented a change in trend and how much could be dismissed as the outcome of exceptional events that would not recur. On top of that, we had to assess the changes in trend that devaluation would bring about and plan the reallocation of resources that would be required if devaluation was to do all we wanted.

Looking back in 1967, we first needed to know what had gone wrong. So far as the domestic economy was concerned, we judged that output had grown rather faster than we expected, except in the final quarter of 1967. We had forecast an expansion at an annual rate of 1 per cent in GDP in the first half of 1967, and 2.5 per cent in the second. Our picture at the end of 1967 was of rather higher percentages – 1.4 and 3.25.

It was not the rise in output that was to blame for the exchange crisis, however, but the collapse of the trade balance and, behind that, the upsurge in investment. It is not only in conditions of full employment that investment has to be balanced by savings. If investment increases, as in 1967 by nearly 9 per cent with no corresponding rise in savings, the strain is inevitably taken by the balance of payments (i.e. by foreign savings). In the public sector where the increase in investment in 1967 reached $11\frac{1}{2}$ per cent, there was a particularly large shortfall in finance of £1400 million, associated with a borrowing requirement of £1860 million – twice as high as in 1966. How this affected the balance of payments may not be instantly apparent. But it would seem that the engineering industries, for example, could only meet domestic requirements by absorbing more imports and cutting down on exports. In other circumstances, higher investment would have been met from an expansion in output with higher savings and less impact on the balance of payments.

THE BALANCE OF PAYMENTS

Whatever the consequences of higher investment, the change in the trade balance was disastrous. By the fourth quarter of 1967 exports had fallen in four successive quarters (seasonally adjusted), imports had risen in three successive half years, and the trade balance was showing a deficit of £343 million where in the last quarter of 1966 there had been a surplus of £100 million. Foreign markets had lost their buoyancy in 1967; unemployment was higher in nearly every industrial country, world industrial production was lower until the final quarter than in the final quarter of 1966; and world trade in manufactures remained flat or falling. The closure of the Suez canal, combined with higher freights and oil prices, helped to limit both exports and imports. While the fall in exports was disappointing, there were some grounds for expecting a cyclical recovery later and our pre-devaluation forecast showed a rise in 1968 of 7 per cent in volume.

It was imports that were to prove the real difficulty in 1968. Before devaluation we thought that imports might be growing at about 5.5 per cent per annum by the second half of 1968. But after devaluation, in the expectation that import prices would rise by about 13 per cent we assumed some check to the demand for imports and put this check at 5 per cent by the middle of 1969. Instead, the volume of imports *rose* by no less than 10 per cent in 1968. This was not only quite unforeseen and the source of many of our difficulties during the year but is very hard to explain even now.

The rate at which the balance of payments improved was central to our whole strategy. The more rapidly it improved, the more pressure there would be on existing resources and the more rapidly slack would disappear in rising output. We should then have to cut out competing demands in one form or another in order to allow exports to go on expanding and to keep the demand for imports under control. We had to aim for a large and early improvement in the balance of payments in order to repay our debts before the competitive advantage conferred by devaluation melted away. We had decided that it would be reasonable to aim at the injection of at least an additional £500 million in resources into the balance of payments in 1968, and a balance of payments surplus of £500 million in 1969. But the injection was not in the control of the government: it would reflect the efforts of businessmen to find additional markets abroad and displace foreign imports in the domestic market, profiting from the price advantage conferred by devaluation.

The trade balance did improve much as we had planned but more slowly. From a deficit of £343 million (seasonally adjusted) in the final quarter of 1967 it dwindled to £137 million a year later and £17 million a year later again. By the end of 1969 the current account was showing a surplus approaching £700 million a year and in 1970–1 was even larger. But it took longer than we had planned to develop the surplus. Instead of a surplus on current account of £100 million in the second half of 1968, as both the Treasury and the National Institute predicted, there was a deficit now estimated at £72 million (£150 million as published in 1969). This failure to meet a target given to the IMF was one, but by no means the only reason, why there was no restoration of confidence in sterling but a drain on the reserves in 1968 comparable with the drain of the previous year. 1968 can be regarded along with 1967 as the first of the years of turbulence in currencies that ended in a régime of floating exchange rates all over the world.

THE PACE OF EXPANSION

An early controversy occurred over the pace of expansion. The TUC was agitating for a 6 per cent expansion rate, largely to give substance to their private norm for wages. At the meeting of Working Party No. 3 in Paris in December, on the other hand, the British representatives were taken to task for aiming at such a high rate of expansion as 4 per cent. Since the rate of growth of productive potential was at least 3 per cent, this hardly represented a very fast rate of taking in slack; but there was a natural fear that resources once absorbed before exports had had time to adjust would not be available later when they were needed. There had been a surge in consumer buying in anticipation of higher prices and taxes when it was evident that a substantial part of any surrender of resources would have eventually to come from consumers. (It will be recalled that earlier calculations of the adjustments needed by 1970 or 1972 treated consumer spending almost as a residual and pointed to massive reductions in it as the price of regaining external balance and repaying debts.) We considered the possibility of raising indirect taxes at once to quell the panic buying but it was so near Christmas that it would have caused the maximum of inconvenience.

When the forecasts were produced in mid-December they showed a rate of expansion of $5\frac{1}{2} - 6\frac{1}{2}$ per cent per annum in GDP, mainly under the influence of a 10 per cent increase in exports reinforced by a 5 per cent increase in fixed investment. This rate of expansion seemed likely to continue into 1969, with exports growing rather more slowly and investment speeding up. The balance of payments, after working up to the surplus £200 million mentioned in the Letter of Intent in the second half of 1968, would cease to increase thereafter and might soon decline under the pressure of competing claims on resources. All this was highly speculative but it served to emphasise the risk of dissipating a strong competitive position by headlong expansion. We thought it a mistake to set a pace appreciably higher than was sustainable after the elimination of existing slack and tried to envisage the consequences of a 4 per cent rate of expansion in 1968 and $4\frac{1}{2}$ per cent in 1969. To get down to 4 per cent would require a cut in demand of £850 million (or, say, £1000 million in extra taxation or less public expenditure).

The results of our tentative calculations still pointed to a balance of payments surplus on current account of £100 million in the second half of 1968 (although we very soon became increasingly sceptical of this forecast) and a surplus of over £250 million in the second half of 1969 (which seemed much more likely). Where we went wrong was not on exports, for our assumption of a 10 per cent volume increase was near the mark, but on imports. We exaggerated the limiting effect that higher import prices would have on the volume of imports. Instead of falling as we assumed, they increased in 1968 by 10 per cent. The result was that the balance of payments stayed obstinately in the red all through 1968. We had also hoped to see a marked check to consumer spending from a combination of the hire-purchase restrictions introduced after devaluation, higher import prices and the higher taxation to be expected in the Budget. Consumer spending, however, was particularly heavy after devaluation precisely because prices were expected to rise, and it continued to remain above the relatively high level reached in the second half of 1967, showing an increase that averaged 2 per cent in the second half of 1968 in spite of all efforts to keep it down (Table 11.1). This should not have surprised us. But we had grown accustomed to treating consumer expenditure as a residual in forward looks at the economy and had thrown the whole burden of adjusting from $5\frac{1}{2}$–$6\frac{1}{2}$ to 4 per cent growth in demand on consumer spending as a convenient first step in our calculations (as we had done also in earlier medium-term projections). On this basis, a fall of 2 per cent in consumption was the price of moderating the growth rate; in practice, other elements in demand would have to share the adjustment.

The fact is that it took more than a transfer of £500 million per annum in resources into the balance of payments to remove the deficit. A deficit of £279 million in the second half of 1967 was reduced to one of £73 million in the second half of 1968, an improvement of £200 million per half-year or over £400 million per year. This was quite rapid progress which, if continued for another year at the same rate, would yield a satisfactory surplus in the second half of 1969 of £133 million and in fact yielded a surplus of £327 million. What delayed the emergence of a surplus was the J-curve effect – the automatic setback from less favourable terms of trade. In the first quarter of 1968, for example, the terms of trade had swung 5 per cent against the United Kingdom which added about £300 million a year to the import bill: it needed an extra £300 million in resources to eliminate the deficit. Similarly, between the second half of 1967 and the second half of 1968, a 3 per cent shift in the terms of trade added nearly £200 million a year to the resource requirement. The total shift in resources over the year was thus about £600 million. Exports in 1968 absorbed nearly half the increase in GDP. But it was not enough: we were still in deficit. An improvement from a large deficit to a smaller deficit is never so impressive as a move from deficit to surplus. We had made bold promises and those who disbelieved them felt fully justified.

TABLE 11.1 Preliminary forecasts, December 1967

	Forecast changes from 2nd half 1967 to 2nd half 1968 (%)	'Actual' changes (%)	Forecast changes from 2nd half 1968 to 2nd half 1969 (%)	'Actual' changes (%)
Consumer spending (residual)	−1.9	+1.8	3.0	+1.1
Public consumption	+2.5	−0.5	3.5	−1.5
Fixed investment	+4.3	+4.6	5.4	+1.1
Exports of goods and services	+10.6	+18.7	6.8	+10.1
Stockbuilding				
Total final expenditure	+2.3	+5.4	+4.5	+1.7
Import of goods and services	−2.5	+5.7	+5.6	+2.3
Factor cost adjustment	−1.4		+2.6	
GDP at factor cost	+4.0	+5.9	+4.5	1.6

FIRST MEASURES

Let us turn next to the succession of measures taken by the new Chancellor, Roy Jenkins. Devaluation had got off to a bad start. The press soon decided that the measures announced were quite insufficient. A consumer spending spree added to their concern. Spending had already increased in response to earlier reflationary measures and was now swollen by expectations that devaluation, whatever the Prime Minister might say, would shortly push up prices quite substantially. Consumers in adding to their spending did no more than the government had been doing for some time: public expenditure was leaping up to the accompaniment of increased government borrowing. The money stock had also been inflated in 1967 through a rise of £1200 million in bank advances – a record rate.

We had hoped that Callaghan would take sufficiently strong measures in November to ensure that confidence in sterling at the reduced parity was not disturbed. I had pressed him to take no chances and announce right away the full extent of the measures he proposed to take for the restoration of external balance. I had been rebuffed on the grounds that the timing of government measures was a political decision. Now things had fallen out as we feared and there was little sign of any reflux of funds. On the contrary, Australia, Kuwait, Malaysia and other holders of sterling balances were beginning to make withdrawals that we had somehow to finance while still in deficit.

In December, the increase in consumer spending continued unchecked. We hesitated to use the regulator so near Christmas but we might have extended the existing hire-purchase restrictions. The new Chancellor felt that it was more important to concentrate on cutting public expenditure and reserve tax changes for an early budget. It also seemed possible that after an initial burst of spending, consumers would return to a more normal pattern of saving.

We had no difficulty in persuading the Chancellor of the need for drastic measures. At first he had been rather sceptical of talk of over-rapid expansion. But he soon grasped the possibilities as a consumer boom developed. At Christmas, William Armstrong assured me that Ministers appeared to be in agreement on the biggest cuts they could make in public expenditure. They had taken note of the public reaction to the November measures and the criticisms from the Bank, the IMF, the Treasury and the Press of their inadequacy. Unable to act at once, the Chancellor was all the more determined to make sweeping cuts in public expenditure and concentrated his efforts on that object in December and January. After January he could turn his attention to taxation and scale up the package; but in advance of the Budget he had to begin with the job of pruning public expenditure.

Jenkins was fortunate in taking office when the economy was in such peril that he could count, as Callaghan could not, on full support for the measures he judged necessary, however distasteful to his party. On the other hand, he was anything but fortunate in having to navigate through a succession of economic hurricanes. He did so with great skill and determination and in my judgment was undoubtedly the ablest of the Chancellors of the 1960s. He weighed the alternatives carefully, took time to make up his mind and tried to ensure that the measures he took were fully commensurate with his objectives. Once he had decided what to do he would give us his reasons in logical sequence, in a way no other Chancellor ever did. He had the advantage, too, of being at home in economic problems and, more important, of bringing a careful judgment to bear on them. On several occasions he shamed his officials by being the first to draw attention to dangers that they had overlooked.

On the basis of the December forecasts I did a hasty note for the Chancellor suggesting £500 million in extra taxation and £300 million in expenditure cuts. It was urgent to take action to limit demand and for this purpose public expenditure was likely to act relatively slowly. More weight ought, therefore, to be attached to increased taxation. Later, I suggested that the Budget might be brought forward to February or the expenditure cuts might be accompanied by a statement of the tax increases to be introduced in the Budget.

On 16 December the Chancellor asked the Cabinet to approve cuts of £800 million and two days later the Prime Minister announced 'a wide-ranging review of public expenditure' and on 3 January he told the NEDC that, over the next two years there must be a switch of resources amounting to £1000 million from consumption and public expenditure to investment and the balance of payments. On 16 January spending cuts of £700 million in the next financial year were announced after a series of eight Cabinet meetings lasting in all 32 hours. These were additional to the cuts already included in the devaluation package and gave effect to major changes of policy such as the cancellation of a large order for F111 military aircraft from the United States, an accelerated withdrawal from defence posts east of Suez and the postponement to 1973 of an increase in the school-leaving age. The cuts were widely spread between defence, road construction, housing and local authority expenditure, national health service charges (including the reintroduction of prescription charges), overseas aid and investment grants. Simultaneous provision was made for the additional expenditure of £165 million in assistance to private industry for modernisation.

The Chancellor had hoped to follow the announcement of the cuts with a Budget in February but it was delayed until 19 March, immediately after the gold crisis. By that time the outflow from the reserves over the six winter months was already in excess of £1000 million. Of that horrific total, the deficit on current account formed about a third, the outflow of capital about half and most of the rest – some £200 million – losses on the forward transactions falling due after devaluation. We were a long way from the current account surplus of £500 million a year, set up as a target by the Chancellor in January. Fresh debt had to be incurred to foreign central banks and what remained of the portfolio of dollar securities, to the value of £204 million, had to be taken into the reserves for early disposal. There could be no question of the need for a budget of exemplary stringency.

Just such a budget was introduced on 19 March. The additional taxation imposed added up to £923 million in a full year – far more than we, or anyone else, expected. My first thought thought had been for an increase of £600 million, half of it indirect, half direct, with perhaps £100 million held over until the 1969 Budget. I judged that an extra £600 million in taxation would slow down expansion in 1968 to about 4 per cent or less and in 1969 to about $2\frac{1}{2}$ per cent – rates that should satisfy OECD and the IMF. But I had not dared to suggest £900 million. In urging the Chancellor to take no chances, I summed up in my Budget submission:

> It seems highly unlikely that we can hope to do better than balance our international accounts this year unless restrictive action is taken. In the meantime we are surrounded by anxious creditors many of them contemplating withdrawal of funds or seeking early repayment of debts due to them. If they are not convinced that we have acted resolutely, covered ourselves against possible misfortunes that cannot at present be foreseen, and done our best to ensure a radical improvement in our balance of payments within the next twelve months, they could easily push us into a disastrous situation very different from the limited slowing down in the rate of expansion that a substantial increase in taxation would involve.

The National Institute in February took much the same view as we did. They started from the assumption that expansion in 1968 would be limited to 4 per cent by budgetary measures. Their estimates then showed an even more dramatic improvement in the balance of payments than ours, with a swing over the two years up to the fourth quarter of 1969 of no less than £950 million (at annual rates). From our point of view, this corroboration of our long-term optimism was decidedly helpful. So too was their prescription of strong measures in the Budget to raise taxation by £400–650 million. We did not, however, expect quite so rapid an expansion in exports and fixed investment as they did; and we both made the same mistake of predicting a fall in consumer spending in 1968 when no such fall occurred.

The tax increases in the Budget were more or less equally divided between direct and indirect taxation. The latter, in the form of increased purchase tax and higher duties on wine, spirits and tobacco, was expected to yield £314 million in revenue while the changes on direct taxation, including a one-year investment income levy, a rise in corporation tax by $2\frac{1}{2}$ per cent, the introduction of taxation of family allowances, were expected to bring in £331 million. The remainder was divided roughly equally between a 50 per cent increase in SET and a rise in motor vehicle duties. No change was made in the standard rate of income tax.

Legislation was also to be introduced to limit increases in wages and dividends to $3\frac{1}{2}$ per cent (except for productivity agreements) with a nil norm – not a measure in which we had much confidence. Two days after the Budget, bank rate was cut from 8 to $7\frac{1}{2}$ per cent.

These measures brought the Budget into overall surplus by the end of 1968 for the first time since the late 1940s. The distrust in the pound, however, now ran so deep that financial markets continued to unload sterling on the authorities. The spot rate of exchange, no longer supported by forward purchases, fell below par early in 1968 and headed for its floor, remaining under par until the end of 1969.

THE GOLD RUSH OF MARCH 1968

Throughout the year the success of devaluation remained in the balance. The trade balance, after an initial improvement once the dock strikes were settled, lurched further into the red in April and May creating fresh alarm. Another source of trouble had already emerged in March. The devaluation of the pound threw doubt on the other reserve currency, the dollar, and in due course made gold seem a better bet. Those who wished to protect themselves against a change in the value of the dollar, or speculate for a fall, could do so by buying gold on the London market (purchases in the United States were illegal). Uncertainty attaching to the dollar was only too likely to weaken sterling; once the gold market felt the weight of dollar sales, sterling, too, would begin to flow into the market. The possibility that the United States might have to acquiesce in a higher price for gold created turmoil in the London gold market and rebounded on sterling.

Alternatively, if the US government decided to suspend gold sales was it not likely that we would suffer most, since people would flog sterling more than dollars? Would Blessing, the President of the Bundesbank, stockpile dollars or let the DM appreciate? When I put these questions to Van Lennep, the Chairman of Working Party No. 3, he had no hesitation in dismissing my fears and implying that in such circumstances sterling would be given support, but not the dollar. The EEC would not accept a dollar standard and Blessing would undoubtedly revalue the DM. I was not so sure that we would escape the sidewinds of any disturbance in the dollar.

Efforts to stabilise the London gold price went back to November 1960 when it shot up to $38–40, encouraging speculative buying. There had already been heavy purchases of gold from the US by foreign monetary authorities at the official price of $35. These had contributed to a fall in the US gold stock by $5 billion in the three years 1958–60 but they had ceased in conformity with the Fund's Articles of Agreement when the market price rose above the official price. The United States and seven other countries then began selling gold on the London market in order to push the price down to the official level. These arrangements grew into the gold pool which fed in gold, in periodic contributions from each member of $50 million each, so as to maintain a free market at a price close to $35 per ounce. In some years such as 1962 and 1963 it was possible to make net purchases in the market but in 1967 sales up to November reached $400 million, mainly in October.[2] At that stage the pool was in substantial net credit, i.e. the total gold reserves of the members had increased since 1961.

In November 1967, pool sales reached $800 million but the market became calmer after a meeting in Frankfurt on 26 November of the governors of the central banks concerned (now seven since France had dropped out in the summer, but without publicising her withdrawal until a carefully timed leak on 21 November). They agreed to continue pool sales and to support the existing pattern of exchange rates. Restrictions were also imposed, notably in Switzerland, on forward buying of gold and buying on credit, but these could be easily circumvented by borrowing elsewhere.

Although sales subsided in January and February, the feeling grew that the gold pool would soon be abandoned. The United States still had large holdings of gold but had to provide gold cover against Federal Reserve notes (until Congress eliminated the requirement in mid-March) and the free margin on which attention was concentrated was shrinking rapidly. At the end of February, Senator Javits proposed the suspension by the US of convertibility into gold and the ending of the gold pool. Speculative purchases of gold rose to a much higher rate from $250 million a month, sales on a single day, 8 March, reaching $180 million. At a meeting of central bankers in Basle on 9–10 March Governor Martin persuaded his colleagues to continue pool operations. But not only had France opted out: Belgium had been earmarking gold contributions to the pool for some time (which was tantamount to withdrawal) and Italy was likely to follow suit.

In all, the central banks lost $3 billion of gold through the gold pool between devaluation and the closing of the pool on 15 March 1968. Of the total $2.2 billion was supplied by the United States.[3] This was an outright loss of reserves. Other countries when they sold gold through the pool were paid in dollars, so that their reserves were undiminished. From the United Kingdom's point of view it was not the loss of gold that was disturbing but the unloading of sterling in an atmosphere of currency uncertainty.

I was made aware by Roy Reierson, just before Senator Javits's statement, of American feeling against continuing gold sales. At the meeting of the Economic Policy Committee of OECD on 5 March, Hay, the Swiss banker, argued that the gold fever was unlikely to die down. If one Senator could cause a loss of 70 tons of gold in a few days, people must have persuaded themselves that a rise in price was inevitable and would be difficult to persuade to the contrary. Milton Gilbert, of the BIS, had long argued that without a rise in the gold price, the international monetary system was no longer viable. He and others at the BIS had had a big influence on Eastern European bankers and created widespread distrust in the fixed price of $35 an ounce. Kessler, the Netherlands delegate, had a scheme for the maintenance of similar gold ratios in the reserves of all countries in order to show conclusively that the price of gold would remain fixed.

This did not look a likely starter, least of all from the US point of view. There were two possible schemes apart from a rise in the price of gold, which seemed the only one likely to be sustainable. One was the gold certificate plan devised by Robert Solomon of the Federal Reserve and backed by the US. This would have involved the creation of new reserve assets in the form of gold certificates to take the place of gold disposed of through the market. No extinction of reserves would then accompany pool sales and speculators would have no reason to expect that the market would be closed down to stem the loss. The alternative was Governor Carli's plan to abandon the gold pool and split the gold market in two: into sales between monetary authorities at $35 an ounce and private sales in a free market at a fluctuating price.

The crisis blew up very quickly while we were drafting passages for the Chancellor's Budget speech. It was on 14 March that things got out of hand. There was a large discount on forward dealings in sterling but the Bank continued to stay out of the market as it had done since devaluation. The discount reflected distrust of sterling and meant that we were likely to face heavy losses in the spot market, which up to that point had been relatively small but amounted to $250 million on the 14th. Governor Martin had rung that morning (at 4:30 a.m. Washington time) to say that the Americans were summoning a conference of central bankers and were proposing to adopt the Carli plan. Treasury officials after discussion agreed that the plan would not work and that the consequent rise in the free market price would cause large withdrawals of sterling. To my mind any course other than a straight increase in the price of gold was full of danger to sterling.

We discussed possible responses to pressure in the sterling exchange market: blocking, floating and US credits. There was also the possibility of a US embargo on gold sales which Nicky Kaldor supported, but which seemed to me likely to set off an international credit contraction. The Bank was reported to be against further borrowing and to favour floating. Nicky Kaldor, whose dream for many years had been to see the pound floating, was unexpectedly against an immediate float, which he thought would be disastrous in advance of the Budget. He wanted blocking *followed* by floating 'after a decent interval of a fortnight or so' (to give the US time to float too!). He also favoured a US embargo.

When we saw the Chancellor we found that Bill Martin had reported a division of opinion in Washington with an increase in the price of gold not ruled out. The idea of a Bank Holiday was mooted – possibly on both Monday and Tuesday –but if other markets remained open it was not clear how a second day would help sterling – indeed it was more likely to intensify distrust. The Chancellor thought that we had $1500 million in reserves to see us through but the Governor put the total at $1200 million after allowing for losses. The Chancellor expressed himself strongly against floating.

On Friday the 15th, Nicky Kaldor drew our attention to a fall in the exchange rate to 2.374 in spite of an assurance from Governor Martin that if we suspended gold dealings the rate would be looked after and held above the floor. To let this continue was to invite heavy losses after the week-end but it was only after considerable pressure that the Bank made representations to the Federal Reserve. It emerged next day that their argument that we were saving a large outlay in dollars was without foundation. When the Federal Reserve entered the market on the 15th they were able to push the rate up above 2.38 at a cost of only $3 million. Earlier in the day, however, there had been quite large conversions of sterling in New York by Libya and Singapore.

On the Friday morning there was a long debate between Treasury and Bank officials on blocking and floating against the background of a possible failure of the conference of central bankers in Washington that weekend and no aid from the US. Three schemes for blocking had been devised, named Brutus I, Brutus II and Brutus III in honour of the Ides of March, and the Treasury was backing Brutus I, the only version sufficiently advanced to be feasible. The Bank, on the other hand, thought that we had no option but to float. Maurice Allen insisted that reserves were not $1200 million but negative: the till was empty. Kit MacMahon argued that once we blocked we would never revive the sterling system and would pay for the decision for a whole generation. Blocking would still leave us with all our forward commitments to honour. Others pointed out that nobody would help us if we blocked, while if we floated it would be in their interest to do so. I argued strongly that at least we should not block on Sunday night, should aim to get through Monday and Tuesday (i.e. till after the Budget) without blocking or floating, but might find ourselves without the option. The situation, as I confessed to Burke Trend, was more frightening than in the run-up to devaluation, perhaps more than in any economic crisis in the past twenty years.

The Ides of March was indeed an eventful day. A Bank Holiday was declared, precipitating the resignation of George Brown, who was not consulted; the Stock Exchange was closed and dealings in gold were suspended. The Governor went off to the Washington Conference and was joined by William Armstrong who found himself for the first time admitted as a Treasury official to the haggling of central bankers.

From the start it was clear that if agreement was reached it was almost certain to be on the Carli plan; and so it proved. As had happened in 1950 when I attended a meeting of the EPU on Germany, Carli used Ansiaux to push through an agreed settlement. The Conference opened with a statement by Fred Deming that the US administration ruled out a rise in the official price of gold. It ended with acceptance of the Carli Plan for a two-tiered gold market. Sir Leslie O'Brien took the occasion to declare his unwillingness to ask for or receive further short-term assistance. Longer-term aid, he was told, would require consultation with governments. An IMF standby could, however, be activated within twenty-four hours and this, together with $1.4 billion of unexhausted credits and $2 billion in extra aid if available under Basle Arrangements, would yield nearly $5 billion.

There had been talk in Washington of closing the London gold market indefinitely, but a compromise was reached that it should be shut for a fortnight only. The low point in the conference came on Sunday 17 March when the European bankers were unwilling to provide further assistance for sterling and Bill Martin then told the meeting that if no further progress could be made 'we shall have to impose an embargo on gold dealings and our plans for this are all ready' – a threat that proved to be effective. It was thus on sterling, not the dollar, that much of the discussion turned.

The gold crisis was not a reassuring experience. We had been caught ill-prepared and were unconvinced that an enduring solution had been found. No paper had been prepared in advance of the crisis reviewing alternative lines of action. Even when a paper was submitted by the economic advisers, it failed to address itself to what the Chancellor regarded as the main issue: 'how bad did things have to be to make it right to block or float?' As for the Washington agreement, what assurance could there be that the two markets for gold would remain segregated from one another? It was only too likely that we would yet see an embargo.

Fortunately, attention was diverted from the gold market by other events: the resignation of George Brown, the appalling riot in Grosvenor Square. Fortunately, too, it was thought of as a *dollar* crisis. Even more fortunately, the Budget was only a day or two away and did everything and more than everything that one could have wished for to reassure opinion. But had there been a run after the budget we should have had no option but to block and almost certainly float as well.

12 A Long Hard Slog, 1968

When we took stock of the situation in April, two indicators – consumer spending and imports – were particularly disturbing. In the first quarter of 1968, the consumer boom was more swollen than ever: consumer spending was running nearly 5 per cent in volume above the level in the middle of 1967. Yet we had held out the prospect to the IMF after devaluation of finding resources for the balance of payments at the expense of consumption and on those grounds had argued in Economic Trends that 'there can be little if any scope for an increase in personal consumption next year'.[1]

Imports were also disturbingly high. They had risen in volume by 8 per cent in 1967. In the first quarter of 1968 they rose above the 1967 level by a full 10 per cent. Some of this might be due to the delayed importation of goods held up by dock strikes in 1967 estimated at £135 million. But there was no mistaking the strong upward trend. Imports of finished manufactures in the first quarter of 1968 were more than one-third higher by value than a year previously, and in the next three quarters the increase on the corresponding period in 1967 was just under one-third. The rise in imports prolonged and increased the deficit in the balance of payments. The press talked of the J curve: but it was something more than a J curve that produced an actual increase in the volume of imports after a 14 per cent devaluation.

Before the April trade figures appeared, the Chancellor sought to make another $\frac{1}{2}$ per cent cut in bank rate in order to stop the building societies from raising their rates. This seemed to me an odd and futile proceeding but I felt confident that it would be opposed by the Bank. It was in the middle of the holiday season with most senior staff (and the Chancellor) away and action left to a new Second Secretary (David Serpell) who was uninstructed in the appropriate procedure. By the time the Chancellor returned, annoyed by an inadequate minute against the move, the Federal Reserve had put up their rate and on the same day the building societies raised theirs. That put paid to a cut but it did not prevent quite unnecessary advice to the press that the Treasury did not approve the action of the building societies.

In May and June the international temperature rose with the student riots in Paris and the assassination of Robert Kennedy in Los Angeles.

The visible trade deficit in both months was unexpectedly high. The forward discount on sterling at three months rose to 7 per cent. The spot rate, which had fallen steadily since January, remained close to its floor in June. Meanwhile speculation against the franc beginning in April had disturbed currency markets and brought pressure on sterling (as well as other currencies). Funds had been transferred on a large scale into Deutschmarks and when they flowed out again they tended to be reinvested in Eurodollars for which US banks were bidding strongly at high rates of interest.

To make matters worse, the National Institute was calling for import quotas and predicting a current account deficit until the middle of 1969. Estimates of the borrowing requirement had risen from the figure of £364 million in the Budget to £750 million without a word to the Chancellor, who, once he recovered his calm, let the IMF know that the deficit would be cut down again, but without specifying how. There was also a contretemps over a fresh credit squeeze. On 23 May the Bank of England imposed a limit of 4 per cent on the increase in private sector bank lending (including export credit) above November 1967, much to the annoyance of the City and contrary to official advice.

The publication of the May trade figures showing an undiminished deficit of £165 million (seasonally adjusted) made it imperative to prepare contingency plans. We could no longer assume that the economy was headed for a healthy surplus which we would reach without any further change in policy. What measures were open to us? There seemed little to be said for further deflation: unemployment, contrary to what the Chancellor had ill-advisedly announced in April, was rising gently. More direct measures were needed: import restrictions, import deposits or a surcharge for a limited period. I came to the conclusion, with which my colleagues among the economic advisers agreed, that if the June figures showed no improvement the best course would be to introduce a 5 per cent import surcharge for six months. This might help to slow down stockbuilding and was unlikely to aggravate fears of a fresh devaluation. None the less, the market would no doubt go through much the same train of thought as we had and, fearing bad June figures, might take the precaution of importing more before import restrictions were imposed. Meanwhile, the exchange rate continued to fall (see Figure 12.1).[2]

On 17 June the Chancellor told a meeting of Treasury and Bank that Ministers had been told of the advice in favour of a temporary surcharge given by the economic advisers, but they had concluded that a scheme of import deposits was preferable and that no action should

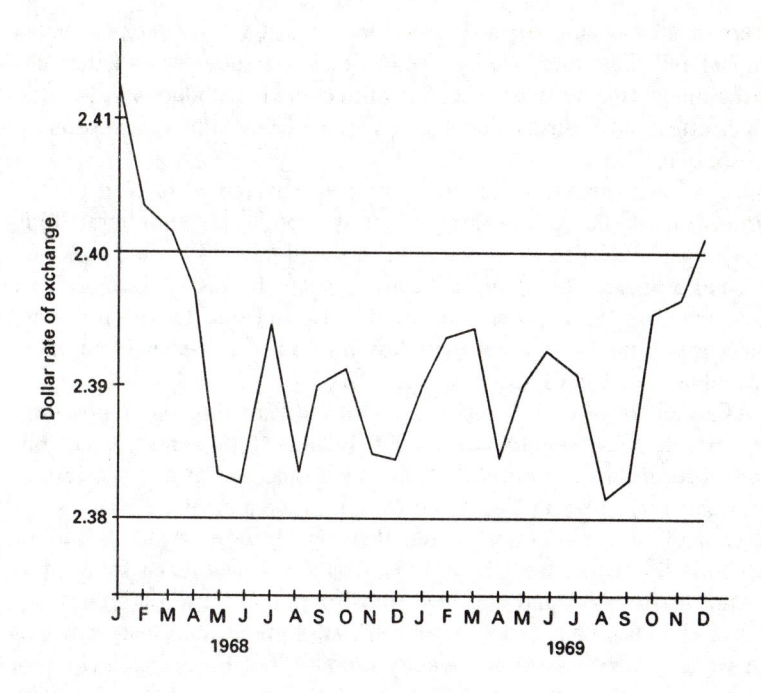

FIGURE 12.1 *Dollar rate of exchange, 1968–9*

be taken in June. This ruling had the backing of Kaldor, Goldman and the Bank, but was opposed by Harold Lever, Under-Secretary of State in DEA, and Douglas Allen, who had succeeded William Armstrong as Permanent Secretary. They felt that if the news in July was very bad, neither a surcharge nor import deposits would be enough, while if the news was not too bad, either scheme would destroy our chances of further financial support. In any event, as Jeremy Morse pointed out, there was no way of moving towards either scheme and continuing with the negotiations in Basle for sterling guarantees. Nor had we received yet from the IMF the stand-by of $1400 million for which we had asked. It emerged also that a scheme of import deposits would require the immediate appointment of a staff of over 200 to get the scheme ready in a month's time; the surcharge could be got ready in 4–7 days. Consultation in advance of either scheme raised major difficulties since the talk would get round and some of those who would have to be consulted were notoriously insecure.

From then on, a variety of schemes was under constant examination.

There was a scheme for a 25 per cent deposit for six months and a gradual fall thereafter. Nicky Kaldor, however, doubted whether deposits amounting to a mere £250 million or thereabouts would have much effect on industrial and commercial firms holding deposits of £20 billion.

Three days later at a second meeting it was agreed to plan for the earmarking of staff and printing of forms. Douglas Allen reiterated his objections: if we had to move at all it would have to be to something still more drastic, involving a new approach. It was fairly clear that the announcement of the scheme would have to coincide with the latest trade figures on 11 July but that Customs could not be ready so soon. I concluded that both schemes were dead.

As usual, however, discussion continued, growing more pointless and prolix. Nicky could never confine himself to a set agenda but wanted to discuss everything at the same time and at every meeting. He wanted us to begin by setting ourselves the aim of a £100 million per month saving in imports and then decide how to do it. But of course if that had been our aim we would not have been saying 'no change in strategy' and starting from the possible use of import deposits. His cure had always been to float, preferably a float in which the United States joined and ideally a float of all European currencies against the dollar but pegged to the mark, with the German authorities operating to smooth fluctuations in the $/Dm rate – in fact the ERM (Exchange Rate Mechanism).

The latest forecast added £600 million to the February estimate of the balance of payments deficit, of which £400 million was for additional imports. But by this time we were sceptical of forecasts. For that matter we had cause to be just as sceptical of the records of the past as of forecasts of the future. In the summer of 1968 the current account deficit in the fourth quarter of 1967 was estimated at £370 million; now it is put at £235 million – over one-third less. Similarly for 1967, a deficit that once stood at £514 million dwindled later to £359 million. We were to find the same overstatement of deficits in 1968. We had given the IMF a target surplus for the current account in the second half of the year of at least £100 million; the result was first announced as a deficit of £150 million – a shortfall of £500 million a year. Now the deficit is put at £68 million, bringing the shortfall down by a third.

When we met the Chancellor to discuss the forecasts at the end of June, he gave full vent to his annoyance. The latest forecasts showed how little faith could be put in them. It had been a mistake to delay the Budget until March instead of having it in February ('as he had wanted'); the need to wait for the forecasts that had been urged as grounds for delay had ended in more being done than the forecasts indicated as necessary so that the delay had been pointless. The moral of it all he took to be the need for forecasts at shorter intervals so as to avoid sudden shocks.

Much of this surprised me since I had been the first to press for a February Budget. Ministers had little reason to complain of the forecasts which were little more than the corollary of the monthly visible deficit which they had been receiving regularly and which showed us to be moving away from balance, not approaching it. Forecasts were merely a way of organising current information so as to throw light on the future. But it was wrong to think that frequent forecasts would give a truer picture of prospects or do away with shocks: on the contrary they would give free rein to timid imaginations. Only a major forecasting exercise got people down to working out systematically the full implications of what was going on.

The Chancellor had been comforted by information from the Bank that in the second quarter the identified deficit, together with a large positive balancing item, came within £50 million of balance. When I tried to pour cold water on the story, which hung on a big swing in the balancing item (by definition unexplained), I was surprised to find him obstinate in the comfort he derived from it. The current account was in almost as big a deficit in the second as in the first quarter (whatever vintage of statistics one uses) and the estimate of the balancing item of +£42 million first issued had been cut in half a few months later. What the Bank could have pointed to by way of comfort was an addition to reserves and evidence of a big fall in the net outflow of funds.

In any event, the Chancellor was determined to hold his hand until the Basle Arrangement (discussed below) had been settled. He could not deflate further because he could not hope to carry his colleagues. As for monetary policy he could not tighten monetary policy again after what had happened in May.

He went on to ask us what we would suggest doing if the French devalued that weekend. Not that he supposed they would. But we had lost $170 million that day and couldn't afford to let another $1000 million ooze away. We agreed that there would be no alternative to floating. But it was disconcerting that it was left to the Chancellor to pose the question and to find that we hadn't given the matter a thought.

The import deposit scheme kept being brought up for discussion.

Douglas Allen was steadfastly against it, arguing that a loss of confidence would lose us far more than the scheme could save. At the beginning of July, the Financial Secretary showed us a memorandum full of the dangers of the scheme and suggesting vague alternatives that came down to credit restriction and stopping pre-payment for imports. But he went on to propose a continuing scheme for 20 per cent deposits if the deficit were prolonged. After a discussion of the probable monetary effects, the Chancellor asked us whether the scheme could be a bridge to quantitative restrictions or whether a surcharge was preferable. Jasper Hollom, Deputy Governor, favoured a surcharge. If people were afraid of quotas they would pay high rates for money to furnish deposits, recognising that they would have a gilt-edged and highly profitable investment. I observed that no one spoke up for credit restriction although there was evidence that money was beginning to get tight.

After this discussion, Sam Goldman and I agreed with the Financial Secretary that the best contingency plan might be a low deposit scheme with a wide coverage and lasting a year. This would be designed to bring about a mild degree of deflation concentrated on imports. Nothing came of this. It was rejected by the Board of Trade as ineffective and by the Treasury on that and other grounds; Douglas Allen was turning more and more to import quotas.

By this time I had argued in turn for a surcharge, a 50 per cent deposit scheme, a 25 per cent deposit scheme and against *any* deposit scheme. I had dithered in sheer desperation over a type of device that I had hitherto taken for granted to be inappropriate to use in the United Kingdom. A scheme that bit severely on imports would be sure to have the wrong effect on confidence; if it bit mildly it could be dismissed as inadequate. Yet all the time, as Nicky Kaldor kept urging, we were importing more that we could pay for and hesitating to use the obvious and legitimate device of import quotas.

On 5 July circulation of our report on the forecasts was held up and we were asked to withdraw drafts from 'peripheral' departments and suspend circulation of the statistical annexes. Our own copies came to us marked *Top Secret* and a meeting called to discuss them was cancelled. Ministers appeared to be in a funk. But as the Prime Minister told SEP, in withholding the forecasts he was chiefly influenced by the knowledge that everything was liable to appear next day in the *Manchester Guardian*. The longer the figures remained in quarantine, however, the greater our difficulty in preparing for a further IMF review of progress due at the end of July. We knew that the IMF was distinctly worried: they were sending Dick Goode to head the Mission and threatening to make the meeting formal.

At this point, the June trade figures brought relief with a drop of over £100 million in the unadjusted trade deficit. This was entirely due to an erratic fall in imports which, however, was more than made good in July (in the seasonally adjusted figures). But there was also a small increase in exports for the first time since January and from June onwards the rise in exports accelerated. On the strength of this improvement the forecasts were at last released to a pruned circulation. Ministers seemed unaware that outside forecasts were showing the same tinge of gloom as had affected ours. The London and Cambridge Economic Service in the last week of July issued a forecast of no more than £100 million for the balance of payments surplus in 1969; and in August the National Institute revised its May forecasts of the current account down by about £100 million both for the second half of 1968 and the first half of 1969, but still showed a surplus in 1969 as a whole of £350 million on current account and £250 million in the basic balance. However, when I spoke in Working Party No. 3 at the end of July I was able to indicate that we expected the balance of payments to reach a surplus of £500 million a year in the course of 1969 (presumably in the final quarter when the surplus is now estimated at £163 million or £650 million a year). The IMF, I was glad to find, suspected that our forecasts were too cautious and had suggested that our surplus in 1969 might reach £350 million (the current account in fact reached £470 million).

The good news encouraged the Governor to propose a cut of $\frac{1}{2}$ per cent in bank rate. This seemed to have the support of the Chancellor and the Treasury but looked to me to show unseemly haste after one good set of trade figures and was also opposed within the Bank. At least money was flowing into sterling and in July there was a net intake of foreign exchange – an almost incredible change in a month. The inflow, however, dried up, the IMF Mission frowned on a cut in bank rate, the US delayed cutting *their* rate and the Governor changed his mind. So action was put off and the July trade figures finally killed the proposal.

There was some danger in July that Ministers might be carried away and start to reflate: they were so given to reflating in summer and early autumn that, as Douglas Allen put it, we needed 'seasonally adjusted Ministers'. However, the Governor had written to the Chancellor stressing the need for restraint and it seemed unlikely that anything would be done without a second month of good trade figures.

In the meantime, the Basle Agreement had been concluded on 8 July and was expected to lead to a substantial increase in deposits in sterling by members of the sterling area. The agreement allowed the United Kingdom to draw on stand-by facilities of $2 billion, provided by 12 countries and the BIS, to implement a dollar guarantee of each member country's sterling reserves less 10 per cent of its total reserves. The members entered into a reciprocal guarantee to maintain an agreed minimum proportion of their reserves in sterling. The effect of the agreement was to bring to an end the wholesale withdrawals that were taking place earlier in 1968 and add to sterling balances as the reserves of member countries grew.

The IMF Mission saw the Chancellor two days before the July trade figures gave us another shock on 8 August. They were inclined to think that our policies were working better than we allowed, but reserved judgment and the power to ask for them to be reinforced. They were disappointed by the increase in consumer spending and felt that it should still be reined back. But their most important point was that private credit to residents and non-residents had risen in the second quarter by nearly £500 million. The stock of money (£M3) had also increased by about £500 million; and the government's borrowing requirement was of the same order of magnitude. It hardly added up to a squeeze on liquidity. But all these variables were undergoing rapid change and would be quite different in 1969. In the second quarter of 1969 the stock of money *fell* and the government's borrowing requirement was negative.

In the light of the IMF's favourable verdict, it was a blow to find imports in July at an all-time record and the trade deficit almost back to the April/May level. The Chancellor, who was on holiday in Cyprus, took some comfort from the thought that if there had to be a bad month's figures, it was best if it came in August. The market took the news calmly, but there were rumours in the City of an intensification of the credit squeeze which was not part of our programme.

There were more grounds for concern over the gilt-edged market: the market weakened in May and June and the Bank was unable to offer support by taking in stock. There had been hints that might have come from the Bank that bank rate might be reduced in spite of the trade figures and such hints, if from official sources, did not tally with tighter money. Fortunately the unemployment figures were still more or less flat so that the itch to reflate could be suppressed.

In August came the Soviet attack on Czechoslovakia. There were also rumours of a deutschmark revaluation that were without foundation but were enough to produce a run on the pound. The British authorities were also said to be bringing pressure on the Germans in Basle and London. There was no truth in any of this and it all looked like an inspired leak in the British press. Our interpretation was that Peter Jay and Sam Brittan were strongly in favour of a revaluation and wanted to get on the record so that if it happened they could claim to have urged it in good time. According to Douglas Allen, the French thought that we had started the rumour because the Basle negotiations were going badly and by alarming continental opinion we might find it easier to win support. This was even more absurd since it was the holders of sterling such as Australia on whom we would have had to operate, not the Six.

That the negotiations were proving difficult was not in question. Frank Figgures had so much trouble with the Australians that the Governor had to go out and lend his support. The difficulties with Malaysia and Singapore were still unresolved.

Contingency planning continued. The Treasury became hesitant about using import deposits because it was so difficult to judge in advance what effect they would have. Quotas seemed a better bet with perhaps a surcharge as a run in over the first two months. But as exports rose and the trade deficit fell I found it difficult to take the planning seriously. Nicky Kaldor, however, still hankered after a float, although he admitted that he was thinking of action in two to three months' time but not if things either got rapidly better or we had a sudden deterioration. It was neither easy to visualise the circumstances he had in mind nor to reconcile what he proposed with earlier arguments that we simply couldn't afford what we were importing and should cut imports first before floating. Nicky was confident that a float would not take sterling below 2.20 to the dollar. That seemed optimistic to me. Why should holders of sterling think that a further small reduction would do what a larger one had failed to do? Would there not be a strong desire to get out of sterling at all costs? And what of our undertakings to the IMF?

Poor Nicky! When I said that it would be a mistake to float just as soon as the Basle agreement was signed he told me that previously he had been told to wait until the agreement was signed. This too was now represented as the wrong time. But the agreement, he maintained, safeguarded our right to float. Import deposits he could understand, since at least they aimed at the excess of liquidity from which we suffered. But quotas were a cul-de-sac and would be resented abroad.

In mid-September, the atmosphere in the Treasury became rather listless as if there ought to be a crisis but none had occurred. There was no longer an over-full work-load pressing on every minute of the working day but unexampled leisure to reflect on the next move. Bank rate was cut by another $\frac{1}{2}$ per cent – the first since March – but I was not told until it was all but settled. Most of the press wanted another $\frac{1}{2}$ per cent but the IMF and the Federal Reserve were said to share the hostility of *The Economist*. The press continued to discuss quotas, Peter Jay confessing to being in favour after all and Alan Day reviving the idea of auctioning them.

By this time we had a series of running forecasts, the latest of which showed unemployment rising to 3 per cent by the end of 1969 with no corresponding improvement in the trade balance. I was sceptical and held up all copies for other departments except one for Donald MacDougall. When the Chancellor saw the forecast, it was the 3 per cent level of unemployment that seized his attention. How could we reconcile ourselves to 3 per cent? Would it really be 3 per cent? He had no faith in our forecasts but worried about them. He refused to let us send the running forecast even to the Prime Minister. In other respects the latest forecast was much like the last, which events had borne out. The Chancellor was no doubt brooding on the forthcoming Party Conference. But for the first time since he took office our expectations, as reflected in the forecasts, were not too different from current trends in the economy.

It was about this time that the first green shoots of monetarism appeared in the press. Peter Jay had begun plugging the money supply as the root of inflation in *The Times* and other papers, especially Sam Brittan in the *Financial Times*, soon joined in. When I asked Paul Bareau why the English press was making such a fool of itself over Milton Friedman he said that he assumed that it must all be Treasury inspired. It made me laugh to think of the Treasury putting Peter Jay up to publishing an article appealing to us for help in refuting Milton Friedman. But as I was to discover at a seminar with the IMF a week later, there *were* some closet monetarists in our midst.

In the third quarter of 1968 the drain from the reserves virtually ceased. There were occasional flutters and in the first week in September a flight into deutschmarks cost us £100 million; but this, however bad, was small by past standards. In early October things looked a great deal better than at any time in 1968. We seemed to be near balance and closer to our Budget forecast than I had expected. Unemployment was falling and this could hardly be due to rising consumption: perhaps after all we were enjoying some export-led growth. The likelihood of our using import quotas had also receded. A muddle between

A Long Hard Slog, 1968

Customs and the Board of Trade ruled them out before November and it was hard to see how we could justify using them then after refraining from using them at critical times earlier in the year.

This was not, however, the general view. At a dining club of senior civil servants and top business men on 10 October, I found that nobody took seriously the idea that we would have a surplus at the rate of £500 million per annum by the end of 1969, and there were laughs when I pointed out that this was not the same as £500 million *during* 1969. Gordon Richardson said to me afterwards: 'I can't see how we can get through 1969 without import restrictions.' Equally, there was no expectation of a revival in industrial investment. Yet the very next day *The Times* published figures pointing to a 15 per cent increase in 1969 (manufacturing investment turned out to be 14 per cent up on 1967 but only 7 per cent on 1968 because, contrary to press comment all through the year, it rose quite substantially in 1968).

In mid-October the Chancellor was taking an optimistic view of the balance of payments thinking that we were near to balance on current account – as indeed later figures, seasonally adjusted, imply that we were. He was troubled, however, about the level of consumption which was above the level in mid-1967 instead of 2 per cent below it. He put in a paper in late October suggesting a tightening of hire-purchase restrictions, but the proposal was resisted and our forecast quoted against him. The Board of Trade urged on their Minister (Crosland) that it was better to use the regulator than hire purchase and in this judgment I concurred. Ministers pointed out to him that there could be no guarantee that, if he made use of hire purchase, he would have no need to raise taxes in a month. The proposal continued to be resisted but was finally accepted at Cabinet and came into force on 1 November. It raised the minimum deposit and contracted the maximum repayment period for cars, motorcycles, furniture, radio and TV sets, and domestic appliances. Whatever other effects it had, it arrested throughout 1969 what had been a sharp upward trend in sales of motor cars and motorcycles and effected a small reduction in hire-purchase debt.

This was an instance, but not the only one, in which Roy Jenkins felt let down by his officials while they complained of erratic and inadequate consultation. We were glad to have so intelligent and decisive a Chancellor but were uneasy to find him discussing policy with his private advisers and then calling in officials to hear his judgement before inviting their views. Throughout my time in the Treasury I could never count on seeing the papers or knowing what papers had been circulated, much less on being consulted or even informed: there were no clear terms of reference for advisers and the administrative machine was never adequately co-ordinated so that who was consulted was at times a matter almost of chance. There could be long periods when I never set eyes on the Chancellor and other times when I was deeply involved with him on similar matters. Under Roy Jenkins the machine was less fragmented and the Chancellor more open but officials still encountered difficulties.

One example occurred when the Monthly Economic Report that I submitted regularly to Ministers came back to me much later, unseen by Ministers. There were good reasons for withholding it as I discovered: but I was unaware that it *had* been withheld. What made it rather absurd was that Ministers had taken a decision on short-term policy on the one occasion when they had no short-term report and were now demanding to be provided with the latest *short-term* forecast before deciding on *medium-term* strategy (public expenditure in 1970/1) just when we had already provided a *medium-term* projection (in the form of documents on a new plan).

As 1968 drew to an end it was clear that our earlier forecasts had not been borne out. There was no current surplus of £100 million in the second half of 1968; instead, there was a deficit of £68 million – above the deficit in the first half of 1967. Had we then failed to secure some transfer of resources into the balance of payments? The answer was that with devaluation import prices had risen about 4.7 per cent more than export prices so that we needed about £1000 million in additional resources to pay for the same quantity of imports. Resources *were* moving into the balance of payments and if the terms of trade moved no further (and they might even improve) we needed only a continuation of the movement for another year to be in really substantial surplus.

We had also been in error over the change in consumer spending. From devaluation onwards we kept forecasting a fall in consumer spending that never occurred. It was perhaps reasonable to expect that a rise in import prices of at least 12 per cent would reduce what con-sumers could buy out of unchanged incomes – and make them buy less imports in particular. But in practice we were wrong on both counts. There was an immediate consumer boom at the end of 1967 as it was realised that price rises lay ahead; and in 1968 consumer spending rose above 1967 by over 3 per cent instead of remaining at the 1967 level as our forecasts implied. In the second half of the year, however, there was little increase and it was easier to appreciate that the hoped for transfer of resources was in progress.

THE NON-DEVALUATION CRISIS

Another major crisis hit us in November: not because of anything we did or news of a change for the worse in our circumstances. The cause of the crisis was an expected devaluation of the franc and revaluation of the deutschmark. The uncertainties went far back. A devaluation of the franc had been the talk of the City ever since the 'events of May' and the large wage settlements that followed. In the year to August 1968 wages rose by 15.3 per cent in France compared with 6 per cent in the United Kingdom, 4.4 per cent in Germany and 3.5 per cent in Italy. An increase of 2 per cent in the French minimum wage was due in a few weeks. At the beginning of October Sam Goldman attended a meeting in the Netherlands of a group of financial experts from the leading countries – a kind of inner, inner circle – to discuss the 'impending' devaluation. The French had already lost over one-third of their reserves (i.e. over $2 billion) and were still losing about $100 million a week. A devaluation was not expected until the spring, but might occur earlier. The financial experts were in agreement that it would de desirable to accompany a franc devaluation by an upvaluation of the deutschmark and perhaps also the lira. Sam told them that if the Germans did *not* move and the dollar and the pound were still in trouble, there was likely to be a flight from both currencies.

When the October trade figures were issued early in November they showed an erratic jump in the visible deficit. If the government wanted to be seen to be on top of events, should not such an apparent change for the worse precipitate drastic action of some kind? But what? We were back with the old possibilities. New forecasts were just becoming available and, to make matters worse, they showed no balance of payments surplus in 1969 and very little even in early 1970. A week later a franc/mark storm blew up as the week-end approached.

On November 12 the French raised their bank rate and restricted credit. The move backfired, alerting markets to a deteriorating situation. Gold sales in Paris increased and the mark broke through its ceiling in Paris. The chances of a revaluation of the mark attracted funds out of sterling and traders doing business with Germany found it prudent to hold marks rather than pounds. London dealers began to regard a revaluation of the mark as almost inevitable and the prospects for the mark rather than the franc became the dominant preoccupation. In the New York market there was little expectation of a franc devaluation after de Gaulle dismissed it as an 'absurdity' but the mark, now above its ceiling in New York too, was seen differently.

Contingency plans had been prepared and were very similar to the ones we had in July. Import deposits and import quotas were obvious possibilities, but we were still hesitant to use them. Since the reserves were very low we contemplated floating for a day or two until we could establish whether the United States would rally round. We also had in mind a substantial increase in taxation, either through the use of the regulator or, if we could wait, in the next Budget. Peter Jay got wind of this and told the readers of *The Times* on Saturday 16 November after turmoil in the markets that the government was considering raising purchase tax and tightening credit.

During the week-end of the 16th, central bank governors met in Basle. Before the return of the Governor on the afternoon of the 18th there was further discussion in the Treasury of possible action. One suggestion which at first had some appeal was a 5 per cent devaluation. But on reflection we all (including the Chancellor) came down against it on the grounds that the immediate effect would be to aggravate the deficit and, in addition, it might be seen as only a first instalment. Another proposal was to tighten credit at once instead of at a later stage. Douglas Allen was still in favour of deflation alone while the Chancellor, although in favour of deflation by January, was convinced that some form of import restriction would be necessary before the winter was over and was drawn towards import deposits. It would be politically inacceptable, he said, to deflate without some more direct action on the balance of payments. Later in the day he was doubtful about import deposits and Douglas Allen emphasised that nobody could estimate what impact import deposits would have on the balance of payments. My colleagues in the Economic Section doubted whether tight credit would do much more than was already assumed in the forecast especially when any cut in bank advances would be more than offset by an additional £700 million of extra fixed-rate credit for exports. They regarded the use of the regulator immediately as the most important weapon the Chancellor had and one that might improve the balance of payments in a year by £100 million.

All this was put to the Chancellor and an increase in bank rate was suggested. The Chancellor, although initially favourable, changed his mind and in the afternoon received support from the Governor who wanted to jack up long rates of interest and stop the market sagging but told us this could be done without raising bank rate. The Chancellor contemplated immediate action all along the line including the use of the regulator.

It was not until later that he decided firmly to include import deposits. The scheme involved the deposit before Customs clearance of 50 per cent of the value of imported goods, to be repaid after 180 days and to apply to about one-third of total imports. The other two items were deflationary. The clearing banks were to reduce their loans to the private sector to 98 per cent of the November 1967 total by March 1969; and the regulator was to be applied to the full extent of 10 per cent. Thus even a year after devaluation further measures were still being added in a package that would have been denounced earlier as another dose of stop–go.

The Chancellor remarked at one point that he was confident that the package would be approved by Cabinet even without import deposits. But when it did run the gauntlet of Ministerial criticism on Friday 22 November, while the Chancellor was in Bonn and the President in Vienna, it was very doubtful whether it would have been accepted in the absence of this magic device which few understood.

The Governor on his return form Basle called on the Chancellor and gave us an account of the state of play. Brunet, the French governor, had taken the line that France was not prepared to borrow her way out of her difficulties like us. The General was prepared to eat his words on devaluation. What the French proposed was a unilateral move by 15 per cent unless the Germans were prepared to go part of the way to meet them. Blessing, the Governor of the Bundesbank, was prepared to recommend outright a 5 per cent revaluation to his government but had nothing to say on a $7\frac{1}{2}/7\frac{1}{2}$ proposal and advised that a 10 per cent revaluation was out of the question. The French were speaking of a move within a week but were unlikely to move at once. The French Prime Minister, Couve de Murville, would be broadcasting that evening at 8 p.m. in answer to some pre-arranged questions.

The Germans had a Bank Holiday on Wednesday 20 November and for this reason a joint move on Tuesday night seemed to the Governor possible and desirable. He expected Brunet to tell him that night (Monday) if the French were going to close their markets next day. If they did, we should close ours and support the pound in New York and elsewhere pending a clarification of German intentions. He had left the others in no doubt that we should be obliged to float if the deutschmark stayed put and that this was his professional opinion not what his political masters were threatening. The Governor argued that if the French and Germans both moved we should not then do 'frightful things' since this would be a breach of faith. But he agreed when I pressed him, that this did not cover Import Deposits nor even perhaps import quotas, although this would be much more distasteful: he was thinking primarily of floating. He wanted us to be prepared to use foreign exchange to avoid floating on Tuesday and Wednesday if the French moved at once. We felt that we *had* to support the rate until we were sure that the Germans couldn't be prevailed on to move even by 5 per cent.

Couve de Murville in his broadcast never so much as mentioned the rate. Starting with the warcry of speculation, he went on to the 'malady' of the international financial system, the need for budgetary equilibrium and a rousing assurance that France disposed of all the means necessary for the support of the franc. Later I learned from a reliable source that Couve had told journalists that the franc would be devalued but that the formal announcement would come later.

On Tuesday morning the Chancellor told us that he had read through all the papers on import deposits and decided in favour of using them on three grounds: (a) that apart from presentational advantages there was the solid support of a united Cabinet to be won; (b) that there would be a prolonged controversy in the press over any failure to restrict imports directly when he was deflating and he ran the risk of having to do in December what had been repudiated as unthinkable a couple of weeks before; (c) there might well be forestalling based on the expectation of direct limitation of imports. Nevertheless, he was confident that he could carry the Cabinet without import deposits if this seemed right: the Prime Minister was half against and so was Crosland. By the afternoon the die was cast; the banks had been told of the additional demand for credit they would have to meet.

We started Tuesday well, with no market pressure and the knowledge that our fears of Monday had not been fulfilled. But by 4.30 p.m. we had lost $155 million, and two or three days at that rate were more than we could endure, especially with an inevitable escalation. It was agreed during the day that all the leading foreign exchange markets would close for the next three days, but for some unexplained reason New York remained open, continuing to support the pound. It was estimated by *The Times* that about $1150 million had flowed into German marks over the past few days and the turnover in the Paris gold market was estimated at Fr.2 billion. In the evening the German Chancellor, Schiller, called a conference of the Group of Ten to consider the position of the mark and the franc, beginning at 4 p.m. on Wednesday in Bonn. The conference would include both finance ministers and central bankers and would be chaired by Schiller. What the conference was to do was obscure since the German government almost simultaneously announced categorically that there would be no revaluation of the mark but that, in what was represented as a compromise, it would seek powers to make tariff reductions and lower tax rebates on exports so as to achieve results equivalent to those produced by a devaluation estimated later at 4 per cent.

In the course of Tuesday, many of us scattered to various European capitals: Sam Goldman to Bonn in the hope of bringing home to the Americans the urgency of the situation (to which they alleged we were overreacting); myself to Paris for a meeting of Working Party No. 3 that was cancelled (but succeeded by a meeting of the Economic Policy Committee); Tony Crosland, President of the Board of Trade, to a meeting of EFTA in Vienna at which he could say not a word about our intentions; and the Chancellor next day with Douglas Allen to the conference in Bonn.

In Paris I found it hard to believe that in a day or two we might be floating and that we had no power to intervene at the source of our difficulties. Five days previously Jeremy Morse had asked 'Why are we wasting time on all this? There isn't the faintest chance of the French moving.' The day before, René Larre said we could rest assured that no devaluation of the franc was contemplated and we had to ring through to Basle to make sure that the French position was unchanged. By Tuesday, Emminger was saying that the Bundesbank had lost the battle: there would be no revaluation of the mark – at most some adjustment to the turnover tax in favour of imports.

When I got back to London I found that we were in a state of comprehensive ignorance. On Friday morning, we knew little or nothing of what conclusions, if any, had been reached in Bonn. We did not know whether

> the Cabinet would agree on the measures, nor who would sign the Regulator Order, nor when the Chancellor would leave Bonn, nor when a communiqué would be issued (if at all), nor who would make a statement in the House, nor indeed whether we could count on a statement before the weekend.

Some of this comprehensive uncertainty was dissipated by 12.30. It was agreed between the Chancellor and Prime Minister that the President should be allowed to tell EFTA and the Chancellor should give the Group of 10 an outline before leaving. If he got back in time he would speak; if not, the PM. The statement would be made at about 4 p.m. if the communiqué was out. If it was not out, a statement should be issued in writing from No. 10 in the course of the evening.

We were still unaware after the Chancellor's speech in the House of Commons whether the French intended to devalue. On the contrary, Frank Figgures was busy arranging for a possible statement on Saturday about a devaluation of the franc that was likely to be by 11.1 per cent. When the question was raised as to what we should do if there were no franc devaluation, nobody took it very seriously. One day later, on Saturday night, however, the General announced to universal 'stupefaction' that there would be devaluation. Larre was right after all; and those who told me at OECD that it would end with a $2 billion package for France also proved right. Those who knew least – the Americans – guessed right.

It was hard to see what France gained from these manoeuvres except that, like ourselves, they were enabled to take fairly drastic fiscal and other measures (cuts of Fr.5 billion in the budget deficit, reimposition of exchange control, etc.) that allowed them to prolong the current rate of exchange into 1969. It was probable, too, that, had the franc been devalued, the French unions would have demanded (and won) a 10 per cent rise in wages that would have offset much of the gain in competitiveness.

The Bonn Conference had been a waste of time and unbelievably badly handled. Once the German measures were announced there was no point in holding it but the German administrative machine was powerless to call it off. Lou Rasminsky, returning by plane to Canada, said that he could remember no conference so badly managed except Savannah in 1946. He, Brunet and Raymond Barre were pushed out and had to sit on a bench awaiting news. 'Goodbye, Mr Barre', said Schiller, 'we don't need you'. Strauss, however, remained in the meeting with a claque of about forty other Germans whom he addressed as if he were still in the Bundesrat. Schiller, who was a hopeless chairman, obviously wanted them there. When Roy Jenkins enquired what the Governors had agreed at Basle to be desirable, Schiller waved aside what the bankers thought, saying it was for governments to decide and brought pressure on Blessing to make statements in line with the position that he (Schiller) was taking.

What the German press was told openly, other countries were asked to keep secret. Sam Goldman had to ring London to find out what the German measures were. He created quite a scene at Schiller's press conference by asking in English, at the end of a string of questions in German, why on earth the conference had ever been called.

I discovered later that Larre had made repeated attempts to find some other currency that would move with the franc. He proposed to

Douglas Allen that France and the United Kingdom should devalue by, say, 5 per cent while Germany, Italy and the Netherlands should revalue. When told that this was unacceptable he approached Sam Goldman with the suggestion that France and the United Kingdom should 'move together', up or down! It was just conceivable that the Germans might have moved if they had had an assurance that the French and perhaps the Italians would move with them. But neither would consider moving alone.

When we took stock at the end of the month, the losses in foreign exchange added up to £300 million, with the heaviest losses on Friday, Monday and Tuesday (15–19 November). This was quite as much as in March at the time of the gold rush. When all the European exchange markets were closed there was good reason to fear further losses (for example, through New York) since it invited the expectation of a general re-alignment of currencies. But things calmed down; and when the third quarter balance of payments showed a current account deficit down to £80 million – now reduced to £21 million – sentiment improved. A dramatic improvement in the November trade balance made the position secure.

Could the crisis have been avoided? Not easily by any action on the part of the United Kingdom. *The Times* on 25 November attacked the Chancellor for failing to act in time. It is, of course, desirable to be ahead of events; and we were quite conscious before the crisis that the government ran the risk of seeming to be obliged to react to events rather than dominate them. But how to prevent a flight into marks that has not yet begun? To float or introduce import quotas or deflate *before* the crisis rather than when it happened did not make much sense unless one thought that we would continue out of balance in the absence of such measures. We did, in fact, urge the regulator earlier on the Chancellor but he thought the political risks too great: correctly in the light of Cabinet reactions on 22 November.

The November crisis was barely over when pressure built up again, this time because of news that was completely without foundation. On Friday 5 December the rumour spread that first the Chancellor and then the Prime Minister had resigned. The exchange market ad the gilt-edged market plunged and $100 million drained away. The fact that there had been no resignations made no difference. The newspapers exuded gloom all through the weekend. On Monday the pound remained weak and on Tuesday was still weaker with a loss of another $100 million in the first forty minutes and yet another $100 million later in the morning. Since the November trade figures were known and showed a marked improvement, there was a natural temptation to release them at once to calm the markets. Such a move might, however, look like an act of desperation and misfire. It was decided to wait. Fortunately, the mood of the market changed in the afternoon and the outflow ceased. It would almost seem as if the crises of the period were self-limiting and exhausted themselves when precautions had been taken by a limited group of commercial concerns. On Wednesday the Bank was able to carry out a bear squeeze and $100 million flowed back to the reserves.[2] One more crisis was over.

After the November crisis attention concentrated on the Budget, beginning with public expenditure. The Chancellor was conscious that every major service had expanded by 50 per cent since Labour took office in 1964. But it was only he and the Prime Minister who were alive to the electoral drawbacks of the high taxes to pay for the expenditure; his colleagues took pride in the increase as their one major achievement. They failed to see that all the cuts that resulted from the battles in Cabinet did not prevent a steady rise in the total. It grew all the time without fresh decisions and still faster because decisions implying higher expenditure were taken without the struggle accompanying a cut. Even in 1968, after all the cuts at the beginning of the year, public expenditure, as then measured, increased by nearly 10 per cent at current prices.

Meetings of the Budget Committee had formerly led to a submission to the Chancellor by the Chairman at his own discretion covering an economic assessment by the Director of the Economic Section. Under Douglas Allen, the membership was widened and we now had quite a number of non-Treasury members who did most of the talking but were the least well equipped to discuss fiscal policy. At a preliminary meeting on 12 December, everybody wanted to cut consumption in 1969 and favoured a corresponding rise in taxation. I entered a mild dissent. I thought that the balance of payments might be slower to improve than we forecast, that the gain from general deflation would be small in comparison with the loss in output and the extra social friction, and that it would be preferable to aim at a bigger cut in public expenditure in 1970/1. We were likely to find many local bottlenecks in capacity pushing up imports or limiting exports and that, given time, these would cost themselves out. In that event it would be best to stretch out the cut in consumption too.

When I looked back on 1968 I could distinguish three successive explanations of the rise in imports. First, it had looked as if it could be attributed to high stockbuilding and would prove to be temporary;

then it seemed as if there had been a marked rise in the propensity to import; now we were faced with a more alarming possibility – that although there ought to be no shortage of resources, capacity constraints made it impossible to push up exports without dragging up imports at the same time. This was how it looked before the crisis, with rising capacity utilisation, overtime and unfilled vacancies, and sharply falling unemployment; and it was these indications that made us press for deflationary measures. The capacity limitations might be temporary and pass; and in some parts of industry they clearly did not exist. But we might be wise to show caution in planning for a swing in the balance of payments as large as £1000 million between 1968 and the second half of 1969. If we did achieve a surplus on current account such as we aimed at, there would be no need to fear for the capital account: we would be able to borrow abroad at long term to fund at least some of our debts while we repaid the rest out of the surplus.

However, my colleagues were not much impressed by this argument. Douglas Allen pointed out that it would be easier to get agreement on tax increases in 1969 than in an election year like 1970. In any event, it seemed a little premature to be deciding what advice to give to the Chancellor in two months' time about the shape of the Budget.

In the event, production did slow down perceptibly in the first half of 1969 and grew over the year as a whole by less than 2 per cent. The swing in the balance of payments was far in excess of expectations. The volume of exports grew about twice as fast as we were predicting before the 1969 Budget and the current account improved by over £800 million a year between the second half of 1968 and the second half of 1969, so that the resources needed in order to restore external balance were at last transferred.

The government's outstanding medium and short-term debts had risen during 1968 from under $5000 million to over $8000 million. Right to the end of 1968 the reserves continued to drain away, the loss in the final quarter reaching £346 million. The three successive crises in March, July and November produced heavy losses in three out of four quarters and a total for the year that was twice as high at £1410 million as in any previous year, including the year of devaluation in 1967.

13 Success at Last, 1969

1969 was the second of the 'two years of hard slog' that Roy Jenkins had warned in his 1968 Budget would be needed to get the country back into balance. But if the slog continued would the promised surplus appear? There was every likelihood of a substantial improvement in the current balance of payments in 1969, but the promised surplus of £500 million at the end of the year was beginning to look to commentators like 'pie in the sky'.[1] The pound was expected to remain weak and undergo the same kind of speculative batterings that had raged in 1968. So long as the mark and the franc exchange rates remained misaligned, currency uncertainties would issue in periodic crises like that of November 1968 and would envelop sterling even if they did not originate in sterling's difficulties. If the current account improved steadily, a flight from the pound into deutschmarks could still scupper all chances of holding to the parity when the exchange reserves had fallen so far and further borrowing was increasingly difficult.

It was in his second Budget of 1969, not in 1968, that the Chancellor confessed that he 'could not dismiss without thought the views of those who urge some entirely different strategy'. As late as mid-May he sketched out to himself the new policies to which he would be driven if the trade figures for May and June showed no decisive improvement. They included blocking all sterling balances (including blocking the convertibility of foreign holdings into dollars), letting the pound float knowing that it would fall – perhaps heavily – in value, imposing severe quantitative restrictions on imports and taxing consumer goods still more heavily: in fact, nearly all the measures, except an import surcharge, that we had revolved in our minds in 1968.[2]

Why should the uncertainty have been so great when the position was so much improved? After all, the deficit on current account in the second half of 1968 had been no more than £68 million and over the six winter months was estimated £31 million. Since the first quarter of 1968 the net outflow of long term capital had been negligible. On the other hand, British exports, although growing faster than before were still growing more slowly than world trade in manufactures, which grew by 40 per cent (at current prices) in the two years from the end of 1967 to the end of 1969. There was no assurance that a really de-

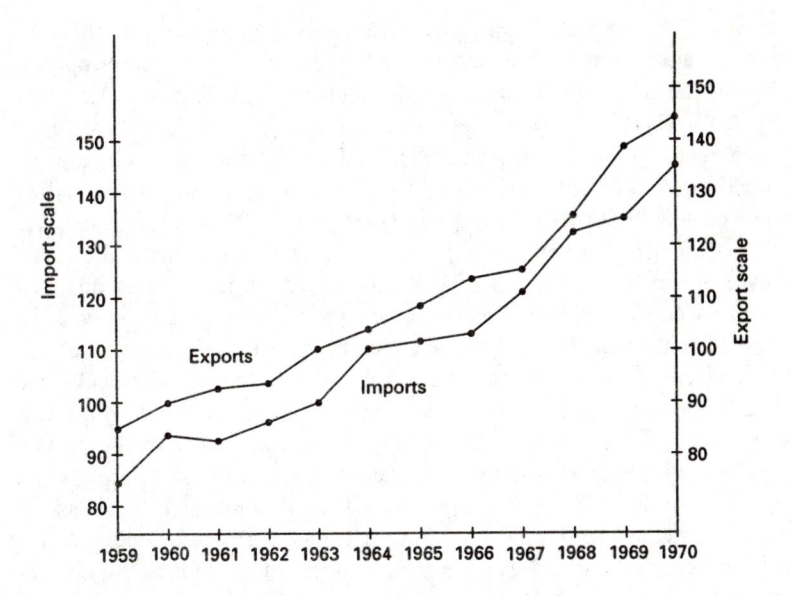

FIGURE 13.1 *Volume of exports and imports, 1959–70*

cisive and lasting change had taken in Britain's competitive position. Moreover, the basic balance of payments had been in deficit for seven successive years and in that time heavy external debts had accumulated. In the five years from 1964 to the end of 1968 debts to the IMF had risen by over £1000 million and borrowing from other monetary authorities by £2621 million including about £500 million from the sale of the dollar portfolio.[3] At the end of 1968 the basic balance was still in substantial deficit, even after adding in the (positive) balancing item and large foreign credits were still being sought. It is understandable that sterling ended the year not far above its floor at $2.3844 (Figure 13.1).

On top of the economic uncertainty there was political uncertainty. There was constant talk of divisions in Cabinet, of a change of Prime Minister, even at times of a coalition. It was symptomatic that the December rumours discussed in Chapter 12 of the resignation of Prime Minister and Chancellor should have been given such wide credence.

In January the government issued an important White Paper, *In Place of Strife*, designed to give the Department of Employment and Productivity enlarged powers and to contribute to a more effective incomes policy. The proposals gave rise to prolonged dispute within the Labour Party and were never enacted. We shall discuss the proposals later against the background of the collapse of incomes policy (see pp. 239–41).

In February the Treasury found their efforts to tighten credit by placing a ceiling on advances resisted by the clearing banks. An earlier ceiling had been withdrawn in the April Budget in 1967 (excluding finance for exports) and a new ceiling of 100 per cent of the November 1967 level of advances was introduced after devaluation. This in turn had been succeeded in May 1968 by a ceiling of 104 per cent, reduced to 98 per cent of 22 November 1968, the first of these including and the second excluding export finance. At the end of January the banks had been reminded by the Bank of England of the new ceiling which was due to come into force in March 1969. Bank advances to the private sector had continued to increase rapidly in 1968 and to the public sector a good deal less rapidly. The parallel increase in the stock of money was not to the liking of the IMF and contrary to undertakings in the Letter of Intent. In its greater reliance on tight money the government was not only seeking to satisfy the IMF and find a credible alternative to still more taxation, but was also responding to financial opinion that was increasingly monetarist. The clearing banks, unfamiliar with monetary theory, seem to have assumed that the limitation of credit had as its purpose a reduction in consumer spending and pointed out that very little bank lending was to private individuals. *The Economist*, on the other hand, attributed the increase in the stock of money to the Bank's support for the gilt-edged market, not to lending by the clearing banks.

We shall deal more fully below with these issues too (see pp. 236–7). The immediate result of the dispute was a rise in Bank Rate on 27 February from 7 to 8 per cent, a level at which it was maintained for just over a year. Independently of the dispute with the banks, it made sense, in the circumstances of 1969, to use monetary policy rather than higher taxation as a means of limiting the growth of demand. Taxes had already been raised by £1173 million in March and November 1968 while bank rate had twice been reduced from the 8 per cent rate announced on 18 November 1967. The influence of tighter money and of operations in the gilt-edged market is discussed later (below, pp. 249ff.).

THE 1969 BUDGET

In his Budget on 15 April, however, the Chancellor did not blench at a further increase in taxation of £340 million. Consumer spending had increased in each half-year since 1966 and in the second half of 1968 was 4.5 per cent above the level eighteen months previously. The trade figures, after a big improvement in January, had slipped back in February and March. It was seventeen months since devaluation and something had to be done to speed up the slow march to an acceptable balance.

The increases in tax were widely spread: corporation tax was increased by a further $2\frac{1}{2}$ per cent to 45 per cent and this, less concessions in the form of income tax allowances, was expected to raise £55 million in 1969–70; SET was to be increased yet again, this time by 28 per cent, bringing in an estimated £130 million in a full year; purchase tax was extended, and duties on wine, oil and betting increased with an expected addition of £90 million in revenue in 1969–70. It was a long and complicated budget in pursuit of a strategy still in the balance and aroused little of the enthusiasm that had greeted the budget of 1968. It had a bad press, *The Times* in particular attacking it as inadequate and uninspiring although it provided for a public sector surplus (of £243 million) for the first time since the days of Stafford Cripps.

On the day after the Budget the exchange rate stood at 2.3969 – about as close to parity as it got in 1969. The Bank had taken in £272 million from the market in the first quarter and had allowed the rate to rise gently from 2.3844 at the end of 1968 to 2.3895 on 1 April. In spite of the bad trade figures it began to look as if the worst was over.

On 28 April, however, General de Gaulle resigned. Expectations of a franc devaluation were re-awakened and soon there were rumours of an impending revaluation of the mark. Sterling at once began to slide and had reached 2.3825 early in May, while the forward discount at three months went over 15 per cent. The renewed crisis shook the nerve of the Chancellor. Was there to be no end to the threats to the new parity, no return of confidence, after all that had been done? On May 16, as he tells us in his memoirs, he reached the low point intellectually in his Chancellorship and asked himself whether it might not be wise to adopt a fundamentally different approach to the pressure on sterling.[4] At that point the crisis was beginning to subside with a recovery in the rate to 2.3894 by 21 May and a reduction in the forward discount to 7 per cent, but it was not until the end of June that the exchange market recovered to the February level with a forward discount under 3 per cent.

The exchange losses during the crisis reached over $200 million on 10 May and totalled some $750 million. Of that total, however, about two-thirds had come back by the middle of June. As in November, most of the movement of funds in the crisis was direct from the United States ($4 billion moved into deutschmarks according to *The Economist*) while the movement inside Europe was nearly all of commercial credit, especially pre-payment for German exports or pre-ordering of goods from Germany.

In mid-June the government received a piece of good news. It was discovered that for some years there had been a substantial under-recording of exports. It was estimated that this amounted to about £10 million per month and in September the export figures for the first six months of 1969 were revised upwards by £70 million. This carried with it a corresponding reduction in the balancing item, which had usually been quite a large positive item, for reasons now evident. Since many commentators made a practice of adding in the balancing item and so reducing the apparent deficit, the discovery did not necessarily call for a revision of earlier assessments that took account of the balancing item. But it was of course highly important to less expert opinion.

Shortly afterwards, when the United Kingdom sought to refinance the $1 billion it had still to repay of its drawing of $1.4 billion in December 1965, the IMF concluded another visit of inspection. As a result of its enquiries a fresh Letter of Intent was supplied. This modified the (basic) balance of payments target to a surplus of £300 million in 1969–70, accepted a limit to the increase in real terms of public expenditure in 1969–70 of 1 per cent above the level planned for 1968–9 and agreed to restrict the growth in domestic credit to £400 million in 1969–70 compared with £1175 million in 1968–9. The last of these pledges related to a new concept, domestic credit expansion, which was supposed to purge the money stock of the influence on it of surpluses and deficits in the current balance of payments (and private sector borrowing overseas).

The Fund had obviously been taken aback to find that the money stock had grown nearly as fast in 1968 as in 1967 (in 1968 at about 8 per cent per annum) and that the Bank of England, by supporting the gilt-edged market, especially in the final quarter of 1968, was adding to the liquidity of the system when what was needed was a spell of tight money. As *The Economist* put it in February 'the Bank was pumping out money by buying gilts', and it was still a buyer in April and May.[5] The gilt-edged market had gone on rising for nearly a year after devaluation and there had been no great need for support from the Bank but towards the end of the year sentiment changed as the crisis lengthened, and a fall began that continued throughout 1969.

The fall reflected not just a change in sentiment but a gradual shift in opinion towards greater reliance on monetary policy. If fiscal policy was so slow in bringing the economy into balance and was nearing the limits of what was politically feasible, perhaps it was time to see what tighter money could do. There were those who thought that money, and only money, could bring inflation under control and among them some who had no use for incomes policy and little use even for fiscal policy. The Labour government was not of their number: but it did come in 1969 to look to monetary policy for reinforcement of the measures it had taken and tried to lever long-term interest upwards when a budget surplus might have been expected to lever them down. In the six weeks after the Budget and covering the period of the IMF visit, gilt-edged prices fell by 10–15 per cent. The new issue market was left with a large quantity of unabsorbed stock and needed support from the Bank. Rates of interest continued to rise and domestic credit creation eventually began to contract, ending the fiscal year lower than at the beginning, not £400 million higher as in the Letter of Intent.

The news since May had been almost consistently good. The trade balance had remained under £100 million in deficit, the exchange rate had risen slowly but fairly steadily, and the Bank had taken in £63 million from the market in the second quarter in spite of the losses in May. A decisive change was just ahead in the switch in the trade balance from a deficit of £95 million in July to a surplus of £99 million in August.

A fresh shock came on 8 August with a devaluation of the franc. The French took action promptly and before there was any sign of speculative pressure on the pound. Nevertheless, the devaluation of the franc delivered a severe blow. The pound sank from $2.3914 on 6 August to $2.3811 on the 12th – the lowest point reached in 1968-9. On that one day the exchange losses reached $247 million. Yet as Roy Jenkins explains, Wednesday 12 August was the day on which the remarkable August trade figures were released and it was their release that was the paradoxical cause of much of the haemorrhage. The Bank had decided, uninstructed by higher authority, to let the rate take the strain on the Tuesday and allowed it to fall to $2.3817. This was interpreted by the market as a sign that the Bank had very good trade figures and had let the rate drop as a prelude to a bear squeeze. The surplus in the trade balance when announced, however, was received with utter disbelief; and to make matters worse the Bank were now under instructions to push up the rate to the previous minimum of $2.3825. The result was something of a stampede out of sterling.

For the rest of August and the first half of September the forward rate against the dollar was at a discount fluctuating around 8–9 per cent at three months. Such a situation was only possible in spite of a trade surplus, because a German revaluation was thought to be imminent and there was no expectation that the pound would show a comparable appreciation. When the mark was allowed to float on 28 September, and inevitably floated upwards, the forward rate began to fall. By the time a new parity for the mark was announced on 24 October the forward rate had fallen to about $1\frac{1}{2}$ per cent and the spot rate had risen to 2.3925. From then until the end of the year the Bank allowed the spot rate to rise slowly but kept it under par, while the forward discount almost disappeared. As the trade balance remained in surplus and the surplus on current account was now well above the derided target of £500 million per annum, foreign exchange flowed into the reserves. In the third quarter the prolonged crisis of August and September had produced an unexpected drain of £80 million. In the fourth quarter £432 million flowed the other way, into the reserves.

It had been a long and anxious struggle, but balance had at last been achieved, and achieved with a margin in hand. It had not been achieved without cost. The measures required imposed fresh imbalances and sacrifices whose after-effects had yet to be felt. A heavy burden of debt remained. The international financial system had been badly shaken and was in decay. Some of the aftermath we must pass over. The repayment of debt was accomplished in full by the spring of 1972, just before a crisis in which the pound began its long float. Within a few years, the Bretton Woods international financial system had disappeared. But what of the domestic changes that had helped to restore balance? Were these of a lasting character or would efforts be made to reverse them and restore previous relationships? In particular, would the holding down of disposable incomes with such determination have explosive effects in the years to follow?

INCOMES POLICY

The long-run success of devaluation depended on the maintenance of competitive power, and this in turn, in the 1960s, was largely a function of wage behaviour. If nominal wages kept being jacked up by inflationary wage settlements the competitive advantage conferred by devaluation would soon be dissipated. But devaluation itself injected inflation into the economy through its effects on import and export prices. The danger was that it would spread through the system levering up domestic prices and perhaps going on to set off a wage–price spiral. It was precisely these considerations that caused such hesitation to resort to devaluation if it could be avoided. The failure to prevent wage inflation had made devaluation inevitable. Would devaluation be made futile by a renewal of the very forces that caused it?

The Labour government had relied on incomes policy to give some stability to money wages, but with only limited success. When there was a freeze, as in July 1966, it was for a limited time successful because it operated on all incomes alike and was purged of the taint of unfairness that attended interference in individual settlements. But a freeze was not a true incomes policy.

In 1969 an attempt was made to curb trade-union power and make it subject to legal constraints, beginning with the issue of *In Place of Strife* on 17 January. This deliberately did not concern itself with wage norms but with the procedures and powers of trade unions and with unofficial strikes. All collective and procedural agreements entered into by firms employing over 5000 workers would have to be registered with the Department of Employment and Productivity, the grand new title for the Ministry of Labour. The Department could then refer them to a new institution, the Commission on Industrial Relations under the chairmanship of George Woodcock. It was proposed also to empower the Department to issue orders for a secret ballot before an official strike could be called; to order workers engaged in an unofficial strike to desist for up to 28 days while a procedure for settling the issue was authorised; to order employers to recognise or refuse recognition to particular unions after a report from a court of enquiry appointed by the Commission on Industrial Relations. An industrial Board would be responsible for the imposition of financial penalties in enforcement of these powers. It would hear complaints of 'unfair or arbitrary action by trade unions resulting in substantial injustice' and of failure to recognise trade union rights to negotiate. Fines could be imposed on employers, trade unions and strikers if they disobeyed orders for secret ballots or conciliation pauses.

The proposals came under attack from the trade unions whose powers it was proposed to reduce, and from other critics who wanted more far-reaching changes. *The Economist*, for example, dismissed the provisions for dealing with unofficial strikes, of which about 2000 occurred annually, as applying only to a tiny minority and wanted legally enforceable labour contracts as in the United States, with a ban on wildcat strikes.[6] The fundamental problem arose from the attempt to inject legal procedures and penalties into a system that was more informal and left it to the parties to reach agreement without legal sanctions. As an American consultant on industrial relations commented, British management enjoyed no 'predictability' in its day-to-day relations with employees: the British manager 'doesn't know when the hell he's going to be hit by a strike and he has even less idea how to settle it, except by giving in'.[7]

The Labour Party National Executive joined in the attacks on the proposals, rejecting on 11 February its penal provisions, strike ballots and the cooling-off period for unofficial strikes. The former Chancellor, James Callaghan, came out publicly against the whole scheme and on 26 March supported a critical resolution in the National Executive Committee. Roy Jenkins, who had his doubts about trade-union reform under a Labour government, urged in Cabinet from the start that there should be no delay and that the legislation should be carried through 'on the run'.[8] Barbara Castle, the Minister responsible, took a different view and had the backing of the Prime Minister. Faced with Callaghan's campaign of opposition, both of them changed their mind and it was agreed that Roy Jenkins would introduce into his Budget speech an announcement that an Industrial Relations Bill would be pushed through in the current parliamentary session, and that, on the other hand, the Prices and Incomes legislation would not be renewed in its existing rigour in the autumn. This agreement was confirmed by the Budget Cabinet on 14 April. It was not until two days later, however, and not in the Budget, that the new proposals were announced. It was Barbara Castle, not the Chancellor, who made them. While they envisaged an Industrial Relations Bill, it was no longer to provide for strike ballots or imprisonment of strikers.

Negotiations continued while opposition continued to build up. But the TUC made no concessions and support in the Cabinet oozed away.[9] On 18 June the Prime Minister entered into a deal with the TUC, announced the same day, to abandon the proposed bill and accept the TUC alternative proposals, including their plan for dealing with unofficial and inter-union strikes. It was a humiliating defeat for the government and put an end to any further efforts by the Labour government at trade union reform.

The episode was re-examined at a conference in Glasgow in 1991 at which Lord Callaghan and Lord Jenkins were both present.[10] It had been a deliberate policy decision by the Government, according to Lord Jenkins, to go for trade union reform rather than incomes policy, on the basis that there was a direct trade-off between the two. The government had agreed to go ahead quickly with the necessary legislation but never did. It did relax 'the stringency of the wage-freeze' and that probably had some adverse effect on wage movements. But it was a mistake to suggest that the whole issue of dealing with trade-union power was a diversion, and that incomes policy should always have priority. In this Lord Callaghan concurred, recanting the opposition he had expressed to the government measures in 1969. He had then taken the view that it was for the trade unions to reform themselves, which, given Bevin-type leadership they could have done, rather than let a Labour government reform them by the law, which was so inherently opposed to everything in which the trade-union movement had believed from 1904 onwards. The behaviour of the trade unions in the 1970s, he said, had made him change his views.

An acceleration in wage increases at the end of the 1960s was common to all, or nearly all, industrial countries. There were undoubtedly international factors at work affecting them all. But the experience of different countries differed widely and domestic influences could be of greater importance. In Germany, for example, the increase in hourly earnings rose to a peak of 13 per cent in 1970 from which it fell throughout the 1970s. In the United Kingdom there was a sudden spurt in the last quarter of 1969 which increased hourly earnings in manufacturing in that one quarter by nearly 3.5 per cent – a rate of increase which continued into the early 1970s and led to a rise in hourly earnings by 62 per cent between 1969 and 1973 compared with 30 per cent in the previous four years. It was the start of the great inflation of the 1970s.

Various explanations have been given of this acceleration. It is difficult to see it as the direct result of devaluation after a two-year lag. Hourly wage-rates in 1968 and 1969 rose by 6.8 and 5.4 per cent respectively over the previous year after an average annual increase of 5 per cent between 1959 and 1966.[11] It is possible, however, to see the acceleration as a reaction to the austerity that devaluation made necessary, as is suggested below. It may also owe something to an increasing awareness of inflation since there had been a distinct acceleration in the rise in consumer prices from a low 2.5 per cent in 1967 (compared with 1966) to 5.3 per cent in 1969 (compared with 1968). There had certainly been a strong *consumer* reaction after devaluation to the expectation of higher prices in the winter of 1967–8 but it is hard to see why *producers* should suddenly react at the end of 1969 when consumer prices were rising at a steady rate with no particular reason to expect an early acceleration.

A more plausible line of explanation is that of Sir Henry Phelps Brown who traces the discontinuity to a gradual shift in the balance of power within trade unions away from an older generation, with memories of the 1930s and a strong attachment to job security, in favour of a younger and more militant generation, typified earlier by Frank Cousins. The enhanced role of shop stewards told in the same direction. The 'events of May 1968' in France can be cited as an example of the change in attitudes at this time. What happened in France may have exercised a powerful demonstration effect.

Lastly there is a popular view that it was the collapse of incomes policy that opened the way to faster inflation. That view is difficult to square with the equally popular view that incomes policy was largely ineffective. If that were so, why should its collapse produce any larger effect? Perhaps, after all, incomes policy did have a moderating influence on wage claims and the forces that led to its collapse became more unbridled by virtue of their success. Perhaps also, once the balance of payments was safely in the black, trade unions may have felt less need to hold in check the ambitions of their members.

The influence of devaluation made itself felt through the increases in taxation to which it led. These bore heavily on the average worker. The earnings of the average male worker, after deduction of tax and national insurance contributions and an addition for family allowances, were no higher in real terms in 1969 than three years earlier. The experience of those years contrasts strikingly with that of the three years that followed when there was a rise of over 13 per cent.[12] It was not the first time in post-war history that the struggle to restore external balance was won at the expense of a deferment of improvements in the standard of living. The same thing had happened between 1945 and 1950.

Was there a link between this halt in the growth of the worker's standard of living and the more inflationary outcome of wage-bargaining in the 1970s? It is at least a possibility that the faster rise in money wages that began towards the end of 1969 and continued into the 1970s was a reaction to the pressure on real incomes that accompanied the transformation in the balance of payments. That transformation required higher taxation and lower take-home pay. It also raised import prices relative to export prices and so imposed a further loss of real income. It is conceivable that those burdens underlay the beginnings of rapid inflation in the 1970s as wage-earners attempted to restore their real incomes to the level to which they felt entitled.

14 Monetary and Financial Policy in the 1960s

In the 1960s monetary policy had only a limited contact with the monetary policy discussed in textbooks. It was largely a collection of administrative devices intended to improve the balance of payments and moderate excess demand. It was neither aimed at controlling the stock of money nor was it much relied upon to combat inflation. From 1961 onwards, incomes policy was regarded as a more appropriate weapon for that purpose and fiscal policy had for many years been the favoured instrument of demand management. Raising interest rates had the disadvantage of being particularly discouraging to investment, which was regarded as of major importance to economic growth.

The monetary authorities were also inclined to doubt the effectiveness of monetary policy in controlling domestic activity. In 1960 the Radcliffe Committee had only recently reported and the views expressed in its Report were in keeping with Treasury experience in the 1950s. That experience, especially in 1955–7, did not dispose the Treasury to put great weight on monetary policy as an instrument of economic stabilisation, especially if quick responses were required. For that purpose they preferred to rely on fiscal policy, supplemented from time to time by hire-purchase restrictions, although raising taxation was a much more political and dramatic act than putting up bank rate. Hire-purchase restrictions were almost instantly effective but told on a limited range of goods and, as the Radcliffe Committee warned, could progressively reduce the competitive power of the industries affected.

Given the strong expansionary momentum of the economy, in common with the whole world economy in this period, the government had far more occasion to restrain economic activity than to boost it. The sole occasion when the government felt compelled to take decisive action to speed up recovery was in the 1963 budget when the additional purchasing power released in the form of tax concessions was no more than 1 per cent of GDP in the current financial year (although substantially more in 1964). Action to slow down an over-rapid expansion was much more frequent; and for this purpose higher interest rates were a more flexible weapon than additional taxation.

There was thus little occasion to bring down interest rates sharply so as to provide a stimulus and frequent occasion to tighten credit to limit demand. Nevertheless, bank rate changes were remarkably few except in 1967 when there were six changes – three up, then three down – and in 1960–2 when there were ten in all. In the remaining six years there were only eight changes. Moreover the changes were nearly always small – usually $\frac{1}{2}$ per cent – the exceptions being in July 1961 and November 1964 when the rate was raised (on both occasions) from 5 to 7 per cent, and in November 1967 when the pound was devalued and the rate went up from $6\frac{1}{2}$ to 8 per cent.

As these three cases illustrate, changes in bank rate were much more powerful in their external than in their domestic impact and large changes were normally confined to crisis conditions in the exchange market. This had long been recognised and corresponds to the far greater ease with which the capital balance can be changed by varying interest differentials than the current account can be made to respond to monetary or fiscal policy.

While monetary policy was thought of in the 1960s largely in terms of bank rate and bank advances, there were monetary influences of a quite different kind associated with the management of public sector debt. There were various ways in which the Bank of England, as the agency for debt management, could extend or shorten the average maturity of public sector debt with perceptible effects on the structure of interest rates and the liquidity of the system. These effects were interwoven with changes in expectations inseparable from operations in the bond market. Debt management which made bond prices fluctuate could exercise much more far-reaching influence on financial markets than operations confined to the short end of the market.

In the 1960s, management of the national debt was dominated by two main influences. One was the growth in the debt as the government borrowing requirement grew from a negligible figure in 1959 to £1150 million in 1967.[1] This fresh debt had to be disposed of along with the re-financing of about £1500 million annually in maturing debt. A second influence was the desire to fund the debt, substituting long-term obligations for short-term liquid debt. The difficulty was to engage in funding at the same time as finding a market for all the debt that had to be sold annually. Such a market had to be long-term and cultivated with care so that it could be maintained and expanded from year to year. To put an abnormal weight of debt on the market and trust to a cut in price to dispose of it risked disturbing the confidence of buyers and might even lead them to make sales instead of purchases.

A government running a large deficit, so far from funding any of its debt, risked being unable to borrow enough to cover the deficit and being forced to *unfund*, borrowing from the Bank of England or selling more short-term debt, and laying the basis for monetary expansion. *Per contra*, a government wanting to pursue a restrictive monetary policy could not put too great a load of debt on the market and was correspondingly limited in the deficit it could run. Monetary policy and fiscal policy were interconnected.

Interest rates were far from the only instrument of monetary and financial policy. Governments sought to exercise control over financial transactions by more direct means. In external intervention policy, borrowing and exchange control were of more importance than changes in bank rate. In domestic policy, control over bank lending also relied on administrative controls and requests rather than on the classical weapons of open market operations and changes in bank rate.

MEASURES TO IMPROVE BALANCE OF PAYMENTS

Borrowing Abroad

The measures employed by the government to deal with balance of payments difficulties in the 1960s are dealt with in detail by Brian Tew in *British Economic Policy, 1960–74* (pp. 325–80) and need no lengthy treatment here. These measures did not, however, eliminate the difficulties. There was a steady drain on the reserves in every year in the 1960s except three: 1960 when there was a large inflow of short-term funds from abroad; 1962 when the economy was depressed; and 1969 when devaluation at last brought a large surplus on current account. As a result, it was necessary to borrow heavily from the IMF and foreign bankers, the debt incurred rising to a peak of $8 billion at the end of 1968. Foreign borrowing was at times of more importance than exchange control in dealing with balance of payments difficulties; but it did nothing to get rid of the deficit it financed.

Of the borrowing in which the Bank of England engaged, most came from the IMF up to devaluation and thereafter most came from foreign monetary authorities who were rapidly repaid in 1969–70. There was a limit to what the IMF could supply from its own funds. In August 1961 it made $2 billion available to the UK and what was drawn was soon repaid. After 1961 it could supplement its resources from the

Group of Ten under the General Arrangements to Borrow. The first activation of the GAB was in August 1964 when a stand-by of $1 billion was renewed, and drawn upon during the November 1964 crisis. Subsequent drawings were agreed in May 1965 ($1.4 billion) and in November 1967 (a further $1.4 billion, after repayment of the 1964 drawing). On each occasion a Letter of Intent was submitted to the IMF indicating the policies which the government intended to follow and the targets it pledged itself to adopt.

Borrowing from other central banks took the form of swaps or foreign currency deposits under the Basle Arrangements of March 1961. These were intended to deal with speculative transfers of funds between one currency and another and were usually for a period of three months only. Failing a return of the funds transferred within that time, repayment was to be made out of a longer-term loan from the IMF. These arrangements were used to advance $900 million to the UK between March and July 1961, most of this being repaid out of the August drawing on the IMF. Swap credits from the Group of Ten were supplemented by similar arrangements on a reciprocal basis by the Federal Reserve Board. Credit was also provided by the BIS and by Switzerland. Assistance from other monetary authorities was of particular importance in 1967–8: in the eighteen months from June 1967 to December 1968, $4.7 billion was borrowed in this way.[2]

Recourse was also made to foreign central banks under the Basle Group Arrangements, the first negotiated in June 1966, the second in September 1968. The first of these provided swap facilities to offset most of any reduction in UK reserves caused by withdrawals of sterling balances. Under the second, central banks and the BIS provided a medium-term facility of $2 billion from which to offset fluctuations below an agreed level in the sterling balances of sterling area holders. This was followed by negotiations with individual members of the sterling area for the holding of a specific proportion of their reserves in sterling against a dollar-value guarantee.

No attempt was made to borrow abroad at long-term. In 1968 the Norwegians drew my attention to their regular use of the Euro-dollar market and asked why we did not follow their example. In January 1968, after a good deal of argument, it was agreed to let nationalised industries and local authorities borrow abroad with forward cover from the Treasury and a beginning was made in 1969 with loans amounting to £56 million.

Official Intervention in the Forward Market

Akin in many ways to borrowing was support of the forward market in sterling. It had not been the practice of the Bank of England in the 1950s to offer such support but when the pressure on the pound became intense in 1964 and it was necessary to avoid letting the reserves reflect all too clearly the losses that were occurring, there was a strong case for intervening to attract more funds to London by sustaining the forward rate. The transfer of uncovered funds might increase the interest return but ran the risk of capital depreciation if the spot rate fell, particularly if it fell heavily because of a devaluation of the pound. Funds held temporarily in sterling could, however, be protected against these risks if covered by a forward sale. Apart from the desirability of encouraging an inflow of funds, there was also a need to avoid the danger that if the forward rate were allowed to fall it would drag down the spot rate and cause general alarm. Those who engaged in forward sales of sterling were not just investors seeking cover for their funds but speculators selling forward sterling outright at a price they expected to see fall before delivery. By sustaining the forward rate the Bank could bear the weight of speculative pressure without forfeiting the reserves that would be required if the pressure moved to the spot rate.

If, however, the pound had to be devalued, the forward contracts that the Bank had then to honour would involve a loss equal to the depreciation. Just such a loss, amounting to £356 million, was incurred after the devaluation of 1967, indicating the enormous scale of the transactions in which the Bank had engaged. A fall in the rate from 2.80 to 2.40, implying a loss of one-seventh, points to outstanding transactions of seven times the loss or £2492 million. It would have been quite impossible to engage in the *spot* market in transactions of that value.

Import Control by Surcharge, Deposits, Quotas

The normal method of import limitation for the sake of the balance of payments was through the use of quota restrictions. This method had been extensively used in the 1940s and 1950s but after convertibility in 1958 was never revived. Although it remained legal, the IMF and the main industrial countries were strongly against quantitative restrictions. Schemes were prepared by the Board of Trade in 1961 and (more elaborately) in 1964, but were never put into use. Instead, in 1964 an import surcharge was introduced, following the example of Canada, and the British example was later copied by the United States. It was a far more attractive and sensible arrangement than quota restrictions but aroused intense opposition in EFTA and GATT and although considered in 1968 was never again adopted.

A device that was also contrary to international agreement but had been used by other countries was the scheme for temporary import deposits introduced for a year in November 1968 and prolonged into 1970. This called for the deposit for six months of, at first half, then lower proportions, of the value of manufactured imports in advance of their importation and could be regarded as a form of credit restriction confined to imports. It was open to the importer to seek the necessary credit from the exporter and it is likely that at least a quarter of the outstanding total was advanced from abroad, While estimates of the impact of the surcharge on the volume of imports have been made – usually of the order of £100–200 million per annum – similar estimates of the reduction in imports resulting from the deposit scheme have no firm basis.

Capital Controls[3]

Exchange control in the 1960s was mainly over investment of capital abroad. There were no legal restrictions on investment within the sterling area but a voluntary scheme intended to limit long-run investment there was included in the 1966 Budget. Firms seeking to make a direct investment outside the sterling area could apply for the necessary foreign currency from the Bank of England but only in special circumstances would it be supplied. They were free, however, for most of the decade, to borrow in foreign currency and could make use of profits arising overseas to extend their business there. They could also from 1962 raise funds by purchasing 'investment currency' in the 'switch market'. This was a market in which portfolio investments abroad could be bought and sold for a form of sterling called 'investment currency' that commanded a premium over official sterling varying from 10 per cent or less in 1961–2 to 40 per cent or more in 1968. From the Budget of 1965 onwards, 25 per cent of the proceeds of all sales of foreign currency securities, wherever the sales were made, had to be sold on the official exchange market and so accrued to the reserves. Institutional investors from the latter part of the 1960s were also allowed to acquire foreign securities out of foreign currency borrowing.

In spite of the restrictions, private investment outside the sterling area remained substantial, increasing from £121 million in 1960 to £373 million in 1968 and £293 million in 1969. Direct investment reached a total of £1936 million in ten years, of which the oil companies alone accounted for £600 million, the unremitted profits of other companies for £790 million and direct investment financed by other means for £580 million. Fortfolio investment, on the other hand, was negative at –£34 million. It is clear that exchange control bore heavily on portfolio investment, but that private direct investment was much less restricted.

Another measure intended to limit investment abroad was taxation. It was expected that the corporation tax introduced in 1965 would be a deterrent to investment overseas; and much argument went to the justification of more severe treatment of foreign than of domestic investment. The proponents of the argument, including in particular Nicky Kaldor, were taken aback in the spring of 1965 to be told by the Inland Revenue that the tax would involve the loss of £40–60 million in foreign exchange. American and other companies would cease to pay income tax and under the OECD code it would not be possible to levy more than a 5 per cent withholding tax on profits remitted.

Other Measures

Other measures introduced to improve the balance of payments were the limitation of the travel allowance to £50 for travel outside the sterling area in the years 1966–70, and the export rebate scheme from October 1964 to March 1968 (which refunded indirect taxes on exports to the value of about £80 million a year).

DOMESTIC MONETARY POLICY

Monetary policy in the 1960s was conducted partly by the Bank of England as the agent and financial adviser of the government and partly through a series of 'requests' from the Chancellor to the clearing banks and other financial institutions. These 'requests' had two purposes: to limit bank lending to certain types of borrower (for example, for speculation or consumer spending) and give precedence to others (for example, exporters in the form of export credit); and to keep bank advances within some specified ceiling. Both types of request went back many years: the first type to the early post-war years, the second to Rab

Butler's call for a substantial reduction in bank advances in 1955 (and to earlier proposals by the Economic Section which the Bank opposed).

For almost the whole period of Labour government, starting in April 1965, there was a ceiling on bank advances, or on the rate of increase in advances. The ceiling was discontinued in the 1967 Budget and reimposed in November 1967 as part of the devaluation package. At that point the ceiling, which applied to commercial bills as well as advances, was the November level. This proved to be too strict a limit and was relaxed in May 1968 to allow a 4 per cent increase in November 1968 to the actual level in May. In November 1968 a new ceiling was introduced: total loans to the private sector were to be reduced to 98 per cent of the November 1967 level by March 1969. Again, this was more than the banks were able to accomplish and caused an uproar in the ensuing months, with the Bank of England applying pressure by cutting the interest on Special Deposits in half. Eventually lending was brought down to the prescribed level; but opposition to the operation of monetary policy through requests, ceilings, and negotiations grew to the point at which it was clear that the system of control had had its day.[4]

The Bank of England operated alongside these efforts at quantitative control. It made use of operations in the money market and the gilt-edged market and experimented with a new device first used in 1960: special deposits. The traditional means of monetary control was through operations designed to affect bank reserves and react on bank lending. But in the 1960s, as the Radcliffe Report made clear, the Bank of England had lost the power to control bank reserves and so limit the growth of the money stock. Not that the aim of policy was directed towards control of the money stock: the focus of policy was the complex of interest rates: at the short end, in the market for Treasury Bills, by acting as the residual supplier of finance to the discount houses; at the long end, in the market for gilts, by dealings intended to smooth the movement of interest rates upwards or downwards. The Bank's practice from 1960 until near the end of the decade was to 'lean against the wind', buying as sales pushed prices down and selling as prices rose, so as to maintain an orderly market in government debt and contribute in that way to higher long-term sales of debt. To that extent interest rate policy was subordinate to the long-term aims of debt management and could not be used simultaneously for purposes of demand management; indeed operations in the market in gilts rarely served that purpose.[5]

When the Bank seized the opportunity of a buoyant market in gilts in the second half of 1962 to engage in extensive funding of government debt, this created something of a famine in Treasury Bills, especially in the first quarter of 1963 when the supply fell by £547 million, leaving the clearing banks in temporary difficulties when the government had no wish to tighten credit. In March 1963 the banks were allowed to show a liquid assets ratio of between 29 and 30 per cent and in September this was lowered to 28 per cent (which was still well in excess of what the banks judged to be operationally desirable).

In the course of the 1960s, funding operations reduced the total of outstanding Treasury Bills held by the market from £3267 million in 1960 to £1723 million in 1967 (although there was then a large increase back to £3217 million in 1969, entirely absorbed by foreign central banks and monetary institutions).[6] The London clearing banks reduced their holdings from £941 million in 1960 to £310 million in 1969 but made up for most of the reduction by substituting commercial and other bills and loans at call to the discount market. The discount market moved in the same direction, reducing their holdings of Treasury bills by half, so that within the banking sector as a whole liquid assets came to consist increasingly of private rather than public debt.

How far the increase from year to year in the money stock was governed by the increase in public sector indebtedness is a matter of dispute. Professor Kaldor argued at one time that they matched almost pound for pound. Professor Artis thought that the relationship 'held true in a rough and ready way of the 1960s' but not of later years. The figures he gives for the 1960s offer some support to this proposition.

But there was no close relationship between M3 and the PSBR (see Table 14.1). Even if one deducts sales of public sector debt to the non-bank public there is very little connection except in years in which borrowing was particularly heavy, as in 1965 and 1967. After all, the extent to which borrowing could be covered by sales of public sector debt varied erratically from year to year and the contribution made by bank lending was subject at times to lending ceilings that had little connection with changes in the public sector borrowing requirement (PSBR). A striking example of the volatility of the first of these influences on monetary expansion was the sale of over £1000 million of (central) government stocks in the six winter months of 1966–7 compared with the taking in from the market of £900 million in the six winter months of 1968–9 (see Table 14.2).

The same conclusion applies to the monetary indicator favoured by the IMF, domestic credit expansion (DCE). It is true that the PSBR is

TABLE 14.1 *Public borrowing and monetary growth, 1960–9 (£ million)*

Year	PSBR	− Sales of public sector debt to non-banks	+ Bank lending to private and overseas sector	= Domestic credit expansion[a]	External financing of public sector	Increase in money stock (M3)
1960	710	1082	757	385	−119	182
1961	704	510	319	513	117	262
1962	546	831	560	275	−330	275
1963	824	575	791	1040	104	697
1964	999	513	1028	1514	657	597
1965	1190	469	409	1130	98	915
1966	965	263	88	790	416	536
1967	1826	626	566	1766	505	1309
1968	1318	79	669	1908	1114	1075
1969	−474	338	631	−181	−593	454

[a] Domestic credit expansion exceeds the increase in the money stock by the sum of external financing of the public sector (for example, borrowing abroad to cover an external deficit) and two other items not shown but less variable than those included: the addition to Banks' non-deposit liabilities less additions to bank deposits of overseas residents.

SOURCE: *Bank of England Statistical Abstract 1970*, Table 12.

TABLE 14.2 *Net sales of government stocks, 1960–9 (£ million)*

	Total net sales	Sales to non-banks	Sales to banking sector	Sales to overseas holders
1960	+148	−	−365	−
1961	−218	(+55)	−162	(−111)
1962	+599	(+269)	+328	(+2)
1963	−137	−126	−12	+1
1964	−114	+13	−215	+88
1965	+222	+152	+73	−3
1966 (June–September)	−194	−119	−101	+26
1966–67 (October–March)	+1011	+519	+516	−24
1967 (April–December)	−71	−10	−63	+2
1968 (January–September)	−101	−14	−49	−38
1968–69 (October–March)	−911	−389	−549	+27
1969 (April–December)	+689	+550	−26	+165

SOURCE: *Bank of England Statistical Abstract, 1970*; *Financial Statistics, December 1966*.

one of three factors determining the magnitude of DCE but the other two varied widely and often in the opposite direction. Moreover, although DCE may be an interesting analytical concept as a guide to the net effect of influences that are almost entirely domestic, it may not be the most significant indicator from the point of view of monetary management. It is not altogether surprising that no fresh target was set for DCE after April 1971 when sterling was in a much stronger position.

The setting of targets for the money stock and DCE in Letters of Intent to the IMF did imply that, whether through additional sales of gilts or in some other way, the Bank was in a position to control the growth in the quantity of money. The Bank came under pressure, therefore, to change its tactics and give priority to reaching an agreed level of sales over so conducting its operations as to maintain an orderly market conducive to long term confidence in marketability. When it took in stock on the grand scale in the winter of 1968–9 it inevitably contravened the targets for the money stock and DCE and was attacked as the source of the rapid increase in the money supply then in progress.[7] The Bank responded by continuing to wait for a rising market in order to make sales of gilts but did become more cautious about offering support to a weak market. In 1969–70, when DCE was negative, there was no difficulty in meeting the monetary targets but the following year the targets were again exceeded and for the next five years no fresh targets were issued.

The alternative to trying to match the creation of government debt with sales of debt to the public was to operate more directly on bank reserves through a call for Special Deposits. This was a device first mentioned in evidence to the Radcliffe Committee and brought into use soon after it reported. The calls were usually for $\frac{1}{2}$ per cent of London clearing bank and Scottish bank deposits to be placed in the keeping of the Bank of England until such time as the Bank thought proper to release them. There might be further calls until 2 per cent, 3 per cent or an even higher proportion of bank deposits were held by the Bank of England. After the July measures in 1961, for example, Special Deposits reached 3 per cent on 20 September and remained there until June 1962. They were not all released until late December 1962 when the economy was plainly in recession.

Special Deposits were next used at the end of April 1965. Calls were made of $\frac{1}{2}$ per cent in mid-May and mid-June in advance of the July measures that year. In July and August 1966 two further calls of $\frac{1}{2}$ per cent were made, bringing the total up to 2 per cent. Again they were announced ahead of the measures taken later in July. No further calls were made until 1970, but neither was there any release of the 2 per cent on deposit with the Bank of England until 1971. It would not appear that Special Deposits were a particularly effective weapon of monetary control. The device passed out of use in the 1970s and was superseded by the 'corset' (Supplementary Deposits) in 1973.

For most of the 1960s domestic monetary policy was something of an afterthought, offering some slight reinforcement of other policies but not regarded by the authorities as a prime mover in economic management. Towards the end of the decade, however, much more importance came to be attached to the resolute use of tighter credit and to letting long rates of interest respond more freely to market pressure. The Treasury was not much influenced by monetarist ideas, but its perception of the usefulness of a more flexible monetary policy in a more inflationary economy changed decisively.

INTERNATIONAL LIQUIDITY

As far back as 1956, the IMF had begun to interest itself in the growth of international liquidity: that is, the aggregate holdings by monetary authorities of the means of international payment. The reserves held by central banks and other monetary authorities consisted of gold, dollars and sterling, supplemented by drawing rights on the IMF. Of these, gold was much the largest component. At the beginning of 1960 official holdings totalled just under $38 billion compared with a little over $9 billion in dollars and $7 billion in sterling. Aggregate drawing-rights on the IMF were almost as large as the total holdings of reserve currencies.

What caused anxiety was neither the level of international reserves, nor their composition, but their rate of growth. The fear was that if reserves grew too slowly in comparison with world trade and the scale of the imbalances accompanying its growth, there would be a deflationary pressure on the world economy. The quantity of gold in monetary reserves had been increasing slowly, and in some years not at all (Table 14.3). The price was fixed at $35 an ounce and the USA had no intention of raising it. The United Kingdom had no wish to encourage a further increase in sterling balances which far exceeded its own reserves. The growth in international reserves in the 1950s had been heavily dependent, therefore, on the growth in dollar balances from $4.2 billion in 1951 (about half the size of official holdings of sterling) to $11 billion in 1961 (more than 50 per cent in excess of ster-

TABLE 14.3 *Total international reserves in 1949, 1955, 1969 (end of year, $billion)*

	1948	1955	1969
Gold reserves			
US	25	21	12
Other countries	8	17	27
Total ($billion)	33	38	39
Total as percentage of world imports	55	38	15
Dollars and other currencies			
Dollars	3	10	16
Sterling and other currencies	10	10	24
Total ($billion)	13	20	40
Total as percentage of world imports	22	20	16

SOURCE: Brian Tew, based on R. Triffin, *Banca Nazionale del Lavoro, Quarterly Review*, September 1982; IMF *Annual Reports*.

ling holdings). But would the growth in dollar holdings survive a situation in which the United States, instead of running a perennial deficit, moved into chronic surplus?

It was a question pressed strongly by Robert Triffin and taken up by 1958 in the Treasury.[8] Others thought that there was quite enough liquidity – enough to sustain international inflation – and that countries in difficulty in finding the means to settle their international accounts had only themselves to blame. The outcome of the debate at that stage was international agreement to add to the resources of the IMF through a 50 per cent increase in quotas and so provide more *conditional* liquidity (borrowing from the IMF in excess of quota requiring approval by the Fund).

An enthusiastic convert to the thesis of a coming shortage of international liquidity was Harold Macmillan.[9] Indeed he argued at times as if the shortage was already responsible for some of Britain's difficulties.

By 1960 he was raising the subject with his colleagues. In a paper to the Export Group of Ministers in August 1960 he brooded over Britain's recurrent balance of payments difficulties. 'We can rule out devaluation', he wrote, 'but what about floating? [Should we] consider multilateral action to increase the international credit base?' Should President Kennedy be encouraged to think about raising the price of gold? Or 'some triffin-type development?'[10]

International liquidity featured in Macmillan's first letter to Kennedy in the winter of 1960, and in his first meeting with the President in the spring of 1961.[11] He had advised an increase in the price of gold early in 1961 but, as Robert Hall warned him, it was not a starter. He returned to the subject in May 1962 when he complained to Selwyn Lloyd that the last eighteen months had been wasted in 'playing about with approaches to the problem of world credit'.[12] The City, he said, was buying gold shares, knowing that 'the Almighty Dollar must yield'. In a letter to the Chancellor he warned him not to be caught holding dollars. 'Watch and pray' he admonished him 'and sell dollars – all the dollars you have', taking care to repay outstanding debt to the IMF.[13]

In February 1961, Frank Lee was sent to Washington to discuss financial policy but was told in his brief that 'the crucial problem at this time is *not* one arising from a shortage of liquidity'.[14] As Bernstein had been arguing, it was an imbalance in international payments not a general failure of reserves to increase that was the difficulty. It was agreed to continue discussion at the Annual IMF meeting, held in Vienna, where Per Jacobsson raised a proposal that the IMF should be enabled to borrow from surplus countries what it needed to help out deficit countries. The European and other surplus countries did not take to the proposal with any enthusiasm but accepted it, so permitting a second method of enlarging the resources of the IMF through what became the GAB (General Arrangements for Borrowing).

In the winter of 1961–2 there were lengthy exchanges with the US Treasury over the earmarking of gold. Having borrowed £535 million from the IMF, the British government's liability to make repayment was in terms of gold and would be inflated by any rise in the price of gold. What had been drawn, however, included £450 million made available to the IMF by the United States and it had been agreed that this should not be converted into gold. Since sterling was a reserve currency it was necessary to be in a position to meet demands for gold and the Treasury sought, therefore, to earmark its gold obligation to the IMF. In November the Americans agreed that an initial earmarking of £250 million should be made. But as the US continued to lose gold to creditor countries, Dillon, the US Secretary of the Treasury, complained of the strain that Britain was putting on the dollar. The matter was settled with an assurance that earmarking would be confined to dollar holdings in excess of a normal working balance plus the undischarged debt to the IMF. This experience heightened concern over a possible lack of international liquidity.[15]

At the beginning of 1962 Frank Lee paid another visit to Washington and reported on his return that no new major initiative on liquidity was possible in 1962. What could be explored was the possibility of loans from surplus countries like Germany and of greater transferability of currencies made available under the GAB.[16]

After the fall in Wall Street in June 1962 Macmillan wrote again to Selwyn Lloyd (then in his last few weeks in office) urging him to propose 'radical changes' in international payments' arrangements (i.e. more international liquidity). A World Economic Conference might not be the best way of proceeding since panic might be caused by a 'mere meeting' of such a conference. Perhaps it would be better to use the machinery of OECD with Heads of Government taking part behind the scenes.

The moves in the early 1960s did not take the form of an international conference or debate in OECD. Instead, they consisted in the development of a system of international swaps through the Basle Arrangements and bilateral agreements with the United States, beginning in 1961. These were designed to cope with short-term speculative pressure by currency swaps that would offset monetary flows without drawing on reserves. Agreement was also reached after the annual meeting of the IMF in Vienna in 1961 to reinforce the power of the IMF to draw additional resources from the Group of Ten by borrowing under the GAB.

In September 1962, Maudling produced his scheme for a Mutual Currency Account (MCA), proposing the deposit in such an account, with the benefit of a gold guarantee, of sterling or dollars accumulated by surplus countries. The scheme appeared to be based on the principle of earlier swap arrangements but on an international rather than a national footing. The Americans objected to it on two grounds. On the one hand, it cut across a scheme to strengthen the dollar through the development of 'Roosa bonds'. This proposed to couple US holdings of foreign currencies with foreign holdings of US obligations denominated in the currency of the holder (and thus providing an automatic exchange guarantee). What Roosa envisaged was that other countries would go on adding to the dollar holdings in their reserves, with or without an American balance of payments deficit, while the United States acquired other currencies in return. More important, it was feared that the Maudling plan would 'permit holders of sterling or dollars to "run" from them into a special deposit account in the IMF on their own initiative'.[21]

Without American support the scheme was not a starter. Maudling represented it as a means of enabling 'world liquidity to be expanded without additional strains on the reserve currencies'. But what was really needed, by the United Kingdom at least, was a way of reassuring holders of sterling balances through some form of international guarantee; and this was later found in the Basle Group Arrangements in 1968.

A working party of US/UK officials reviewed the liquidity problem in the spring of 1963, the British still pressing the idea of a Mutual Currency Account. Reporting this to the Prime Minister, Maudling expressed doubts about 'the practicability and indeed the desirability' of the American proposals to set up a long-term network of credit outside the IMF, 'to a large extent becoming the world's banker'. A Mutual Currency Account, on the other hand, could undermine confidence in the dollar and make it more difficult to finance the US deficit by offering creditor countries a more attractive asset.[22]

The outcome of the discussion was agreement to call for a study by the Group of Ten of the adequacy of international liquidity over the long run. A group under Roosa's chairmanship was appointed at the annual meeting of the IMF in 1963 and reported in June 1964. The French members of the group argued for the replacement of reserve currencies by a 'collective reserve unit' (CRU) while the Americans laid stress on the role of credit facilities in the provision of international liquidity and the British continued to argue for a Mutual Currency Account. It was agreed that 'the need may in time be felt for some additional kind of international reserve asset' and a study group was set up on the creation of reserve assets under Rinaldo Ossola of the Bank of Italy.

On receipt of the Roosa report, Ministers agreed on a further enlargement of quotas by 25 per cent, and this was approved in April 1965. Meanwhile interest in international liquidity continued to grow. The IMF pursued its own studies, summarising its conclusions in its 1964 Annual Report. A group of academic economists led by Fritz Machlup met in Princeton, USA and Bellagio, Italy, and issued a statement at its final meeting in June 1964. By the time the IMF held its annual meeting in Tokyo in 1964, discussion of international monetary reform was the centre of interest. A clear line of division between the French and the American positions had emerged. British representatives were in general agreement with the Americans but there is no published account of the development of British views.

The French emphasised the role of gold and wanted a new international asset linked to gold. Their interest in a new asset was fundamentally as a replacement for the dollar rather than as a means of alleviating a shortage of liquidity. Within a few months of the Tokyo meeting, in February 1965 de Gaulle was denouncing reserve currencies and cashing French dollar holdings for gold. The Americans and British, on the other hand, looked forward to eliminating their deficits and to a diminishing role for reserve currencies in consequence of this. Their concern was to defend the existing system and they laid emphasis on the contribution of international credit to it in financing balance of payments deficits and surpluses.

The Ossola Group analysed various techniques for the creation of reserve assets: first, the creation of new reserve assets by a limited group of countries, either outside the Fund like the CRU, or associated with the Fund; second, the creation of drawing rights or a new asset in the IMF; and third, the creation of reserve assets in the Fund in exchange for countries' currency holdings as in Maudling's MCA. The first of these – or at least the CRU variant of it – was a thinly disguised scheme for raising the price of gold and received no support. Nor did the Maudling plan. The more hopeful proposal was for the creation of reserves in the form of drawing rights on the IMF automatically usable by Fund members. Countries would use such supplementary reserves in order to draw currency from the Fund and in doing so would transfer reserves to the country whose currency was drawn. Alternatively the new reserves could take the form of a claim on the Fund that could be freely transferred between Fund members. This alternative was what became the SDR or Special Drawing Right.

The Ossola Group's report was completed in May 1965 but agreement on a contingency plan for the creation of SDRs was not reached until its approval at the Rio meeting of the IMF in September 1967 and it was not until January 1970 that the first distribution of SDRs was made. Although the earlier discussions had been in meetings of the Deputies of the Group of Ten under Roosa or in the Group of Ten's Study Group under Ossola (both including observers from the IMF), the later expert discussions in 1966–7 were joint meetings between the Deputies and the Executive Board of the IMF, Schweitzer chairing two meetings in Washington and Emminger two meetings in Europe. There were many issues to be resolved but two were of particular importance. The Deputies had conducted their early discussions largely on the assumption that only the countries they represented would qualify to receive SDRs and make the key decisions, whereas the IMF had to carry the developing countries with it and ensure that the scheme was universal and non-discriminatory. This issue was settled in favour of universality. The second issue related to the French insistence that no new unit to rival gold should be created: the most they would agree to was that the proposed special drawing rights should be a *credit*.

When the joint Ministerial meeting was held in London in 17–18 July 1967 the Chancellor asked for a draft to be prepared overnight. Dewey Daane, who claimed to be used to working all night offered to produce one but failed to show up in time. Emminger, unable to sleep because of continued thunder, provided the Chancellor with a draft that formed the basis of eventual agreement (so far as there was agreement). Later he got a draft communiqué ready with brackets round disputed passages, knowing after sounding out the Deputies what concessions were necessary to the various points of view. The draft was agreed in ten minutes without brackets by the Ministers. Débré, however, got very excited when he heard Emminger say that he would have to invent a 'zebra' (i.e. it would be a new reserve asset to please the Americans and at the same time an extension of credit to please the French). The Belgian Minister tried to soothe Débré by saying that it was 'un mouton à cinq pattes' but this only made Débré explode that the scheme was neither a zebra nor a sheep but *'un crédit'*. Although the French claimed that 'the question of creating new money was discarded', special drawing rights were freely transferable like gold and unlike existing IMF drawing rights.

Other matters had still to be settled: the French insisted on a formula to require countries using drawing rights to do so no more heavily than their other reserves over a given period; and on a specific limitation on the amount of drawing rights that countries could use in a given period. A second Ministerial meeting in London on 26 August was necessary to resolve these difficulties.

This was not the end. After the gold rush in March 1968 yet another Ministerial meeting was held at French insistence, this time in Stockholm. President de Gaulle was still harping on the need for a gold standard and seems to have thought that the end of the gold exchange standard was at hand. The meeting opened with a restatement of the French position and an attempt to raise the question of the price of gold. At the end France was still unable to accept the final package in spite of efforts to accommodate the French point of view wherever possible.

Two final comments can be made on the whole debate. The first is that although the United Kingdom could claim to have initiated the debate in 1958, and attached great importance to a successful outcome, it did not, so far as I am aware, take up a distinctive position thereafter at variance with the American position except in proposing a Mutual Currency Account. The second point relates to the disappearance of the SDR from the political agenda for many years. Looking back from the 1990s it is difficult to understand the extraordinary concentration on a potential shortage of international liquidity. As Jacques Polak has pointed out, 'with free capital markets, creditworthy countries – like creditworthy corporations – can borrow the amount of liquidity they need', so that a shortage in today's circumstances is a non-problem.

> The supply of liquidity is a global problem . . . set by the monetary policies of the major industrial countries whose currencies are used in reserves. These policies may, at any moment of time, be unduly tight or unduly lax by some world standard. . . . But the possibility that the sum of the monetary policies of a small number of key countries may not be optimal does not create the need for a collective power to create or destroy money, such as that provided by the SDR mechanism. If the main central banks agreed that more money was needed, they would supply it themselves; if not, they would have the votes to block SDR creation in the Fund.[23]

It can be argued, however, that a shortage of international liquidity was indeed a potential problem in the circumstances of the 1960s. There were indications, especially in the mid-1960s, of a slowing down in the creation of reserve assets that could become progressively more restrictive. Nor was it so easy for governments to borrow abroad in order to reinforce their reserves. A small country like Norway could make use of the international capital market to meet its reserve requirements, But larger countries would have had difficulty in the years before commercial banks found themselves in the 1970s looking for a use for large petro-dollar deposits.

15 Economic Management in the 1960s: A Summing-up

Like most other decades in British post-war history, the 1960s can be made to seem in retrospect a long series of economic disasters. Two unsuccessful attempts to enter the European Community, the collapse of the National Plan, the abandonment of incomes policy in disillusion, one balance of payments crisis after another ending in the devaluation of sterling in 1967 when so much had been staked on maintaining the parity: these episodes left little to enthuse over. The hopes of sustained expansion with which the decade opened soon faded in the July measures of 1961; Britain's share of world trade in manufactures continued to decline year after year without interruption; and from 1964 onwards the energies of the government were concentrated on the twin problems of wage inflation and a sagging balance of payments.

On the other hand, economic performance in the 1960s was by no means altogether a failure. Economic growth was in fact a good deal faster than in the 1950s and much faster than in the 1970s. Over the decade as a whole (1959–69), GDP increased by over 38 per cent compared with 28 per cent in the previous decade and 25 per cent in the decade following. Moreover, a larger proportion of the increment in output took the form of capital investment. In spite of the balance of payments difficulties during the decade, there was a healthy surplus in 1970 in place of a considerable deficit in 1960.

There were many new departures in policy, not all of which proved successful or survived. Domestically, there were novel attempts to reduce inflation by various forms of incomes policy, starting with Selwyn Lloyd's 'pay pause' in July 1961; a renewed enthusiasm for economic planning making use from 1962 of a new tripartite institution, the National Economic Development Council which lived on into the 1990s; an attempt with the help of a newly created Department of Economic Affairs, to plan for faster economic growth and a better balance between the different regions of the country.

There were also important developments affecting international economic policy: a switch over the decade in the direction of trade from

Commonwealth markets with preferential tariffs to the more rapidly expanding but more competitive markets on the continent; more frequent discussion of economic affairs at the international level and more continuous international co-operation in the framing of economic policy, with wider participation by Ministers and officials in what became the OECD after the entry into the OEEC (Organisation for European Economic Co-operation) of the United States and Canada in 1961 and Japan in 1963; a major attempt in 1961–3 and again in 1967 to gain entry to the European Community; a more active role for the BIS and the IMF, including the development of a system of currency swaps under the Basle Arrangement of 1961; the first creation of Special Drawing rights in the IMF on 1 January 1970.

There were many experiments, too, with the tax system: the introduction of corporation tax and capital gains taxation; fiscal innovations which have not survived such as the use of a tax 'regulator' between budgets, i.e. an adjustment by up to 10 per cent in indirect taxation up or down; the selective employment tax and the regional employment premium; the replacement of investment allowances by grants in support of industrial investment.

In retrospect, all these developments do little to change the common picture of the 1960s as a decade of continuous crisis. Governments repeatedly misjudged the situation, delayed action to deflate or devalue and overdid action to expand. An atmosphere of crisis hung particularly heavily over the Labour government with exchange crises in each successive year and a sense of crisis even in 1969 when the balance of payments had moved into increasing surplus.

Governments were only able to handle these crises with extensive help from abroad: some from the IMF, some from European banks, but most of all from the United States. The assistance took the form of swaps and short-term credit: no attempt was made until near the end of the decade to raise long-term finance, not even through borrowing abroad by publicly owned undertakings as in the 1970s. As a result no adequate reserves were built up and one crisis was soon succeeded by another.

Nor do the events of the period leave one with much admiration for the direction of affairs. The organisation of government, as described in Chapter 5, was at its lowest in point of efficiency in the early days of the Labour government in 1964–6. The triumvirate of those years conducted business in a way that blurred responsibility for policy and did not make for the careful consideration of policy alternatives. The Chancellor retained nominal control over the main instruments of economic policy but with little freedom to decide how and when they should be used. Macmillan and Wilson both sought to maintain an influence on economic policy that took from the authority normally enjoyed by the Chancellor. Macmillan badgered Selwyn Lloyd, bombarding him with notes in extravagant terms and taking over from him responsibility for incomes policy. Wilson went much further and required decisions to be approved, without submission to the Cabinet, by a triumvirate in which the last word rested with himself and it became extremely difficult to take issue with his judgment. It was notable that he and he alone held unwaveringly until the end to the maintenance of the existing parity. It was only when Roy Jenkins became Chancellor that the authority of the Treasury over economic policy was restored. As with all matters of economic policy, Jenkins still needed the Prime Minister's backing. But it lay with him, without operational interference, to frame economic policy and pilot it through Cabinet and Commons.

Yet the government included many outstanding figures and looked distinctly more impressive intellectually than its predecessor. Even in economic affairs, the triumvirate were all highly experienced politicians. But the system of government in the early days of the Labour government did not augur well for the framing and execution of appropriate policies.

A FINAL ASSESSMENT

It remains to examine the government's success in relation to four of the main aims of policy discussed in Chapter 1, beginning with faster growth.

1 Faster Economic Growth

The main aim of both Conservative and Labour governments was faster economic growth but neither of them had an adequate grasp of how to promote it. Both took for granted that an expanding level of demand was indispensable.

Economic growth was a new objective of policy in the 1960s and understanding of its causes was still very imperfect. It was recognised that it was liable to be in conflict with other aims of policy such as stable prices and external balance and there were marked differences of view as to the priority it should be accorded. Inflation, it was thought, could be held at bay through the newly introduced instrument of incomes policy and if external balance was disturbed there were those who thought it could be instantly restored by letting the pound float downwards.[1] There was no parallel emphasis on the limitations of incomes policy in conditions of labour shortage as this had yet to be put to the test of experience; nor was there much emphasis on the inconveniences, and indeed dangers, of resort to devaluation or uncontrolled floating. Both Selwyn Lloyd in 1961 and the Labour government in 1964 were inclined to the view that if only they could raise the pressure on available resources and ride out any resulting deficit in the balance of payments there would be a break-through to higher levels of productivity and faster growth.

Selwyn Lloyd drew back when warned that he was heading for a devaluation but when Maudling took over he soon made up his mind, with the Prime Minister's enthusiastic support, to meet any similar exchange crisis by letting the pound float. The Labour government when it took office – and particularly the Chancellor – had no such intention but persevered for nearly two years with policies that added to, rather than took from, the pressure on resources, relying on foreign borrowing and additional measures of exchange control to support the parity. Eventually they were obliged to take deflationary action, with evident reluctance, by the scale on which funds were draining away. Even so, the measures of July 1966, so clumsily announced, were followed by such a surge in public expenditure, and particularly public investment, that a deficit soon reappeared and pressure on sterling built up again, aggravated by a falling-off in export demand. The government neither took the measure of what was required to maintain the parity nor did it frame a strategy that gave the necessary precedence to their objective.

After 1967 the government's priorities were completely different. Exchange crises continued to occur and with them went large-scale foreign borrowing – in those respects 1968–9 out-distanced 1964–7 – but the government was determined to restore external balance at the new parity, even if the scale of deflationary action required – and with it the abandonment of priority for economic growth – went far beyond what would have been acceptable earlier. The result was to procure a swing in the balance of payments greater than any since 1945–50 and to permit repayment in a remarkably short time of the enormous foreign debts that had built up.

If the economic record of the Labour government was redeemed in the years after 1967 there was no similar transformation in its political fortunes. The continued prosperity of 1964–6 had secured the return to power of the Labour government in spite of its steady drift into deeper indebtedness to foreign bankers. On the other hand, the restoration of external balance weighed less with the electors than the sacrifices that it involved for the taxpayer – sacrifices that contributed powerfully to Labour's loss of office in 1970. Economic virtue is not always translated into political success.

There was also no breakthrough to faster economic growth. There was an undoubted acceleration in the growth of productivity in the early 1960s, i.e. in the years of Conservative government. But somehow the acceleration ceased under Labour in spite of the National Plan and there was no further improvement in the rate of growth in the second half of the decade, not because labour productivity ceased to improve in fact it accelerated slightly but because employment, which increased fairly rapidly in the first half of the 1960s, fell slightly in the second half. Harold Wilson might promise a technological revolution (although he spoke of science rather than technology) but governments are rarely in a position to dictate the pace of technological advance. The Labour government did try to modernise British industry through investment grants, changes in the tax system, the establishment of the Industrial Reorganisation Commission and in other ways. But the outcome as reflected in the statistics was disappointing.

There is no doubt that growth was faster in the 1960s than in the 1950s – indeed faster than in any previous decade. But there is equally no doubt that this was not the outcome of deliberate government policy. After the Second World War, economic growth had quickened all over the world, almost irrespective of the policies pursued; and there had already in post-war years been an advance in productivity in most countries over earlier years before the Second – or for that matter, the First World War.

But except within the public sector, governments have no direct influence on productivity. In the private sector, productivity growth is the outcome of decisions by managements and workers in many thousands of businesses which the government can influence only indirectly. How governments can best exert their influence is a matter to which economists had begun to give thought in the 1950s but there is little evidence that governments did more than accept the traditional panaceas of higher investment, export-led growth and more research and development without much reflection on other factors at work such as competitive pressure, management capability, education and training, labour relations and incentives of various kinds. The need to accelerate growth was given far more attention than the way in which government could contribute.

The absence of an adequate understanding of the forces at work was an important handicap. Targets were set and plans prepared that presumed some almost automatic acceleration in the rate of growth but were unsuccessful in bringing it about. There was a tendency to dissociate faster growth from greater individual effort or acceptance of the need to abandon restrictive practices. Too little thought was given to how innovation could be encouraged, often on the assumption that it would come about of itself or after the government had peppered the economy with the right incentives. There was no mass enthusiasm to do better and earn more by personal endeavour such as the citizens of continental countries had displayed in post-war years when their very survival depended on higher output.

When Selwyn Lloyd proclaimed a target of 4 per cent growth it was almost a matter of indifference to him whether he picked on 4 or 5 per cent. The important thing to him was a target, not the policy proposals that would result in raising the growth of production to the target rate. These were left for consideration by NEDC. Similarly when DEA also adopted a target of 4 per cent (of which 3.2 per cent represented productivity growth and 0.8 per cent growth in employment), the measures required in order to give effect to it were left for incorporation in the National Plan. Both NEDC and DEA could point to lines of action that would improve productivity; but neither could ensure that the necessary actions would be taken or that these would suffice to raise growth to the target rate of 4 per cent.[3] In some quarters it was argued that the mere enunciation of the target by the government would secure its fulfilment; and the National Plan assumed that once the 4 per cent target was translated into sub-targets for each activity, it would facilitate a combined effort of employers and employed to reach the higher levels of output indicated.

In this respect the procedure differed from that followed by the Commissariat au Plan in France which started from the average rate of growth already achieved and sought to continue that rate over the next five years, not to accelerate it. In Britain the tendency to regard planning as a means of accelerating growth encouraged a different practice and was accompanied by much argument that an acceleration was already in progress and would continue.

It was not, however, unrealistic assumptions about the government's powers to speed up economic growth that proved fatal to the National Plan. It was rather its treatment of the uncertainty attached to a weak balance of payments and overvalued exchange rate. If Ministers were not prepared to devalue, the Plan could not assume openly that it would. Yet in the absence of devaluation the government was likely to be driven to deflate and reduce output well below planned levels. The measures taken in July 1966 discredited the National Plan although they did not put an end to economic planning.

The Plan was not fulfilled. But did it do any harm? The mere setting of targets, whether in the form of Selwyn Lloyd's 4 per cent target or the more articulated National Plan might seem relatively harmless and even capable of acting as a spur. But if the target was excessive, as it usually was, it obliged the government to refrain from action to restrain demand so long as the target level had not been reached, even when excessive pressure was clearly building up. Both under the Conservative and the Labour governments planning contributed to the inflation of those years.

The Conservative government, for example, felt compelled to gear public investment to its announced target of 4 per cent and sanctioned large programmes, notably in electric power generation, that put a strain on the economy, created a great deal of excess capacity, and did little to speed up the growth of productivity. The difficulty of abandoning the target was also an important element in the failure to slow down the expansion of the economy in the budget of 1964.

The Labour government's efforts to raise productivity in the National Plan had a similar tendency to lead to acquiescence in excess demand. The idea was still widespread that a sustained pressure on resources would eventually lead into a new world of rising productivity. Those who held such views made little of difficulties with the balance of payments and more rapid inflation, assuring doubters that a breakthrough lay ahead. The sceptics then found difficulty in persuading Ministers to take more resolute action to curtail demand.

There were, of course, many specific ways in which the government sought to raise productivity quite apart from plans and targets. The Labour government in particular made great efforts to raise industrial productivity through the mergers arranged by the Industrial Reconstruction Corporation, the work of the little Neddies, and in other ways. It sought the support of the trade unions in getting rid of restrictive practices in industry and used investment grants and various forms of subsidy as a stimulus to higher efficiency. The expansion of higher education and increased provision for labour training were intended to contribute to the same purpose. But it is hard to find in the record of those years evidence of the more rapid growth in productivity for which the government hoped.

The anxiety of the government to speed up economic growth was coupled with a desire to be in the forefront of technological progress. That there is a powerful link between innovation in technology and economic grwoth no one would deny. But it is not a link easily forged by government and all forms of innovation have to adapt to market opportunities. British governments in the 1960s tended to go for innovations on the grand scale, such as supersonic jets and nuclear power stations, in which the comparative advantage of the United States was outstanding, and to pour out vast amounts of capital to little avail, while doing little to ease risk-taking in the innumerable smaller improvements that were the mainstay of economic growth.

The government's enthusiasm for nuclear power led it to promote the building of Advanced Gas Cooled Reactors long before the design for such reactors had been fully developed. Not only so but it then sought to use them to strengthen the exchange rate, when devaluation was only months away, by setting on foot (in order to save imports) the construction of three aluminium smelters in Britain although Canada and Norway, with access to cheap hydro-electric power, were the natural sources of supply. The aim was to substitute home-produced aluminium for imports; and the justification offered was that if each smelter had the exclusive use of a nuclear reactor (or, in one case, a coal-burning station) the electricity generated would be extremely cheap. In fact, work did not start until well after devaluation; and as for the extremely cheap electricity, the AGRs that were built proved far more expensive to operate than had been expected.

The very urgency of the British desire to match continental rates of growth (which in the 1980s fell *below* the British level) risked pushing the government into policies that had the perverse effect of slowing growth down. Short of that, the constant harping on growth and the expectation that it would be accelerated through government action, not the enterprise of individuals, gave an inflationary tilt to the economy. The more firmly unrealistic expectations of faster growth took root, the greater the inflationary pressure both in the form of excessive wage settlements and in the tendency for governments to let expansion proceed unchecked and overheat the economy.

2 Inflation

The 1960s were also the subject of a determined but largely unsuccessful attack on inflation. The July measures of Selwyn Lloyd in 1961 were aimed as much at inflation as at improving the balance of payments; and in the ensuing years of Conservative government both

Macmillan and Maudling hoped to find ways of moderating wage settlements either through the National Incomes Commission or through agreement with the trade unions. Their hopes were not fulfilled; and Selwyn Lloyd's 'pause', so far as it affected wage settlements, proved less effective than the rise in unemployment that followed. Wage increases did slow down for a time in 1962–3 and so, in consequence, did the rise in prices. But by 1964 excess demand was back at work and wages and prices were rising as fast as in 1960–1.

What moved Conservative governments to action that checked inflation was usually the swing in the balance of payments into deficit in which inflation resulted rather than the inflationary movement in consumer prices itself. A growing balance of payments deficit exerted a more peremptory influence and usually prompted, sooner or later, a rise in bank rate. This did not, however, lead the government to view monetary policy as the natural remedy for inflation. On the contrary, it tended to regard direct action to restrain increases in money wages as a more appropriate way of intervening or, if all else failed, measures to check the growth of demand.

When Labour came to power they placed their faith in incomes policy in the struggle to limit inflation but with excess demand still continuing and eating into unemployment, they had only limited success. The labour shortage was simply too acute. Between 1964 and 1970 hourly wages rose at an average rate of 6.5 per cent per annum – modest by comparison with rates of increase in the 1970s but well above the average of 4.5 per cent in the previous six years. The rise in prices quickened correspondingly; the average annual rise in consumer prices increased from 2.3 to 4.3 per cent. Labour too, made little use of interest rates as an anti-inflationary weapon, changing bank rate only once in 1965, 1966 and 1969 and twice in 1968, and in 1967 never moving it by more than $\frac{1}{2}$ per cent except after the devaluation in 1967. In no year was bank rate raised above 8 per cent and indeed until devaluation in 1967, 7 per cent was regarded as a crisis rate. Short-term interest rates were thought to be of limited influence except in international movements of funds and increases in long-term rates tended to be viewed largely in terms of the additional burden on government debt, with a bias against any deliberate attempt to raise them. Even after the IMF seminar in 1968 the Treasury remained sceptical, on the basis of its experience in the 1950s, of the influence of monetary policy on the rate of inflation and was anxious to keep rates as low as possible in the interests of holding down interest on government debt and encouraging fixed investment.

In one respect the 1960s were lucky in their efforts to limit inflation. There was no dramatic rise in world commodity prices such as had pushed inflation in Britain into double figures in 1951 and was again a major influence in 1973 even before the great rise in oil prices. Not only did the absence of a major rise in import prices contribute to stability in the price level; it contributed also to a favourable shift in the terms of trade over the decade that was helpful to the standard of living.

While the rise in wages and prices in the 1960s was by later standards limited it was followed almost at once by an acceleration that raised inflation to a record rate in the mid-1970s. It is natural to ask whether the acceleration did not have its roots in earlier events and Chapter 13 drew attention to one possible connection. Between 1966 and 1969 devaluation and the subsequent efforts by Roy Jenkins to bring the economy back into balance raised levels of taxation to such an extent that real wages, after deducting tax and national insurance, showed no increase. By the time incomes policy was abandoned in 1969 workers were in an increasingly militant mood and seeking to recover lost ground in higher wage settlements. As a result hourly wages, which had risen at under 5 per cent per annum in 1969 suddenly accelerated to over 13 per cent in 1970 and continued at very high rates for the next few years before the oil shock and the boom in commodity prices. It is hard to resist the conclusion that the trail for this wage explosion had been laid in earlier years in the 1960s when the government was thought to be holding down wages and when the readjustments that were necessary under Roy Jenkins took away in taxes what had been gained in higher wage settlements.

3 High Employment

The aim of high employment had been pursued since the war with a success that dazzled the public. But what had governments contributed to the achievement? Their efforts had been mainly directed towards holding down an over-buoyant economy, rarely to getting rid of unemployment and reviving an economy in depression. In the 1950s they had never had to consider releasing through the budget in any single year more than an extra £150 million in order to combat a temporary depression and had had far more trouble (for example in 1955-7) in putting an end to a most persistent boom. Demand management had become one of the main tasks of the Treasury and the budget was recognised as the principal instrument of demand management.

The 1960s were in some ways an echo of the 1950s. As in 1951–2, the decade began with full employment that set off an exchange crisis. This was followed by depression in 1962–3 and a renewed boom that proved just as long lasting in 1964–7 as the boom of the middle 1950s. The turning point in 1967 with devaluation in the autumn parallelled developments in 1957 although in that year there was no actual devaluation; the last years of the decade were devoted to readjustment.

The problem in both decades was rarely one of maintaining a high level of employment. Leaving aside the bitter weather in the early months of 1963, unemployment never exceeded 2.5 per cent at any time in the 1960s and in a large region like the South-East remained below 1 per cent for long periods in 1964–6. The difficulty was rather to pursue full employment without damage to some other objective such as stable prices or a fixed exchange rate. The efforts to sustain a high and rising level of employment in 1966, for example, brought the exchange rate into renewed crisis and forced the government to take measures which two years previously they would never have contemplated. As explained in the next section, the effort to protect employment levels in face of disappearing reserves could not be continued indefinitely.

The major failure to stabilise employment in the 1960s was in 1962–3 when earlier and more vigorous action to expand demand should have been taken. The then Chancellor (Selwyn Lloyd) did not greatly mind if unemployment remained at a rather higher level than in mid-1961; and on the information available and the expectation of a large expansion in exports it was defensible to refrain from reflating in the 1962 Budget. By mid-summer, however, it was clear that it had been a mistake to expect an early recovery and some action to boost demand would have been appropriate. It so happened that there was a change of Chancellor for reasons unconnected with the mistake and that the new Chancellor was unwilling to take immediate action that would have seemed to reflect on his predecessor. When he did act in the autumn of 1962 the regulator would have been a more appropriate instrument to use rather than a measure benefiting car production only. That apart, the episode was a mixture of bad forecasting, bad luck and Ministerial misjudgment. Selwyn Lloyd was not too perturbed by developments in the first half of 1962; Reggie Maudling was content to wait when he might have done more earlier.

The main trouble in 1962–3 was not that production went down too far but that it was made to bounce back too high. Here again there was an element of luck. By the summer of 1964 it was obvious that trouble was building up and there was a firm promise from the Chancellor to act in July. But he thought (wrongly, as the Economic Section argued) that the economy was stuck; and an election was due in a few months (an election that, had it rested with him, he would have preferred to hold months earlier). The Treasury was to blame in asking for only a rather modest addition to taxation in the 1964 Budget and in encouraging a highly expansionist budget in 1963. But there was time to put on the brakes if the Chancellor had been willing to apply them instead of simply standing by as the reserves began to drain away. So once again there was a mixture of bad (expansionary) advice, bad luck in the proximity of the election and Ministerial misjudgment.

Although these were both major errors, the consequences up to September 1964 were not really disastrous. Unemployment never rose as high as 2.5 per cent at any time; the rise in the number wholly unemployed from the lowest point in 1961 to the highest point in 1963 was 270,000 much of it due to the appalling weather in the spring of 1963. Industrial production rose in each successive year. The main loss was in manufacturing investment which fell in 1962 by about 20 per cent. In comparison with later depressions it was a rather minor affair.

4 External Balance

Throughout the post-war period the balance of payments has been the main source of weakness in the British economy. It continued to be the subject of controversy and anxiety in the 1960s.

Even under the Conservatives in the early 1960s there was pressure to devalue or float. In the Press economists attacking stop–go policies publicly advocated resorting to devaluation whenever a balance of payments deficit seemed likely to give rise to deflation. There was a readiness to believe that devaluation would put an end to balance of payments deficits almost at once by raising the price of foreign exchange and that the process could be repeated endlessly without ill effects on the trade of the country. The Prime Minister in 1963 urged his Chancellor to consider floating and Maudling, had the Conservatives won the 1964 election, might very well have opted for a float once it became apparent that the import surcharge could have only a limited life.

Whatever they might eventually have done, it was entirely wrong to let the months go by in the summer and autumn of 1964 without any response to the growing deficit – not even an increase in bank rate or the promised use of special deposits. Action should have been taken not later than July and reinforced, if necessary before the election put a stop to further intervention. If the Labour government was irresponsible in doing little or nothing to arrest the outflow of funds when they took office, so too were the Conservatives in earlier months. It is difficult to choose between the fatuity of the Prime Minister's notes to Maudling (above, p. 73) and the equal fatuity of the discussions at No. 10 in the early days of Labour government (above, pp. 100–1). Whatever the case against devaluation in 1964 – and it rested heavily on the presumption that the Labour government would balk at the deflationary measures that should accompany it (as they showed signs of doing even in 1967) – there could be no excuse for two of the key ministers concerned insisting that officials must treat devaluation as unmentionable while the third regarded devaluation as calling for his immediate resignation. On a matter of such cardinal importance the Labour government took a position that was neither wise nor realistic.

Even after 1964 the government's policy remained unrealistic. Until 1967 there was simply no alternative strategy and by then it was too late. Various measures were taken to strengthen the pound but their inadequacy can be measured by the constant need to seek further help from other central banks and the IMF. The threat to the economy may have been even more serious in 1968–9 than it was in 1964–7 but at least the Cabinet was by that time willing to give the Chancellor its full backing for the measures he judged necessary.

The failure to devalue earlier resulted from the concentration of responsibility on a small group of Ministers – the Prime Minister, First Secretary and Chancellor – who made it clear that they wanted no official advice on the matter and disregarded all advice in favour of devaluation. Papers submitted by the advisers they had themselves brought into government went unread. No earlier remonstrance much before November 1967 would have received attention. Apart from that, there were serious doubts whether it would be possible to count on the necessary accompanying measures once a decision to devalue had been taken. There was no inclination to take such measures in 1964 and even in 1967 the measures taken were quite insufficient. It is often suggested that devaluation should have accompanied the measures of July 1966 and, given the more buoyant state of world trade, that might well have been preferable to November 1967. Alternatively it would have been possible to couple a devaluation with the second application for entry to the European Community in May 1967.

CONCLUSION

The picture that emerges of the 1960s is one of considerable success mixed with near disaster. Growth in productivity continued over the decade at a rate that remained well below continental rates in spite of all the efforts to make the British hippopotamus move faster. Governments, as is their way, showed little wisdom in spite of the high intellectual calibre of some of their members and took extraordinary risks with the balance of payments. As they were baled out one after another with foreign credits, the impression of disastrous mismanagement deepened. Yet the credits were repaid, the standard of living rose faster than ever before and unemployment remained remarkably low. What allowed the economy to remain so buoyant?

The answer would seem to lie outside the United Kingdom in the even greater buoyancy of the world economy. Between 1959 and 1969 world industrial production increased by 30 per cent and world trade in manufactures expanded (in real terms) to more than two and a half times its initial amount. In so propitious a world economic environment and with friends so willing to come to the rescue, it is hardly surprising that at the end of the decade Britain shared some of her neighbours' success.

Appendix
An Economic Anatomy of the 1960s

This note is intended to supplement the narrative by an analysis of national income data on the main forces affecting economic activity. Table A.1 shows the increments from year to year in the main elements in GDP at constant 1985 prices as estimated by the Central Statistical Office. Since all estimates of the variables can be no more than approximations, incremental changes in them over short periods are subject to large margins of error. The figures in Table A.1 should be regarded as rough guides to the main changes at work.

While the figures in Table A.1 (and most of the figures in this volume) represent the latest judgment of the CSO, they may differ widely from the earlier official figures that formed the basis of advice to Ministers and ministerial decision. Countless examples could be given: but two will suffice.

Few estimates were of more importance than those of the balance of payments on current account but the official estimates when first published were often very different a few years later and might still undergo amendment twenty or thirty years after publication. Table A.2 compares the figures first published with those now in use.

A second example relates to the index of industrial production: an aggregate of year-on-year increases as first announced yields a total increase between 1959 and 1964 of about 10 per cent while later estimates put the increase at 17 per cent.

One important reason for the changes over time is that more complete data became available. The export figures, for example, were revised upwards systematically when it was discovered in 1969 that there had been serious under-recording.

What matters is not just that the figures kept being changed but that the changes from year to year might be altered and give a different indication of the trend. The direction of change in the balance of payments might be reversed, as in 1963, and the magnitude of the change from one year to the next might shrink as in 1968 or balloon as in 1966. If forecasts set traps for the unwary so do the records of the past.

Table A.1 shows the growth of GDP as the average of three different measures of growth: in output, income and expenditure. As the last two lines of Table A.1 show, the volume of output, whether at market prices or at factor cost, increased in every year, with peaks in 1960, 1964 and 1968 and low points in 1962 and, to a lesser extent, 1966. Of the constituents of GDP, the largest was consumer spending which absorbed 48 per cent of the total increase in income (measured at market prices). In most years consumer spending moved fairly closely with GDP but there were some notable divergences of which the most obvious was in 1969 when higher taxation in the post-devaluation budgets effected a marked slow-down in consumer spending. In other years the fluctuations in consumers' expenditure were much smaller than in national

TABLE A.1 *Changes in the allocation of resources (increase from year to year in £billion at constant 1985 prices)*

	1960	1961	1962	1963	1964	1965	1966	1967	1968	1969	Increase 1959–60
Consumers' expenditure	4.6	2.7	2.8	5.9	4.1	2.1	2.5	3.5	4.1	0.8	33.4
Public authorities' final consumption	0.9	1.6	1.4	0.8	0.8	1.3	1.4	3.0	0.2	−1.0	10.4
Gross domestic fixed capital formation	2.6	3.0	0.2	0.5	5.8	2.1	1.1	3.8	3.0	−0.3	21.8
Value of physical increase in stocks and work in progress	2.5	−1.9	−1.7	1.0	3.4	−1.5	−1.1	−0.3	0.9	0.2	1.4
Exports of goods and services	1.9	1.1	0.6	1.8	1.3	1.7	2.2	0.2	5.5	4.9	21.2
Total final expenditure	13.0	6.3	3.0	10.4	15.5	5.5	6.0	9.3	14.0	5.1	88.7
Imports of goods and services	4.0	−0.3	0.8	1.6	4.2	0.4	1.1	3.1	3.7	1.7	20.3
Gross domestic product (at market prices)	10.6	5.2	2.7	8.2	11.9	5.9	4.5	5.5	10.0	5.3	69.7
Gross domestic product (average at factor cost)	9.2	4.7	2.6	7.1	10.4	5.8	3.9	4.6	9.3	5.5	63.2

SOURCE: *Economic Trends Annual Supplement* (1990 edn) Tables 2 and 3. The figures for GDP are *average* estimates while the others are *expenditure* estimates. Aggregates differ from sum of the components.

TABLE A.2 *Balance of payments estimates then and now (£ million)*

Year	Balance on current account	
	As estimated in the following May	As estimated in 1990
1960	−344	−237
1961	−70	+35
1962	+67	+143
1963	+121	+114
1964	−374	−372
1965	−136	−77
1966	−61	+128
1967	−514	−281
1968	−419	−264
1969	+366	+482

SOURCE: *National Institute Economic Review*; *Economic Trends Annual Supplement 1990*.

income as, for example, in 1962 when the dip of nearly 50 per cent in the growth of GDP was accompanied by a slight *increase* in consumption.

The economic expansion of the 1960s was driven primarily by the growth of fixed investment on the one hand and exports on the other, with imports acting as a damper and stock-building usually inflating the fluctuations that occurred. Figure A.1 shows how fixed investment plus exports dominated the growth of GDP: there is a slight falling off in 1961, a sharp dip in 1962, followed by a boom that developed in 1963–4, an easing of pressure in 1965–6, some renewal of expansion in 1967, and a new boom in 1968 that subsided a little in 1969. Very similar fluctuations occurred in GDP. In fact the fluctuations in activity, largely initiated by changes in fixed investment and exports, produced parallel fluctuations in imports, consumption and even stockbuilding, while the changes in public expenditure on goods and services were usually too small to make much difference except in 1967–9, when the budgets of those years were first inflationary in 1967 and then strongly deflationary in 1968–9.

If we compare the dynamic elements in the 1960s with those in the 1950s, it is clear that expansion in the 1960s was more powerfully driven by the growth in exports and investment. Over the decade as a whole, exports absorbed over 30 per cent of the growth in output compared with 21 per cent in the previous decade and grew in volume in the 1960s by 64 per cent, well above the rate of 40 per cent in the 1950s. The contrast between the two decades is mainly attributable to the setback in exports during the years of rearmament in 1951–2 and the re-emergence of foreign competitors on the one hand, and the stimulus of devaluation in the late 1960s on the other: nearly half the increase in exports in the 1960s took place in the last two years and accounted for three-quarters of the increase in output in those years. The growth of imports, although it, too, accelerated in the 1960s, lagged a little behind the growth of exports by the end of the decade. No doubt the growth of exports was disappointing in comparison with other industrial

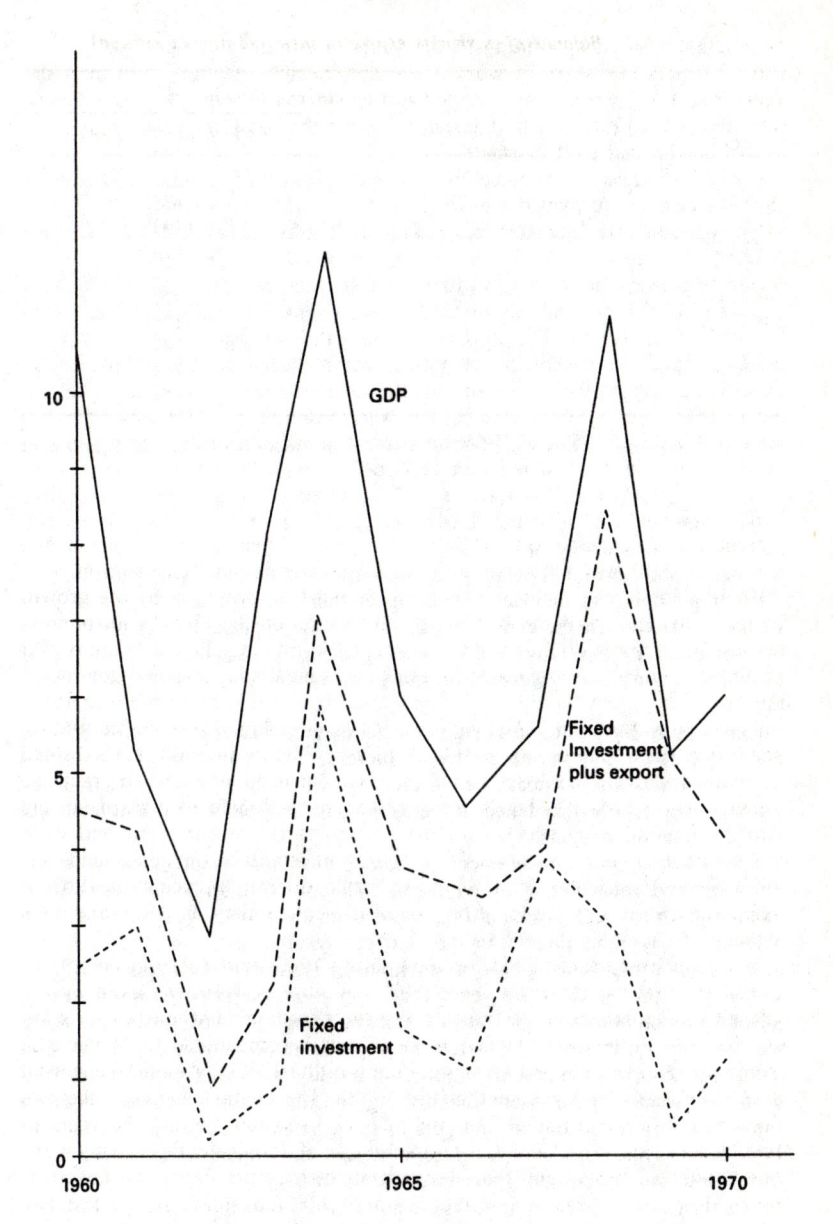

FIGURE A.1 *Annual increase in fixed investment, exports and GDP, 1960–70*

countries – very disappointing in the years before devaluation – so that the United Kingdom's share of world trade continued to decline, even after devaluation. The contribution of exports to expansion over much of the decade was decidedly limited; but it became by far the most important source of growth at the end of the decade.

Fixed investment took much the same proportion of resources as exports over the decade but played a more prominent part in maintaining activity up to devaluation and fluctuated more widely. It grew rather faster than in the previous decade – by 76 per cent compared with 65 per cent – and continued to rise in the proportion of total resources devoted annually to it. A large part of the growth was in public investment especially in the years up to 1967 when, for the first and only time (at 1975 prices but not at 1985 prices!), fixed investment in the public sector exceeded fixed investment in the private sector. The buoyancy of public investment, first in the steel industry then in electricity, was perhaps the most important single factor behind the booms of 1959 and 1964. Investment in manufacturing industry peaked in 1961 but fell to a low point in 1963 before expanding again almost without interruption to a fresh peak in 1970. Whatever else went wrong after 1964, manufacturing investment was nearly 20 per cent higher in the second half of the decade than in the first.

Stocks, both absolutely and as a proportion of output, were on a downward trend over the decade, but as usual there were sharp fluctuations in stockbuilding, much the most volatile of the aggregates. It was positive in the booms of 1959–60 and 1963–4 and again in the recovery in 1968, to all of which it contributed powerfully, but in all other years except 1969 it was falling off.

Expenditure by public authorities on goods and services was another item that expanded faster in the 1960s. It increased most in 1967 when public investment was also at peak, i.e. in the year when the struggle to avoid devaluation was finally abandoned. It increased least in 1968–9 after Roy Jenkins's post-devaluation budgets.

Table A.1 suggests an element of competition for resources between investment and the balance of payments. The pressure in 1964, when both fixed investment and stockbuilding were expanding fast, was relieved by a balance of payments deficit. In the next two years a more moderate growth to fixed investment and a fall in stockbuilding allowed the balance of payments to improve. In those years the fluctuations in imports were largely offset by fluctuations in the rate of stockbuilding. In 1967, however, there was no increase in stocks to match the surge in imports; it was fixed investment that absorbed the resources released by the balance of payments. In the next two years exports were the driving force and the resources required came first from extra output and cuts in government expenditure and then in 1969 from a marked check to investment and the impact of fiscal retrenchment on consumption and government spending.

We turn next to the changes in employment, unemployment and wages and the interactions between them, which go some way to explaining the generation of inflation in the 1960s. Figure A.2 shows the movement in unemployment and hourly wages, the latter serving as a proxy for inflation. The movements in consumer prices, which measure inflation directly, are

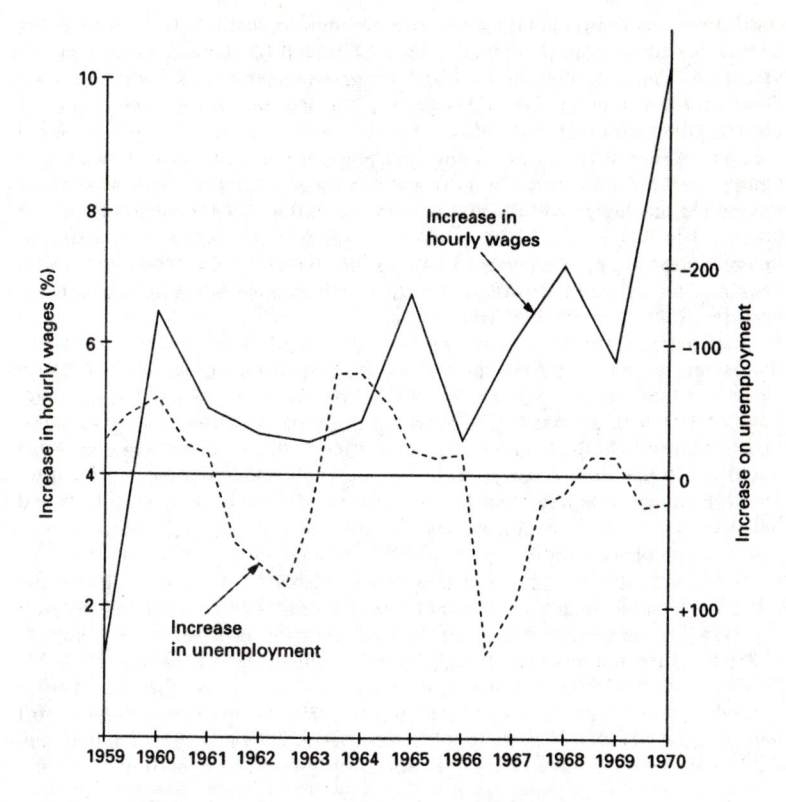

FIGURE A.2 *Unemployment and hourly wages, 1959–70*

not shown, because, although they reflected wage changes they were also affected by many other things: the rise in productivity, changes in import prices, harvest fluctuations (especially the potato harvest). Over the decade as a whole, consumer prices rose by just under 40 per cent, much the same as in the previous decade. Hourly wages increased by 67 per cent so that there was a rise of about 20 per cent in real wages per hour – and a much larger increase in real earnings.

Employment grew in each of the first six years and fell in each of the last four. There were increases in 1960 and then in 1963–5, with a peak in 1964, and a big fall from the middle of 1966 to the middle of 1968, after which the changes were quite minor. Unemployment follows a parallel course the other way round, with a substantial fall in 1960 and a fall from the middle of 1963 to the middle of 1966 succeeded by a rise over the next two years and only small changes in the last two years. The main divergence occurs in 1962 when the employment figures show first a sharp recovery in the first half of the year, then a remarkable reversal in the second half of the year, while the unemployment figures rise steadily in both halves of the year. There are also some divergences in 1961 and 1963, with a sudden drop in the employment figures in 1961 and an equally sharp turnaround in the first half of 1963 without any corresponding fluctuations in unemployment.

The fluctuations in unemployment are reflected in the changes in hourly wages (Figure 1.5). As unemployment begins to mount in 1961, wages rise more slowly and continue to do so until the second half of 1963 when unemployment has begun to fall. Wages then rise faster as unemployment remains low and falling until mid-1966 when a wage-freeze reinforced by rising unemployment almost succeeds in halting the rise in wages. The rise picks up again in the second half of 1967 as the climb in unemployment slackens and continues in 1968–9 after devaluation.

The annual rise in hourly wages had slowed down gradually in each quinquenium since the end of the war, falling from an average of 6.9 per cent in 1945–9 to 5.1 per cent in 1960–4. It was in the 1960s that the downward trend was reversed. The working population, which had grown by a million in the 1950s, began to fall after 1966, and this may have contributed to labour's bargaining power, but more probably reflects greater difficulty in finding suitable employment. It is something of a paradox that wages should begin to rise faster simultaneously with the most determined effort to introduce an incomes policy.

It is hardly surprising that wages should respond, like prices, to the pressure of demand. Indeed what is surprising is that a long sustained period of full employment did not produce an accelerating rise in wages but, until the 1960s, rather the reverse. If employment remains at one level for a long period and then falls to a lower level for an equal period the rise in wages may be quite unaffected. Variations in pressure, and the rate at which workers see their mates lose their jobs, have an effect on wage demands quite different from a change of regime, involving prolonged operation at a higher or lower level of unemployment.

Notes

Notes to Chapter 1: Introduction

1. 'Policies for Faster Growth', *National Institute Economic Review*, February 1962, p. 55.
2. *The Economist*, 28 October 1961, p. 313.
3. 'Sustainable Growth' and 'Waiting for Exports, by R. C. Tress and J. Miles Fleming, in the *London and Cambridge Economic Bulletin*, June 1961, pp. iii–v and June 1962, pp. i–iv.
4. 'Policies for Faster Growth', *National Institute Economic Review*, February 1962, pp. 55–56.
5. The membership of EEC and EFTA expanded over time. The figures quoted above relate to the original members so that they understate the increase in the importance of trade links with both groups.
6. This view is contested in J. K. Bowers, P. C. Cheshire, A. E. Webb and R. Weeden, 'Some Aspects of Unemployment and the Labour Market, 1966–71', in *National Institute Economic Review*, November 1972, pp. 75–88.
7. These figures are all taken from Table 138 in *British Labour Statistics*. They are strictly comparable and have not been extended to 1970 from other sources in case changes in the industrial classification might upset comparability.
8. These figures are at current prices. At 1975 prices public investment in 1967 was over 50 per cent of the total.

Notes to Chapter 2: The First Cycle, 1957–61

1. For the early history of the Economic Section, see Alec Cairncross and Nita Watts, *The Economic Section, 1939–61* (London: Routledge, 1989). For an account of the development of economic advising in the United Kingdom since 1939, see the chapter I contributed to *The Role of the Economist in Government*, ed. J. A. Pechman (Hemel Hempstead: Harvester Wheatsheaf, 1989).
2. A brief first-hand account of the development of policy between 1957 and the spring of 1961 is given in *The Robert Hall Diaries, 1954–61*, ed. Alec Cairncross (London: Unwin Hyman/Routledge, 1991). I have drawn also on an unpublished Treasury study of demand management between 1958 and 1964 by R. F. Bretherton.
3. *The Robert Hall Diaries, 1954–61*, p. 127.
4. Ibid.
5. These figures relate to wholly unemployed, excluding school-leavers, as given in *British Labour Statistics: Historical Abstract 1886–1968*, Table 165.
6. 'Economic Prospects in July 1959', Note by Sir Robert Hall, 28 July 1959 in PRO T 171.506.

7. 'The Lessons of Reflation', EA(63)2, 16 January 1963.
8. Robert Hall, minutes and memorandum of 6 February, 9 February and 19 February 1960 in PRO T 230/419.
9. 'The Chancellor thinks of little else than the menace of returning inflation', *The Robert Hall Diaries, 1954–61*, p. 217, Nov. 19, 1960.
10. *The Robert Hall Diaries, 1954–61*, p. 223.
11. Ibid., p. 221; minutes and briefs of 25 November, 1 and 3 December 1959, by Hall and Makins in PRO T 230/387, 'Development of Monetary Policy'.
12. *The Robert Hall Diaries*, p. 222.
13. Ibid., p. 228.
14. Ibid., p. 229.
15. Ibid., p. 231.
16. Ibid., p. 232.
17. Meeting of Budget Committee, 16 February 1960, in PRO T 171/506.
18. Ibid.
19. Meeting of Budget Committee, 21 April 1960, in PRO T 171/506; *The Robert Hall Diaries, 1954–61*, p. 236.
20. D. R. Thorpe, *Selwyn Lloyd* (London: Jonathan Cape, 1989) p. 337.
21. Ibid., p. 360.
22. Meeting of Cabinet on 20 July 1961 in PRO CC (61) 61.
23. The reader should be warned that all estimates of rates of change of production, especially over very short periods, are dependent on impossibly exact measurement at two different dates, and are necessarily, therefore, very approximate. This is indeed obvious from the large retrospective changes cited above.

Notes to Chapter 3: The July Measures and After, 1961–2

1. Working Party on Balance of Payments Trends, 9 May 1961, in PRO T230/553.
2. Ibid.
3. 'Economic Growth and National Efficiency?' C (61) 94, 10 July 1961 in PRO CAB129/105.
4. *Control of Public Expenditure*, Cmnd 1432.
5. Five Year Plan for Public Expenditure: Memorandum by the Chancellor of the Exchequer, C (61)88, 29 June 1961 in PRO CAB 129/105. For the earlier Cabinet discussions see CC(61)19, 28 March 1961 in CAB 128/35; and for the report by officials, 'Public Expenditure and Resources 1961–2 to 1965–6', C(61)43 in CAB 129/105.
6. Why Selwyn Lloyd changed his mind on the second regulator is not clear, especially as he had successfully fought off criticisms, for example that it would raise industrial costs. Opposition had been expressed before the April Budget by John Boyd Carpenter, Minister of National Insurance, who threatened to resign. His objection was that it would show how easily the employer's contribution could be increased and that it would give rise to claims for higher benefits. After Selwyn Lloyd wrote to the Prime Minister (PRO PREM 11/3762) Boyd Carpenter was squared by the inclusion of an agreed paragraph in the Budget speech. Similar

objections may have continued to be urged by other ministers.
7. PRO PREM 11/3883, Prime Minister to Chancellor, 5 November 1961.
8. Ibid. Prime Minister to Chancellor, 11 April 1962.
9. PRO PREM 11/4202, Prime Minister to Chancellor, 11 April 1962.
10. Ibid. Prime Minister to Chancellor, 14 June 1962 and 11 April 1962.
11. Ibid. Prime Minister to Chancellor, 4 July 1961.
12. Correspondence between PM and Chancellor of the Exchequer on Financial Policy in PRO PREM 11/3883, 4201.
13. Letter from PM to Chancellor, 23 June 1962 in PRO PREM 11/4201.
14. Note from Chancellor to PM, 4 July 1962, covering Treasury reply to Macmillan's letter of 23 June 1962 in PRO PREM 11/4201.
15. Letter from Maudling to Macmillan, 2 July 1962, in PRO PREM 11/4201.
16. Table 13, *British Labour Statistics*. If one uses the figures from the April and October earnings enquiries (Table 85) the increase in wage-rates from October 1961 to April 1962 was 1.4 per cent compared with 3.0 the year before and 1.4 the year after.
17. 'Economic Growth and National Efficiency', C(61)94, 10 July 1961 in PRO 129/105.
18. Cmnd/1432.
19. 'Planning by Whom?', *The Economist*, 29 August 1961, p. 773.
20. 'No Mr Lloyd', *The Economist*, 7 October 1961, p. 13.
21. 'Plan for 1962', *The Economist*, 9 December 1961, p. 997. The writer suggests a rise of 4–5 per cent in output and 2–3 per cent in wages with a probable expansion in exports by 6 per cent.
22. There was some disagreement as to what the current rate was. The rate of growth in productivity in the 1950s had averaged 2 per cent but there had been some acceleration, certainly to $2\frac{1}{2}$ per cent, in the course of the decade. The Neddy staff was more optimistic than the Economic Section about the continuation of this acceleration and regarded a 4 per cent growth in output (allowing for an expansion of 0.7 per cent in employment) as no great improvement on current performance.
23. In May 1963 Selwyn Lloyd told me that according to Henry Brooke, the Chief Secretary, the rise in government expenditure was deliberately calculated to make things difficult for the Labour Party if they got in in 1964.

Notes to Chapter 4: The Maudling 'Dash for Growth'

1. *The Economist*, 10 November 1962, p. 544.
2. PRO PREM 11/4202.
3. Ibid.
4. Ibid.
5. Ibid.
6. Prime Minister to Chancellor, 20 February 1963, in PRO PREM 11/4202.
7. Discussion between Prime Minister and Chancellor, 21 February 1962, in PRO PREM 11/4202.

Notes to Chapter 5: A Change of Government, 1964

1. See p. 105.
2. F. Blackaby (ed.), *British Economic Policy, 1960–74* (Cambridge: Cambridge University Press for National Institute Economic and Social Research, 1978) pp. 34–5.

Notes to Chapter 6: A Strategy for the Pound?

1. Brian Tew, in F. Blackaby (ed.), *British Economic Policy, 1960–74*, p. 334.
2. S. Howson and D. Winch, *The Economic Advisory Council, 1930–1939* p. 89 (Cambridge: Cambridge University Press, 1977) p. 89.

Notes to Chapter 7: The Exchange Crisis of 1965

1. Hansard, 6 April 1965, col. 287.
2. The figures in Table 7.1 differ slightly because of later amendment.
3. *Financial Statistics*, April 1965, Table 4.
4. F. Blackaby (ed.), *British Economic Policy, 1960–74*, p. 35.
5. As the *National Institute Economic Review* pointed out, no public investment programme had been published so that 'cuts of an unknown size are being made in an unknown sum, to take effect at an unknown time' (August 1965, p. 8).
6. The cuts made were smaller than intended but apparently fully implemented. The *net* effect, however, would appear to have been much smaller (Blackaby, op. cit., pp. 35, 113–4).
7. *National Institute Economic Review*, August 1965, p. 18.
8. *London and Cambridge Economic Bulletin*, March 1966, p. v.
9. Ibid., September 1965, p. xvi.
10. *National Institute Economic Review*, January 1966, p. 4.
11. Ibid., August 1965, p. 5. The National Institute predicted that gross fixed investment would peak in the first quarter of 1966 and decline gently thereafter.
12. The National Institute forecast an increase in output in 1966 of 1 per cent in August, 2.2 per cent in January 1966 and 2.6 per cent in May.
13. 'Two Views about the Labour Market', *London and Cambridge Economic Bulletin*, March 1966. For adult men the fall was from 47.7 hours in October 1964 to 47.0 hours in October 1965.

Notes to Chapter 10: The Countdown to Devaluation

1. F. Blackaby (ed.), *British Economic Policy, 1960–74*, p. 41.
2. J. Callaghan, *Time and Chance* (London: Collins, 1987) pp. 218–19.
3. H. Wilson, *The Labour Government, 1964–1970: A Personal Record* (London: Weidenfeld & Nicolson and Michael Joseph, 1971) p. 456.
4. Ibid., p. 449.
5. Ibid., p. 451.
6. Ibid., p. 452.

Notes to Chapter 11: From Devaluation to the Gold Rush

1. For a review of estimates of the impact of the 1967 devaluation see A. Cairncross and B. Eichengreen, *Sterling in Decline* (Oxford: Blackwell, 1983) pp. 197 *et seq*. Estimates of the effect on the current balance of payments in 1970 vary between £425 million and £1036 million. There is close agreement as to exports but marked disagreement on imports, four estimates putting the reductions in volume at the absurd level of zero. Estimates of the effect on invisibles are generally agreed on an estimate of about £300 million. My own assessment would be that virtually the whole of the improvement in the balance of payments of £1070 million between 1967 and 1970 can be attributed to devaluation.
2. Robert Solomon, *The International Monetary System 1945–76* (New York: Harper & Row, 1977), pp. 36, 104, 114.
3. Ibid., p. 119.

Notes to Chapter 12: A Long Hard Slog, 1968

1. *Economic Trends*, December 1967, p. ii.
2. Roy Jenkins, *A Life at the Centre* (London: Macmillan, 1991) pp. 270–1.

Notes to Chapter 13: Success at Last, 1969

1. *The Economist*, 18 January 1969, p. 16. *The Economist* was no more optimistic in May.
2. Roy Jenkins, op. cit., p. 277.
3. These figures are derived from *Economic Trends Annual Supplement*, 1981 edition, p. 126. The figures given in *Financial Statement and Budget Report 1969–70*, Table 6 attribute about £100 million more to the IMF.
4. Roy Jenkins, op. cit., p. 276.
5. *The Economist*, 8 February 1969 and 17 May 1969; *Bank of England Quarterly Bulletin*, September 1969, p. 288.
6. *The Economist*, 25 January 1969.
7. Ibid.
8. Roy Jenkins, op. cit., p. 287.
9. Ibid., pp. 288–90.
10. F. and A. Cairncross (eds), *The Legacy of the Golden Age* (London: Routledge, 1992) Ch. 2, especially pp. 70–1 and 75–6.
11. 'Some Aspects of the Present Inflation', *National Institute Economic Review*, February 1971, p. 38.
12. *National Institute Economic Review*, May 1974, p. 20.

Notes to Chapter 14: Monetary and Financial Policy in the 1960s

1. This figure relates to borrowing by the central government, not by the entire public sector (the PSBR) which borrowed £1826 million in 1967.
2. Blackaby, op. cit., p. 308. Nearly all of this was borrowed *after* devaluation in November.
3. For a fuller treatment, see Brian Tew, 'Policies Aimed at Improving the

Balance of Payments', in F. Blackaby, op. cit., pp. 325–38.
4. For a fuller account of requests and ceilings in the 1960s, see C. D. Cohen, *British Economic Policy, 1960–69* (London: Butterworths, 1971) pp. 130–3.
5. The best full account of monetary policy in the 1960s is in Chapter 5 by Brian Tew and Chapter 6 by Michael Artis in Blackaby, op. cit.
6. These figures are for end-March dates.
7. Sales were discontinued when the IMF drew them to the attention of the Treasury as incompatible with the target for DCE.
8. *The Robert Hall Diaries, 1954–61*, p. 149.
9. Ibid., p. 261.
10. Governor to Chancellor/Prime Minister, PRO PREM 11/3285.
11. Macmillan to Ormsby-Gore, 3 July 1962 in PRO PREM 11/4201.
12. Macmillan to Selwyn Lloyd in PRO PREM 11/3883.
13. Ibid., letters of 9 May, 22 May, 1962.
14. PRO PREM 11/4201, Minute by P. de Zulueta, 29 June 1962.
15. PRO PREM 11/4203.
16. Ibid.
17. Correspondence between PM and Chancellor of the Exchequer on Financial Policy in PRO PREM 11/3883, 4201.
18. Letter from PM to Chancellor, 23 June 1962 in PRO PREM 11/4201.
19. Note from Chancellor to PM, 4 July 1962, covering Treasury reply to Macmillan's letter of 23 June 1962 in PRO PREM 11/4201.
20. Letter from Maudling to Macmillan, 2 July 1962, in PRO PREM 11/4201.
21. Robert Solomon, op. cit., pp. 63–4.
22. Maudling to Macmillan, 15 May 1963, in PRO PREM 11/4201.
23. Jacques J. Polak, 'The International Monetary Issues of the Bretton Woods Era: Are They Still Relevant?' (from a symposium in honour of Rinaldo Ossola).

Notes to Chapter 15: Economic Management in the 1960s: A Summing-up

1. For an economic history the reader should consult *British Economic Policy 1960–74* (ed. F. Blackaby; Cambridge University Press for National Institute, 1978) and, for an assessment of the policies of the Labour government, *The Labour Government's Economic Record 1964–1970* (ed. W. Beckerman; Duckworth, 1972). Some aspects of the problems of the 1960s are considered in *The Legacy of the Golden Age: The 1960s and their economic consequences* (ed. A. and F. Cairncross; Routledge, 1992).
2. In *The Labour Government's Economic Record: 1964–1970* (p. 12) Andrew Graham and Wilfred Beckerman assert that 'a deficit can be *corrected instantly*' [their italics] by 'floating' – a statement easily misunderstood. Other economists held a similar view of the equilibrating power of exchange depreciation.
3. The improvement in productivity growth depends on the periods chosen for comparison. It rose by about 50 per cent in manufacturing between the 1950s and the first half of the 1960s and continued to improve up to 1968 but grew rather little in the next two years. Averaged over 1964–70

the growth in productivity in manufacturing was hardly any faster than between 1960 and 1964. Measured over the whole economy, the growth in productivity accelerated between 1960–4 and 1964–8 from 2.3 to 2.8 per cent per annum. Again the improvement would be very much less if the comparison were with 1964–70.

Bacon and Eltis in *Britain's Economic Problem* argue that output per man-hour in manufacturing industry accelerated from 2.2 per cent per annum in 1951–62 to 4.1 per cent per annum in 1962–75 (and so *exceeded* the rate assumed in the National Plan) and that this potential for growth was thrown away by failure to make the necessary investment in manufacturing capacity. The figures appearing in the National Institute Economic Review indicate an acceleration in 1962–75 to 3.7 per cent rather than 4.1 per cent per annum. They also imply a cumulative improvement at 3.6 per cent per annum in 1960–5 leaving a negligible further improvement after 1965. These rates relate only to manufacturing which is a limited part of the whole economy. Estimates for the growth of GDP indicate a somewhat slower rate of growth and a similar tendency for the acceleration in the first half of the 1960s to peter out in the second half of the decade.

Calendar of Main Events, 1960-9

1960
10 January	End of eight months' steel strike in the United States.
14 January	46 collieries to be closed.
21 January	Bank rate raised to 5 per cent.
25 February	Bank of England reduces support price for gilt-edged.
3 March	Report of Guilleband Committee on railway pay.
13 March	Development Assistance Group set up.
4 April	Budget raises profits tax and tobacco duty.
28 April	First call for Special Deposits; hire-purchase restrictions reimposed.
2 May	European Free Trade Area begins to operate.
23 June	Bank rate raised to 6 per cent.
27 July	Selwyn Lloyd becomes Chancellor of the Exchequer.
12 August	Federal Reserve discount rate reduced to 3 per cent.
30 August	Abandonment of over 1000 restrictive agreements in the UK.
14 September	Foundation of OPEC.
22 September	W. Germany budgets for a 6 per cent increase in the GNP in 1961.
27 October	Bank rate reduced to $5\frac{1}{2}$ per cent.
8 November	Election of John F. Kennedy as President of USA.
14 November	Ford Motor Co. bids £129 million for its English affiliate.
8 December	Bank rate falls to 5 per cent.

1961
19 January	Hire purchase restrictions eased.
15 February	Ten European countries move to convertibility under Article 8.
5 March	Deutschmark revalued by 5 per cent; Dutch guilder follows; British reserves fall by £50 million in a day.
1 April	Graduated state pension scheme comes into operation.
17 April	UK Budget introduces two tax 'regulators' and reduces surtax on earned incomes.
31 May	South Africa leaves Commonwealth.
1 July	Lord Cromer succeeds Mr Cobbold as Governor of Bank of England.
20 July	Plowden Report on *Control of Public Expenditure* (Cmnd 1432).
25 July	UK mini budget imposes indirect tax regulator, raises bank rate to 7 per cent and announces 'pay pause' in the public sector. Planning Council to be appointed.

Calendar of Main Events, 1960–9

31 July	Fourth and final report of Council of Prices, Productivity and Incomes.
4 August	UK obtains credit of $2 billion from IMF.
10 August	UK applies for membership of the EEC. Negotiations begun in Brussels on 8 November.
30 September	OEEC becomes OECD with the United States and Canada as full members.
2 November	Bill to limit number of Commonwealth immigrants; bank rate reduced to 6 per cent (6½ per cent on 5 October).
16 November	Electricity Council breaks the 'pay pause': rebuked by Prime Minister.
17 November	OECD members accept target of 50 per cent growth in output between 1960 and 1970.
22 November	TUC defer agreement to join NEDC because of disagreement with pay policy.
18 December	Sir Robert Shone appointed Director General of NEDC.

1962

1 January	IMF obtains drawing rights of $6 billion from ten member countries under the General Agreement to Borrow (GAB).
24 January	TUC votes to join NEDC.
2 February	Publication of *Incomes Policy: the next step* (Cmnd 1626) indicating 'guiding light' of 2–2½ per cent or wage increases.
14 March	Government loses seat to Liberals at Orpington.
22 March	Bank rate reduced to 5 per cent (5½ per cent 8 March).
31 March	End of 'pay pause'.
9 April	Budget. Abolition of schedule of tax on owner-occupiers.
17 April	Talks on European treaty union broken off indefinitely.
4 May	Canada reverts to fixed rate of exchange after floating.
9 May	NEDC to examine implications of annual 4 per cent growth from 1961 to 1966.
28 May	Sharpest fall on Wall St since 1929.
29 May	*Financial Times* index of industrial ordinary shares falls 18 points but recovers 15 points to 258 next day.
31 May	Reduction in Special Deposits from 3 to 2 per cent.
4 June	Hire-purchase relaxation but not on cars.
3 July	Engineering unions accept 3 per cent increase in pay for 3 million workers.
13 July	Seven Ministers leave Cabinet including the Chancellor. Reginald Maudling takes over.
24 July	National Incomes Commission to be set up; opposed by trade unions.
30 July	William Armstrong succeeds Sir Frank Lee as Joint Permanent Secretary of the Treasury.
31 July	All debts to IMF discharged.
1 August	First stage of Common Agricultural Policy comes into force.
19 September	UK proposal of Mutual Currency Account at Annual Meeting of IMF: opposed by USA.

27 September	Special Deposits reduced from 2 to 1 per cent.
3 October	Chancellor announces reflationary measures: release of post-war credits, additional public investment and removal of ceiling on bank advances.
11 October	President Kennedy signs Trade Expansion Act.
23–28 October	Cuban Missile Crisis.
5 November	Increased investment allowances; purchase tax on cars cut from 45 to 25 per cent.
19 November	Release of last 1 per cent of Special Deposits.
26 December	Cold spell begins, lasting over two months.

1963

1 January	Cuts in purchase tax from 45 to 30 per cent on television and radio sets, records and cosmetics.
4 January	Bank rate reduced to 4 per cent.
14 January	De Gaulle vetoes UK membership of EEC; President Kennedy proposes $6 billion tax cut in 1963.
11 February	Unemployment (including temporarily stopped) reaches 878,000.
14 February	Harold Wilson elected leader of Parliamentary Labour Party in succession to Hugh Gaitskell (died 18 January).
11 March	Sterling below dollar parity for first time since August 1961; outflow of short-term funds.
3 April	Expansionary budget in UK. 'Free' depreciation in development districts; abolition of Schedule A; new 'guiding light' of 3–3½ per cent. Net effect in full year +£460.
15 April	NEDC publishes *Conditions Favourable to Faster Growth*.
21 June	P. P. Schweitzer succeeds Per Jacobson as Managing Director of IMF.
18 July	President Kennedy announces new measures to improve US balance of payments including 15 per cent tax on purchases of foreign securities and request for $500 million standby credit from IMF.
26 July	Japan joins OECD.
29 September	IMF agrees to set up two enquiries into world liquidity requirements.
19 October	Lord Home succeeds Harold MacMillan as Prime Minister.
23 October	Robbins Report on Higher Education.
14 November	Industrial Training Bill sets up seven new training boards.
22 November	Assassination of President Kennedy.
18 December	UK public spending to increase by 4.1 per cent annually over next four years.

1964

27 January	UK school-leaving age to be raised to 16 in 1970.
5 February	TUC rejects NEDC draft of a prices and incomes policy statement.
25 February	Resale Price Maintenance Bill introduced: becomes law on 16 July.

Calendar of Main Events, 1960–9

3 March	Ministry of Transport agrees to Beeching proposals for railway closures.
16 March	President Johnson submits $1000 million 'attack on poverty' bill to Congress.
14 April	UK budget raises taxes; aims to reduce rate of growth from 5.6 to 4 per cent.
4 May	Kennedy Round opens in Geneva,
28 July	IMF renews stand-by credit of $1000 million to the United Kingdom.
10 September	Governors of IMF agree to 25 per cent increase in quotas.
15 October	Labour party wins General Election with overall majority of five.
16 October	Brezhnev succeeds Khrushchev as First Secretary of Soviet Communist Party.
16 October	China explodes her first nuclear device.
26 October	UK government announces measures to reduce external deficit estimated at £70–800 million; surcharge of 15 per cent on all manufactured imports and system of export rebates.
3 November	Lyndon Johnson elected President of the United States.
11 November	UK budget raises taxes and national insurance contributions and announces increase in pensions in 1965.
19 November	EFTA Council not satisfied of need for surcharge without consultation.
23 November	UK bank rate raised to 7 per cent.
25 November	Bank of England announces credits of $3000 million from banks of sixteen countries and the Bank of International Settlements (BIS).
16 December	Joint 'Statement of Intent' on prices and incomes policy signed by Government, CBI and TUC.
18 December	GATT Council declares UK import surcharge a violation of the Treaty.

1965

5 January	French government to convert dollar holdings into gold.
25 January	Biggest increase in US social expenditure since the New Deal.
29 January	EFTA demands immediate cut in 15 per cent import surcharge.
4 February	General de Gaulle demands abandonment of reserve currencies and return to gold standard.
10 February	President Johnson announces plan for reducing US balance of payments deficit.
17 February	India imposes 10 per cent import surcharge.
18 February	Board of Trade orders end of all resale price maintenance.
22 February	UK import surcharge to be cut in April to 10 per cent.
22 February	UK public expenditure to be limited to increase of 4.25 per cent per annum.
26 February	IMF quotas to be raised by 25 per cent (more for larger countries).

17 March	TUC agrees to 3–3.5 per cent norm for wage increases.
6 April	UK budget introduces (long-term) capital gains tax and corporation tax. Increased taxation of £164 million in 1965/6, £217 million in a full year.
29 April	Call for 1 per cent Special Deposits.
30 April	Publication of steel nationalisation White Paper.
6 May	London clearing banks to limit increase in lending to 5 per cent in 1965–6.
6 May	First meeting of National Board for Prices and Incomes.
12 May	The United Kingdom draws $1.4 billion from IMF.
3 June	Bank rate cut from 7 to 6 per cent; hire-purchase deposits increased.
1 July	France decides to block further progress on Common Market.
27 July	Restrictive financial measures in the United Kingdom. Cuts in public investment of £200 million per annum. Tighter exchange controls and hire-purchase restrictions. Building licences for some private projects over £100,000.
9 September	General de Gaulle calls for revision of Treaty of Rome, repudiating supra-national provisions.
16 September	Publication of *The National Plan*.
22 September	TUC sets up 'early warning system' for wage claims (White Paper issued 11 November: Cmnd 2808).
11 November	Southern Rhodesia declares unilateral independence.
18 November	NCB to close 150 collectives in next 2–3 years.

1966

17 January	Investment allowances to be replaced by 20 per cent cash grant on new plant and machinery in manufacturing industry.
25 January	UK government to set up Industrial Reorganization Corporation to encourage mergers.
1 February	London clearing banks asked to limit advances to 105 per cent of March 1965 level.
8 February	Hire-purchase restrictions lightened.
10 March	France withdraws from NATO.
31 March	UK General Election gives Labour increased majority of ninety-seven.
3 May	UK budget introduces Selective Employment Tax and seeks voluntary restraints on investment in developed sterling area countries.
13 June	$2000 million credits to the United Kingdom arranged at BIS annual meeting.
3 July	Frank cousins resigns as Minister of Technology.
20 July	Harold Wilson announces measures to reduce home demand by £500 million and overseas spending by £150 million: voluntary wage freeze.
14 July	Bank rate raised to 7 per cent; Special Deposits doubled.
9 August	George Brown moves to foreign office; replaced by Michael Stewart.

Calendar of Main Events, 1960–9

25 August	Group of Ten issue *Report on International Liquidity*.
4 October	Compulsory provisions of Prices and Incomes Act are actuated.
22 November	White Paper on wages and prices policy during period of severe restraint (Cmnd 3150).
30 November	Import surcharge removed: record trade surplus.
31 December	Final reduction to zero in EFTA of internal tariffs on industrial goods.

1967

11 January	President Johnson asks Congress for $4500 million in new taxes for Vietnam War.
20 January	Finance Ministers of the United States and four main European countries agree at Chequers to co-operate in keeping interest rates down.
26 January	Bank rate reduced to $6\frac{1}{2}$ per cent.
16 February	UK government spending to be £660 million higher in 1967–8.
13 March	Loan of $1 billion from BIS renewed for one more year.
21 March	White Paper on Prices and Incomes Policy (Cmnd 3235). Voluntary vetting system by TUC and CBI to replace compulsory notification.
11 April	Neutral UK budget aiming at 3 per cent growth in 1967–8; ceiling on bank advances removed.
4 May	Bank rate falls to $5\frac{1}{2}$ per cent (from 6 per cent on 16 March).
11 May	United Kingdom applies to join EEC.
31 May	PWLB introduces market rates for local authority borrowing.
5 June	Yom Kippur War between Israel and neighbours; fighting ends 12 June.
9 June	White Paper on Regional Employment Premium (Cmnd 3310): to be operative 4 September.
30 June	End of period of severe (wage) restraint; period of moderation to follow.
30 June	Kennedy Round tariff agreements signed.
19 July	Large natural gas strike off Norfolk coast.
24 July	Cutback in UK government spending to 3 per cent average over next three years.
28 August	Michael Stewart gives up post; Harold Wilson takes personal charge of DEA.
29 August	United Kingdom relaxes hire-purchase restrictions.
1 September	Arabs restore fuel oil supplies to West.
11 September	Group of Ten agree to create SDRs to supplement reserves.
2 November	Test rate of discount for nationalised industries fixed at 8 per cent (Cmnd 3437).
9 November	Bank rate raised to $6\frac{1}{2}$ per cent (6 per cent, 19 October).
18 November	Devaluation of pound sterling from $2.80 to $2.40; bank rate increased to 8 per cent; target of £500 million improvement in balance of payments.

Calendar of Main Events, 1960–9

29 November	James Callaghan (Chancellor) and Roy Jenkins (Home Secretary) exchange places; IMF agrees to standby credit of $1400 million; Letter of Intent next day fixes limits for government borrowing and 'domestic credit creation'.
29 November	Federal Reserve Bank of New York announces increase in swap facilities to $6780 million after pressure on dollar.
12 December	Informal central bank agreement to limit demands for gold from gold pool countries.
19 December	France vetoes discussions by EEC of applications to join by the United Kingdom, Eire, Denmark and Norway.
21 December	Chancellor announces further cuts of £600 million to be made after Christmas in government spending.
21 December	Fiftieth Report from Prices and Incomes Board.

1968

1 January	President Johnson announces restrictions on foreign spending designed to save $3000 million in 1968.
16 January	UK Prime Minister announces cuts in government spending to save £700 million in 1968–9.
16 January	Industrial Expansion Bill to provide aid for industrial modernisation (Cmnd 3509).
12 February	Basle credits renewed for a further year.
29 February	OECD calls for 5.5 per cent economic growth in 1968 in France, Germany and Italy to offset US restrictions.
7 March	OECD Working Party No. 3 urges cut in the United Kingdom official target from 4 to 3 per cent growth.
15 March	London Stock Exchange, foreign exchange and gold market closed; George Brown resigns as Foreign Secretary.
18 March	After meeting in Washington, two-tier gold system is established.
19 March	Stringent UK budget to raise £923 million in new taxation in 1968–9; legislation to follow enforcing maximum increase in wages and dividends of 3.5 per cent in year from end July.
21 March	Bank rate reduced to $7\frac{1}{2}$ per cent.
25 March	Chancellor rejects TUC Economic Committee's call for 6 per cent growth target.
1 April	London gold market re-opens.
3 April	White Paper on Productivity, Prices and Incomes Policy in 1968 and 1969 (Cmnd 3590) announces legislation to freeze wages for twelve months, enforce price reductions and control rents and dividends.
11 April	Restrictive Trade Practices Bill.
6 May	Demonstrations by Sorbonne students in Paris; general strike on 14 May; riots continuing on 24 May.
29 May	Pompidou announces agreement with French trade unions and employers.
5 June	Senator Robert Kennedy assassinated in Los Angeles.
7 June	Douglas Jay calls for withdrawal of application to join EEC.

Calendar of Main Events, 1960–9

26 June	France announces temporary import quotas, export aids and price controls for second half of June; GATT accepts quota restrictions.
1 July	Kennedy Round tariff cuts implemented.
8 July	'Basle facilities' of $2 billion agreed to help the United Kingdom offset sterling balance fluctuations.
9 July	Monopolies Commission rejects merger between Lloyds, Barclays and Martins by six votes to four; Martins accept takeover bid from Barclays on 25 July.
13 August	French budget aims at 7 per cent growth in 1969.
21 August	Invasion of Czechoslovakia by Warsaw Pact.
19 September	Bank rate reduced to 7 per cent.
30 September	Labour Party Conference votes by large majority for repeal of Prices and Incomes Act.
16 October	Seminar at UK Treasury with IMF on monetary policy.
25 October	Sterling finance of trade between non-sterling countries forbidden.
1 November	New restrictions on hire purchase in the United Kingdom.
6 November	Richard Nixon elected President of the United States.
16 November	Deutschmark exceeds dollar ceiling in Zurich.
20 November	Flight from the franc: main foreign currency markets closed for three days. Group of Ten Finance and Economic Ministers meet with central bankers in Bonn, extend $2000 million standby credits to France on 22 November; De Gaulle rejects widely expected 10 per cent franc devaluation and cuts Budget deficit by Fr. 5000 million.
22 November	UK Chancellor announces import deposit scheme; use of tax regulator; reduced ceiling on bank lending.
15 December	NEDC accepts 3 per cent growth target for 1969 but TUC reasserts its 6 per cent target next day.
21 December	The United States launches Apollo spacecraft with crew of three to circle the moon.

1969

17 January	White Paper on *In Place of Strife: a Policy for Industrial Relations* (Cmnd 3888).
29 January	100th Report of Prices and Incomes Board.
31 January	Bank of England reminds banks of 98 per cent ceiling to lending.
10 February	Labour Party Executive rejects provisions of *In Place of Strife*.
14 February	Government to encourage nationalised industries to raise capital abroad.
27 February	Bank rate raised to 8 per cent in response to overlending by banks.
2 March	Concorde's maiden flight in France; 9 April in the United Kingdom.
17 March	Gas Council borrows £31 million on German capital market.
4 April	US bank rate raised to 6 per cent: highest for forty years.

15 April	UK budget raises additional £345 million in new taxation.
28 April	Resignation of de Gaulle.
12 May	Danish bank rate at 9 per cent.
2 June	Bank of England halves interest paid on Special Deposits to clearing banks for failure to restrict lending to 98 per cent.
12 June	British exports reported under-recorded by £10 million per month.
18 June	British government drops Industrial Relations Bill.
19–20 June	Six National Board for Prices and Incomes reports issued.
23 June	New Letter of Intent to IMF giving targets for balance of payments surplus, public expenditure and domestic credit creation.
17 July	Germany increases minimum reserve ratios of commercial banks by 10 per cent.
21 July	Armstrong steps onto the moon.
22 July	The United Kingdom imposes tariffs on Commonwealth imports of textiles.
8 August	France devalues franc by 11.1 per cent.
19 August	Test rate of discount raised to 10 per cent.
3 September	TUC votes for complete repeal of Prices and Incomes Act.
11 September	West German bank rate raised to 6 per cent.
21 September	IMF Annual Report opposes floating rates of exchange.
28 September	Deutschmark floats temporarily.
5 October	Department of Economic Affairs abolished.
8 October	French bank rate reaches 8 per cent.
17 October	Arthur Burns succeeds William McChesney Martin at Federal Reserve Board.
21 October	Willy Brandt becomes West German Chancellor.
24 October	Deutschmark revalued by 9.29 per cent.
6 November	Expansionary monetary measures in Germany.
2 December	EEC Summit Conference on agricultural finance, monetary co-operation and applications for membership from the United Kingdom and others.
12 December	Monopolies Commission and National Board for Prices and Incomes to be merged.
30 December	Increase in IMF quotas of over 35 per cent (pound rises above $2.40 for first time since April 1968).

Dramatis Personae, 1960–70

Allen, Douglas (1917–), Under-Secretary, Secretary Treasury, 1960–2; Third Secretary, 1962–64; Deputy Under Secretary of State, Dept. of Economic Affairs, 1964–6; Permanent Under Secretary of State, 1966–68; Permanent Secretary Treasury, 1968–74.

Allen, Maurice (1908–88), Executive Director, Bank of England, 1964–70.

Amory, Heathcoat (1899–1981), Chancellor of the Exchequer, January 1958–July 1960; High Commissioner in Canada, 1961–3.

Ansiaux, Hubert (1908–), Governor, National Bank of Belgium, 1957–71; Governor for Belgium, IMF, 1957–71.

Armstrong, William (1915–80), Third Secretary Treasury, 1958–62; Joint Permanent Secretary 1962–68; Head of Home Civil Service, 1968–74.

Atkinson, Fred (1919–), Economic Section, Treasury, 1955–62, 1963–9; Economic Adviser, Foreign Office, 1962–3; Deputy Director, Economic Section, 1965–9.

Balogh, Thomas (1905–85), Reader in Economics, University of Oxford 1960–73; Economic Adviser to Cabinet 1964–7; Consultant to Prime Minister 1968.

Barber, Anthony (1920–), Economic Secretary to Treasury 1959–62; Financial Secretary to Treasury 1962–3; Minister of Health 1963–4; Chancellor of the Exchequer 1970–4.

Barre, Raymond (1924–), Professor in Faculty of Law and Economics, University of Paris, 1962– ; Vice President of EEC Commission 1967–72.

Bator, Francis (1925–), Economic Adviser, AID, US State Department 1963–4; Staff, National Security Council, White House 1964–5; Department Special Assistant US President for National Security Affairs 1965–7; Special Consultant US Secretary of Treasury 1967–9.

Berrill, Kenneth (1920–), Fellow and First Bursar King's College, Cambridge 1962–9; Special Adviser Treasury 1967–9; Chairman UGC 1969–73.

Boyd-Carpenter, John (1908–), Minister of Pensions and National Insurance 1955–62; Chief Secretary to Treasury 1962–64; Chairman Public Accounts Committee 1964–70.

Boyle, Edward (1923–81), First Secretary to Treasury 1959–62; Minister of Education 1962–4.

Brooke, Henry (1903–84), Chief Secretary to Treasury and Paymaster General 1961–2; Home Secretary 1962–4.

Brown, George (1914–85), Deputy Leader of Parliamentary Labour Party 1960–70; First Secretary of State for Economic Affairs 1964–6; Foreign Secretary 1966–8.

Brunet, Jacques (1901–), Governor, Bank of France, 1960–9.

Butler, R. A. (1902–82), Home Secretary 1957–62; First Secretary of State and Deputy Prime Minister 1962–3; Secretary of State for Foreign Affairs 1963–4.

Callaghan, James (1912–), Shadow Chancellor 1961–4; Chancellor of the Exchequer 1964–7; Home Secretary 1967–70.

Carli, Guido (1914–93), Director General and Governor of Banca d' Italia 1959–75.

Castle, Barbara (1910–), Minister of Overseas Development 1964–5; Transport 1965–8; First Secretary of State and Secretary of State for Employment and Productivity 1968–70.

Clarke, R. W. B. (Otto) (1910–75), Third Secretary Treasury 1955–62; Second Secretary 1962–6; Permanent Secretary Ministry of Aviation 1966; Minister of Technology 1966–70.

Cobbold, Cameron (1904–87), Governor of the Bank of England 1949–61.

Couve de Murville, Maurice (1907–), French Minister of Foreign Affairs 1958–68; Prime Minister of France 1968–9.

Cromer, Earl of (1918–), Head of UK Treasury Delegation to Washington and UK Executive Director IMF and IBRD 1959–61; Governor of Bank of England 1961–66.

Crosland, Anthony (1918–77), Minister of State for Economic Affairs 1964–5; Secretary of State for Education and Science 1965–7; President of the Board of Trade 1967–9; Secretary of State for Local Government and Regional Planning 1969–70.

Crossman, R. H. S. (1907–74), Minister of Housing and Local Government 1964–6; Leader of House and Lord President of Council 1966–8; Secretary of State for Social Services 1968–70.

Dramatis Personae, 1960–70

Deane, Dewey (1918–), Assistant to Secretary of US Treasury 1960–1; Department Under Secretary of Treasury for Monetary Affairs 1961–3; member Board of Governors of Federal Reserve System 1963–74.

Débré, Michel (1912–), Minister of Justice 1959–62; Prime Minister of France May 1963; Minister of Economics and Finance 1966.

Deming, Frederick (1912–), President Reserve Bank of Minneapolis 1957–65; Under Secretary for Monetary Affairs, US Treasury 1965–9.

Diamond, John (1907–), Chief Secretary to the Treasury 1964–70.

Dow, J. C. R. (1916–), Deputy Director National Institute of Economic and Social Research 1954–62; Treasury 1962–3; Assistant Secretary General OECD 1963–73.

Emminger, Otmar (1911–86), Member, Board of Governors, Bundesbank 1953–69; Deputy Chairman Monetary Committee of EEC 1958–67; Chairman Deputies Group of Ten 1964–67.

Figures, Frank (1910–90), Secretary-General EFTA 1960–5; Third Secretary Treasury 1965–8; Second Permanent Secretary 1968–71.

Fowler, Henry (1908–?), Under-Secretary US Treasury 1961–4; Secretary 1965–8.

Godley, W. A. H. (1926–), Economic Section, Treasury 1956–70; Deputy Director 1967–70.

Goldman, Samuel (1912–), Under Secretary Treasury 1960–2; Third Secretary 1962–8; Second Permanent Secretary 1968–72.

Hall, Robert (1901–88), Economic Adviser to HMG 1953–61; part-time Economic Adviser to Minister of Transport, 1961–4.

Heath, Edward (1916–), Parliamentary Secretary to the Treasury and Government Chief Whip 1955–9; Minister of Labour 1959–60; Lord Privy Seal with Foreign Office responsibilities 1960–3; Secretary of State for Industry, Trade and Regional Development and President of the Board of Trade 1963–4; Leader of the Opposition 1965–70; Prime Minister 1970–4.

Helsby, Laurence (1908–78), Permanent Secretary Ministry of Labour 1959–62; Joint Permanent Secretary Treasury and Head of Home Civil Service 1963–8.

Heller, Walter (1915–?), Chairman Council of Economic Advisers, USA 1961–4; Consultant, Executive Office of the President, 1965–9.

Hollom, Jasper (1917–), Chief Cashier, Bank of England 1962–6; Director 1966–70.

Hopkin, W. A. B. (1914–), Deputy Director Economic Section 1958–65; Economic Planning Unit, Mauritius 1965; Min. of Overseas Development 1966–69 (Dir. Gen. of Economic Planning 1967–69); Dir. Gen., Dept. of Economic Affairs 1969.

Jay, Douglas (1907–), President, Board of Trade 1964–7.

Jenkins, Roy (1920–), Minister of Aviation 1964–5; Home Secretary 1965–7; Chancellor of the Exchequer 1967–70.

Jukes, John (1907–), Economic Adviser to UK Atomic Energy Authority 1954–64; Deputy Director-General, DEA, 1964; Deputy Under-Secretary of State, DEA, 1967; Director General Research and Economic Planning, Ministry of Transport, 1969–70.

Kaldor, Nicholas (1908–86), Reader in Economics, University of Cambridge 1952–65; Professor 1968–75; Special Adviser to Chancellor of the Exchequer 1964–8.

Larre, René (1915–), Cabinet of French Minister of Finance 1957–8; financial adviser at French embassy Washington 1961–3; financial director, French Ministry of Economics and Finance 1967–71.

Lee, Frank (1903–71), Permanent Secretary Ministry of Food 1959–61; Joint Permanent Secretary to the Treasury 1960–2.

Lennep, Emil van (1915–), Chairman, Monetary Committee of EEC 1958– ; Chairman, Working Party No. 3 of OECD 1961– .

Lloyd, Selwyn (1904–1978), Secretary of State for Foreign Affairs 1955–60; Chancellor of the Exchequer 1960–2; Lord Privy Seal and Leader of the House of Commons 1963–4.

MacDougall, Donald (1912–), Economic Director NEDO 1962–4; Director General DEA 1964–8; Head of Government Economic Service and Chief Econ. Adviser to the Treasury 1969–73.

MacMahon, C. J. (Kit) (1927–), Fellow and Tutor, Magdalen College Oxford 1960–4; entered Bank of England 1964; Adviser to Governors 1966–70.

Macmillan, Harold (1894–1986), Prime Minister 1957–63.

Makins, Roger (1904–), Joint Permanent Secretary of Treasury 1956–9; Chairman Atomic Energy Commission 1960–4.

Marjolin, Robert (1911–1986), Vice-President EEC Commission 1958–67.

Martin, William McChesney (1906–), Chairman Federal Reserve Board 1951–70.

Dramatis Personae, 1960–70

Maudling, Reginald (1917–79), President of the Board of Trade 1959–61; Secretary of State for the Colonies 1961–2; Chancellor of the Exchequer 1962–4.

Morse, C. J. (1928–), Executive Director Bank of England 1965–72.

Neild, Robert (1924–), Deputy Director National Institute of Economics and Social Research 1958–64; MIT Center for International Studies, New Delhi 1962–3; Economic Adviser to Treasury 1964–7; Director Stockholm International Peace Research Institute 1967–71.

O'Brien, Leslie (1908–), Chief Cashier, Bank of England 1955–62; Executive Director 1962–4; Deputy Governor 1964–6; Governor 1966–73.

Padmore, Thomas (1909–), Second Permanent Secretary Treasury 1953–62; Permanent Secretary Ministry of Transport 1962–8.

Plowden, Edwin (1907–), Chairman Committee on Public Expenditure 1959–61; on Aircraft Industry 1964–5.

Posner, Michael (1931–), Director of Economics, Ministry of Power 1966–7; Economic Adviser to Treasury 1967–9; Economic Consultant to Treasury 1969–71.

Powell, Richard (1909–), Permanent Secretary Board of Trade 1960–8.

Rasminsky, Louis (1908–), Governor, Bank of Canada 1961–73.

Rawlinson, Anthony (1926–86), Treasury 1960–75; Assistant Secretary 1963–8; Under Secretary 1968–72.

Rickett, Denis (1907–), Second Permanent Secretary Treasury 1960–8; Vice President World Bank 1968–74.

Roll, Eric (1907–), Deputy Secretary Ministry of Agriculture 1959–61; Dep. Leader, UK Delegation for negotiations in the EEC 1961–3; Head of Treasury Delegation, Washington, and Executive Director IMF and IBRD 1963–4; Permanent Under Secretary of State, Department of Economic Affairs, 1964–6.

Roosa, Robert V. (1918–), Federal Reserve Bank of New York 1946–60; Under Secretary for Monetary Affairs, US Treasury 1961–4.

Roy, A. (1920–), Economic Consultant, Treasury 1962–4; Senior Economic Adviser 1964–69; Under-Secretary 1969–72.

Schiller, Karl (1911–), Member Bundestag 1965–72; Federal Minister of Economics 1966–71.

Serpell, David (1911–), Deputy Secretary Ministry of Transport 1960–3; Second Secretary Board of Trade 1963–6; Second Permanent Secretary Treasury 1966–8; Permanent Secretary Board of Trade 1968–70.

Shone, Robert (1906–92), Director General National Economic Development Council 1962–6.

Shore, Peter (1924–), Head of Research Department Labour Party 1959–64; PPS to Prime Minister 1965–6; Joint Parliamentary Secretary Ministry of Technology 1966–7; Department of Economic Affairs 1967; Secretary of State for Economic Affairs 1967–9; Minister without Portfolio and Deputy Leader of House of Commons 1969–70.

Stewart, (Lord) Michael (1906–90), Minister of Education 1964–5; Foreign Secretary 1965–6 and 1968–70; Secretary of State for Economic Affairs 1966–8.

Stewart Michael (1933–), Secretary to Council on Prices Productivity and Incomes 1960–1; Economic Adviser Treasury 1961–2; Cabinet Office 1964–7.

Thorneycroft, Peter (1909–), Minister of Aviation 1960–2; Minister of Defence 1962–4; Secretary of State for Defence April–October 1964.

Watkinson, Harold (1910–), Minister of Defence 1959–62; Member, British National Export Council 1964–70.

Wilson, Harold (1916–95), Chairman Public Accounts Office 1959–63; Leader, Labour Party 1963–76; Prime Minister 1964–70.

Woodcock, George (1904–79), General Secretary TUC 1960–9; Member NEDC 1962–9; Chairman Commission on Industrial Relations 1969–71.

Index

accompanying measures, 92, 183–4, 188–90
advanced gas-cooled reactors, 270
advance warning of wage claims, 139
agricultural subsidies, 49
aid to developing countries, 114
Allen, Douglas (later Lord Croham), Treasury, 92, 182–3, 213–14, 216–19, 224, 227, 230–1
Allen, Maurice, Bank of England, 82, 209
aluminium smelters, 115, 270
Amory, Heathcoat (later Lord), Chancellor (1958–60), 34–41
Ansiaux, Hubert Governor, National Bank of Belgium, 210
Arab–Israeli War, 180
Armstrong, William (later Lord), Perm. Sec. Treasury (1962–5), 39–40, 93–4, 97–8, 101, 111, 124, 130, 139, 143, 145–6, 148, 152, 161, 165, 169, 175, 181, 184–5, 191, 209
Artis, Prof. Michael, 251
Atkinson, Fred, Economic Section, Treasury, 32, 97
auction of import quotas, 220
automation, 101

balance of payments, 3, 4, 8, 12, 18–22, 64; crises, 5, 19, 32, 263; in **1961**, 45–8; in **1964**, 72–80, 84–7, 91; in **1965**, 128–31; in **1966**, 150–4; in **1967**, Ch. 10 *passim*; in **1968**, 197–8, 208–10, 223–9; in **1969**, 235–8; in the **1960s**, 274–5; deficit, 45, 93–4; impact of deflation, 161; measures to protect, 112–16; relation to domestic savings, 197; surplus, 195, 263; targets, 147, 188, 191, 214, 238; Letter of Intent, 191

balancing item, 215
Baldwin, Peter, Treasury, 155
Ball, George, US Department of State, 170
Balogh, Thomas (later Lord), Cabinet Office, 87, 97, 101–2, 145–6, 170, 173, 188
Bank for International Settlements, 151, 154, 207, 213, 224, 246
Bank of England, x, 33, 36–7, 48, 50–1, 53, 56, 67, 76, 86, 101; borrows $3 billion, 105, 113, 137, 147, 177, 216, 230, 237; *Quarterly Bulletin*, 144; *see also* gilt-edged market
bank lending, 124; restrictions on, 33–4, 123, 146, 212, 225, 234, 249–50; *see also* credit squeeze
bank minimum liquidity ratio, 76, 86
bank rate, 8, 33, 37, 40, 45, 51, 54, 56, 67, 72, 82–3, 86–7, 91; raised to 7 per cent, 105, 108, 123–5, 146–7, 151, 164, 205, 217, 220, 234; frequency of charges in, 244; Tribunal, 33
Barber, Anthony, Econ. Fin. Sec., Treasury, 48–50, 55
Bareau, Paul, 220
Barre, Raymond, Vice-President of EEC Commission, 228
Basle Arrangements, 45, 48, 72, 169, 177, 255; Group Arrangements, 210, 218–19, 246
Bator, Francis, 171
Bernstein, Edward, 256
Berrill, Kenneth, 166–8
bisques under the Loan Agreement, 114, 141
Blackaby, Frank, National Institute, 112
Blessing, Karl, Governor of Bundesbank, 164, 206, 225, 228
blocked sterling, 208–10, 237

305

Bonn Conference of 1968, 226–9
Borrowing, long-term, 13, 92, 112; short-term, 42, 105, 108
Borrowing requirement of central government, 86, 121, 156, 212
Boyd Carpenter, John, Minister of National Insurance, 285–6
Boyle, Sir Edward, Fin. Sec. Treasury, 39, 45, 50
Bretherton, Russell, Treasury, 35
Bretton Woods System, 238
Brittan, Sam, *Financial Times*, 219–20
Britton, Andrew, National Institute, 32
Brooke, Henry, Chief Secretary, 30, 286
Brown, George, First Secretary DEA, 96, 103–4, 110, 124–5, 126–7, 130–1, 138; Foreign Secretary, 154, 186, 189; resigns, 209–10
Brunet, M., Governor, Bank of France, 187, 225, 228

Callaghan, James, first impressions, 95; raises bank rate, 105; **1965** Budget, 110–11; aims to save foreign exchange, 112–14; increases borrowing requirements, 120–3, monetary policy, 123–5; attacks national plan, 125–8; crisis of **1965**, 128–31; Great Bear Squeeze, 137–8; contemplates new measures, 141–3, 145–7; and new publications, 143–4; includes SET in 1966 Budget, 148–50; contemplates resignation, 153; develops new strategy, 159; seeks to reduce interest rates, 163–6; resists evaluation, 185; but changes his mind, 186; defends inadequate package, 189–90; moves to Home Office, 191; opposes trade union reform, 240–1
capital controls, 13, 70, 112–14, 248–9

capital flows, viii, 8, 13, 18–19, 33, 42, 45, 110–11, 132–3, 232; *see also* Balance of payments; Investment overseas
car licence duties, 44
car registration, 58, 68, 79
Carli, Guido, Governor, Bank of Italy, 120–1, 123, 208, 210
Castle, Barbara, Sec. of State for Employment and Productivity, announces Industrial Relations Bill, 240
Central Statistical Office (CSO), 22, 30, 70; on trend in balance of payments, 162–3
Chequers, meetings at, 100, 110
Clarke, R. W. B. ('Otto'), Treasury, 45, 49, 101, 107
coalition rumour, 233
Cobbold, Cameron (later Lord), Governor of Bank of England, 33, 39 41 48, 50
Collective Reserve Unit (CRU), 259–60
Commission on Industrial Relations, 239
Common Agricultural Fund, 169
Common Market, 56, 180; *see also* European Economic Community
competitive power, 4, 8, 15–16, 31, 52, 92, 94, 103, 238
concordat (with DEA), 98
Concorde, 93
Confederation of British Industries (CBI), 167–8
Coombs, Charles, Federal Reserve Board, 137
Couéism, 12
Council on Prices, Productivity and Incomes (COPPI), 58
Cousins, Frank, 152
Couve de Murville, 169, 185, 225–6
credit squeeze, 149, 151, 153, 216, 218, 224
Cripps, R. Stafford, 56
Cromer, Earl of, Governor Bank of England, 50–1, 55, 124–5, 130–1, 146–8, 150

Crosland, Anthony, 130, 189, 191, 221, 227
Crossman, R. H. S., 100, 107
currency, common, x, 169, 171; convertibility 21, 36, 232; investment (switch dollars), 111, 113, 150; misalignment, 232; overvaluation, 13–14, reserve, 13, 53, 109, 205, 259; swaps, 66, 86, 105, 246, 258
cycle of 1957–61, 33–43

Daane, Dewey, Federal Reserve Board, 260
Daily Worker, 56
Dalton, Hugh, 96
Day, Alan, 220
Débré, Michel, 156, 169, 260
Debt, external, 20–1, 43, 233, 245; management, 244; repayment of, 118–19, 138, 158, 238
defence expenditure, 48, 111, 141–2; overseas, 114
deflation, 16; in **1961**, 47; in **1965**, 131; in **1966**, 151–2; *see also* packages of deflationary measures
demand, excess, 8, 15–16, 45, 52, 70, 78, 243, 269; management, 11, 16, 98, 104, 272
Deming, Fred, US Treasury, 210
Department of Economic Affairs, 31, 96, 102, 110, 142, 263
Deutschmark revaluation, 42, 223, 235, 238
devaluation of sterling, ix–x, 4, 13–14, 20–1, 52–3, 56, 70, 92–5, 99–100; 'unmentionable', 105; urged in July 1965, 130, 143; ministerial doubts in 1966, 146–8; 'virtually certain', 186; devaluation to $2.40 on 18 September 1967, 180–8; effects, 195–6; devaluation of 5% proposed, 224; of the franc, 237; impact in wages and prices, 241–2
Diamond, John, Chief Secretary, 148, 177

Dillon, Douglas, US Secretary of State, 256
discrimination in trade, 21–2
dockers' pay, 61
dollar portfolio, 47, 75, 141, 223
Domestic credit expansion (DCE), 236–7, 251–3
Douglas-Home, Sir Alec, Prime Minister 1963–4, 78, 82
Dow, J. C. R. (Christopher), 32, 81, 110
Downie, Jack, 32

economic advisers after 1964, 97
economic cycle of 1957–61, 33–43
Economic Policy Committee (UK), 34, 80
Economic Section of the Treasury, 29–32, 102, 105, 224
economic strategy in 1967, 159–62, 178
Economic Survey, 7
Economic Trends 143
Economist, The, 7–8, 51, 57, 62–3, 65, 81, 86, 144, 234, 236, 257
Electricity Council, 60; investment in, 106–7, 269
Emminger, Otmar, 227, 259–60
Euro-dollar market, xiii, 153, 246
European Economic Community (EEC), ix, 6, 21; first application to join, 51, 54, 58, 72, 107, 148; renewed application, 165, 168–72, 180, 186, 263; Monetary Committee, 123
European Monetary Union (EMU), 171
Exchange Rate Mechanism (ERM), 214
exchange rates, variations in, ix, 141, 213; *see also* devaluation; floating
exchange reserves, 8, 13, 45, 47–8, 86, 94, 105, 107, 128, 132; international, 254–5
exports, 6, 36, 54, 133; boom in 1969, 231–2; rebate, 53, 114–15, 249; subsidies, 13; *see also* world trade

Far East, 48
Federal Reserve Board, 137–8, 154, 208–10, 211
Federation of British Industries (FBI), 52; conference in 1960, 45, 62
Figgures, Frank, Treasury, 219, 228
Financial Times, 220
Fleming, Miles, 9
floating, ix–x, 7, 49, 65, 73, 92, 186, 208–9, 219, 224, 232
forecasting arrangements, 81, 144, 214–15
forecasts, 7, 38, 47, 50, 55, 58, 69, 77, 107, 133, 142, 155, 184, 196, 216
foreign-currency borrowing by nationalised industries, 246
foreign-travel allowance, 48, 114, 153, 249
forward sales of sterling, 86, 105, 113–14, 132, 153, 185, 205, 247; forward discount, 235, 238
Fowler, Henry, Secretary of US Treasury, 137–8, 165, 184, 191
free depreciation, 24, 75
Friedman, Milton, 219
funding, 37, 72, 76, 244–5, 251

GATT, 91, 94
Gaulle de, Charles, 51, 109, 138, 169, 223, 236, 259–60
Gilbert, Milton, 135, 207
gilt-edged market, 150, 180, 191, 218, 234, 236–7, 249
Godley, Wynne, Treasury, 32, 108, 174–5; works out devaluation package, 188
gold crisis in 1968, 205; embargo, 171, 208; price, 57, 206–8, 254–7; reserves, 255
Goldman, Sam, Treasury, 213, 46, 223, 227–8
Goode, Dick, IMF, 217
Government Economic Service, viii, 29
Great Bear Squeeze of 1965, 137–8
group system, 137; Bonn Conference, 226, 259

growth, economic, 5, 14–15; hurts to decelerate, 7–8, 14, 70; exports, 220; faster in 1960s, 263, 265–70; potential in 1961, 42–3, sustainable, 9; targets, 64, 87, 147, 268
'Guiding Light', 35, 60–1, 76

Hailey, Sir W., editor, *The Times*, 62
Hall, Sir Robert, Economic Adviser to HMG, 33–7, 41, 50, 69, 144, 256
Harrod, Sir Roy, 110
Hay, Alexander, 207
Healey, Denis, 189
Heath, Edward, 147
Heller, Walter, 164
Helsby, Laurence (later Lord), Treasury, 102, 139
hire-purchase restrictions, 16, 40, 50, 124–5, 131, 141–2, 145–6, 152, 160, 179–80, 200, 221, 243
Hollom, Jasper, Bank of England, 216
Home, *see* Douglas-Home
Hopkin, W. A. B. (Bryan), Treasury, 32, 34
house-building, 106–7, 130–1, 156, 175

import controls, 13, 52, 92, 222, 247–8; deposits, 13, 155, 212, 224–5; factors behind increase in 1968, 230–1; prices, 197, 199–200, 222, 230; quotas, 13, 49, 74, 91, 212, 216, 225; surcharge, 13, 74, 91–4, 105, 150, 212–13, 226
incomes policy, 8–9, 56, 58–62, 78, 96, 103–4, 137–40, 166–8, 240–1, 263, 265
industrial production, 5–6, 41, 67, 87
Industrial Relations Bill, 240
Industrial Reorganisation Commission, 267
industrial structure, 3–4, 24–5
inflation, 4–5, 8, 15–18, 270–2; in **1957**, 33, 38; in **1961**, 41; in **1964**, 92, 140; cost, 9

innovation, 10, 31, 270
interest, rate of, 16, 243; long term, 37–9, 56, 72, 161, 224; international action to reduce, 163–5; *see also* bank rate
international liquidity, 31, 57, 66, 254
International Monetary Fund (IMF), 13, 16, 21, 42, 47, 51, 73, 75, 108–9, 123, 126, 169, 191, 210, 213, 216–8, 256, 260; Letters of Intent of **1967**, 191; **1968**, 218; **1969**, 236
investment:
 allowances, 68, 75, 101
 boom in **1959–61**, 36; in **1965**, 133–4; in **1966–7**, 155; in **1960s**, 15, 263; fall in, 54, 66, 69
 grants, 101, 143, 269
 intentions, 5, 58
 in the sterling area, 146
 manufacturing, 15, 54, 66–7, 83, 107, 134, 136, 221, 274
 over-, 78–80;
 overseas, 13, 18–19, 49, 51, 112–13, 146
 public, 26, 64, 67; in **1962**, 58; in **1963–4**, 78–9, 83; in **1965**, 131, 135–6; in **1966**, 152; in **1967**, 155
 see also currency
invisible income, fall in, 45

J curve, 200, 211
Jacobson, Per, IMF, 256
Javits, Senator, 207
Jay, Douglas, President Board of Trade, 146
Jay, Peter, *The Times*, 219–20, 224
Jenkins, Roy, 130; 191; cuts public expenditure, 202–3, raises taxation, 204–5; opposes floating, 208–9; attends Bonn Conference, 225–7; rumours of resignation, 229; contemplates very different strategy, 232, 235; 1969 budget, 235; faces fresh crisis, 237–8; urges no delay in labour legislation, 240–1, 264

Johnson, Prof. Harry, 170
Johnson, L. B., US President, 181, 187
Jukes, John, DEA, 145–6
July measures of 1961, 45, 54, 263

Kahn, Richard (later Lord), 166–8
Kaldor, Nicholas (later Lord), 87, 93, 103, 128, 145–8; proposes SET, 148–9; 153; 157; 161; develops New Cambridge view, 173–5; urges Regional Employment Premium, 176–7; 188, 206, 209, 213–14, 216, 219, 249, 257
Kennedy, John F., US President, 255–6
Kennedy, Robert, 170; assassinated, 211
Kessler, 207
Keynes, Lord, 116
Khrushchev, N., 91

labour shortage, 4, 16, 60, 104, 136
Larre, René, 227–9
Lawson, Nigel (later Lord), 83
Lee, Sir Frank, Perm. Sec. Treasury, 32, 41, 50, 60, 256–7
Lee, Fred, Chancellor of the Duchy of Lancaster, 182
Lever, Harold, 216, 231
liquidity, excess in 1967, 157–8, 172
Lloyd, Selwyn (later Lord), 7, 8, 17, 40–1, 44, 63–5, 69–70, 96, 116, 151, 256–7, 262–72
local authority borrowing, 122–3
London and Cambridge Economic Bulletin, x, 133, 217
Long Term and the Short in Economic Planning, The, 98

M-rate 60
McDermot, Niall, Financial Secretary to the Treasury, 177
Macdougall, Sir Donald, 97, 102, 145, 161, 220
MacMahon C. M. (Kit), Bank of England, 183, 209

Macmillan, Harold, Prime Minister, 3, 9, 35, 39–41, 56–7, 63, 78, 96; fears shortage of international liquidity, 155–8, 264–5, 273–4
Macrae, Norman, *The Economist*, 8, 9, 144–5
Machlup, Prof. Fritz, 256
Makins, Roger (later Lord Sherfield), 37
Manchester Guardian, 216
Marjolin, Robert, EEC, 171
Martin, William McChesney, Governor of Federal Reserve Board, 82, 164, 207–10
Martinière, G. de la, 169
Maudling, Reginald, Chancellor (1962–4), 19, 24, 49, 57–8, 62, 64 *passim*, 91, 94, 96, 105–6, 109, 155, 257–8, 265, 273
Meade, James, viii
Ministry of Economic Planning, 78, 98
monetarism, x, 5, 16, 220, 234
monetary policy, 16, 31, 123–5, 146, 254, Chapter 14 *passim*
money, quantity of, 5, 202, 218, 220, 250
Morrison, Herbert, ex-Lord President, 96
Morse, Jeremy, Bank of England, 164, 227
Mutual Currency Account, 66, 258–61

National Board for Prices and Incomes, 17, 103, 138–40, 167–8
National Economic Development Council (NEDC), 7, 41, 49, 51, 55, 63, 70, 78, 263
National Incomes Commission, 17, 62
National Institute of Economic and Social Research, x, 32, 36, 73, 76, 85, 87, 108, 126, 133, 144, 204, 212, 217; conference on economic planning in 1961, 45
National Insurance contributions, 44, 104, 148–9
nationalised industries, finance of, 5, 63, 69, 92, 122–3; foreign-currency borrowing, 92, 113, 246; *see also* prices
Neild, Robert, 102, 124, 145–7, 175–6
'New Cambridge', 173, 175
New Statesman, 87
No. 10, meetings at in 1964–5, 100–1, 107
nuclear power, 270
Nuffield College Conference of Forecasting, 145
nurses' pay, 61

O'Brien, Leslie (later Lord), Governor Bank of England, 50, 150–1, 164, 179, 181, 183, 190–1, 210, 217, 224–5
Oppenheimer, Peter, 133
Organisation for European Co-operation and Development (OECD), 18, 56, 71, 94; Economic Policy Committee, 151, 207, 227; Working Party No. 3, 110, 123, 128–9, 217
Ormsby Gore, David (Lord Marlech), British ambassador to USA, 170
Ossola, Rinaldo, Bank of Italy, 258; group, 259
overheating, 78, 94, 188

packages of deflationary measures, 8; in **1961**, 51; in **1965**, 131; in **1966,** 151–2; in **1967**, 190; of expansionary measures in **1963**, 67
Padmore, Sir Thomas, Treasury, 50–1
Phelps Brown, Henry, 63, 242
Plan, National, 9, 18, 98, 103, 126–8, 137, 145, 147, 156, 162, 263, 268–9
planning economic, 6–8, 98, 263; in 1961, 58, 62–64; in France, 6–8, 62, 268; different conceptions of, 11; targets, 7–8, 11, 63
plant bargaining (on wages), 166
Plowden, Lord Treasury, 49;

Committee on Public Expenditure, 46, 62
Polak, Jacques, 261
Political and Economic Planning (PEP), 45
Pompidou, Georges, 169
Posner, Michael, Treasury, 182
post-war credits, 67-8
prescription charges, 104
Prices, commodity, 17; consumer, 18, 244; retail, 8; of nationalised industries, 54-5, 139-40, 142; control, 142; freeze of 1966, 153; *see also* import inflation; terms of trade
Prices and Incomes Act 1966, 166
productivity growth, 10, 13, 31, 46, 61, 64, 70, 127, 140, 147, 264
profits, increase in (1967-8), 157
publications, 143-4
public expenditure, planning and control, 46, 49, 51, 109; cuts in overseas, 152; outgrows limits in 1966-7, 156-7; continues to rise in 1968, 230
Public Sector Borrowing Requirement (PSBR), 172, 193, 251-3
Public Sector, surplus in 1968-8, 235
Public Sector, Survey Committee (PESC), viii, 64
Public Works Loan Board, 123, 164

Radcliffe Report, x, 5, 16, 31, 60, 144, 243, 250, 253
Rasminsky, L., 228
rationing, 5
Raw, Rupert, Bank of England, 138
Rawlinson, Anthony, Treasury, 111
Reflation in **1958**, 33-4; in **1962-3**, 66-7; in **1967**, 177-9, 180-1
regional differences in unemployment, 23-4, 71; policy, 263
Regional Employment Premium, 24, 176-7
Regulators, tax, 16, 41, 44, 50, 58, 67, 69, 86, 138, 141, 152, 224

Reierson, Roy, 207
Repurchase agreements, 76
resale price maintenance, 49
resource transfers, 188, 198, 200, 222, 231
restrictive practices, 31, 49, 269
Richardson, Gordon (later Lord), 221
Rickett, Sir Denis, Treasury, 101, 124, 175, 187
Roll, Sir Eric (later Lord), Perm. Sec. of Economic Affairs, 95, 97, 101, 147
Roosa, R. V., 66, 82, 257-8
Rose, Brian, 121
Rostow, Eugene, 171
Rostow, Walt, 171

Schedule A, 74
Schiller, Karl, German Minister of Economics, 226, 228
Schweizer, Pierre Paul, IMF, 169, 187, 259
Serpell, Sir David, 211
'shake out of labour', 67
Shone, Sir Robert, 63
Shore, Peter, 182
Soames, Christopher, Minister of Agriculture, 49
Solomon, Robert, Federal Reserve Board, 208
special deposits, 36, 39-40, 51, 56, 68, 86, 123-4, 151, 253-4
State, role of the 25-6
Stafford, Jack, Board of Trade, 179
sterling area, 13, 21, 91, 246
sterling balances, 13, 202, 246
Stevens, John, Treasury representative in Washington, 170
Stewart, Michael (later Lord), Foreign Secretary and briefly First Secretary, 154
stockbuilding, 36-7, 42, 55, 66, 78, 106, 230
'stop-go', 8, 10, 13, 45, 49, 74, 92, 225
Strategic Economic Policy Committee, 99-100, 154-5
strikes, 239-40

structural change, 3-4, 24-5
Suez Canal closed, 130-1, 196

tax, capital gains, 49, 104; corporation, 104, 143, 235; fuel oil, 189; income, 104; payroll, 44, 148; profits, 148; purchase, 67, 148, 235; petrol, 44, 104, 149; Selective Employment Tax (SET), 148-9, 172, 174-6, 205, 235; surtax, 44; value added tax, 142; on services, 148
Tax Reserve Certificates, 17
terms of trade, 18, 200, 222
test rate of discount, viii
Tew, Prof. Brian, 112, 245
Thompson-McCausland, Lucius, 66
Thorneycroft, Peter (later Lord), ex-Chancellor, 5, 8, 53
Times, The, 82, 220, 224, 226, 229, 235
Trade balance, 128, 198, 211, 217-18, 237
trade unions, 4, 152, 239-42, 269; militancy, 4, 18, 242
training, 14, 16
Treasury bills, 37-40, 46, 251; shortage of, 122, 124
Treaty of Rome, 21
Trend, Sir Burke, Cabinet Secretary, 185, 209
Triffin, Prof. Robert, 255
Triumverate of 1964-66, 99-100
TSR2, 111
TUC, 8, 36, 52, 58-9, 63, 76, 103, 167, 198, 240
Tydings, Senator, 170

unemployment, 3, 8, 22-4; in **1957**, 33; in **1960**, 41; in **1962**, 54, 67; in **1963**, 71; in **1964**, 87; in **1965**, 125-6; in **1966-7**, 155, 159; in the **1960s**, 272-4; strategy to avoid devaluation, 159, 161-3

Van Lennep, Emil, Chairman of Working Party No. 3, 10, 110, 129, 156, 206
voluntary limitation of investment of sterling area, 109, 113
Vote on the Account 1967, 173

Wadsworth, Midland Bank, 108
wage acceleration in 1970, 242, 272; bargaining, 5, 9, 56; freeze, 17, 139; of 1966, 17, 61, 150, 152, 166; inflation, 17, 36, 139-41; pause, 17, 51, 58-60, pressure, 8; real, 139; stationary after tax, 166-9 242, 272; restraint, 7, 17 36, 51, 76
Wall Street fall, 54, 57
Watkinson, Harold, Minister of Defence, 219
Wilson, Harold, Prime Minister, viii, 91, 93-4, 99-101, 105, 110-11, 123-5, 127-9, 130-1, 138, 141-2, 145-9; accepts need for deflation, 151-3; appoints SEP Committee, 154; launches fresh attempt to enter EEC, 168 *passim*; applies to enter, 180-1; takes charge of DEA, 182, 185; suggests floating the pound, 186, 189, 216; rumour of resignation, 214, 233, 266, 274
Woodcock, George, Secretary General TUC, 60-1, 239
world trade in manufactures, 67, 197; British share of 6, 18-19, 67, 93, 232, 263